William Ware

Palmyra

Letters of Lucius M. Piso from Palmyra to his Friend Marcus Curtius at Rome

William Ware

Palmyra

Letters of Lucius M. Piso from Palmyra to his Friend Marcus Curtius at Rome

ISBN/EAN: 9783744770064

Printed in Europe, USA, Canada, Australia, Japan

Cover: Foto ©ninafisch / pixelio.de

More available books at **www.hansebooks.com**

PALMYRA

BEING

LETTERS OF LUCIUS M. PISO

FROM PALMYRA

TO HIS

FRIEND MARCUS CURTIUS AT ROME

REPUBLISHED FROM CHAMBERS'S PEOPLE'S EDITIONS

WILLIAM AND ROBERT CHAMBERS
LONDON AND EDINBURGH
1860

PUBLISHERS' PREFACE.

The present work, which is of American authorship, was first published in New York, in two volumes duodecimo, several years ago; and both from the able manner in which the subject was treated, and the exceeding elegance of the style, it soon attracted universal attention. It has since passed through several editions in America, and been reprinted in London, but at such an expense as to place it beyond the means of the more ordinary class of purchasers, and, in point of fact, to keep it from being generally known in Britain. The present PEOPLE'S EDITION will, it is hoped, bring the work within the reach of every one who possesses a taste for a pure and elevating kind of reading, and give it that place in our popular literature which it so eminently deserves. In, perhaps, no instance has English literature received so valuable an accession from the western shores of the Atlantic.

With respect to the nature and character of the work, we may be permitted to quote the following notice from the North American Review, for October 1837:—

"This work seems to be rapidly gaining the reputation which it so well deserves. It is an historical romance. Piso, the imagined author of the Letters, is supposed to have visited Palmyra towards the close of the third century, to have become acquainted with Zenobia and her court, to have seen the city in its glory, and to have witnessed its destruction by Aurelian. (A. D. 273.)

The scene, the characters, and the historical events, are finely selected; for they abound with striking images and associations. We are carried back to Palmyra, a city the history of which is unknown, rising in the desert, shown to the world but for a single age, in the height of its almost unparalleled splendour, and then becoming the spoil of a Roman army and its savage leader, who laid waste in a few days what was never to be restored. After this, a cloud of obscurity settled over it, and its ancient glories were almost regarded as fabulous; till, in the latter part of the seventeenth century, a few English merchants, from the factory at Aleppo, found their way to its wonderful ruins, and brought back a tale, for which they scarcely obtained credit—which, indeed, caused their veracity to be questioned. Zenobia, the queen of this city, has been a name for poetry and painting, and history represents her as a woman of extraordinary intellect and beauty, united with great strength of character; an Asiatic princess, with Grecian refinement and Roman hardihood. Her principal minister, who is very happily introduced in the present work, was the philosopher Longinus. Her victor, Aurelian, was the son of a Pannonian peasant, originally an adventurer, a common soldier; who, by his courage, ferocity, bodily strength, power of control, and skill in war, had raised himself to be the military despot of the Roman empire, and kept himself at its head almost five years, before his turn for assassination came. With perhaps occasional outbreaks of something like a generous impulse, he was on the whole only less hateful than some of his predecessors, because he did not, like them, mix up his atrocious cruelties with the utter vileness of the most loathsome sensuality.

The complete ruin of Palmyra followed its destruction by Aurelian. As regards that city, he might have rivalled the boast of Attila, that *the grass grew not where his horse's hoofs had trod.* Lying as an oasis in the desert, between the Euphrates and the Mediterranean, and favoured with an abundant supply of water, it rose rapidly to wealth and civilisation, as an emporium of the commerce of the East. Its Grecian name, Palmyra, and its Eastern name, Tadmor, were equally expressive of the great number of palm-trees which flourished around it. In the middle of the last century, there was but one remaining; the sands of the desert had encroached to its walls, and only a few Arab huts were to be found among its ruins.

At that time (in 1751), it was visited by the travellers Dawkins and Wood, to whom we are indebted for our principal information respecting its present state. Their published drawings and measurements are satisfactory, but are accompanied with only a very brief narrative. After a journey of six days from Aleppo, through the desert, the travellers arrived about noon in view of 'Tadmor's marble wastes.' 'The hills opening,' says Mr Wood, 'discovered to us all at once the greatest quantity of ruins we had ever seen, all of white marble; and beyond them, towards the Euphrates, a flat waste, as far as the eye could reach, without any object which showed either life or motion. It is scarcely possible to imagine any thing more striking than this view.' The remains of the city lay within a circuit of about three miles, which appeared as if it had been filled with public edifices. The whole ground was covered with heaps of marble; yet among them the ruins of vast buildings were still conspicuous, the greatest and most entire, says Wood, which the travellers had seen. Among these, two were preeminent;—one of them, the Temple of the Sun, standing in a court, more than 700 feet square, which was enclosed by a wall; adorned on the outside with pilasters, and originally with a double row of interior columns, forming as it were cloisters; the temple itself being in the midst of the area, surrounded by columns fifty feet high :—the other, an open portico, stretching three quarters of a mile in length, many of the pillars of which are yet standing. All the edifices, of which any considerable ruins are extant, are supposed to have been erected during the period of less than three centuries which intervened between the Christian era and the destruction of the city. The style of architecture is almost throughout Corinthian; but the vastness of the buildings has an Egyptian character.

It was this city which Piso, the supposed author of the Letters, is imagined to have seen in its glory, and also to have seen destroyed and left a desert waste.

One characteristic of the 'Letters from Palmyra,' from which they derive much of their interest, consists in the just views they afford of the condition of mankind during the period to which they relate. Facts are brought distinctly before us, so as to produce a right impression of the age;—the merciless and rapacious character of its continual wars, the widely-spread miseries of private slavery, the absence of a true standard of right, and the religious darkness of the pagan world. Nor are these painful features made too prominent; a benevolent and cheerful tone of feeling pervades the work; the picture is brightened by the conception of the holiday joyousness of Palmyra, by the amiable or generous traits of character ascribed to most of the principal personages, and especially by the light of Christianity, which appears as having risen above the horizon. Ancient history has often been so written in modern times that the reader, unless he be more than commonly attentive and thoughtful, will gain no correct notion of its proper subject, of the men of former times of whom it proposes to give an account. He will learn little more than names, events, and dates. He will have little idea of the real state of civilisation, of the forms of society, of the modes of life, the feelings, occupations, and enjoyments of the generality of men, of the passions, vices, impulses, and principles by which they were governed, of the point to which intellectual culture had attained, and of the extent of its diffusion, or, consequently, of the aspect under which human nature presented itself, so widely different from what it has assumed in modern times. The historian wants a philosophical comprehension of what he is relating. The facts of the age of which he treats are insulated in his mind, not grouped together so as to form a consistent and striking picture, not seen in their relations, not viewed comparatively with those of other periods and different states of our race. He has not imagination to discern the details necessarily involved in general statements; nor penetration, knowledge of human nature, and moral sensibility, to appreciate as he ought the particulars which he brings together. He cannot withdraw himself from the circle of the age in which he lives. His modern associations cling round the events and characters of antiquity, and hide their real features. He limits his views to prominent individuals, concerning whom our information is often so uncertain, and overlooks the actual character and state of the mass of men which, for the most part, there are documents enough to illustrate. As shown by him, a veil lies over it, beneath which only the common outline of humanity is to be seen.

When the veil or the pall is lifted from the age to which the 'Letters from Palmyra' relate, we behold the Roman world overspread with armies. Everywhere are war, seditions, massacres, slavery, and cruelty. The Roman armies, formed, like the Free Companions or the troops of the *Condottieri*, of mercenaries of different nations, and resembling them in rapacity and savageness, were the true rulers of the empire. The emperors were those whom they chose for a time to acknowledge as their masters; either military leaders, like Aurelian, whose fierce and hardy qualities commanded their admiration, and gave them promise of success in war; or worthless profligates, like Gallienus, who, by unbounded largesses and bribes, purchased from them the privilege of indulging in the most detestable excesses. Among the nobles and the rich, there was generally that reckless and shameless abandonment to vice, that sole care for safety and selfish gratifications, which can result only from the absence of all sense of morals in a community where life and fortune are constantly at hazard. 'He loved his friends,' says the contemporary historian

Trebellius, 'a thing in our age to be compared to a prodigy.'

But amid this state of things, which seemed to threaten the dissolution of civil society, a new element had been and was still working. Christianity had been introduced; and there cannot be a contrast more striking than what appeared during the first three centuries of our era, between the pagan world and the new brotherhood of Christians. In becoming acquainted with the true history of the Christians of this period, we become conversant with men who, whatever might be their mistakes or failings, or the vices of some of their number, present a wholly different character from that of the multitudes around them. We discern the high qualities and powers of our nature unfolding. A history that should fairly represent the age—a history, in consequence, unlike that of Gibbon in almost every feature—would constitute one of the most powerful arguments for the divine origin of our religion; for it would show the impossibility of its having had its source in those causes which had been and were operating upon the condition of men everywhere without the sphere of its influence.

We have been led into these remarks, because in the volumes before us the contrast between Christianity and paganism is beautifully exhibited. Though never obtrusively brought forward, it runs through the work, and constitutes one of its principal charms. Of this no quotations which our limits admit would afford a fair specimen; and we shall give but a single extract from a very interesting conversation. In the course of the story we are introduced to an individual in extreme old age, a hermit, who, having been a preacher of our religion, had now, that his strength failed him, retired from the world to die. He is visited by Piso, who writes the account, in company with Fausta and with Julia, the daughter of Zenobia. The old man is speaking.

'Till age dried up the sources of my strength, I toiled night and day in all countries and climates, in the face of every danger, in the service of mankind; for it is by serving others that the law of Christ is fulfilled. This disinterested labour for others constituted the greatness of Jesus Christ. This constitutes true greatness in his followers. I perceive that what I say falls upon your ear as a new and strange doctrine; but it is the doctrine of Christianity. It utterly condemns, therefore, a life of solitary devotion. It is a mischievous influence, which is now spreading outwards from the example of that Paul, who suffered so much under the persecution of the Emperor Decius, and who then, flying to the solitudes of the Egyptian Thebais, has there in the vigour of his days buried himself in a cave of the earth, that he may serve God by forsaking man.'

'I am obliged to confess that it is,' I replied. 'I have heretofore lived in an easy indifference towards all religions. The popular religion of my country I early learned to despise. I have perused the philosophers, and examined their systems, from Pythagoras to Seneca, and am now, what I have long been, a disciple of none but Pyrrho. My researches have taught me only how the more ingeniously to doubt. Wearied at length with a vain inquiry after truth that should satisfy and fill me, I suddenly abandoned the pursuit, with the resolve never to resume it. I was not even tempted to depart from this resolution when Christianity offered itself to my notice; for I confounded it with Judaism, and for that, as a Roman, I entertained too profound a contempt to bestow upon it a single thought. I must acknowledge that the reports which I heard, and which I sometimes read, of the marvellous constancy and serenity of the Christians, under accumulated sufferings and wrongs, interested my feelings in their behalf; and the thought often arose, Must there not be truth to support such heroism? But the world went on its way, and I with it, and the Christians were forgotten. To a Christian, on my voyage across the Mediterranean, I owe much for my first knowledge of Christianity. To the princess Julia I owe a larger debt still. And now from your lips, long accustomed to declare its truths, I have heard what makes me truly desirous to hear the whole of that, which, in the little glimpses I have been able to obtain, has afforded so real a satisfaction.'

'If you studied the Christian books,' said the recluse, 'you would be chiefly struck, perhaps, with the plainness and simplicity of the doctrines there unfolded. You would say that much which you found there, relating to the right conduct of life, you had already found scattered through the books of the Greek and Roman moralists. You would be startled by no strange or appalling truth. You would turn over their leaves in vain in search of such dark and puzzling ingenuities as try the wits of those who resort to the pages of the Timæus. A child can understand the essential truths of Christ. And the value of Christianity consists not in this, that it puts forth a new, ingenious, and intricate system of philosophy, but that it adds to recognised and familiar truths divine authority. Some things are indeed new; and much is new, if that may be called so, which, having been neglected as insignificant by other teachers, has by Christ been singled out and announced as primal and essential. But the peculiarity of Christianity lies in this, that its voice, whether heard in republishing an old and familiar doctrine, or announcing a new one, is not the voice of man, but of God. Philosophers have long ago taught that the only safe and happy life is a virtuous life. Christianity repeats this great truth, and adds, that it is such a life alone that conducts to immortality.'

Our general estimate of the 'Letters from Palmyra' appears in what we have already said. It is not a work of an ordinary character. It is the production of a thoughtful, able, imaginative, and, above all, a pure and right-minded author, of clear thoughts and sound sense."

PALMYRA.

LETTER I.

It is with difficulty that I persuade myself, that it is I who am sitting and writing to you from this great city of the East. Whether I look upon the face of nature, or the works of man, I see every thing different from what the West presents—so widely different, that it seems to me, at times, as if I were subject to the power of a dream. But I rouse myself, and find that I am awake, and that it is really I, your old friend and neighbour Piso, late a dweller upon the Cœlian hill, who am now basking in the warm skies of Palmyra, and, notwithstanding all the splendour and luxury by which I am surrounded, longing to be once more in Rome, by the side of my Curtius, and with him discoursing, as we have been wont to do, of the acts and policy of the magnificent Aurelian.

But to the purpose of this letter, which is, in agreement with my promise, to tell you of my fortunes since I parted from you, and of my good or ill success, as it may be, in the prosecution of that affair which has driven me so far from my beloved Rome. Oh, humanity! why art thou so afflicted? Why have the immortal gods made the cup of life so bitter? And why am I singled out to partake of one that seems all bitter? My feelings sometimes overmaster my philosophy. You can forgive this, who know my sorrows. Still I am delaying to inform you concerning my journey and my arrival. Now I will begin.

As soon as I had lost sight of you weeping on the quay, holding in your hand the little Gallus, and the dear Lucilia leaning on your arm, and could no longer, even by mounting upon the highest part of the vessel, discern the waving of your hands, nor cause you to see the fervour with which I returned the sign of friendship, I at once left off thinking of you, as far as I could, and, to divert my thoughts, began to examine, as if I had never seen them before, the banks of the yellow Tiber. At first the crowds of shipping, of every form, and from every part of the world, distracted the sight, and compelled me to observe what was immediately around me. The cries of the sailors, as they were engaged in managing different parts of their vessels, or as they called out in violent and abusive terms to those who passed them, or as their several galleys struck against each other in their attempts to go up and down the river, together with the frequent roarings and bellowings of whole cargoes of wild beasts from the deserts of Asia and Africa, destined to the amphitheatre, intermingled with the jargon of a hundred different barbarian languages, from the thousands who thronged the decks of this fleet of all nations—these sights and sounds at first wholly absorbed me, and for a moment shut all the world beside—even you—out of my mind. It was a strange yet inspiring scene, and gave me greater thoughts than ever of the power and majesty of Rome. Here were men and ships that had traversed oceans and continents to bring the offerings of their toil, and lay them at the feet of the mistress of the world. And over all this bustle, created by the busy spirit of commerce, a splendour and gaiety were thrown by numerous triremes and boats of pleasure, which, glittering under the light of a summer's morning sun, were just setting out upon some excursion of pleasure, with streamers floating from the slender masts, music swelling up from innumerable performers, and shouts of merry laughter from crowds of the rich and noble youths of the city, who reclined upon the decks, beneath canopies of the richest dyes. As these Cleopatra barges floated along with their soft burdens, torrents of vituperative epithet were poured upon them by the rough children of Neptune, which was received with an easy indifference, or returned with no lack of ability in that sort of warfare, according to the temper or breeding of the parties.

When the novelty of this scene was worn out, for though often seen it is ever new, and we had fallen a few miles below the city, to where the eye first meets the smiling face of the country, I looked eagerly around, first upon one, and then upon the other, bank of the river, in search of the villas of our fortunate citizens, waiting impatiently till the well-known turn of the stream should bring me before yours, where, with our mutual friends, we have passed so many happy days. It was not long before I was gratified. Our vessel gracefully doubled the projecting point, blackened with that thick grove of pine, and your hospitable dwelling greeted my eyes; now, alas! again, by that loved and familiar object, made to overflow with tears. I was obliged, by one manly effort, to leap clear of the power of all-subduing love, for my sensibilities were drawing upon me the observation of my fellow passengers. I therefore withdrew from the side of the vessel where I had been standing, and moving to that part of it which would best protect me from what, but now, I had so eagerly sought, sat down and occupied myself in watching the movements and the figures of the persons whom chance had thrown into my company, and with whom I was now, for several weeks, to be shut up in the narrow compass of our merchant-barque. I had sat but a little while, when the master of the ship, passing by me, stopped, and asked if it was I who was to land at Utica—for that one, or more than one, he believed, had spoken for a passage only to that port.

"No truly," I replied; and added, "Do you, then, cross over to Utica?—that seems to me far from a direct course for those bound to Syria."

"Better round-about," rejoined he, in his rough way, "than risk Scylla and Charybdis; and so would you judge, were the bowels of my good ship stored with your wealth, as they are, it may be, with that of some of your friends. The Roman merchant likes not that narrow strait, fatal to so many, but prefers the open sea, though the voyage be longer. But with this wind —once out of this foul Tiber, and we shall soon see the white shores of Africa. Truly, what a medley we seem to have on board! Jews, Romans, Syrians, Greeks, soldiers, adventurers, merchants, pedlars, and, if I miss not, Christians too; and you, if I miss not again, the only patrician. I marvel at your taking ship with so spotted a company, when there are these gay passenger boats, sacred to the trim persons of the capital, admitting even not so much as a case of jewels beside."

"Doubtless it would have been better on some accounts," I replied, "but my business was urgent, and I could not wait for the sailing of the packet-boats; and besides, I am not unwilling to adventure where I shall mix with a greater variety of my own species, and gain a better knowledge of myself by the study of others. In this object I am not likely to be disappointed, for you furnish me with diverse samples, which I can contemplate at my leisure."

"If one studied so as to know well the properties of fishes or animals," rejoined he, in a sneering tone, "it would be profitable, for fishes can be eaten, and animals can be used: but man! I know little that he is good for, but to bury, and so fatten the soil. Emperors, as being highest, should be best, and yet, what are they? Whether they have been fools or madmen, the Tiber has still run blood, and the air been poisoned by the rotting carcases of their victims. Claudius was a good man, I grant; but the gods, I believe, envied us our felicity, and so took him."

"I trust," said I, "that the present auspices will not deceive us, and that the happiness begun under that almost divine ruler, will be completed under him whom he designated as most worthy of the sceptre of the world, and whose reign—certainly we may say it—has commenced so prosperously. I think better of man than you do, and I cannot but believe that there will yet rise up among us those who shall feel what power, almost of a god, is lodged in the will of a Roman emperor, and will use it like a god to bless, not curse mankind. Why may not Nature repeat the virtuous Antonines? Her power is not spent. For myself, I have faith that Aurelian will restore not so much the greatness, as the peace and happiness, of the empire."

"So have not I," cried the master of the ship: "is he not sprung from the loins of a peasant? Has not the camp been his home? Was not a shield his cradle? Such power as his will craze him. Born to it, and the chance were better. Mark a sailor's word: he will sooner play the part of Maximin, than that of Antonine or Severus, or of our late good Claudius. When he feels easy in the saddle, we shall see what he will do. So far, the blood of barbarians, slain in battle, has satisfied him: when once in Rome, that of citizens will be sweeter. But may the gods befriend us!"

At this point of our discourse we were interrupted by loud vociferations from the forward part of the vessel, where I had long observed a crowd of the passengers, who seemed engaged in some earnest conversation. The tones now became sharp and angry, and the group suddenly dispersed, separating this way and that, as the hoarse and commanding voice of the master of the ship reached them, calling upon them to observe the rules of the vessel, which allowed of no riot or quarrelling. Towards me there moved one whom I hardly know how to describe, and yet feel that I must. You will here doubtless exclaim, "Why obliged to describe? Why say so much of accidental companions?" But you will answer yourself, I feel persuaded, my

Curtius, by supposing that I should not particularly notice a mere companion of the voyage, unless he had connected himself in some manner with my fortunes. Such has been the case with this person, and one other whom I will shortly introduce to you. As I was saying, then, when that group dispersed, one of its number moved towards me, and seated himself near me. He was evidently a Roman and a citizen. His features were of no other nation. But with all the dignity that characterised him as a Roman, there were mixed a sweetness and a mildness, such as I never remembered to have seen in another; and in the eye there was a melancholy and a deepness, if I may say so, more remarkable still. It was the eye of one who was all sorrow, all love, and all purity; in whom the soul had undisputed sway over the passions and the senses. I have seen an expression which has approached it in some of our priests, but far below it in power and beauty. My first impulse was to address him, but his pallid and thoughtful countenance, together with that eye, restrained me; and I know not how I should have overcome this strange diffidence, had not the difficulty been removed by the intervention of a third party. This was no other than one of those travelling Jews, who infest all cities, towns, and regions, and dwell among all people, yet mixing with none. He was bent almost double by the weight of large packages of goods, of all descriptions, which he carried, part before and part behind him, and which he had not yet laid aside, in the hope, I suppose, of effecting some sales among the passengers.

"Here's old Isaac the Jew," cried he, as he approached towards where I sat, and then stood before me resting his pannier of articles upon a pile of merchandise, which lay there—"here's old Isaac the Jew, last from Rome, but a citizen of the world, now on his way to Carthage and Syria, with all sorts of jewellery and ornaments: nothing that a lady wants that's not here—or gentleman either. Most noble sir, let me press upon you this steel mirror, of the most perfect polish: see the setting, too; could the fancy of it be better? No. You would prefer a ring: look then at this assortment—iron and gold rings; marriage, seal, and fancy rings—buckles, too: have you seen finer? Here, too, are soaps, perfumes, and salves for the toilet—hair-pins and essences. Perhaps you would prefer somewhat a little more useful. I shall show you, then, these sandals and slippers: see what a charming variety, both in form and colour: pretty feet alone should press these—think you not so? But, alas! I cannot tempt you."

"How is it possible," said I, "for another to speak when thy tongue wags so fast? Those rings I would gladly have examined, and now that thou hast discharged that volley of hoarse sounds, I pray thee open again that case. I thank thee for giving me an occupation."

"Take care!" replied the voluble Jew, throwing a quick and mischievous glance towards the Roman whom I have already mentioned—"take care how my friend here of the new faith hears thee or sees thee, an thou would'st escape a rebuke. He holds my beauties here and my calling in high contempt; and as for occupation, he thinks one never need be idle who has himself to converse with."

"What you have last uttered is true," replied the person whom he addressed: "he need never want for employment who possesses the power of thought. But as to thy trade, I object not to that, nor to what thou sellest: only to being myself a buyer."

"Ha! thou wilt not buy? Trust Isaac for that. I keep that which shall suit all, and enslave all. I would have made thee buy of me before, but for the uproar of those soldiers."

While uttering these words, he had placed the case of rings in my hands to examine them, and was engaged himself in exploring the depths of a large package, from which he at length triumphantly drew forth a parchment roll.

"Now open all thine eyes, Nazarene," cried the Jew, "and thou shalt see what thou shalt. Look!"

And so saying, he unfolded the first page of the book, upon which the eye of the Roman had no sooner fallen, than his face suddenly glowed as if a god shone through him; and reverently seizing the book, he exclaimed,

"I thank thee, Jew; thou hast conquered: I am a customer too. Here is my purse—take what thou wilt."

"Hold, hold!" interrupted the Jew, laughing, "I have not done with thee yet; what thou hast bought in Greek, I would now sell thee again in Latin. Thy half convert, the soldier Macer, would greet this as a cordial to his famishing soul. Take both, and thou hast them cheaper."

"Your cunning hardly deserves such a reward," said the Christian, as I now perceived him to be, "but you have said well, and I not unwillingly obey your suggestions. Pay yourself now for both, and give them to me, carefully rolled up."

"No better sale than this shall I make to-day, and that too to a Jew-hating Nazarene. But what matters it whom I tax for the upholding of Jerusalem? Surely it is sweeter, when the cruel Roman or the heretic Christian is made unconsciously to build at her walls."

Thus muttered the Jew to himself, as he skilfully bound into a parcel the Christian's books.

"And now, most excellent sir," said he, turning towards me, "what do you find worthy your own or your lady's finger? Here is another case—perhaps these may strike you as rarer for their devices or their workmanship. But they are rather better suited to the tastes of the rich Palmyrenes, to whom I am bearing them."

"Ah!" I exclaimed, "these are what I want. This seal ring, with the head of Zenobia, for which I sought in vain in Rome, I will buy, nor care for its cost, if thou canst assure me of its resemblance to the great queen. Who was the artist?"

"As I stand here, a true son of Abraham," he replied, "it was worked by a Greek jeweller, who lives hard by the Temple of Fortune, and who has engraved it after a drawing made by a brother, an inhabitant of Palmyra. Two such artists in their way are not to be found. I myself, moreover, bore the original drawing from Demetrius to his brother in Rome, and that it is like the great queen I can well testify, for I have often seen her. Her marvellous beauty is here well expressed, or as well as that which partakes so much more of heaven than of earth can be. But look at these, too. Here I have what I look to do well with. See! Heads of Odenatus! Think you not they will take well? These also are done with the same care as the others, and by the same workmen. Nothing of the kind has as yet been seen in Palmyra, nor indeed in Rome. Happy Isaac!—thy fortune is made! Come, put them on thy finger, and observe their beauty. King and queen—how lovingly they sit there together! 'Twas just so when Odenatus was alive. They were a noble and a loving pair. The queen yet weeps for him."

"Jew," said I, "on thy word I purchase these. Although thy name is in no good repute, yet thy face is honest, and I will trust thee so far."

"The name of the unfortunate and the weak is never in repute," said Isaac, as he took my money, and folded up the rings, his whole manner suddenly changing. "The Jew is now but a worm, writhing under the heel of the proud Roman. Many a time has he, however, as thou well knowest, turned upon his destroyer, and tasted the sweetness of a brief revenge. Why should I speak of the massacres of Egypt, Cyrene, and Syria, in the days of Trajan? Let Rome beware! Small though we seem, the day will yet arrive when the glory of Zion shall fill the whole earth—and He shall yet arise, before whom the mighty emperor of Rome shall tremble in his palaces. This is what I say. Thanks to the great Aurelian, that even a poor son of Abraham may speak his mind and not lose his head. Here's old Isaac: who'll buy of old Isaac—rings, pins, and razors —who'll buy?"

And so singing, he turned away, and mixed with the

passengers in the other parts of the vessel. The wild glare of his eye, and deep, suppressed tone of his voice, as he spoke of the condition and hopes of his tribe, startled and moved me, and I would willingly have prolonged a conversation with one of that singular people, about whom I really know nothing, and with none of whom had I ever before come in contact. When I see you again, I shall have much to tell you of him; for during the rest of the voyage we were often thrown together, and, as you will learn, he has become of essential service to me in the prosecution of my objects.

No sooner had Isaac withdrawn from our company, than I embraced the opportunity to address myself to the remarkable-looking person whom I have already in part described.

"It is a great testimony," I said, turning towards him, "which these Jews bear to their national religion. I much doubt if Romans, under similar circumstances of oppression, would exhibit a constancy like theirs. Their attachment, too, is to an invisible religion, as one may say, which makes it the more remarkable. They have neither temples, altars, victims, nor statues, nor any form of god or goddess, to which they pay real or feigned adoration. Towards us they bear deep and inextinguishable hate, for our religion not less than for our oppressions. I never see a Jew threading our streets with busy steps, and his dark, piercing eye, but I seem to see an assassin, who, with Nero, wishes the Roman people had but one neck, that he might exterminate the whole race with a single blow. Towards you, however, who are so nearly of his own faith, I suppose his sentiments are more kindly. The Christian Roman, perhaps, he would spare."

"Not so, I greatly fear," replied the Christian. "Nay, the Jew bears a deeper hatred towards us than towards you, and would sooner sacrifice us; for the reason, doubtless, that we are nearer him in faith than you; just as our successful emperors have no sooner found themselves securely seated, than they have first turned upon the members of their own family, that from this, the most dangerous quarter, there should be no fear of rival or usurper. The Jew holds the Christian, though in some sort believing with him, as a rival, a usurper, a rebel; as one who would substitute a novelty for the ancient creed of his people, and, in a word, bring ruin upon the very existence of his tribe. His suspicions, truly, are not without foundation, but they do not excuse the temper with which he regards us. I cast no imputation upon the virtues of friend Isaac, in what I say. The very spirit of universal love, I believe, reigns in his soul. Would that all of his race were like him!"

"What you say is new and strange," I replied. "I may possibly bring shame upon myself by saying so, but it is true. I have been accustomed to regard Christians and Jews as in effect one people; one, I mean, in opinion and feeling. But in truth I *know* nothing. You are not ignorant of the prejudice which exists towards both these races on the part of the Romans. I have yielded, with multitudes around me, to prevailing ideas, taking no steps to learn their truth or error. Our writers, from Tacitus to the base tools, for such they must have been, who lent themselves to the purposes of the bigot Macrianus, and who filled the city with their accounts of the Christians, have all agreed in representing your faith as a dark and mischievous superstition. I have, indeed, been struck with the circumstance, that while the Jews make no converts from among us, great numbers are reported to have joined the Christians; and of those, not a few of the higher orders. The late Emperor Philip, I think it clear, was a Christian. This might have taught me that there is a wide difference between the Christian and the Jew. But the general hatred towards both the one and the other, together with the persecutions to which they have been exposed, have made me more than indifferent to their merits."

"I trust the time will come," replied the Christian, "when our cause will be examined on the ground of its merits. Why may not we believe that it has now come? The Roman world is at peace. A strong and generous prince is upon the throne. Mild and just laws restrain the furious bigotry of an ignorant and sanguinary priesthood. Men of intelligence and virtue adorn our profession, from whom those who are anxious to know the truth can hear it; and copies of our sacred books, both in Greek and Latin, abound, whence may easily be learned the true principles of our faith, and the light of whose holy pages would instantly dispel the darkness by which the minds of many, even of the virtuous and well disposed, are oppressed. It is hardly likely that a fitter opportunity will soon offer for an examination of the claims of Christianity. We have nothing to dread but the deadness and indifference of the public mind. It is not credible that Polytheism should stand a day upon any fair comparison of it with the religion of Christ. You yourself are not a believer, (pardon my boldness) in the ineffable stupidities of the common religion. To suppose you *were*—I see by the expression of your countenance, would be an unpardonable offence. I sincerely believe, that nothing more is wanting to change you, and every intelligent Roman, from professed supporters of the common religion (but real infidels), into warm believers and advocates of the doctrine of Christ, but simply this, to read his sayings, and the delineation of his character, as they have been written down by some of his followers. You are, I see, incredulous, but not more so than I was myself only a year ago; yet you behold me a Christian. I had to contend against, perhaps, far more adverse influences than would oppose you. You start with surprise that I should give evidence that I know you; but I have many a time seen you at the shop of Publius, and have heard you in your addresses to the people. I am the son of a priest of the Temple of Jupiter—son of a man, who, to a mildness and gentleness of soul that would do honour to the Christian, added a faith in the religion of his fathers, deep-struck and firm-rooted as the rocks of ocean. I was his assistant in the duties of his office. My childish faith was all he could wish it; I reverenced a religion which had nurtured virtues like his. In process of time, I became myself a father. Four children, more beautiful than ever visited the dreams of Phidias, made my dwelling a portion of Elysium, as I then thought. Their mother—but why should I speak of her? It is enough to say, she was a Roman mother. At home, it was my supreme happiness to sport with my little ones, or initiate them into the elements of useful knowledge. And often, when at the temple preparing for the days of ceremony, my children were with me; and my labours were nothing, cheered by the music of their feet running upon the marble pavements, and of their merry voices echoing among the columns and arches of the vast interior. Oh days thrice happy! They were too happy to last. Within the space of one year, one cruel year, these four living idols were ravished from my arms by a prevailing disease. My wife, broken-hearted, soon followed them, and I was left alone. I need not describe my grief: I will only say, that with bitter imprecations I cursed the gods. 'Who are ye,' I cried, 'who sit above in your secure seats, and make your sport of human woe? Ye are less than men. Man though I am, I would not inflict upon the meanest slave the misery ye have poured upon my defenceless head. Where are your mercies?' I was frantic. How long this lasted, I cannot tell, for I took no note of time. I was awakened, may I not say saved, by a kind neighbour whom I had long known to be a Christian. He was a witness of my sufferings, and with deep compassion ministered to my necessities. 'Probus,' said he, 'I know your sorrows, and I know your wants. I have perceived that neither your own thoughts, nor all the philosophy of your venerable father, have brought you peace. It is not surprising: ye are but men, and ye have but the power and the wisdom of men. It is aid from the Divinity that you want. I will not discourse with you; but I leave with you this book, which I simply ask you to read.' I read it, and read it again and again; and I am a Christian. As the Christian grew up within me, my pains were soothed, and days once days of tears and unavailing complaints are now days of calm and cheerful duty:—I am a new man."

I cannot describe to you, my Curtius, the effect of this little narrative upon myself, or upon those who, as he spoke, had gathered round, especially those hard-featured soldiers. Tears flowed down their weather-beaten faces, and one of them—Macer, as I afterwards learned—cried out, "Where now are the gods of Rome?" Probus started from his seat, apparently for the first time conscious of any other listener beside myself, and joined the master of the vessel at the helm. I resigned myself to meditation; and that night fell asleep, thinking of the Christian and his book.

Five days brought us in sight of the African coast, but quite to the west of Utica. So, coasting along, we presently came off against Hippo, and then doubling a promontory, both Utica and Carthage were at once visible—Utica nearer, Carthage just discernible in the distance. All was now noise and bustle, as we rapidly drew near the port. Many of our passengers were to land here, and they were busily employed, with the aid of the sailors, in collecting their merchandise or their baggage. The soldiers destined to the African service here left us, together with the Jew Isaac, and the Christian Probus. I was sorry, indeed, to lose them, as besides them there was not one on board, except the governor of the ship, from whose company or conversation I could derive either pleasure or knowledge. They are both of them, however, destined to Palmyra, as well as myself, and I shall soon expect them to join me here. You smile at my speaking thus of a travelling Jew and a despised Christian, but in the issue you will acknowledge your as well as my obligations to them both. I confess myself attached to them. As the Jew turned to bid me farewell, before he sprang on shore, he said,

"Most noble Piso, if thou forsakest the gods of Rome, let it be for the synagogue of the children of Abraham, whose faith is not of yesterday. Be not beguiled by the specious tongue of that heretic Probus. I can tell thee a better story than his."

"Fear not, honest Isaac," I cried; "I am not yet so weary of the faith of my ancestors. That cannot be altogether despicable, which has had power to bind in one mass the whole Roman people for so many ages. I shall be no easy convert to either you or Probus. Farewell, to meet in Tadmor." Probus now passed me, and said, "If I should not see you in the Eastern capital, according to my purpose, I trust I shall in Rome. My dwelling is in the Livian Way not far from the Pantheon, opposite the well-known house of Vitruvius, still so called; or at the shop of the learned Publius I may be seen every morning, and may there be always heard of." I assured him that no affairs could be so pressing, after I should return to Rome, as not to allow me to seek him, but that I hoped the fates would not interpose to deprive me of the pleasure of first seeing him at Palmyra. So we parted. And very soon after, the merchandise and passengers being all landed, we set sail again, and stood out to sea. I regretted that we were not to touch at Carthage, as my desire had always been strong to see that famous place. An adverse wind, however, setting in from the north, drove us farther towards the city than the pilot intended to have gone, and I thus obtained quite a satisfactory glimpse of the African capital. I was surprised at the indications of its vastness and grandeur. Since its attempted restoration by Augustus, it has advanced steadily to almost its former populousness and magnificence. Nothing could be more imposing and beautiful than its long lines of buildings, its towers, walls, palaces, and columns, seen through the warm and rosy mist of an African sky. I could hardly believe that I was looking but upon a provincial city, a dependent upon almighty Rome. It soon sank below the horizon, as its glory had sunk once before.

I will not detain you long with our voyage, but will only mark out its course. Leaving the African shore, we struck across to Sicily, and coasting along its eastern border, beheld with pleasure the towering form of Ætna, sending up into the heavens a dull and sluggish cloud of vapours. We then ran between the Peloponnesus and Crete, and so held our course till the Island of Cyprus rose like her own fair goddess from the ocean, and filled our eyes with the beautiful vision of hill and valley, wooded promontory, and glittering towns and villas. A fair wind soon withdrew us from these charming prospects; and after driving us swiftly and roughly over the remainder of our way, rewarded us with a brighter and more welcome vision still, the coast of Syria and our destined port Berytus.

As far as the eye could reach, both towards the north and the south, we beheld a luxuriant region, crowded with villages, and giving every indication of comfort and wealth. The city itself, which we rapidly approached, was of inferior size, but presented an agreeable prospect of warehouses, public and private edifices, overtopped here and there by the lofty palm, and other trees of a new and peculiar foliage. Four days were consumed here in the purchase of slaves, camels, and horses, and in other preparations for the journey across the desert. Two routes presented themselves, one more, the other less direct; the last, though more circuitous, appeared to me the more desirable, as it would take me within sight of the modern glories and ancient remains of Heliopolis. This, therefore, was determined upon; and on the morning of the fifth day we set forward upon our long march. Four slaves, two camels, and three horses, with an Arab conductor, constituted our little caravan; but for greater safety we attached ourselves to a much larger one than our own, in which we were swallowed up and lost, consisting of travellers and traders from all parts of the world, and who were also on their way to Palmyra, as a point whence to separate to various parts of the vast East. It would delight me to lay before you, with the distinctness and minuteness of a picture, the whole of this novel, and to me most interesting route; but I must content myself with a slight sketch, and reserve fuller communications to the time, when, once more seated with you upon the Cœlian, we enjoy the freedom of social converse.

Our way through the valleys of Libanus, was like one long wandering among the pleasure-grounds of opulent citizens. The land was every where richly cultivated, and a happier peasantry, as far as the eye of the traveller could judge, nowhere exists. The most luxuriant valleys of our own Italy are not more crowded with the evidences of plenty and contentment. Upon drawing near to the ancient Baalbec, I found, on inquiry of our guide, that we were not to pass through it, as I had hoped, nor even very near it, not nearer than between two and three miles; so that in this I had been clearly deceived by those of whom I had made the most exact inquiries at Berytus. I thought I discovered great command of myself, in that I did not break the head of my Arab, who, doubtless to answer purposes of his own, had brought me thus out of my way for nothing. The event proved, however, that it was not for nothing; for soon after we had started on our journey, on the morning of the second day, turning suddenly round the projecting rock of a mountain ridge, we all at once beheld, as if a veil had been lifted up, Heliopolis and its suburbs, spread out before us in all their various beauty. The city lay about three miles distant. I could only, therefore, identify its principal structure, the Temple of the Sun, as built by the first Antonine. This towered above the walls, and over all the other buildings, and gave vast ideas of the greatness of the place, leading the mind to crowd it with other edifices that should bear some proportion to this noble monument of imperial magnificence. As suddenly as the view of this imposing scene had been revealed, so suddenly was it again eclipsed, by another short turn in the road, which took us once more into the mountain valleys. But the overhanging and impenetrable foliage of a Syrian forest shielding me from the fierce rays of a burning sun, soon reconciled me to my loss, more especially as I knew that in a short time we were to enter upon the sandy desert, which stretches from the Anti-Libanus almost to the very walls of Palmyra.

Upon this boundless desert we now soon entered. The scene which it presented was more dismal than I can describe. A red, moving sand—or hard and baked by the heat of a sun, such as Rome never knows—low, grey rocks, just rising here and there above the level of the plain, with now and then the dead and glittering trunk of a vast cedar, whose roots seemed as if they had outlasted centuries—the bones of camels and elephants, scattered on either hand, dazzling the sight by reason of their excessive whiteness—at a distance occasionally an Arab of the desert, for a moment surveying our long line, and then darting off to his fastnesses—these were the objects which, with scarce any variation, met our eyes during the four wearisome days that we dragged ourselves over this wild and inhospitable region. A little after noon of the fourth day, as we started on our way, having refreshed ourselves and our exhausted animals, at a spring which here poured out its warm but still grateful waters to the traveller, my ears received the agreeable news, that towards the east there could now be discerned the dark line which indicated our approach to the verdant tract that encompasses the great city. Our own excited spirits were quickly imparted to our beasts, and a more rapid movement soon revealed into distinctness the high land and waving groves of palm-trees which mark the site of Palmyra.

It was several miles before we reached the city, that we suddenly found ourselves—landing, as it were, from a sea upon an island or continent—in a rich and thickly peopled country. The roads indicated an approach to a great capital, in the increasing numbers of those who thronged them, meeting and passing us, overtaking us, or crossing our path. Elephants, camels, and the dromedary, which I had before seen only in the amphitheatres, I here beheld as the native inhabitants of the soil. Frequent villas of the rich and luxurious Palmyrenes, to which they retreat from the greater heats of the city, now threw a lovely charm over the scene. Nothing can exceed the splendour of these sumptuous palaces. Italy itself has nothing which surpasses them. The new and brilliant costumes of the persons whom we met, together with the rich housings of the animals which they rode served greatly to add to all this beauty. I was still entranced, as it were, by the objects around me, and buried in reflection, when I was aroused by the shout of those who led the caravan, and who had attained the summit of a little rising ground, saying, "Palmyra! Palmyra!" I urged forward my steed, and in a moment the most wonderful prospect I ever beheld—no, I cannot except even Rome—burst upon my sight. Flanked by hills of considerable elevation on the east, the city filled the whole plain below as far as the eye could reach, both towards the north and towards the south. This immense plain was all one vast and boundless city. It seemed to me to be larger than Rome. Yet I knew very well that it could not be—that it was not. And it was some time before I understood the true character of the scene before me, so as to separate the city from the country, and the country from the city, which here wonderfully interpenetrate each other, and so confound and deceive the observer. For the city proper is so studded with groups of lofty palm-trees, shooting up among its temples and palaces, and on the other hand, the plain in its immediate vicinity is so thickly adorned with magnificent structures of the purest marble, that it is not easy, nay it is impossible, at the distance at which I contemplated the whole, to distinguish the line which divided the one from the other. It was all city and all country, all country and all city. Those which lay before me I was ready to believe were the Elysian fields. I imagined that I saw under my feet the dwellings of purified men and of gods; certainly they were too glorious for the mere earth-born. There was a central point, however, which chiefly fixed my attention, where the vast Temple of the Sun stretched upwards its thousand columns of polished marble to the heavens, in its matchless beauty casting into the shade every other work of art of which the world can boast. I have stood before the Parthenon, and have almost worshipped that divine achievement of the immortal Phidias. But it is a toy by the side of this bright crown of the Eastern capital. I have been at Milan, at Ephesus, at Alexandria, at Antioch; but in neither of those renowned cities have I beheld any thing that I can allow to approach in united extent, grandeur, and most consummate beauty, this almost more than work of man. On each side of this, the central point, there rose upwards slender pyramids, pointed obelisks, domes of the most graceful proportions, columns, arches, and lofty towers, for number and for form beyond my power to describe. These buildings, as well as the walls of the city, being all either of white marble, or of some stone as white, and being every where in their whole extent interspersed, as I have already said, with multitudes of overshadowing palm-trees, perfectly filled and satisfied my sense of beauty, and made me feel for the moment as if in such a scene I should love to dwell, and there end my days. Nor was I alone in these transports of delight. All my fellow-travellers seemed equally affected: and from the native Palmyrenes, of whom there were many among us, the most impassioned and boastful exclamations broke forth. "What is Rome to this?" they cried: "Fortune is not constant. Why may not Palmyra be what Rome has been—mistress of the world? Who more fit to rule than the great Zenobia? A few years may see great changes. Who can tell what shall come to pass?" These, and many such sayings, were uttered by those around me, accompanied by many significant gestures and glances of the eye. I thought of them afterwards. We now descended the hill, and the long line of our caravan moved on towards the city.

LETTER II.

I FEAR lest the length of my first letter may have fatigued you, my Curtius, knowing, as I so well do, how you esteem brevity. I hope at this time not to try your patience, But however I may weary or vex you by my garrulity, I am sure of a patient and indulgent reader in the dear Lucilia, to whom I would now first of all commend myself. I salute her, and with her the little Gallus. My writing to you is a sufficient proof that I myself am well.

By reason of our delaying so long on that little hill, and at other points, for the sake of drinking in full draughts of the unrivalled beauty which lay spread over all the scenery within the scope of our vision, we did not approach the walls of the city till the last rays of the sun were lingering upon the higher buildings of the capital. This rendered every object so much the more beautiful; for a flood of golden light, of a richer hue, it seemed to me, than our sun ever sheds upon Rome, rolled over the city, and plain, and distant mountains, giving to the whole a gorgeousness altogether beyond any thing I ever saw before, and agreeing well with all my impressions of oriental magnificence. It was seen under the right aspect. Not one expectation was disappointed, but rather exceeded, as we came in sight of the vast walls of the city, and of the "Roman Gate," as it is called, through which we were to make our entrance. It was all upon the grandest scale. The walls were higher, and more frequently defended by square massy towers springing out of them, than those of Rome. The towers, which on either side flanked the gateway, and which were connected by an immense arch flung from one to the other, were particularly magnificent. No sooner had we passed through 'it, than we found ourselves in a street lined as it were with palaces. It was of great width—we have no street like it in this respect—of an exact level, and stretched onwards farther than the eye could distinctly reach, till, as I was told, it was terminated by another gate similar to that by which we had entered. The buildings on each side of it were altogether of marble, of Grecian design—the city is filled with Greek artists of every description—frequently adorned with porticoes of the most rich and costly construction, and the long ranges of private dwellings often interrupted by temples of religion, edifices of vast extent belonging to the state, or by gardens attached to the residences of the luxurious Palmyrene nobility.

"It is well for Palmyra," here muttered my slave Milo, "that the emperor has never, like us, travelled this way."

"Why so, Milo?" said I.

"I simply think," rejoined he, "that he would burn it down; and it were a pity so many fine buildings should be destroyed. Was there not once a place called Carthage? I have heard it said that it was once as large as Rome, and as well garnished with temples, and that for that reason the Romans 'blotted it out.' The people here may thank the desert which we have crossed that they are not as Carthage. Aurelian, I trow, little dreams what glory is to be won here in the east, or else he would not waste his time upon the savage Goths."

"The Romans are no longer barbarians," I replied, "as they were once. They build up now, instead of demolishing. Remember that Augustus rebuilt Carthage, and that Antonius Pius founded that huge and beautiful temple which rose out of the midst of Baalbec; and besides that, if I am not mistaken, many of the noblest monuments of art in this very city are the fruit of his munificence."

"Gods, what a throng is here!" ejaculated Milo, little heeding, apparently, what I had said; "how are we to get our beasts along? They pay no more regard to us, either, than if we were not Romans. Could any one have believed a people existed of such strange customs and appearance? What carriages, what waggons, what animals! and what unheard-of dresses! and from all parts of the earth, too, as it would seem! But it is a pretty sight. Pity, though, but they could move as quick, as they look well. Fellow, there, you will gratify us, if you will start your camels a little out of the way. We wish to make towards the house of Gracchus, and we cannot pass you."

The rider of the camel turned round his turbaned head, and fixing upon Milo a pair of fierce eyes, bade him hold his peace. "Did he not see the street was crowded?"

"I see it is filled with a set of dull idlers," replied Milo, "who want nothing but Roman rods to teach them a quick and wholesome movement. Friend, lend me thy cudgel, and I will engage to set thy beasts and thee, too, in motion. If not, consider that we are new comers, and Romans withal, and that we deserve some regard."

"Romans!" screamed he; "may curses light on you! You swarm here like locusts, and like them you come but to devour. Take my counsel: turn your faces the other way, and off to the desert again! I give you no welcome for one. Now pass on, if on you still will go, and take the curse of Hassan the Arab along with you."

"Milo," said I, "have a care how you provoke these orientals. Bethink yourself that we are not now in the streets of Rome. Bridle your tongue betimes, or your head may roll off your shoulders before you can have time to eat your words to save it."

"I am a slave indeed," answered Milo, with some dignity for him, "but I eat other food than my own words. In that there hangs something of the Roman about me."

We were now opposite what I discovered, from the

c

statues and emblems upon it, and surrounding it, to be the Temple of Justice, and I knew, therefore, that the palace on the other side of the street, adorned with porticoes, and partly hidden among embowering trees and shrubs, must be the dwelling of Gracchus.

We turned down into a narrower street, and after proceeding a little way, passed under a massy arched gateway, and found ourselves in the spacious courtyard of this princely mansion. Slaves soon surrounded us; and by their alacrity in assisting me to dismount, and in performing every office of a hospitable reception, showed that we were expected guests, and that my letters announcing my intended visit had been received. Leaving my slaves and effects to the care of the servants of the house, I followed one who seemed to be a sort of head among them, through walks bordered with the choicest trees, flowers and shrubs, opening here and there in the most graceful manner to reveal a statue of some sylvan god reclining under the shade, and soon reached the rear of the house, which I entered by a flight of marble steps. Through a lofty hall I passed into a saloon which seemed the reception-room of the palace, where I had hardly arrived, and obtained one glance at my soiled dress and sun-burnt visage in the mirror, than my ear caught the quick sound of a female foot hastening over the pavement of the hall, and, turning suddenly, I caught in my arms the beautiful Fausta. It was well for me that I was so taken by surprise, for I acted naturally, which I fear I should not have done if I had had a moment to deliberate before I met her; for she is no longer a girl, as in Rome, running and jumping after her slave to school, but a nearly full-grown woman, and of a beauty so imposing as might well cause embarrassment in a youth of even more pretensions than myself.

"Are you, indeed," said I, retaining each hand in mine, but feeling, that in spite of all my assumed courage, I was covered with blushes, "are you indeed the little Fausta? Truly there must be marvellous virtues in the air of Palmyra. It is but four years since you left Rome, and then, as I remember—shall I mention such a thing?—you were but twelve, and now, though but —"

"Oh!" cried she, "never begin such a speech; it will only trouble you before you can end it. How glad I am to see you! Welcome, dear Lucius, to Palmyra! If open hearts can make you happy here, you will not fail to be so. But how did you leave all in Rome? First your friend Marcus? and Lucilia? and the noble, good Portia? Ah! how happy were those days in Rome! Come sit on these cushions by this open window. But more than all, how does the dear pedagogue and dialectician, the learned Solon? Is he as wise yet as his great namesake? Oh what days of merriment have his vanity and simplicity afforded me! But he was a good soul. Would he could have accompanied you! You are not so far out of leading-strings that you could not have taken him with you as a travelling Mentor. In truth, nothing could have given me more pleasure."

"I came away in great haste, dear Fausta," said I, "with scarce a moment for preparation of any kind. You have but this morning received my letter, which was but part of a day in advance of me. If I could have done it, I should have given you more timely notice. I could not, therefore, look out for companions for the way. It would, however, have been a kindness to Solon, and a pleasure to me. But why have I not before asked for your father? is not the noble Gracchus at home?— and is he well?"

"He is at home, or rather he is in the city," replied Fausta, "and why he makes it so late before returning, I cannot tell: but you will soon see him. In the mean time, let my slaves show you where to find your rooms, that you may rest, and prepare for supper."

So saying, she clapped her hands, and a tall Ethiopian, with a turban as white as his face was black, quickly made his appearance, and took me in his charge.

"Look well after your toilet," cried Fausta, laughing, as I left the room; "we think more of costume here than they do in Rome."

I followed my dark conductor through many passages to a distant part of the building, where I found apartments furnished with every luxury, and already prepared for my use.

"Here I have carefully placed your baggage," said the slave, as I entered the room, "and whatever else I thought you might need. Call Hannibal, when you wish for my services; I am now yours. This door leads to a small room where will lodge your own slave Milo; the others are in the stables." Thus delivering himself, he departed.

The windows of my apartment opened upon the wide street by which we had entered the city, not immediately, but first upon a border of trees and flowers, then upon a low wall, here and there crowned with a statue or a vase, and which separated the house from the street, and last upon the street itself, its busy throngs and noble structures. I stood for a moment enjoying the scene, rendered more impressive by the dim but still glowing light of the declining day. Sounds of languages which I knew not fell upon my ear, sent forth by those who urged along through the crowds their cattle, or by those who would draw attention to the articles which they had to sell. All was new and strange, and tended, together with my reflections upon the business which had borne me so far from my home and you, to fill me with melancholy. I was roused from my reverie by the voice of Milo.

"If," said he, "the people of these eastern regions understand better than we of Rome the art of taking off heads, they certainly understand better, as in reason they should, the art of making them comfortable while they are on: already I have taken a longer draught at a wine-skin than I have been blessed with since I was in the service of the most noble Gallienus. Ah, that was life! He was your true philosopher who thought life made for living. These Palmyrenes seem of his school."

"Leave philosophy, good Milo, and come, help me

dress; that is the matter now in hand. Unclasp these trunks, and find something that shall not deform me."

So desirous was I, you perceive, to appear well in the eyes of the fair Fausta.

It was now the appointed hour to descend to the supper room, and as I was about to leave my apartment, hardly knowing which way to move, the Ethiopian, Hannibal, made his appearance, to serve as my conductor.

I was ushered into an apartment, not large, but of exquisite proportions—circular, and of the most perfect architecture, on the Greek principles. The walls, thrown into panels between the windows and doors, were covered with paintings, admirable both for their design and colour; and running all around the room, and attached to the walls, was a low and broad seat, covered with cushions of the richest workmanship and material. A lofty and arched ceiling, lighted by invisible lamps, represented a banquet of the gods, offering to those seated at the tables below a high example of the manner in which the divine gifts should be enjoyed. This evening, at least, we did not use the privileges which that high example sanctioned. Fausta was already in the room, and rose with affectionate haste to greet me again.

"I fear my toilet has not been very successful, Fausta, said I, "for my slave Milo was too much elated by the generous wines with which his companions had plied him, as a cordial after the fatigues of the journey, to give me any of the benefit of his taste or assistance. I have been my own artificer on this occasion, and you must therefore be gentle in your judgments."

"I cannot say that your fashions are equally tasteful with those of our Palmyrenes, I must confess. The love of the beautiful, the magnificent, and the luxurious, is our national fault, Lucius; it betrays itself in every department of civil and social life, and not unfrequently declines into a degrading effeminacy. If any thing ruins us, it will be this vice. I assure you I was rather jesting than in earnest, when I bade you look to your toilet. When you shall have seen some of our young nobles, you will find reason to be proud of your comparative simplicity. I hear, however, that you are not now far behind us in Rome—nay, in many excesses you go greatly beyond us. We have never yet had a Vitellius, a Pollio, or a Gallienus. And may the sands of the desert bury us a thousand fathoms deep, ere such monsters shall be bred and endured in Palmyra!"

"I perceive," said I, "that your sometime residence in Rome has not taught you to love your native country less. If but a small portion of the fire which I see burning in your eye warms the hearts of the people, it will be no easy matter for any external foe to subdue you."

"There are not many, I believe," replied Fausta, "of your or my sex in Palmyra, who would with more alacrity lay down their lives for their country and our sweet and noble queen, than I. But believe me, Lucius, there are multitudes who would do it as soon. Zenobia will lead the way to no battle-field where Fausta, girl though she be, will not follow. Remember what I say, I pray you, if difficulty should ever again grow up— which the gods forefend!—between us and Rome."

We were now suddenly interrupted by the loud and cheerful voice of Gracchus, exclaiming, as he approached us from the great hall of the palace, "How now!— how now!—whom have we here? Are my eyes and ears true to their report? Lucius Piso? It is he indeed. Thrice welcome to Palmyra! May a visit from so noble a house be an augury of good. You are quick, indeed, upon the track of your letter. How have you sped by the way? I need not ask after your own welfare, for I see it, but I am impatient to learn all that you can tell me of friends and enemies in Rome. I dare say all this has been once told to Fausta, but, as a penalty for arriving while I was from home, it must be repeated for my special pleasure. But come, that can be done while we sit at table; I see the supper waits."

In this pleasant mood did the father of Fausta, and now, as you know, one of the chief pillars of the province or kingdom—whichever it must be called—receive me. I was struck with the fine union in his appearance and manner of courtly ease, and a noble Roman frankness. His head, slightly bald, but cast in the truest mould of manly beauty, would have done honour to any of his illustrious ancestors; and his figure was entirely worthy of that faultless crown. I confess I experienced a pang of regret that one so fitted to sustain and adorn the greatness of his parent country had chosen to cast his fortunes so far from the great centre and heart of the empire. After the first duties of the table had been gone through with, and my hunger—real hunger—had been appeased by the various delicacies which my kind hostess urged upon me, noways unwilling to receive such tokens of regard, I took up the questions of Gracchus, and gave him a full account of our social and political state in Rome, to all which Fausta, too, lent a greedy ear, her fine face sparkling with the intelligence which beamed out from every feature. It was easy to see how deep an interest she took in matters to which her sex are so usually insensible. It is indescribable, the imperial pride and lofty spirit of independence which at times sat upon her brow and curled her lip. She seems to me made to command. She is, indeed, courteous and kind, but you, not with difficulty, see that she is bold, aspiring, and proud, beyond the common measure of woman. Her beauty is of this character. It is severe, rather than in any sense soft or feminine. Her features are those of her father, truly Roman in their outline, and their combined expression goes to impress every beholder with the truth that Roman blood alone, and that too of all the Gracchi, runs in her veins. Her form harmonises perfectly with the air and character of the face. It is indicative of great vigour and decision in every movement; yet it is graceful, and of such proportions as would suit the most fastidious Greek. I am thus minute in telling you how Fausta struck me, because I know the interest you and Lucilia both take in her, and how you will desire to have from me as exact a picture as I can draw. Be relieved, my dear friends, as to the state of my heart, nor indulge in either hopes or suspicions in this direction. I assure you I am not yet a captive at the fair feet of Fausta, nor do I think I shall be. But if such a thing should happen, depend upon my friendship to give you the earliest intelligence of the event. Whoever shall obtain the heart of Fausta, will win one of which a Cæsar might be proud. But to return to our present interview, and its event.

No sooner had I ended my account of the state of affairs at Rome, than Gracchus expressed, in the strongest terms, his joy that we were so prosperous. "It agrees," said he, "with all that we have lately heard. Aurelian is in truth entitled to the praise which belongs to a reformer of the state. The army has not been under such discipline since the days of Vespasian. He has now, as we learn by the last arrival of news from the north, by the way of Antioch, nearly completed the subjection of the Goths and Alemanni, and rumours are afloat, of an unpleasant nature, regarding an eastern expedition. For this no ground occurs to me, except, possibly, an attempt from Persia for the rescue of Valerian, if yet he be living, or for the general vindication of the honour of Rome against the disgraceful successes of the great king. I cannot for one moment believe that towards Palmyra any other policy will be adopted than that which has been pursued for the last century and a half, and emphatically sanctioned, as you well know, by both Gallienus and Claudius. Standing on the honourable footing, as nominally a part of the empire of Rome, but in fact a sovereign and independent power, we enjoy all that we can desire in the form of political privileges. Then, for our commerce, it could not be more flourishing, or conducted on more advantageous terms, even to Rome itself. In one word, we are contented, prosperous, and happy; and the crime of that man would be great indeed, who from any motive of personal ambition, or any policy of state, would disturb our existing relations of peace and friendship with all the world.

To this I replied: "I most sincerely trust that no design, such as you hint at, exists in the mind of Aurelian. I know him, and know him to be ambitious and imperious, as he is great in resources and unequalled in military science, but withal he is a man of wisdom, and, in the main, of justice too. That he is a true lover of his country, I am sure; and that the glory of that country is dearer to him than all other objects, that it rises in him almost to a species of madness, this I know too; and it is from this quarter, if from any, that danger is to be apprehended. He will have Rome to be all in all. His desire is that it should once more possess the unity that it did under the Antonines. This idea dwelt upon, may lead him into enterprises from which, however defended on the ground of the empire's glory, will result in nothing but discredit to himself and injury to the state. I, too, have heard the rumours of which you speak, but I cannot give them one moment's credence; and I pray most fervently, that springing as they do, no one knows whence, nor on what authority resting, they will not be permitted to have the least effect upon the mind of the queen, nor upon any of her advisers. She is now in reality an independent sovereign, reigning over an immense empire, stretching from Egypt to the shores of the Euxine, from the Mediterranean to the Euphrates, and she still stands upon the records of the senate as a colleague, even as when Odenatus shared the throne with her, of the Emperor. This is a great and a fortunate position. The gods forbid that any intemperance on the part of the Palmyrenes should rouse the anger or the jealousy of the fierce Aurelian!" Could I have said less than this? But I saw in the countenances of both, while I was speaking, especially in the honest, expressive one of Fausta, that they could brook no hint of inferiority or of dependence on the part of their country, so deep a place has the great Zenobia secured for herself in the pride and most sacred affections of this people.

"I will not, with you, noble Piso," said Gracchus, "believe that the emperor will do aught to break up the present harmony. I will have faith in him; and I shall use all the influence that I may possess in the affairs of the state to infuse a spirit of moderation into our acts, and, above all, into our language; for one hasty word uttered in certain quarters may lead to the ruin of kingdoms that have taken centuries to attain their growth. But this I say, let there only come over here from the west the faintest whisper of any purpose on the part of Aurelian to consider Zenobia as holding the same position in regard to Rome as Tetricus in Gaul, and that moment a flame is kindled throughout Palmyra that nothing but blood can quench. This people, as you well know, has been a free people from the earliest records of history, and they will sink under the ruin of their capital and their country, ere they will bend to a foreign power."

"That will they, that will they, indeed," cried Fausta; "there is not a Palmyrene who, had he two lives, would not give one for liberty, and the other for his good queen. You do not know Zenobia, Lucius, nor can you tell, therefore, how reasonable the affection is which binds every heart to her as to a mother or a sister."

"But enough of this for the present," said Gracchus; "let us leave the affairs of nations, and ascend to those of private individuals—for I suppose your philosophy teaches you, as it does me, that individual happiness is the object for which governments are instituted, and that they are, therefore, less than this—let us ascend, I say, from the policy of Rome and of Aurelian, to the private affairs of our friend Lucius Piso, for your letter gives me the privilege of asking you to tell us, in all frankness and love, what, besides the pleasure of seeing us, brings you so far from Rome. It is, you hint, a business of a painful nature. Use me and Fausta, as you would in Rome the noble Portia and the good Lucilia, with the same freedom and the same assurance of our friendship."

"Do so, indeed," added Fausta, with affectionate warmth, "and feel, that in addressing us you are entrusting your thoughts to true and long-tried friends."

"I have," replied I, "but little to communicate, but that little is great in its interest, and demands immediate action; and touching what shall be most expedient to be done, I shall want and shall ask your deliberate counsel. You are well aware, alas! too well aware, of the cruel fate of my parent, the truly great Cneius Piso, whom to name is always a spring of strength to my virtues. With the unhappy Valerian, to whom he clung to the last, resolved to die with him, or suffer with him whatever the fates should decree, he passed into captivity; but of too proud a spirit to endure the indignities which were heaped upon the emperor, and which were threatened him, he—so we have learned—destroyed himself. He found an opportunity, however, before he thus nobly used his power, to exhort my poor brothers not at once, at least, to follow his example. 'You are young,' said he, 'and have more strength than I, and the gods may interpose and deliver you. Hope dwells with youth, as it dies with age. Do not despair. I feel that you will one day return to Rome. For myself, I am a decayed trunk at best, and it matters little when I fall, or where I lie. One thing, at least, I cannot bear; it would destroy me if I did not destroy myself. I am a Roman and a Piso, and the foot of a Persian shall never plant itself upon my neck. I die.' My elder brother, thinking example a more powerful kind of precept than words, no sooner was assured of the death of his father, than he too opened his veins and perished. And so we learned had Calpurnius done, and we were comparatively happy in the thought that they had escaped by a voluntary death the shame of being used as footstools by the haughty Sapor, and the princes of his court. But a rumour reached us, a few days before I left Rome, that Calpurnius is yet living. We learn, obscurely, that being favourably distinguished and secretly favoured by the son of Sapor, he was persuaded to live, and wait for the times to open a way for his escape. You may imagine both my grief and my joy on this intelligence. The thought that he should so long have lain in captivity and imprisonment, and no step have been taken towards his rescue, has weighed upon me with a mountain-weight of sorrow. Yet at the same time, I have been supported by the hope that his deliverance may be effected, and that he may return to Rome once more, to glad the eyes of the aged Portia. It is this hope which has brought me to Palmyra, as perhaps the best point whence to set in motion the measures which it shall be thought wisest to adopt. I shall rely much upon your counsel." No sooner had I spoken thus, than Fausta quickly exclaimed,

"Oh, father, how easily, were the queen now in Palmyra, might we obtain through her the means of approaching the Persian king with some hope of a successful appeal to his compassion! and yet ——" She hesitated and paused.

"I perceive," said Gracchus, "what it is that checks your speech. You feel that in this matter Zenobia would have no power with the Persian monarch or court. The two nations are now, it is true, upon friendly terms; but a deep hatred exists in the heart of Sapor towards Zenobia. The successive defeats which he suffered, when Odenatus and his queen took it upon them to vindicate the honour of Rome, and revenge the foul indignities cast upon the unfortunate Valerian, will never be forgotten; and policy only, not love or regard, keeps the peace between Persia and Palmyra. Sapor fears the power of Zenobia, supported, as he knows she would be, by the strength of Rome; and, moreover, he is well aware that Palmyra serves as a protecting wall between him and Rome, and that her existence as an independent power is vital to the best interests of his kingdom. For these reasons harmony prevails; and in the event of a rupture between us and Rome, we might with certainty calculate with Persia as an ally. Still Sapor is an enemy at heart. His pride, humbled as it was by that disastrous rout, when his whole camp, and even his wives, fell into the hands of the royal Odenatus, will never recover from the wound, and will prompt to acts of retaliation and revenge, rather than to any deed of kindness. While his public policy is, and, doubtless, will continue to be, pacific, his private feelings are, and ever will be, bitter. I see not how in this business we can rely with any hope of advantage upon the interposition of the queen. If your brother is ever rescued, it must, I think, be achieved by private enterprise."

"Your words," said I, "have pierced me through with grief, and dispelled in a moment the brightest visions. All the way from Rome have I been cheered by the hope of what the queen, at your solicitation, would be able to attempt and accomplish in my behalf. But it is all over. I feel the truth of what you have urged. I see it—I now see it—private enterprise can alone effect his deliverance, and from this moment I devote myself to that work. If Rome leaves her emperor to die in captivity, so will not I my brother. I will go myself to the den of this worse than barbarian king, and bring thence the loved Calpurnius, or leave my own body there for that beast to batten on. It is now, indeed, thirteen years since Calpurnius left me, a child, in Rome, to join the emperor in that ill-fated expedition. But it is with the distinctness of a yesterday's vision that he now stands before my eyes, as he then stood that day he parted from us, glittering in his brilliant armour, and his face just as brilliant with the light of a great and trusting spirit. As he turned from the last embraces of the noble Portia, he seized me in his arms, who stood jingling his sword against his iron greaves, and imprinting upon my cheek a kiss, bade me grow a man at once, to take care of the household, while they were gone with the good emperor to fight the enemies of Rome in Asia. He was, as I remember him, of a quick and fiery temper, but he was always gentle towards me, and has bound me to him for ever."

"The gods prosper you!" cried Fausta, "as surely they will. It is a pious work to which you put your hand, and you will succeed."

"Do not, Fausta," said Gracchus, "lend the weight of your voice to urge our friend to measures which may be rather rash than wise, and may end only in causing a greater evil than what already exists. Prudence must govern us as well as affection. By venturing yourself at once into the dominion of Persia upon such an errand, it is scarcely less than certain that you would perish, and without effecting your object. We ought to consider, too, I think, what the condition and treatment of Calpurnius are, before too great a risk is incurred for his rescue. He has now, we are to remember, been at the capital of the great king thirteen years. You have hinted that he had been kindly regarded by the son of Sapor. Possibly his captivity amounts to no more than a foreign residence—a sort of exile. Possibly he may, in this long series of years, have become changed into a Persian. I understand your little lip, Fausta, and your indignant frown, Lucius; but what I suggest is among things possible, it cannot be denied; and can you deny it?—not so very unlikely, when you think what the feelings of one must have been to be so wholly forgotten and abandoned by his native country, and that country Rome, the mistress of the world, who needed but to have stretched forth the half of her power to have broken for ever the chains of his slavery, as well as of the thousands who with him have been left to linger out their lives in bondage. If Calpurnius has been distinguished by the son of Sapor, his lot, doubtless, has been greatly lightened, and he may now be living as a Persian prince. My counsel is, therefore, that the truth in this regard be first obtained, before the life of another son, and the only inheritor of so great a name, be put in jeopardy. But what is the exact sum of what you have learned, and upon which we may rely, and from which reason and act?"

"Our knowledge," I replied, "was derived from a soldier, who, by a great and happy fortune, escaped and reached his native Rome. He only knew what he saw when he was first a captive, and afterwards, by chance, had heard from others. He was, he said, taken to serve as a slave about the palace of the king, and it was there that for a space he was an eye-witness to the cruel and insulting usage of both Valerian and Calpurnius. That was but too true, he said, which had been reported to us, that whenever the proud Sapor went forth to mount his horse, the emperor was brought, in the face of the whole court, and of the populace who crowded around, to serve as his footstool. Clothed in the imperial purple, the unfortunate Valerian received upon his neck the foot of Sapor, and bore him to his saddle. It was the same purpose that Calpurnius was made to serve for the young prince Hormisdas. But, said the soldier, the prince pitied the young and noble Roman, and would gladly, at the beginning, have spared him the indignity put upon him by the stern command of his haughty and cruel father. He often found occasion at these times, while standing with his foot upon his neck, to speak with Calpurnius, and to express his regrets and his grief for his misfortunes, and promise redress, and more, if he ever came to the throne. But the soldier was soon removed from the vicinity of the royal palace, and saw no more of either Valerian or Calpurnius. What came to his ears was, generally, that while Valerian was retained exclusively for the use of Sapor, Calpurnius was after a time relinquished as entirely into the hands of Hormisdas, in whose own palace he dwelt, but with what portion of freedom he knew not. That he was living at the time he escaped, he was certain. This, Gracchus, is the sum of what we have heard; in addition only, that the emperor sank under his misfortunes, and that his skin, fashioned over some substance so as exactly to resemble the living man, is preserved by Sapor, as a monument of his triumph over the legions of Rome."

"It is a pitiful story," said Fausta, as I ended: "for a brave man it has been a fate worse than death; but having survived the first shame, I fear me my father's thought will prove a too true one, and that long absence, and indignation at neglect, and perhaps gratitude and attachment to the prince, who seems to have protected him, will have weaned him from Rome. So that we cannot suffer you, Lucius, to undertake so long and dangerous a journey upon so doubtful an errand. But those can be found, bold and faithful, who for that ample reward with which you could so easily enrich them, would venture even into the heart of Ecbatana itself, and bring you back your brother alive, or advertise you of his apostacy or death."

"What Fausta says is just," observed Gracchus, "and in few words prescribes your course. It will not be a difficult thing, out of the multitudes of bold spirits who crowd the capital, Greek, Roman, Syrian, and Arab, to find one who will do all that you could do, and, I may add, both more and better. You may find those who are familiar with the route, who know the customs of Persia, who can speak its language, and are even at home in her capitals, and who would be infinitely more capable than either you or I, or even Fausta, to manage to a happy issue an enterprise like this. Let this then be our decision; and be it now our united care to find the individual to whom we may commit this dear but perilous service. And now enough of this. The city sleeps, and it were better that we slept with it. But first, my child, bring harmony into our spirits by one of those wild, sad airs which you are accustomed to sing to me upon the harp of the Jews. It will dispose Lucius to pleasant dreams."

I added my importunities; and Fausta, rising, moved to an open window, through which the moon was now pouring a flood of silver light, and seating herself before the instrument which stood there, first swept its strings with an easy and graceful hand.

"I wish," said she, "I could give you the song which I am going to sing in the language of the Hebrews, for it agrees better, I think, with the sentiment and the character of the music, than the softer accents of the Greek. But every thing is Greek now."

So saying, she commenced with a prelude more sweetly and profoundly melancholy than even the wailing of the night wind among the leafless trees of the forest. This was followed by—an ode shall I call it? or a hymn?—for it was not what we mean by a song. Nor was the music like any other music I had ever heard, but much more full of passion; broken, wild, plaintive, triumphant, by turns, it stirred all the deepest feelings of the heart. It seemed to be the language of one in captivity, who, refusing to sing one of the songs of his country for the gratification of his conquerors, broke out into passionate strains of patriotism, in which he exalted his desolated home to the heavens, and prophesied, in the boldest terms, her ultimate restoration to power and glory. The sentiment lost nothing coming to the ear clothed in the rich music of Fausta's voice, which rose and sank, swelled and died away, or was full of tears or joy, as agreed with the theme of the poet. She was herself the poet, and the captive, and the Jew, so wholly did she abandon herself to the sway of the thoughts which she was expressing. One idea alone, however, had possessed me while she sang—to which, the moment she paused, I first gave utterance. "And think you, Fausta," said I, "that while the captive Jew remembers his country, the captive Roman will forget his? Never! Calpurnius, if he lives, lives a Roman. For this I thank your song. Melancholy and sad in itself, it has bred joy in my soul. I shall now sleep soundly." So saying, we separated.

Thus was passed my first evening in Palmyra.

D

LETTER III.

With what pleasure do I again sit down, dear Curtius and Lucilia, to tell you how I have passed my time, and what I have been able to accomplish, since I last wrote; thrice happy that I have to report of success rather than of defeat in that matter which I have undertaken. But first, let me thank you for all the city gossip, with which you so greatly entertained me in your joint epistle. Although I pass my hours and days in this beautiful capital as happily as I could any where out of Rome, still my letters from home are a great addition to my enjoyment. After rising from the perusal of yours and my mother's, I was a new man. Let me beg you, which indeed I need hardly do, to send each letter of mine, as you receive it, to Portia, and in return receive and read those which I have written, and shall continue to write to her. To you, I shall give a narrative of events; to her, I shall pour out sentiment and philosophy, as in our conversation we were wont to do. I shall hope soon to have somewhat of interest to say of the state of letters here, and of my interviews with distinguished men. So soon as the queen shall return from her excursion through some of her distant provinces, I shall call upon Gracchus to fulfil his promise, and make me known to the great Longinus, now with the queen absent. From my intercourse with him, I shall look to draw up long and full reports of much that shall afford both entertainment and instruction to you all.

I have now passed several days in Palmyra, and have a mass of things to say. But instead of giving you a confused report, I shall separate one thing from another, and set down each according to the time and manner in which it happened. This is what I know you desire, and this is what I shall do.

I cannot easily tell you how delicious was my slumber after that last day of fatiguing travel, and that evening of to me the most exciting converse. I dreamed that night of Calpurnius rescued and returned; and ever as he was present to my sleeping fancy, the music of Fausta's harp and voice was floating near.

Hannibal was early at my door to warn me of the hour of the morning meal, Milo being still under the influences of the evening's potation. I was shown to a different apartment from that in which we had supped, but opening into it. It was a portico rather than a room, it being on two sides open to the shrubbery, with slender Ionic pillars of purest marble supporting the ceiling, all joined together by the light interlacings of the most gorgeous creeping plants. Their odours filled the air. A fountain threw up in the most graceful forms its clear water, and spread all around an agreeable coolness. Standing at those points where flights of steps led down to the walks and plats of grass and flowers, which wound about the palace, the eye wandered over the rich scene of verdure and blossom which they presented, and then rested where it can never rest too often nor too long, upon the glittering shafts of the Temple of the Sun. This morning prospect, from this single point, I thought was reward enough for my long voyage, and hot journey over the desert. It inspired more cheerful thoughts than the same scene, as I had seen it the evening before from the windows of my chamber. I could not but draw omens of good from the universal smile that beamed upon me from the earth and the heavens. Fausta's little hand suddenly placed within mine, and the cheerful greeting of her voice awoke me from my dreamy state.

"Your countenance shows that you have slept well, Lucius," said she; "it is bright as the morning itself. Your dreams must have been favourable. Or else is it the wonder-working power of a Palmyrene air that has wrought so with you since the last evening? Tell me, have you not slept as you never slept in Rome?"

"I have slept well, indeed," I replied, "but I believe it was owing rather to your harp and Jewish ode, than to any mysterious qualities of the air. Your music haunted the chambers of my brain all night, and peopled them with the forms of those whom I love, and whose memory it last evening recalled so vividly. Mostly I dreamed of Calpurnius, and of his return to Rome, and with him came ever your image dimly seen hovering around, and the strains of your voice and harp. These are to me auguries of good, even as if the voice of a god had spoken. I shall once more embrace a brother —and what is even more, a Roman."

"The gods grant it may be so!" replied Fausta. "A prayer which I repeat," cried Gracchus, as he approached us from the hall, through which I had just passed. "I have thought much of your affair since I parted from you last evening, and am more than ever persuaded that we came to a true decision touching the steps best to be taken. To-day I shall be much abroad, and shall not forget to search in every direction for one who may be entrusted with this nice, and difficult, and withal dangerous business. I can now think of no messenger who bids so fair to combine all the qualities we most desire as the Jew. I know but few of that tribe, and those are among the rich. But, then, those rich are connected in various ways with the poor; for to a marvellous extent they are one people—it is the same, you know, in Rome—and through them I think I may succeed."

"Now have you," I quickly added, "again poured light into my mind. Half our labour is over. I know a Jew whose capacities could not be more fitting for this enterprise. I saw much of him on board the vessel which took us first to the African coast, where, at Utica, it set him on shore, bringing me farther on to Berytus. He is a true citizen of the world—knows all languages, and all people, and all places. He has all the shrewdness of his race—their intelligence, their enthusiasm, and, I may add, their courage. He is a traveller by profession, and a vender of such things as any will buy, and will go wherever he may hope to make large gains wherewith to do his share towards 'building again the walls of Jerusalem,' as he calls it. He has a home in every city of the East. It was towards Palmyra that he was bending his way; and, as I now remember, promised that he would see me here not many days after I should arrive, and have the pleasure, as he trusted, to sell me more of his goods. For you must be told that I did indeed traffic with him, however little it became a patrician of Rome. And here I have about me, in a little casket, some rings which I purchased of him, having upon them heads of Zenobia and Odenatus, resembling the originals to the life, as he assured me, with much asseveration. See, Fausta, here they are. Look now, and tell me if he has spoken in this instance the truth; if so, it will be a ground for trusting him further."

"Beautiful!" exclaimed both Gracchus and Fausta. "He has, indeed, dealt honestly with you. Nothing can be more exact than these resemblances, and the workmanship is worthy the hand of Demetrius the Greek."

"Provincials," said I, "ever know the capital and its fashions better than citizens. Now, never till Isaac, my Jew friend, rehearsed to me the praises of Demetrius the jeweller, had I ever heard his name, or aught concerning his skill, and here in the heart of Asia he seems a household word."

"It is so, indeed," said Gracchus; "I do not doubt that the fashionable artists of every kind in Rome are better known to the followers of fashion in Palmyra, than they are to the patricians themselves. Wanting the real greatness of Rome, we try to surpass her in the trappings of greatness. We are well represented by the frog of Æsop; happy, if our swelling pride do not destroy us. But these rings—they are, indeed, of exquisite art. The head of Odenatus is truer to life, methinks, than that of the queen."

"And how can poor stone and gold set out the divine beauty and grace of Zenobia!" cried Fausta. "This is beautiful to you now, Lucius, but it will be so no longer when you shall have seen her. Would that she were here! It seems as if the sun were gone from the heavens, when she is absent from us on these long excursions among her distant subjects."

"Till then, dear Fausta," said I, "deign to wear on that only finger which I see ungraced by a ring, this head of your so much vaunted queen; afterwards wear it, if you will, not for her sake, but mine."

So saying, upon her finger which she held out to me—and which how beautiful it was I shall not say—I attempted to pass the ring, but alas! it was too small, and would not, with all the gentle force I dared to use, go on.

"Here is an omen, Fausta," said I; "the queen cannot be forced upon your hand. I fear your friendship is threatened!"

"Oh! never entertain any such apprehension," interrupted Fausta; "it is quite needless. Here is plenty of room on this neighbour finger. It is quite right that Aurelian, you know, should give way to Zenobia; so, away with the emperor!"—and she snapped the ring across the pavement of the portico—"and now, Lucius, invest me with that burning beauty."

"And now, do you think you deserve it? I marvel, Gracchus, at the boldness of these little girls. Verily, they bid fair to mount up over our heads. But come, your finger—there—one cannot but say it becomes you better than the fierce Aurelian. As for the deposed emperor, he is henceforward mine. Thus I reinstate him." In saying which, I picked up the discarded ring, and gave to it the most honoured place upon my right hand.

Fausta now, first laughingly bidding me welcome to the ring, called us to the table, where the breakfast, consisting of fruits in greater proportion than with us, awaited us. Much talk now ensued concerning the city, its growth and numbers, power, and probable destiny. I was satisfied from what fell from each, that the most ambitious designs are entertained by both the court and people, and that their wonderful successes have bred in them a real belief that they should have nothing to fear from the valour or power of Rome under any circumstances of collision. When this was through, Gracchus, rising from his seat, and pacing up and down the portico, spoke of my private affairs, and with great kindness went over again the whole ground. The result was the same.

"Our way, then," he said, "is clear. Wait a few days for your fellow-traveller Isaac. If he appears, well—if not, we must then search the quarter of the Jews for one who may do as good service, perhaps. I now leave you, with a suggestion to Fausta that she should take it upon her to drive you round the city, and into the suburbs. No one can perform the office of a guide better than she."

"If Fausta will take that trouble upon her," I replied, "it will give me ——"

"A great deal of pleasure," you were going to say; so it will me. I am sure we shall enjoy it. If I love any thing, it is to reveal to a proud Roman the glories of Palmyra. Take away from a Roman that ineffable air which says 'Behold embodied in me the majesty of Rome!' and there remains a very agreeable person. But for those qualities of mind and manners which fit men and women for society, the Roman men and women must yield to the Palmyrenes. So I think, who have seen somewhat of both, and so think—gainsay my authorities if you have the courage—Longinus and the Bishop of Antioch. I see that you are disturbed. No wonder. Longinus, though a philosopher, is a man of the world, who sees through its ways as clearly as he does through the mysticism of Plato, and that asks for good eyes; and for the bishop, there is not so finished a gentleman in all the East. His appointments are not less exquisite than those of the highest noble either of Antioch or Palmyra. If an umpire in any question of manners were to be chosen, it would be he."

"As for the Greek," I rejoined, "I am predisposed

to admit his superior claims. I will surrender to him
with alacrity my doubts both in manners and philosophy.
For I hold there is a philosophy in manners, nay, even
in clothes, and that the highest bred intellect will on
that very account best perceive the nice distinctions and
relations, in the exact perception and observance of
which the highest manners consist. Such an one may
offend against the last device in costume, and the last
refinement in the recondite art of a bow, but he will
eternally excel in all that we mean by breeding. Your
bishop I know nothing of, but your account of him
strikes me not very agreeably. These Christian bishops,
methinks, are taking upon themselves too much. And,
besides, if what I gathered of the theory of their religion
from a passenger on board the Mediterranean trader
be correct, they depart greatly from the severity of
their principles, when they so addict themselves to the
practices of courts, and of the rich. I received from
this Christian a beautiful idea of his faith, and only
lamented that our companionship was broken off before
I had had time fully to comprehend all he had to say.
The character of this man, and his very countenance,
seemed as arguments to support the strict opinions
which he advanced. This bishop, I think, can scarcely
do his faith the same service."

"I know him not much," said Fausta, "and of his
faith nothing. He has great power over the Princess
Julia, and it would not much amaze me if, by and bye,
she declared herself a Christian. It is incredible how
that superstition spreads. But here is our carriage.
Come, let us forth."

So, breaking off our talk, we betook ourselves to the
carriage. How shall I find language, my Curtius, to
set before you with the vividness of the reality, or with
any approach to it, the pictures which this drive through
and around Palmyra caused to pass successively before
me? You know indeed, generally, what the city is,
from the reports of former travellers, especially from
the late book of Spurius, about which and its specula-

tions much was said a little while since. But let me tell you, a more one-sided, one-eyed, malignant observer never thrust himself upon the hospitalities of a free, open-hearted people, than that same Spurius, poet and bibliopole. His very name is an offence to the Palmyrenes, who, whatever national faults they may have, do not deserve the deep disgrace of being brought before the world in the pages of so poor a thing as the said Ventidius Spurius. Though it will not be my province to treat as an author of the condition, policy, and prospects of Palmyra, yet to you and my friends I shall lay myself open with the utmost freedom, and shall refrain from no statement or opinion that shall possess, or seem to do so, truth or importance.

The horses springing from under the whip of the charioteer, soon bore us from the great entrance of the palace into the midst of the throng that crowded the streets. The streets seen now under the advantages of a warm morning sun, adding a beauty of its own to whatever it glanced upon, showed much more brilliantly than ours of Rome. There is, in the first place, a more general sumptuousness in equipage and dress, very striking to the eye of a Roman. Not perhaps that more wealth is displayed, but the forms and the colours through which it displays itself, are more various, more tasteful, more gorgeous. Nothing can exceed, nothing equals, it is said, any where in the world, the state of the queen and her court; and this infects, if I may use so hard a word, the whole city. So that, though with far less real substantial riches than we have, their extravagance and luxury are equal, and their taste far before us. Then every thing wears a newer, fresher look than in Rome. The buildings of the republic, which many are so desirous to preserve, and whole streets even, of ante-Augustan architecture, tend to spread around here and there in Rome a gloom—to me full of beauty and poetry, but still gloom. Here all is bright and gay. The buildings of marble, the streets paved and clean, frequent fountains of water throwing up their foaming jets, and shedding around a delicious coolness, temples, and palaces of the nobles, or of wealthy Palmyrene merchants, altogether present a more brilliant assemblage of objects than I suppose any other city can boast. Then conceive, poured through these long lines of beautiful edifices, among these temples and fountains, a population drawn from every country of the far east, arrayed in every variety of the most showy and fanciful costume, with the singular animals, rarely seen in our streets, but here met at every turn—elephants, camels, and dromedaries, to say nothing of the Arabian horses, with their jewelled housings, with every now and then a troop of the queen's cavalry, moving along to the sound of their clanging trumpets—conceive, I say, this ceaseless tide of various animal life poured along among the proud piles, and choking the ways, and you will have some faint glimpses of the strange and imposing reality.

Fausta was in raptures at my transports, and in her pleasant but deep meaning way, boasted much over the great capital of the world. So we rode along slowly, because of the crowded state of the streets, and on account of my desire to observe the manners and ways of the people; their shops, which glittered with every rare work of art; and the devices, so similar in all places of trade, by which the seller attracts the buyer. I was engrossed by objects of this sort, when Fausta's voice drew my attention another way.

"Now," said she, "prepare yourself for the glory of Palmyra; look when we shall suddenly turn round the next corner, on the left, and see what you shall see."

The chariot soon whirled round the indicated corner, and we found ourselves in full view of the Temple of the Sun, so famous throughout the world. Upon a vast platform of marble, itself decorated with endless lines of columns—elsewhere of beauty and size sufficient for the principal building, but here a mere appendage —stood in solitary magnificence this peerless work of art. All I could do was, and the act was involuntary, to call upon the charioteer to rein up his horses and let me quietly gaze. In this Fausta, nothing unwilling, indulged me. Then, when satisfied with this the first point of view, we wound slowly around the spacious square upon which it stands, observing it well in all directions, and taking my fill of that exalted but nameless pleasure which flows in upon the soul from the contemplation of perfect excellence.

"This is, if I err not, Fausta, the work of a Greek artist."

"It is," said she: "here both Romans and Palmyrenes must acknowledge their inferiority, and, indeed, all other people. In every city of the world, I believe, all the great works of art are the offspring of Grecian genius and Grecian taste. Truly, a wonderful people! In this very city, our artists, our men of letters, even the first minister of state, all are Greeks. But come, let us move on to the Long Portico, an edifice which will astonish you yet more than even the Temple of the Sun, through your having heard of it so much less. We shall reach it in about half a Roman mile."

This space was soon passed, and the Portico stood revealed with its interminable ranges of Corinthian columns, and the busy multitudes winding among them, and pursuing their various avocations, for which this building offers a common and convenient ground. Here the merchants assemble and meet each other. Here various articles of more than common rarity are brought and exhibited for sale. Here the mountebanks resort, and entertain the idle and lovers of amusement with their fantastic tricks. And here strangers from all parts of the world may be seen walking to and fro, observing the customs of the place, and regaling themselves at the brilliant rooms, furnished with every luxury, which are opened for their use, or else at the public baths which are found in the immediate neighbourhood. The Portico does not, like the Temple, stand upon an elevated platform, but more upon a level with the streets. Its greatness is derived from its extreme length, and its exquisitely-perfect designs and workmanship, as seen in the graceful fluted columns and the rich entablature running round the whole. The life and achievements of Alexander are sculptured upon the frieze, the artist, a Greek also, having been allowed to choose his own theme.

"Fausta," said I, "my soul is steeped in beauty. It will be to no purpose to show me more now. I am like one who has eaten too much—forgive the figure—delicacies are lost upon him."

"I cannot release you yet," cried Fausta: "a little farther on, and you may see the palace of our great queen: give me your patience to that point, and I will then relieve you by a little excursion through the suburbs, where your eye may repose upon a rural beauty as satisfying as this of the city. You must see the palace. There! we are already in sight of it."

It rose upon us, so vast is it, and of so many parts, like a city within a city. A fit dwelling for so great, so good, and so beautiful a woman. Of this you will find a careful and true account, with drawings, which greatly help the imagination, in the otherwise vile book of the traducer Spurius. To that I refer you, and so refrain from all description.

We now left the city, and wound at our leisure among the shady avenues, the noble country retreats, the public gardens, the groves, and woods, which encompass the walls, and stretch away far beyond the sight, into the interior. Returning, we passed through the arches of the vast aqueduct which pours into the city a river of the purest water. This is the most striking object, and noblest work of art, without the walls.

When we had passed in this way nearly the whole day, we at length re-entered the city by the Persian Gate, on the eastern side.

"Now, Fausta," said I, "having given so much of the day to pleasure, I must give the rest, not to pain, but to duty. I will seek out and find, if I can, Demetrius, brother to Demetrius of Rome. From him I can learn, it seems probable, concerning the movements of Isaac."

"You will find the shop of Demetrius in the very heart of the city, midway between the Persian and Roman gates. Farewell for a time, and may the gods prosper you!"

I was not long in making my way to the shop of the Greek. I found the skilful Demetrius busily engaged in putting the last polish upon a small silver statue of a flying Mercury. He looked up as I entered, and saluting me in Greek, invited me to look at his works. I could not for a long time take off my eyes from the figure upon which he was working, and expressed my admiration.

"Ah, it is very well, I think," said he, "but it is nothing compared with the work of my brother at Rome. You know him?"

"Indeed I do not, I am obliged to say."

"What!—a Roman as I perceive, and a patrician also, and not know Demetrius the goldsmith?—he who was the favourite of Valerian, and Gallienus, and Claudius, and now of Aurelian? There is no hand like that of Demetrius the elder. These, sir, are mere scratches, to his divine touch. These are dolls, compared with the living and breathing gold as it leaves his chisel. Sir, it is saying nothing beyond belief, when I say, that many a statue like this, of his, is worth more than many a living form that we see in and out of the shop. Forgive me, but I must say I would rather possess one of his images of Venus or Apollo, than a live Roman—though he be a patrician, too."

"You are complimentary," I said, "but I can believe you. When I return to Rome, I shall seek out your brother, and make myself acquainted with his genius. I have heretofore heard of him chiefly through a travelling Jew, whom I fell in with on the way hither, Isaac as he is called."

"Ah ha!—Isaac of Rome. I know him well," he replied. "He is a good man, that is, he is good for one of that tribe. I look for him every day. A letter from Rome informs me that he is on his way. It is a pleasant thing to see Isaac. I wonder what curiosities he brings from the hand of my brother. He will be welcome. I trust he brings some heads of our late king and present queen, from drawings which I made and transmitted. I am impatient to see them. Saw you any thing of this sort about him?"

"Truly I did; and if by some ill chance I have not left them behind me, in my preparations for a morning excursion, I can show you what you will like to see. Ah! here it is: in this small casket I have, I presume, unless Isaac shall have deceived me—but of which you will be perfect judge—some of your brother's art. Look, here are rings, with heads of your king and queen, such as you have just spoken of. Are they genuine?"

"No instrument but that which is guided by the hand of the elder Demetrius ever did this work," said he, slowly drawing out his words as he closely scrutinised the ring. "The gold embossment might indeed have been done by another, but not these heads, so true to the life, and of an art so far beyond any ability of mine, that I am tempted sometimes to think that he is in league with Vulcan. Gods! how that mouth of the queen speaks! Do we not hear it? Ah, Roman, give me the skill of Demetrius the elder, and I would spit upon all the power of Aurelian."

"You Greeks are a singular people. I believe that the idea of beauty is to you food, and clothing, and shelter, and drink, more than all riches and all power: dying on a desert island, a fragment of Phidias would be dearer to you than a cargo of food."

"That's a pretty conceit enough," said he, "and something near the truth, as must be confessed."

As we were thus idly discoursing, we became suddenly conscious of an unusual commotion in the street. The populace began to move quickly by in crowds, and vehicles of all sorts came pouring along, as if in expectation of something they were eager to see.

"What's all this—what's all this?" said Demetrius, leaving his work, which he had resumed, and running to the door of his shop: "what's the matter, friend?" addressing a citizen hurrying by. "Is Aurelian at the gates, that you are posting along in such confusion?"

"Not Aurelian," replied the other, "but Aurelian's mistress. The queen is coming. Clouds of dust on the skirts of the plain show that she is advancing towards the city."

"Now, Roman, if thou wouldst see a sight, be advised, and follow me. We will mount the roof of yonder market, whence we shall win a prospect such as no eye can have seen that has not gazed from the same point. It is where I go to refresh my dulled senses, after the day's hard toil."

So saying, and pausing a moment only to give some necessary directions to the pupils, who were stationed at their tasks throughout the long apartment, telling them to wait for the show till it should pass by the shop, and not think to imitate their master in all his ways—saying these things in a half earnest and half playful manner, we crossed the street, and soon reached the level roof, well protected by a marble breastwork, of the building he had pointed out.

"We are here just at the right moment," said he; "come quickly to this corner and secure a seat, for you see the people are already thronging after us. There! can Elysium offer a more perfect scene? And look, how inspiring is the view of these two multitudes moving towards each other, in the spirit of friendship! How the city opens her arms to embrace her queen!"

At the distance of about a mile from the walls, we now saw the party of the queen, escorted by a large body of horse; and, approaching them from the city, apparently its whole population, some on foot, some on horse, some in carriages of every description. The plain was filled with life. The sun shooting his beams over the whole, and reflected from the spears and corslets of the cavalry, and the gilding and polished work of chariots and harness, caused the scene to sparkle as if strewed with diamonds. It was a fair sight. But fairer than all, was it to witness, as I did, the hearty enthusiasm of the people, and even of the children, towards their lovely queen. Tears of joy, even, I could see falling from many eyes, that she was returning to them again. As soon as the near approach of Zenobia to the walls began to conceal her and her escort, then we again changed our position, and returned to the steps of the shop of Demetrius, as the queen would pass directly by them, on her way to the palace.

We had been here not many minutes, before the shouts of the people, and the braying of martial music, and the confused sound of an approaching multitude, showed that the queen was near. Troops of horse, variously caparisoned, each more brilliantly, as it seemed, than another, preceded a train of sumptuary elephants and camels, these, too, richly dressed, but heavily loaded. Then came the body-guard of the queen, in armour of complete steel, and then the chariot of Zenobia, drawn by milk-white Arabians. So soon as she appeared, the air resounded with the acclamations of the countless multitudes. Every cry of loyalty and affection was heard from ten thousand mouths, making a music such as filled the heart almost to breaking. "Long live the great Zenobia!" went up to the heavens. "The blessing of all the gods on our good queen!"— "Health and happiness to the mother of her people!" —"Death and destruction to her enemies!"—these, and cries of the same kind, came from the people, not as a mere lip-service, but evidently, from the tone in which they were uttered, prompted by real sentiments of love, such as it seems to me never before can have existed towards a supreme and absolute prince.

It was to me a moment inexpressibly interesting. I could not have asked for more, than for the first time to see this great woman just as I now saw her. I cannot, at this time, even speak of her beauty, and the imposing yet sweet dignity of her manner; for it was with me, as I suppose it was with all—the diviner beauty of the emotions and sentiments which were working at her heart, and shone out in the expressive language of her countenance, took away all power of narrowly scanning complexion, feature, and form. Her look was full of love for her people. She regarded them as if they were her children. She bent herself fondly towards them, as if nothing but the restraints of form withheld her from throwing herself into their arms. This was the beauty which filled and agitated me. I was more than satisfied.

"And who," said I to Demetrius, "is that beautiful being, but of a sad and thoughtful countenance, who sits at the side of the queen?"

"That," he replied, "is the princess Julia—a true descendant of her great mother; and the gods grant that she, rather than either of her brothers, may succeed to the sovereign power."

"She looks indeed," said I, "worthy to reign—over hearts at least, if not over nations. Those in the next chariot are, I suppose, the young Cæsars, as I hear they are called, about as promising, to judge by the form and face, as some of our Roman brood of the same name. I need not ask whose head that is in the carriage next succeeding; it can belong to no other in Palmyra than the great Longinus. What a divine repose breathes over that noble countenance! What a clear and far-sighted spirit looks out of those eyes! But, gods of Rome and of the world! who sits beside him? Whose dark soul is lodged in that fearful tenement?—fearful and yet beautiful, as would be a statue of ebony!"

"Know you not him? Know you not the Egyptian Zabdas?—the mirror of accomplished knighthood—the pillar of the state—the Aurelian of the east? Ah! far may you go to find two such men as those—of gifts so diverse, and power so great—sitting together like brothers. It all shows the greater power of Zenobia, who can tame the roughest and most ambitious spirits to her uses. Who is like Zenobia?"

"So ends, it seems to me," I replied, "every sentence of every Palmyrene—'who is like Zenobia?'"

"Well, Roman," said he, "it is a good ending; may there never be a worse. Happy were it for mankind if kings and queens were all like her. She rules to make others happy, not to rule. She conceives herself to be an instrument of government, not its end. Many is the time, that standing in her private closet, with my cases of rare jewels, or with some pretty fancy of mine in the way of statue or vase, I have heard the wisdom of Aristotle dropping in the honey of Plato's Greek from her divine lips."

"You are all going mad with love," said I; "I begin to tremble for myself as a Roman. I must depart while I am yet safe. But see! the crowd and the show are vanished. Let me hear of the earliest return of Isaac, and the gods prosper you! I am at the house of Gracchus, opposite the Temple of Justice."

I found, on reaching the palace, Fausta and Gracchus overjoyed at the safe and happy return of the queen. Fausta, too, as the queen was passing by, she standing by one of the pillars of the great entrance, had obtained a smile of recognition, and a wave of the hand from her great friend, as I may justly term her, and nothing could exceed the spirits she was in.

"How glad I am, Lucius," said she, "that you have seen her so soon, and, more than all, that you saw her just as you did, in the very heart of the people. I do not believe you ever saw Aurelian so received in Rome—Claudius, perhaps—but not again Gallienus, or his severe but weak father. But what have you done—which is to all of us a more immediately interesting subject—what have you done for Calpurnius? Do you learn any thing of Isaac?"

"I have the best news," I replied, "possible in the case. Isaac will be in Palmyra perhaps this very night, but certainly within a few days, if the gods spare his life. Demetrius is to give me the earliest intelligence of his arrival."

"Now, then, let us," said Fausta, "to the table, which need not offer the delicacies of Vitellius, to insure a favourable reception from appetites sharpened as ours have been by the day's motion and excitement."

Gracchus, throwing down a manuscript he had been attentively perusing, now joined us.

Leaving untold all the good things which were said, especially by Gracchus, while I and Fausta, more terrestrially given, applied ourselves to the agreeable task set before us, I hasten to tell you of my interview with the Jew, and of its issue. For no sooner had evening set in, and Fausta, seated at her harp, was again soothing the soul with her sweet and wild strains, than a messenger was announced from the Greek Demetrius, desiring to have communication with me. Divining at once his errand, I sought him in the anteroom, where, learning from him that Isaac was arrived, and that if I would see him, I must seek him on the moment, as he was but for one night in the city, intending in the morning to start for Ctesiphon, I bade him lead on, and I would follow, first calling Milo to accompany me.

"To what part of the city do we go?" said I, addressing the messenger of Demetrius.

"To the quarter of the Jews, near the Gate of the Desert," he replied. "Be not apprehensive of danger," he added; "the city is as safe by night as by day. This we owe to the great queen."

"Take me where thou wilt, I fear nothing," said I.

"But, methinks, master mine," said Milo, "seeing that we know not the ways of this outlandish capital, nor even who this doubtless respectable person is who invites us to this enterprise, it were more discreet to add Hannibal to our numbers. Permit me, and I will invoke the presence of the Ethiopian."

"No, Milo," I replied; "in thy valour I am ready to put my trust. Thy courage is tried courage, and if need be, I doubt not thou wilt not hesitate to die sword in hand."

"Such sort of confidence I do by no means covet;

I would rather that thou shouldst place it somewhere else. It is true, that when I was in the service of the most noble Gallienus ——"

"Well, we will spare thee the trouble of that story. I believe I do thy virtues no injustice. Moreover, the less talk, the more speed."

Saying this, in order that I might be left to my own thoughts for a space, before I should meet the Jew, we then pressed on, threading our way through a maze of streets, where recollection of place and of compass was soon and altogether lost. The streets now became narrow, filthy, darker and darker, crooked and involved. They were still noisy with the loud voices of the inhabitants of the dwellings, calling to each other, quarrelling, or laughing, with the rattling of vehicles returning home after the labours of the day, and with all that variety of deafening sounds which fall upon the ear where great numbers of a poor and degraded population are crowded together into confined quarters. Suddenly leaving what seemed to be a sort of principal street, our guide turned down into an obscure lane, and which, though extremely narrow and crooked, was better built than the streets we had just left. Stopping now before what seemed a long and low white wall, our guide, descending a few steps, brought us to the principal entrance of the dwelling, for such we found it to be. Applying a stone to the door, to arouse those who might be within, we were immediately answered in a voice which I at once recognised as that of Isaac.

"Break not in the door," shouted he, "with your unmannerly blows. Who are you, that one must live standing with his hand on the latch of the door? Wait, I say, till I can have time to walk the length of the room. What can the Gentiles of Palmyra want of Isaac of Rome, at this time of night?" So muttering, he unbarred and opened the door.

"Come in, come in; the house of Isaac is but a poor house of a poor Jew, but it has a welcome for all. Come in; come —— But, father Abraham! whom have we here? The most noble Piso!—A patrician of Rome in the hovel of a poverty-pinched Jew! That would sound well upon the exchange. It may be of account. But what am I saying? Welcome to Palmyra, most noble Piso, for Palmyra is one of my homes; at Rome, and at Antioch, and Alexandria, and Ctesiphon, and Carthage, it is the same to Isaac. Pray seat yourselves; upon this chair thou wilt find a secure seat, though it promises not so much, and here upon my dromedary's furniture is another. So, now we are well. Would that I had that flask of soft Palmyrene, which but now I sent ——"

"Take no trouble for our sakes," I exclaimed, cordially saluting him; "I am just now come from the table of Gracchus. I have matters of more moment to discuss than either meats or wines."

"But, noble master, hast thou ever brought to thy lips this same soft Palmyrene? The name indicates some delicious juice."

"Peace, Milo, or thou goest home alone, as thou best canst."

"Roman," began Isaac, "I can think only of two reasons that can have brought thee to my poor abode so soon; the one is to furnish thyself with more of that jewellery which gave thee so much delight, and the other to discourse with me concerning the faith of Moses. Much as I love a bargain, I hope it is for the last that thou art come; for I would fain see thee in a better way than thou art, or than thou wouldst be if that smooth Probus should gain thine ear. Heed not the wily Nazarene! I cannot deny him a good heart, after what I saw of him in Carthage. But who is he to take it upon him to sit in judgment upon the faith of two thousand years! Would that I could once see him in the grasp of Simon Ben Gorah! How would his heresy wither and die before the learning of that son of God! Roman, heed him not. Let me take thee to Simon, that thou mayst once in thy life hear the words of wisdom."

"Not now, not now, good Isaac; whenever I apostatise from the faith of the founders of my nation, and deny the gods who for more than a thousand years have stood guardians over Rome, I will not refuse to weigh whatever the Jew has to offer in behalf of his ancient creed. But I come to thee now neither to buy of thee, nor to learn truth of thee, but to seek aid in a matter that lies near my heart."

"Ha! thy heathen god Cupid has ensnared thee! Well, well, the young must be humoured, and men must marry. It was the counsel of my father, whose beard came lower than his girdle, and than whom the son of Sirach had not more wisdom, 'Meddle not nor make in the loves of others. God only knoweth the heart. And how knowest thou that in contriving happiness, thou shalt not engender sorrow?' Howbeit, in many things have I departed from the counsel of that venerable man. Alas for it! Had my feet taken hold, in all their goings, of his steps, I had not now had for my only companion my fleet-footed dromedary, and for my only wealth this load of gilded toys."

"Neither is it," I rejoined, "for any love-sickness that I am come, seeking some healing or inflaming drug, but upon a matter of somewhat more moment. Listen to me, while I unfold."

So saying, I told all that you already so well know, in as few words as I could, but leaving out no argument by which I could hope to work upon either the cupidity, the benevolence, or the patriotism of the Jew. He, with his hands folded under his beard, listened without once interrupting me, but with an expression of countenance so stolid, that when I had ended, I could guess no better than when I began as to the part he would act.

After a pause of some length, he slowly began, discoursing rather with himself than with me: "A large enterprise—and to be largely considered. The way is long—seven hundred Roman miles at the least—and among little other than savage tribes, save here and there a desert, where the sands, as is reported, rise and fall like the sea. How can an old man like me encounter such labour and peril? These unbelieving heathen think not so much of the life of a Jew as of a dog. Gentile, why goest thou not thyself?"

"Thy skill, Isaac, and knowledge of men and countries, are more than mine, and will stand thee in good stead. Death were the certain issue were I to venture upon this expedition, and then my brother's fate were sealed for ever."

"I seem to thee, Roman Piso, to be a lone man in a wide world, who may live or die, and there be none to know or care how it is. It is verily much so. Yet I was not always alone. Children once leaped at the sound of my voice, and clung in sport to my garment. They are in Abraham's bosom. Better than here. Yet, Roman, I am not alone. The God of Israel is with me, and while it is Him I serve, life is not without value. I trust in the coming restoration of Jerusalem: for that I toil, and for that I am ready to die. But why should my bones whiten the desert, or my mangled carcass swing upon a Persian gibbet? Will that be to die for my country?"

"I can enrich thee for thy services, Jew, and thou sayest that it is for wealth, that it may be poured into the general coffers of thy tribe, that thou traversest the globe. Name thy sum, and so it be not beyond reason, I will be bound to pay thee in good Roman coin."

"This is to be thought of. Doubtless thou wouldst reward me well. But consider how large this sum must be. I fear me thou wilt shrink from the payment of it, for a Roman noble loves not money less than a poor Jew. My trade in Ctesiphon I lose. That must be made up. My faithful dromedary will be worn out by the long journey: that, too, must be made good. My plan will require an attendant slave and camel: then there are the dangers of the way—the risk of life in the city of the great king—and, if it be not cut off, the expenses of it. These to Isaac are not great, but I may be kept there long."

"But thou wilt abate somewhat of the sum thou hast determined upon, out of love to thy kind. Is the pleasure of doing a good deed nothing to thee?"

"Not a jot will I abate from a just sum—not a jot. And why should I? And thou art not in earnest to ask the abatement of a feather's weight. What doth the Jew owe the Roman? What hath the Roman done to the Jew? He hath laid waste his country with fire and sword. Her towns and villages he hath levelled with the ground. The holy Jerusalem he hath spoiled and defiled, and then driven the plough over its ruins. My people are scattered abroad among all nations—subject every where to persecution and death. This thou knowest is what the Roman hath done. And what then owe I, a Jew—a Jew—to the Roman? I bear thee, Piso, no ill will; nay, I love thee; but wert thou Rome, and this wheaten straw a dagger, it should find thy heart! Nay, start not; I would not hurt a hair of thy head. But tell me now if thou agreest to my terms: one gold talent of Jerusalem if I return alive with or without thy brother, and if I perish, two, to be paid as I shall direct."

"Most heartily, Isaac, do I agree to them, and bless thee more than words can tell, besides. Bring back my brother alive, and whatsoever thou shalt desire more, shall be freely thine."

"I am content. To-morrow, then, I turn my back upon Ctesiphon and Palmyra, and make for Ecbatana. Of my progress thou shalt learn. Of success I am sure—that is, if thy brother hearken to the invitation."

Then, giving such instructions as might be necessary on my part, we separated.

LETTER IV.

If the gods, dear Marcus and Lucilia, came down to dwell upon earth, they could not but choose Palmyra for their seat, both on account of the general beauty of the city and its surrounding plains, and the exceeding sweetness and serenity of its climate. It is a joy here only to sit still and live. The air, always loaded with perfume, seems to convey essential nutriment to those who breathe it; and its hue, especially when a morning or evening sun shines through it, is of that golden cast, which, as poets feign, bathes the tops of Olympus. Never do we tremble here before blasts like those which from the Appenines sweep along the plains and cities of the Italian coast. No extremes of either heat or cold are experienced in this happy spot. In winter, airs which in other places equally far to the north would come bearing with them an icy coldness, are here tempered by the vast deserts of sand which stretch away in every direction, and which it is said never wholly loose the heat treasured up during the fierce reign of the summer sun. And in summer, the winds which as they pass over the deserts are indeed like the breath of a furnace, long before they reach the city change to a cool and refreshing breeze, by traversing as they do the vast tracts of cultivated ground, which, as I have already told you, surround the capital to a very great extent on every side. Palmyra is the very heaven of the body. Every sense is fed to the full with that which it chiefly covets. But when I add to this, that its unrivalled position in respect to a great inland traffic has poured into the lap of its inhabitants a sudden and boundless flood of wealth, making every merchant a prince, you will truly suppose, that however heartily I extol it for its outward beauties, and all the appliances of luxury, I do not conceive it very favourable in its influences upon the character of its population. Palmyrenes, charming as they are, are not Romans. They are enervated by riches, and the luxurious sensual indulgences which they bring along, by necessity, in their train—all their evil power being here increased by the voluptuous softness of the climate. I do not say that all are so. All Rome cannot furnish a woman more truly Roman than Fausta, nor a man more worthy that name than Gracchus. It is of the younger portion of the inhabitants I now speak. These are without exception effeminate. They love their country, and their great queen, but they are not a defence upon which in time of need to rely. Neither do I deny them courage. They want something more vital still—bodily strength and martial training. Were it not for this, I should almost fear for the issue of any encounter between Rome and Palmyra. But as it is, notwithstanding the great achievements of Odenatus and Zenobia, I cannot but deem the glory of this state to have risen to its highest point, and even to have passed it. You may think me to be hasty in forming this opinion, but I am persuaded you will agree with me when you shall have seen more at length the grounds upon which I rest it, as they are laid down in my last letter to Portia.

But I did not mean to say these things when I sat down to my tablets, but rather to tell you of myself, and what I have seen and done since I last wrote. I have experienced and enjoyed much. How indeed could it be otherwise, in the house of Gracchus, and with Gracchus and Fausta for my companions? Many are the excursions we have together taken into the country, to the neighbouring hills whence the city derives its ample supply of water, and even to the very borders of the desert. I have thus seen much of this people, of their pursuits and modes of life, and I have found that whether they have been of the original Palmyrene population—Persian or Parthian emigrants, Jews, Arabians, or even Romans—they agree in one thing, love of their queen, and in a determination to defend her and her capital to the last extremity, whether against the encroachments of Persia or Rome. Independence is their watchword. They have already shown, in a manner the most unequivocal, and to themselves eternally honourable, that they will not be the slaves of Sapor, nor dependents upon his power. And surely they have given at the same time the clearest proof of .

their kindly feeling towards us, and of their earnest desire to live at peace with us. I truly hope that no extravagances on the part of the queen, or her too ambitious advisers, will endanger the existing tranquillity; yet from a late occurrence, and of which I was myself a witness, among other excited thousands, I am filled with apprehensions.

That to which I allude happened at the great amphitheatre, during an exhibition of games given by Zenobia on the occasion of her return, in which the Palmyrenes, especially those of Roman descent, take great delight. I care, as you know, nothing for them, nor only that, abhor them for their power to imbrute the people accustomed to their spectacles more and more. In this instance I was persuaded by Fausta and Gracchus to attend, as I should see both the queen and her subjects under favourable circumstances, to obtain new knowledge of their characters; and I am not sorry to have been there.

The show could boast all the magnificence of Rome. Nothing could exceed the excitement and tumult of the city. Its whole population was abroad to partake of the general joy. Early in the day the streets began to be thronged with the multitudes who were either pouring along towards the theatre, to secure in season the best seats, or with eager, idle curiosity, pressing after the cages of wild animals drawn by elephants or camels towards the place of combat and slaughter. As a part of this throng, I found myself seated between Gracchus and Fausta, in their most sumptuous chariot, themselves arrayed in their most sumptuous attire. Our horses could scarcely do more than walk, and were frequently obliged to stand still, owing to the crowds of men on horse, on foot, and in vehicles of every sort, which filled the streets. The roaring of the imprisoned animals, the loud voices of their keepers, and of the drivers of the cumbrous waggons which held them, the neighing, or screaming, I might say, of the affrighted horses, every now and then brought into immediate contact with the wild beasts of the forests, lions, tigers, or leopards, made a scene of confusion, the very counterpart of what we have so often witnessed in Rome, which always pains more than it pleases me, and which I now describe at all, only that you may believe, what Romans are so slow to believe, that there are other cities in the world where great actions are done as well as in your own. The inhabitants of Palmyra are as quick as you could desire them to be, in catching the vices and fashions of the great metropolis.

"Scipio, Scipio," cried Gracchus suddenly, to his charioteer, " be not in too great haste. It is in vain to attempt to pass that waggon; nay, unless you shall be a little more reserved in your approaches, the paw of that tawny Numidian will find its way to the neck of our favourite Arab. The bars of his cage are over far apart."

" I almost wish they were yet farther apart," said I, "and that he might fairly find his way into the thickest of this foolish crowd, and take a short revenge upon his civilised tormentors. What a spectacle is this—more strange and savage, I think, looked upon aright, than that which we are going to enjoy—of you, Gracchus, a pillar of a great kingdom; of me, a pillar—a lesser one, indeed, but still a pillar—of a greater kingdom, and of you, Fausta, a woman, all on our way to see wild beasts let loose to lacerate and destroy each other, and, what is worse, gladiators, that is, educated murderers, set upon one another, to die for our entertainment. The best thing I have heard of the Christian superstition is, that it utterly denounces and prohibits to its disciples the frequenting of these shows. Nothing to me is plainer than that we may trace the cruelties of Marius, Sylla, and their worthy imitators, through the long line of our emperors, to these schools where they had their early training. Why was Domitian and his fly worse than Gracchus, or Piso, or Fausta, and their gored elephant, or dying gladiator?"

" You take this custom too seriously," replied

Gracchus; "I see in it, so far as the beasts are concerned, but a lawful source of pleasure. If they tore not one another in pieces for our entertainment, they would still do it for their own, in their native forests; and if it must be done, it were a pity none enjoyed it. Then, for the effects upon the beholding crowd, I am inclined to think they are rather necessary and wholesome than otherwise. They help to render men insensible to danger, suffering, and death; and as we are so often called upon to fight each other, and die in defence of our liberties, or of our tyrants and oppressors, whichever it may be, it seems to me we are in need of some such initiatory process in the art of seeing blood shed unmoved, and of some lessons which shall diminish our love and regard for life. As for the gladiators, they are wretches who are better dead than alive; and to die in the excitement of a combat is not worse, perhaps, than to expire through the slow and lingering assaults of a painful disease. Besides, with us there is never, as with you, cool and deliberate murder perpetrated on the part of the assembly. There is here no turning up of the thumb. It is all honourable fight, and honourable killing. What, moreover, shall be done to entertain the people? We must feed them with some such spectacles, or I verily think they would turn upon each other for amusement, in civil broil and slaughter."

"Your Epicurean philosophy teaches you, I am aware," said I in reply, " to draw happiness as you best can from all the various institutions of Providence and of man, not to contend, but to receive, and submit, and be thankful. It is a philosophy well enough for man's enjoyment of the passing hour, but it fatally obstructs, it appears to me, the way of improvement. For my own part, though I am no philosopher, yet I hold to this, that whatever our reason proves to be wrong or defective, it at the same time enforces the duty of change and reform—that no palpable evil, either in life or government, is to be passively submitted to as incurable. In these spectacles I behold an enormous wrong, a terrific evil ; and though I see not how the wrong is to be redressed, nor the evil to be removed, I none the less, but so much the more, conceive it to be my part, as a man and a citizen, to think and converse, as now, upon the subject, in the hope that some new light may dawn upon its darkness. What think you, Fausta? I hope you agree with me—nay, as to that, I think Gracchus, from his tone, was but half in earnest."

"It has struck me chiefly," said Fausta, "as a foolish custom; not so much in itself very wrong, as childish. It is to me, indeed, attended with pain, but that I suppose is a weakness of my own—it seems not to be so in the case of others. I have thought it a poor, barren entertainment, fit but for children, and those grown children whose minds, uninstructed in higher things, must seek their happiness in some spring of mere sensual joy. Women frequent the amphitheatre, I am sure, rather to make a show of their beauty, their dress, and equipage, than for any thing else; and they would, I believe, easily give in to any change, so it should leave them an equally fair occasion of display. But so far as attending the spectacles tends to make better soldiers and stouter defenders of our queen, I confess, Lucius, I look upon them with some favour. But, come, our talk is getting to be a little too grave. Look, Lucius, if this be not a brave sight! See what a mass of life encompasses the circus! And its vast walls, from the lowest entrances to its very summit, swarm as it were with the whole population of Palmyra. It is not so large a building as your Flavian, but it is not wholly unworthy to be compared with it."

"It is not, indeed," said I ; "although not so large, its architecture is equally in accordance with the best principles, both of science and taste, and the stone is of a purer white, and more finely worked."

We now descended from our carriage, and made our way through the narrow passages and up the narrow stairways to the interior of the theatre, which was already much more than half filled. The seats to which we were conducted were not far from those which were to be occupied by the queen and her train. I need not tell you how the time was passed which intervened between taking our seat, the filling of the theatre, and the commencement of the games—how we all were amused by the fierce strugglings of those who most wished to exhibit themselves, for the best places; by the efforts of many to cause themselves to be recognised by those who were of higher rank than themselves, and to avoid the neighbourhood and escape the notice of others whose acquaintance would bring them no credit; how we laughed at the awkward movements and labours of the servants of the circus, who were busying themselves in giving its final smoothness to the sawdust, and hurrying through the last little offices of so vast a preparation, urged on continually by the voices or lashes of the managers of the games; nor how our ears were deafened by the fearful yellings of the maddened beasts confined in the vivaria, the grated doors of which opened, as in the Roman buildings of the same kind, immediately on the arena. Neither will I inflict weariness upon myself or you, by a detailed account of the kind and order of the games at this time exhibited for the entertainment of the people. The whole show was an exact copy from the usages of Rome. I could hardly believe myself in the heart of Asia. Touching only upon these things, so familiar to you, I will relate what I was able to observe of the queen and her demeanour, about which I know you will feel chiefly desirous of information.

It was not till after the games had been some time in progress, and the wrestlers and mock-fighters having finished their foolish feats, the combats of wild animals with each other had commenced, that a herald announced by sound of trumpet the approach of the queen. The moment that sound, and the loud clang of martial music which followed it, was heard, every eye of the vast multitude was turned to the part of the circus where we were sitting, and near which was the passage by which Zenobia would enter the theatre. The animals now tore each other piecemeal, unnoticed by the impatient throng. A greater care possessed them. And no sooner did the object of this universal expectation reveal herself to their sight, led to her seat by the dark Zabdas, followed by the princess Julia and Longinus, and accompanied by a crowd of the rank and beauty of Palmyra, than one enthusiastic cry of loyalty and affection rent the air, drowning all other sounds, and causing the silken canopy of the amphitheatre to sway to and fro as if shaken by a tempest. The very foundations of the huge structure seemed to tremble in their places. With what queenly dignity, yet with what enchanting sweetness, did the great Zenobia acknowledge the greetings of her people! The colour of her cheek mounted and fell again, even as it would have done in a young girl, and glances full of sensibility and love went from her to every part of the boundless interior, and seemed to seek out every individual, and to each make a separate return for the hearty welcome with which she had been received. These mutual courtesies being quickly ended, the games again went on, and every eye was soon rivetted on the arena, where animals were contending with each other or with men.

The multitude being thus intently engaged, those who chose to employ their time differently were left at full liberty to amuse themselves with conversation or otherwise, as pleased them. Many a fat and unwieldy citizen we saw soundly sleeping, in spite of the roarings of the beasts and the shouts of the spectators. Others, gathering together in little societies of their own, passed all the intervals between the games, as well as the time taken up by games which gave them no pleasure, in discussing with one another the fashions, the news, or the politics of the day. Of these parties we were one; for neither Gracchus, nor Fausta, nor I, cared much for the sports of the day, and there were few foolish or wise things that were not uttered by one of us during the continuance of those tedious, never ending games.

"Well, Lucius," said Fausta, "and what think you now of our great queen? For the last half hour, your eyes having scarcely wandered from her; you must by this time be prepared with an opinion."

"There can be little interest," said I, "in hearing an opinion on a subject about which all the world is agreed. I can only say what all say. I confess I have never before seen a woman. I am already prepared to love and worship her with you, for I am sure that such preeminent beauty exists in company with a goodness that corresponds to it. Her intellect, too, we know is not surpassed in strength by that of any philosopher of the east. These things being so, where in the world can we believe there is a woman to be compared with her? As for Cleopatra, she is not worthy to be named."

As I uttered these things with animation and vehemence, showing I suppose in my manner how deeply I felt all that I said, I perceived Fausta's fine countenance glowing with emotion, and tears of gratified affection standing big in her eyes.

Gracchus spoke. "Piso," said he, "I do not wonder at the enthusiastic warmth of your language. Chilled as my blood is by the approaches of age, I feel even as you do—nay, I suppose, I feel much more; for to all your admiration, as a mere philosophical observer, there is added in my case the fervid attachment which springs from long and intimate knowledge, and from an intercourse, which not the coolness of a single hour has ever interrupted. It would be strange, indeed, if there were not one single flaw in so bright an emanation from the very soul of the divinity, wearing as it does the form of humanity. You know me to allude to her ambition. It is boundless, almost insane. Cæsar himself was not more ambitious. But in her even this is partly a virtue, even in its wildest extravagance; for it is never for herself alone that she reaches so far and so high, but as much or more for her people. She never separates herself from them even in thought, and

F

all her aspirings are, that she herself may be great indeed, but that her country may with and through her be great also, and her people happy. When I see her as now surrounded by her subjects, and lodged in their very heart of hearts, I wish—and fervently would I pray were there gods to implore—that her restless spirit may be at peace, and that she may seek no higher good either for herself or her people than that which we now enjoy. But I confess myself to be full of apprehension. I tremble for my country. And yet here is my little rebel, Fausta, who will not hearken to this, but adds the fuel of her own fiery spirit to feed that of her great mistress. It were beyond a doubt a good law which should exclude women from any part in public affairs."

"Dear father, how do you remind me of the elder Cato, in the matter of the Oppian Law: while women interfered in public affairs only to promote the interests of their worthy husbands, the lords of the world, the great Cato had never thought but to commend them; but no sooner did they seek to secure some privileges very dear to them as women, and clamour a little in order to obtain them, than straightway they were nuisances in the body politic, and ought to be restrained by enactments from having any voice in the business of the state. Truly, I think this is far from generous treatment. And happy am I, for one, that at length the gods in their good providence have permitted that one woman should arise to vindicate her sex against the tyranny of her ancient oppressors. If I might appoint to the spirits of the departed their offices, I could wish nothing merrier than that that same Cato should be made the news-carrier from the kingdom of Zenobia to the council of the gods. How he would enjoy his occupation! But seriously, dear father, I see not that our queen has any more of this same ambition than men are in the same position permitted to have, and accounted all the greater for it. Is that a vice in Zenobia which is a glory in Aurelian? Longinus would not decide so. But see how intent the queen is upon the games."

"I would rather," said I, "that she should not gaze upon so cruel a sight. But see, too, the princess Julia has hidden her head in the folds of her veil."

"Julia's heart," said Fausta, "is even tenderer than a woman's. Besides, if I mistake not, she has on this point at least adopted some of the notions of the Christians. Paul of Antioch has not been without his power over her; and truly his genius is well nigh irresistible. A stronger intellect than hers might without shame yield to his. Look, look, the elephant will surely conquer after all. The gods grant he may! He is a noble creature; but how cruelly beset! Three such foes are too much for a fair battle. How he has wreathed his trunk round that tiger, and now whirls him in the air! But the rhinoceros sees his advantage: quick—quick!"

Fausta, too, could not endure the savage sight, but turned her head away; for the huge rhinoceros, as the elephant lifted the tiger from the ground, in the act to dash him again to the earth, seized the moment, and before the noble animal could recover himself, buried his enormous tusk deep in his vitals. It was fatal to both, for the assailant, unable to extricate his horn, was crushed through every bone in his body, by the weight of the falling elephant. A single tiger remained master of the field, and who now testified his joy by coursing round and round the arena.

"Well, well," said Gracchus, "they would have died in the forest; what signifies it? But why is this blast of trumpets? It is the royal flourish! Ah! I see how it is; the sons of Zenobia, whom none miss not being present, are about to enter the theatre. They make amends by the noise of their approach for their temporary absence. Yet these distant shouts are more than usual. The gods grant that none of my fears may turn true!"

No sooner had Gracchus ended these words, while

his face grew pale with anxious expectation, than suddenly the three sons of the queen made their appearance, and—how shall I say it?—arrayed in imperial purple, and habited in all respects as Cæsars. It seemed to me as if at that very moment the pillars of this flourishing empire crumbled to their foundation. And now while I write, and the heat of that moment is past, I cannot but predict disaster and ruin, at least fierce and desolating wars, as the consequence of the rash act. I know the soul of Aurelian, and that it will never brook what it shall so much as dream to be an indignity—never endure so much as the thought of rivalry in another, whether Roman or foreigner, man or woman. To think it is treason with him—a crime for which blood only can atone.

Having entered thus the amphitheatre, assuming a high and haughty bearing, as if they were already masters of the world, they advanced to the front railing, and there received the tumultuous acclamations of the people. A thousand different cries filled the air. Each uttered the sentiment which possessed him, regardless of all but testifying loyalty and devotion to the reigning house. Much of the language was directed against Rome, which, since the circulation of the rumours of which I have already spoken, has become the object of their most jealous regard. Aurelian's name was coupled with every term of reproach. "Is Aurelian to possess the whole earth?" cried one. "Who are Romans?" cried another; "the story of Valerian shows that they are not invincible." "We will put Zabdas and Zenobia against the world!" shouted others. "The conqueror of Egypt for ever!"—"Long live the great Zabdas!" rose from every quarter. It were in vain to attempt to remember or write down half the violent things which in this hour of madness were uttered. The games were for a long time necessarily suspended, and the whole amphitheatre was converted into an arena of political discussion, from which arose the confused din of unnumbered voices, like the roar of the angry ocean. I looked at Zenobia; she was calm—satisfied. Pride was upon her lip and brow. So like a god was the expression of her whole form, that for a moment I almost wished her mistress of the world. She seemed worthy to reign. Julia was evidently sad, and almost distressed. Longinus, impenetrable as marble. Zabdas, black and lowering as night.

Quiet was at length restored, and the games went on.

A messenger came now from the queen to our seat, with the request that Fausta should join her, not being satisfied with the distant intercourse of looks and signs. So, accompanied by Gracchus, she was soon placed by the side of Zenobia, whose happiness seemed doubled by the society of, I believe, her choicest friend. Left now to myself, I had leisure to think and to observe. A more gorgeous show than this vast assembly presented, I think I never before beheld, no not even in the Flavian. Although in Rome we seem to draw together people of all regions and all climes, yet after all, the north and west preponderate, and we lack the gayer costumes which a larger proportion of these orientals would add to our spectacles. Not to say, too, that here in the east the beauty of woman is more transcendant, and the forms of the men cast in a finer mould. Every variety of complexion is here also to be seen, from the jet black of the slender Ethiopian, to the more than white of the women of the Danube. Here I saw before me, in one promiscuous throng, arrayed in their national dresses, Persians, dark-skinned Indians, swarthy Egyptians, the languishing, soft-eyed Syrian, sylphs from the borders of the Caspian, women of the Jews from the shores of the Mediterranean, Greeks from Asia Minor, the Islands, and Attica, with their classic costume and statue-like forms and faces, Romans, and abounding over all, and more beautiful than all, the richly habited nobles and gentry of Palmyra itself. I enjoyed the scene as a man and a philosopher; nay, as a Roman, too; and could not but desire earnestly, that the state, of whose prosperity it was so clear a token, might last even with Rome itself. I wished you and Lucilia at my side—not to mention the little Gallus—not, as you may believe, to witness the games, but to behold in this remote centre of Asia so fair a show of our common race.

It was not till the sun was already about to sink in the west, that the games ended, and the crowds dispersed, and I once more found myself in the peaceful precincts of home; for so already do I call the hospitable dwelling of Gracchus.

"So, Fausta," said I, "you forsook your old friend Lucius for the companionship of a queen! Truly I cannot blame you, for most gladly would I, too, have gone and made one of your circle. How irksome are the forms and restraints of station, and even of society! how little freedom do they allow in the expression of our real sentiments! Could I have sat with you by Zenobia, can I doubt that by a frank disclosure of my feelings and opinions I could have corrected some errors, softened some prejudices, and at the same time gained her esteem—her esteem for me, I mean, as a sincere well-wisher to her kingdom, although none the less a Roman! It would have been a fortunate moment for such communication as I desire. I trust yet, seeing such a promise has gone forth from you, to see her in her own palace."

"Indeed you shall," said Fausta. "It has only been owing to fatigue, after her long excursion, and to this show of games, that you have not seen her long before this. She is well aware of your rank, and footing of intimacy with Aurelian, and of the object for which you make this visit to her capital, and has expressed frequent and earnest desires of an interview with you. And now have I a great mind not to tell you of the speedy pleasure and honour that await you. What will you give to know the tenor of what I have to say?"

"I will confer the greatest honour in my power," said I; "I will dislodge the emperor from my own finger and replace him upon yours. Here I offer you the head of Aurelian—cut, not indeed by the cunning tool of Demetrius of Rome, but doubtless by some competent artist. Is it not a fair offer, Gracchus?"

"I fear unless you make a different and a better one, you will scarce open the lips of our fierce patriot," answered Gracchus.

"That will he not," said Fausta; "were he to engage by to-morrow to make himself over into a veritable, sound-hearted, queen-loving Palmyrene, it would not be more than he ought to do. I am sure, old Solon toiled hard to make a Roman out of me, and how do I know but it was at your instance? And it having been so, as I must believe, what less can you do in atonement than to plant yourself here upon the soil of Palmyra? A Roman, trust me, takes quick root in this rich earth, and soon shoots up and spreads out into a perfectly proportioned Palmyrene, tall and beautiful as a date tree. Father, how can we bribe him? You shake your head as if without hope. Well, let us wait till Calpurnius returns; when you find him an oriental, perhaps you may be induced to emigrate too. Surely it is no such great matter to remove from Rome to Palmyra? We do not ask you to love Rome any the less, but only Palmyra more. I still trust we shall ever dwell in friendship with each other. We, certainly, must desire it, who are half Roman. But why do I keep you in such painful suspense? Hear, then, my message, which is, that you will appear at the palace of Zenobia to-morrow. The queen desires a private interview with you, and for that purpose will receive no other visitors. Her messenger will in the morning apprise you of the hour, and conduct you to the palace. Ah! I see by your countenance how delighted you are. It is no wonder."

"I am delighted, indeed," said I; "that is a part of my feeling, but not the whole of it. I cannot, accustomed even as I have been to associate with the high in rank and intellect in various countries, without some inward perturbation think of meeting for the first time so remarkable a person; one whose name is known not only throughout Asia, but the world; and whose genius and virtues are the theme of universal wonder and praise. Then, Fausta, Zenobia is a woman, and a woman inspires an awe which man never does; and what is more yet, she is of a marvellous beauty, and before that most perfect work of the gods, a beautiful woman, I am apt to be awkward and dumb; at the least—which perhaps is it—made to think too much of myself to acquit myself well. You may think that I exaggerate these feelings. Possibly I do. Certainly they are not of such strength that I do not gladly seize upon the favour thus extended, and count myself honoured and happy."

"Where, Lucius, tell me where you learned this new dialect, which runs so sweetly when woman is the theme. Sure am I, it is not Roman. Ovid has it not. Nor yet is it Palmyrene. Do we owe it to a rich invention of your own?"

"Fausta, I am in earnest in what I have said. It is my own native dialect—instinctive. Therefore laugh not, but give me a lesson how I shall deport myself. Remember the lessons I have so many times given you in Rome, and now that you have risen into the seat of power, return them as you are bound to do."

"Now are you both little more than two foolish children, but just escaped from the nursery," cried Gracchus, who had been pacing up and down the portico, little heeding, to all appearance, what was going on. " Lucius, ask no advice of that wild school-girl. Listen to me, who am a counsellor, and of age, and ought, if I do not, to speak the words of wisdom. Take along with thee nothing but thy common sense, and an honest purpose, and then Venus herself would not daunt thee, nor Rhadamanthus and the Furies terrify. Forget not, too, that beneath this exterior covering, first of clothes, and then of flesh, there lies enshrined in the breast of Zenobia, as of you and me, a human heart, and that this is ever and in all the same, eternally responsive to the same notes, by whomsoever struck. This is a great secret. Believe, too, that in our good queen this heart is pure as a child's; or, if I may use another similitude, and you can understand it, pure as a Christian's—rather, perhaps, as a Christian's ought to be. Take this also, that the high tremble to meet the low, as often as the low to meet the high. Now ask no more counsel of Fausta, but digest what the oracle has given out, and which now for the night is silent."

In this sportive mood we separated.

At the appointed hour on the following day, the expected messenger appeared; and announcing the queen's pleasure that I should attend her at the palace, conducted me there with as much of state as if I had been Aurelian's ambassador.

On arriving at the palace of the queen, I was ushered into an apartment, not large, but of exquisite architecture, finished and furnished in the Persian taste, where sat Zenobia and Julia. At the feet of the queen, and supporting them, upon an embroidered cushion of silk, there lay crouched a beautiful Indian slave. If it was her office to bear that light and pretty burden, it seemed to be her pleasure too; for she was ever weaving round it, in a playful manner, her jewelled fingers; casting upwards to her mistress frequent glances of most affectionate regard.

"Noble Piso," said the queen, after I had approached and saluted her in the appointed manner, "it gives me pleasure to greet one of your ancient name in Palmyra. I seem already acquainted with you through my fast friends Gracchus and his bright daughter. You have lost nothing, I am sure, in coming to us first through their lips; and if any lips are honest and true, it is theirs. We welcome you to the city of the desert."

"Great queen," I replied, "it is both a pleasure and a pain to find myself in your brilliant capital. I left Rome upon a melancholy errand, which I have as yet but half accomplished. Till success shall crown it, I can but half enjoy the novel scenes, full of interest and beauty, which your kingdom and city present. It was to rescue a brother—if I may speak for one moment of myself—held in captivity since the disaster of Valerian, that I set sail from Italy, and am now a dweller in Palmyra. From this point, I persuaded myself I could best operate for his deliverance. My first impulse was to throw myself at your feet, and ask of you both counsel and aid."

"They should have been gladly yours, very heartily yours. It was a foul deed of Sapor—and a sad fate, that of the great Censor, and of your father the good Cneius Piso. And yet I see not much that I could have done."

"Refuse not my thanks," said I, "for the expression of so generous sentiments. I am sure I should have shared a goodness of which all seem to partake, had I thought it right and necessary to appeal to you. But I was soon convinced, by the arguments of both Gracchus and Fausta, that my chance of success was greater as a private than as a public enterprise. And happy am I to be able to say that I have found and employed an emissary, who, if the business be capable of accomplishment by human endeavours, will, with more likelihood than any other that could easily be named, accomplish it. Aurelian himself could not here do as much nor as well as Isaac of Rome."

"I believe," said Zenobia, "you will readily agree with me in the opinion, that Rome has never respected herself so little as in her neglect of Valerian and his fellow sufferers. But for the scathing got from our arm, the proud Persian had come out of that encounter with nothing but laurels. We, thanks to the bravery and accomplished art of Odenatus, tore off some of those laurels, and left upon the body of the great king the marks of blows which smart yet. This Indian girl at my feet was of the household of Sapor—a slave of one of those women of whom we took a tent full. The shame of this loss yet rankles deep in the heart of the king. But should Rome have dealt so by her good emperor and her brave soldiers? Ought she to have left it to a then new and small power to take vengeance on her mean, base-minded, yet powerful foe? It is not even yet too late, methinks, for her to stir herself, were it only to rescue one of the noble house of Piso. Perhaps it may be with some intent of this kind that we hear rumours of an Asiatic expedition. Aurelian, we learn, having wearied himself with victory in Gaul and Germany, turns his thoughts towards the east. What can his aim be, if not Persia? But I truly rejoice that through efforts of your own you have so good prospect of seeing again your captive brother."

"I have no knowledge of the purposes of the Roman emperor," I replied, "but such as is common to all. Though honoured with the friendship of Aurelian, I am not a political confidant. I can only conjecture touching his designs, from my acquaintance with his character, and the features of the policy he has adopted and avowed as that which is to govern his administration. And this policy is that which has been acted upon by so many of those who before him have been raised to the head of our nation, namely this, that west of the Euphrates to the farthest limits of Spain and Gaul, embracing all the shores of the Mediterranean with their thickly scattered nations, there shall be but one empire, and of that one empire but one head. It is the fixed purpose of Aurelian to restore to the empire the unity by which it was distinguished and blessed under the two Antonines. And already his movements in Gaul show that his practice is to conform to his theory. I feel that you will pardon, nay, that you will commend me, for the plainness with which I impart such knowledge as I may possess. It will be to me the dearest happiness, if I can subserve in any way, consistently with my duty to Rome, the interests of Palmyra and her queen."

"Roman," said Zenobia in reply, "I honour your frankness, and thank you for your faith in my generosity. It is not, I assure you, misplaced. I am glad to know, from so authentic a source, the policy of Aurelian. I surmised as much before. All that I have thought will come true. The rumours which are afloat are not without foundation. Your emperor understands that I have a policy as well as he, and a fixed purpose as well as he. I will never fall from what I have been, but into ruin final and complete. I have lived a sovereign queen, and so I will die. The son of Valerian received Odenatus and Zenobia as partners in empire. We were representatives of Rome in the East. Our dignities and our titles were those of Gallienus. It were small boasting to say that they were worn not less worthily here than in Rome. And this association with Rome—I sought it not. It was offered as a tribute to our greatness. Shall it be dissolved at the will of Aurelian?—and Palmyra, no longer needed as a scourge for the great king, be broken down into a tributary province, an obscure appendage of your greatness? May the gods forsake me that moment I am false to my country! I, too, am ambitious, as well as Aurelian. And let him be told that I stipulate for a full partnership of the Roman power—my sons to bear the name and rank of Cæsar—or the tie which unites Palmyra to Rome is at once and for ever sundered, and she stands before the world an independent kingdom, to make good as she may, by feats of arms, her claims to that high dignity; and the arms which have prevailed from the Nile to the shores of the Caspian, from the Euphrates to the Mediterranean, and have triumphed more than once over the pride and power of Persia, may be trusted in any encounter, if the fates should so ordain, with even Rome herself. The conqueror of Egypt would, I believe, run a not ignoble tilt with the conqueror of a Gallic province."

"Dearest mother," said the princess Julia, in a voice full of earnest entreaty, "do not, do not give way to such thoughts. Heed not these lying rumours. Trust in the magnanimity of Aurelian. We make the virtue we believe in. Let it not reach his ears that you have doubted him. I can see no reason why he should desire to disturb the harmony that has so long reigned—and Aurelian is no madman. What could he gain by a warlike expedition, which a few words could not gain? Noble Piso, if your great emperor would but speak before he acts—if, indeed, any purpose like that which is attributed to him has entered his mind—a world of evil, and suffering, and crime, might possibly be saved. Zenobia, though ambitious, is reasonable and patient, and will listen as becomes a philosopher, and a lover of her people, to any thing he should say. It were a noble act of friendship to press upon him the policy, as well as the virtue, of moderation."

Zenobia gave a mother's smile of love to her daughter, whose countenance, while she uttered these few words, was brilliant with the beauty of strong emotion.

"No act of friendship like this, lady," said I, "shall be wanting on my part. If I have any influence over the mind of Aurelian, it shall be exerted to serve the cause of peace. I have dear friends in Palmyra, and this short residence among her people has bound me to them very closely. It would grieve me sorely to feel, that as a Roman and a lover of my country, I must needs break these so lately knitted bonds of affection. But, I am obliged to say it, I am now full of apprehension, lest no efforts of mine, or of any, may have power to avert the calamities which impend. The scene I was witness of but so few hours ago, seems to me now to cut off all hope of an amicable adjustment."

Julia's countenance fell. The air of pride in Zenobia mounted higher and higher.

"And what was it I did?" said Zenobia. "Do I not stand upon the records of the senate, Augusta of the Roman empire? Was not the late renowned Odenatus, Augustus by the decree of that same senate? And was I not then right to call my own sons by their rightful title of Cæsar, and invest them with the appropriate robe, and even show them to the people as their destined rulers? I am yet to learn that in aught I have offended against any fair construction of the Roman law. And unless I may thus stand in equal honour with other partners of this empire, asking and receiving nothing as favour, I sever myself and my kingdom from it."

"But," said Julia, in her soft persuasive voice, whose very tones were enough to change the harshest sentiment to music, " why put at hazard the certain good we now enjoy, the peace and prosperity of this fair realm, for what at best is but a shadow—a name? What is it to you or me that Timolaus, Herennianus, and Vabalathus, be hailed by the pretty style of Cæsar? For me at least, and so I think for all who love you, it is enough that they are the sons of Zenobia. Who shall heap more upon that honour?"

"Julia," replied the queen, " as the world deems—and we are in the world and of it—honour and greatness lie not in those things which are truly honourable and great; not in learning or genius, else were Longinus upon this throne, and I his waiting-woman ; not in action—else were the great Zabdas king; not in merit, else were many a dame of Palmyra where I am, and I a patient household drudge. Birth, and station, and power, are before these. Men bow before names, and sceptres, and robes of office, lower than before the gods themselves. Nay, here in the east, power itself were a shadow, without its tinsel trappings. 'Tis vain to stand against the world. I am one of the general herd. What they honour, I crave. This coronet of pearl, this gorgeous robe, this golden chair, this human footstool, in the eye of a severe judgment may signify but little. Zeno or Diogenes might smile upon them with contempt. But so thinks not the world. It is no secret that in Timolaus, Herennianus, and Vabalathus, dwells not the wisdom of Longinus nor the virtue of Valerian. What then so crazed the assembled people of Palmyra, but the purple-coloured mantle of the Roman Cæsar! I am for that, fathoms deeper in the great heart of my people. These are poor opinions, so thou judgest, Roman, for the pupil of the chief philosopher of our age, and through him skilled in all the learning of the Greeks. But forget not that I am an oriental and—a woman. This double nature works at my heart with more than all the power of the schools. Who and what so strong as the divinity within?"

This is a poor record, my Curtius, of what fell from this extraordinary woman. Would that I could set down the noble sentiments which, in the midst of so much that I could not approve, came from her lips in a language worthy her great teacher! Would that I could transfer to my pages the touching eloquence of the divine Julia, whose mind, I know not how it is, moves in a higher world than ours. Sometimes, nay many times, her thoughts, strangely enough, raised up before me the image of the Christian Probus, of whom I had till then scarcely thought since our parting. For a long time was this interview continued—an interview to me more stirring than any other of my life, and, owing to the part I was obliged to take, almost painfully so. Much that I said could not but have grated harshly upon the proud and ambitious spirit of Zenobia. But I shrank from nothing that in the least degree might tend to shake her in the designs which now possess and agitate her, and which, as it seems to me, cannot be carried out without great danger to the safety or existence of her kingdom; though I cannot but say, that if a rupture should occur between Palmyra and Rome, imprudence might indeed be charged upon Zenobia, but guilt, deep guilt, would lie at the door of Aurelian. It was a great aid, that Julia, in all I said, was my ally. Her assent gave double force to every argument I used; for Zenobia trusts her as a sister, I had almost said, reveres her as a divinity. Beautiful it was to witness their freedom and their love. The gods avert every calamity from their heads!

When we had in this manner, as I have said, a long time discoursed, Zenobia, at length, rising from her seat, said to me, "Now do we owe you some fair return, noble Piso, for the patience with which you have listened to our treasonable words. If it please you, accompany us now to some other part of our palace, and it will be strange if we cannot find something worthy of your regard."

So saying, we bent our way in company, idly talking of such things as offered, to a remote part of the vast building, passing through and lingering here and there in many a richly-wrought hall and room, till, turning suddenly into a saloon of Egyptian device, where we heard the sound of voices, I found myself in the presence of Gracchus and Fausta, Longinus and Zabdas, with a few others of the chief citizens of Palmyra. I need not say how delighted I was. It was a meeting never to be forgotten. But it was in the evening of this day, walking in the gardens of the palace between Julia and Fausta, that I banqueted upon the purest pleasure of my life.

LETTER V.

You could not but suppose, my Curtius, when you came to the end of my last letter, that I should soon write again, and not leave you ignorant of the manner in which I passed the evening at the palace of Zenobia. Accordingly, knowing that you would desire this, I had no sooner tied and sealed my epistle, than I sat down to give you those minute recollections of incident and of conversation in which you and Lucilia both so much delight, and which, indeed, in the present instance, are not unimportant in their bearing upon my future lot. But this I shall leave to your own conjectures. A tempest of rain makes me a necessary prisoner to the house, but the pleasant duty of writing to you spreads sunshine on all within my room. I trust in the gods that you are well.

Of the banquet in that Egyptian hall, and its immediately attendant circumstances, I need not tell you. It was like other feasts of ceremony, where the niceties of form constantly obtrude themselves, and check too much the flow of conversation. Then, too, one's mind is necessarily distracted, where the feast is sumptuous, by the rarity of the dishes, the richness of the service, and the pomp and stir of the attendance. Never was it my fortune in Rome to recline at a table of more imperial splendour. For Lucilia's sake I will just say, that the service was of pure gold, most elaborately carved, and covered with designs illustrative of points of the Egyptian annals. Our wine cups were also of gold enriched with precious stones; and for each kind of wine, a different cup, set with jewels, typical of the character of the wine for which it was intended. These were by the hand of Demetrius. It was in all respects a Roman meal in its fashions and conduct, though the table was spread with many delicacies peculiar to the orientals. The walls and ceiling of the room, and the carpets, represented, in the colours of the most eminent Greek and Persian artists, scenes of the life and reign of the great queen of Egypt, of whom Zenobia reckons herself a descendant. Cleopatra was all around, above, and beneath. Music at intervals, as the repast drew towards a close, streamed in from invisible performers, and added a last and crowning charm. The conversation was light and sportful, taking once or twice only, and accidentally, as it were, a political turn. These graceful Palmyrenes act a winning part in all the high courtesies of life; and nothing could be more perfect than their demeanour, free and frank, yet never forgetful of the presence of Zenobia, nor even of me, a representative in some manner of the majesty of Rome.

The moon, nearly at her full, was already shining bright in the heavens, when we left the tables, and walking first for a time upon the cool pavements of the porticoes of the palace, then descended to the gardens, and separating in groups, moved away at will among their endless windings. Zenobia, as if desiring some private conference with her great teacher, left us in company with Longinus. It was my good and happy fortune to find myself in the society of Julia and Fausta, with whom I directed my steps towards the remoter and more quiet parts of the garden—for nearer the palace there were still to be heard the sounds of merriment, and of the instruments, furnishing a soft and delicious entertainment for such as chose to remain longer in the palace. Of the rest of the company, some like ourselves wandered among the labyrinthine walks of this vast pleasure-ground, while others, already weary, or satisfied with enjoyment, returned early to their homes.

The evening, shall I say it, was worthy of the company now abroad to enjoy it. A gentle breeze just swayed the huge leaves of the, to me, strange plants which overhung the paths, and came, as it here always seems to come, laden with a sweetness which in Rome it never has, unless added by the hand of art. Dian's face shone never before so fair and bright, and her light, coming to us at frequent turns in our walk, through the spray of numerous fountains, caused them to show like falling diamonds. A divine repose breathed over the whole scene. I am sure our souls were in harmony with it.

"Princess," said I, "the gardens of Nero can have presented no scenes more beautiful than these. He who designed these avenues, and groups of flowers and trees, these frequent statues and fountains, bowers and mimic temples, and made them bear to each other these perfect proportions and relations, had no less knowledge, methinks, of the true principles of taste, and of the very secrets of beauty, than the great Longinus himself. The beauty is so rare, that it affects the mind almost like greatness itself. In truth, in perfect beauty there is always that which overawes."

"I cannot say," replied Julia, "that the learned Greek was the architect and designer of these various forms of beauty. The credit, I believe, is rather due to Periander, a native Athenian, a man, it is universally conceded, of the highest genius. Yet it is at the same time to be said, that the mind of Longinus presided over the whole. And he took not less delight in ordering the arrangements of these gardens, than he did in composing that great treatise, not long published, and which you must have seen before you left Rome. He is a man of universal powers. You have not failed to observe his grace, not less than his abilities, while we were at the tables. You have seen that he can play the part of one who would win the regards of two foolish girls, as well as that of first minister of a great kingdom, or that of the chief living representative and teacher of the philosophy of the immortal Plato."

"For myself," I replied, "I could hardly withdraw myself from the simple admiration of his noble head and form, to attend, so as to judge of it, to what fell from his lips. It seems to me that if a sculptor of his own Greece sought for a model of the human figure, he could hope to find none so perfect as that of Longinus."

"That makes it the foolisher and stranger," said Fausta, "that he should toil at his toilet as he so manifestly does. Why can he not rely, for his power over both men and women, upon his genius, and his natural graces? It might be well enough for the Stagyrite to deck his little person in fine clothes, and to cover his fingers with rings—for I believe there must be something in the outward appearance to strike the mere sensual eye, and please it, either natural or assumed, or else even philosophers might go unheeded. I doubt if upon my fingers there be more or more glowing rings than upon those of Longinus. To be sure, one must admit that his taste is exquisite."

"In the manners and dress of Longinus," said I, "as well as in those of Aristotle, we behold, I think, simply the power of custom. They were both, in respect to such things, in a state of indifference, the true philosophical state. But what happened? Both became instructors and companions of princes, and the inmates of royal palaces. Their manners and costume were left, without a thought, I will dare to say, on their part, to conform themselves to what was around them. Would it not have been a more glaring piece of vanity, if in the palace of Philip, Aristotle had clothed himself in the garb of Diogenes, or if Longinus, in the presence of the great Zenobia, had appeared in the sordid attire of Timon?"

"I think so," said Julia.

"Your explanation is a very probable one," added Fausta, "and had not occurred to me. It is true, the courts may have dressed them and not themselves. But never, I still must think, did a rich dress fall upon more willing shoulders than upon those of the Greek, always excepting, Julia, Paul of Antioch."

"Ah, Fausta," said Julia, "you cannot, do what you will, shake my faith in Paul. If I allow him vain, and luxurious, and haughty, I can still separate the advocate from the cause. You would not condemn the doctrine of Aristotle, on the ground that he wore rings. Nor can I altogether, nor in part, that of Paul, because he rolls through the city in a gilded chariot, with the attendance of a prince. I may blame or despise him, but not therefore reject his teaching. That has a defence independent of him. Policy, and necessity of time and place, have compelled him to much which his reason disproves. This he has given me to believe, and has conjured me on this, as on all subjects, to yield my mind only to evidence, apart from all personal considerations. But I did not mean to turn our conversation in this direction. Here, Piso, have we now arrived in our walk at my favourite retreat. This is my bower for meditation, and frequently for reading, too. Let us take this seat. Observe how through these openings we catch some of the prominent points of the city. There is the obelisk of Cleopatra; there the tower of Antonine; there the Egyptian pyramid; and there a column going up in honour of Aurelian; and in this direction, the whole outline of the palace."

"Yet are we at the same time shut out from all the world," said I. "Your hours must fly swiftly here. But are your musings always solitary?"

"Oh no, I am not so craving as that of my own

society: sometimes I am joined by my mother, and not seldom by my sweet Fausta here," said she, at the same time affectionately drawing Fausta's arm within her own, and clasping her hand; "we do not agree, indeed, upon all the subjects which we discuss, but we still agree in our love."

"Indeed we do, and may the gods make it perpetual! may death only divide us!" said Fausta with fervour.

"And may the divinity who sits supreme above," said Julia, "grant that over that, not even death shall have power. If any thing makes existence valuable, it is love. If I should define my happiness, I should say it in one word, love. Without Zenobia, what should I be? I cannot conceive of existence deprived of her, or of her regard. Loving her, and Fausta, and Longinus, as I do—not to forget Livia and the dear Faustula—and beloved by all in return—and my happiness scarcely seems to admit of addition."

"With what pain," said I, "does one contemplate the mere possibility that affections such as these are to last only for the few years which make up the sum of human life! Must I believe, must you believe, that all this fair scene is to end for ever at death? That you, bound to each other by so many ties, are to be separated, and both of you to be divided from Zenobia, and all of us to fall into nothingness, silence, and darkness? Rather than that, would that the life we now enjoy might be immortal! Here are beautiful objects, among which one might be willing to live for ever. I am never weary of the moon and her soft light, nor of the balmy air, nor of the bright greens of the herbage, nor of the forms of plain and mountain, nor of the human beings, infinite in the varieties of their character, who surround me wherever I go. Here now have I wandered far from my home, yet in what society and in what scenes do I find myself? The same heaven is above me, the same forms of vegetable life around me, and, what is more, friends already dear as those I have left behind. In this very spot, were it but as a humble attendant upon the greatness of the queen, could I be content to dwell."

"Truly, I think you might," cried Fausta; "having chosen for yourself so elysian a spot, and filled it with such inhabitants, it is no great proof of a contented spirit that you should love to inhabit it. But how many such spots does the world present!—and how many such inhabitants! The question I think is, would you be ready to accept the common lot of man as an immortal one? I can easily believe that many, were they seated in these gardens, and waited on by attendant slaves, and their whole being made soft and tranquil, and exempt from care and fear, would say, 'Ensure me this, and I ask no more.' For myself, indeed, I must say it would not be so. I think not even the lot of Zenobia, enthroned as she is in the hearts of millions, nor yet thine, Julia, beloved not less than Zenobia, would satisfy me. I have now all that my utmost desires crave. Yet is there a part of me, I know not what it is, nor where it is, that is not full. I confess myself restless and unsatisfied. No object, no study, no pursuit, no friendship—forgive me, Julia"—and she kissed her hand—"no friendship even, satisfies and fills me."

"I do not wonder," said Julia.

"But how much unhappiness is there spread over the earth," continued Fausta: "I and you, and Piso, perhaps, too, are in a state of dissatisfaction. And yet we are perched, as it were, upon the loftiest heights of existence. How must it be with those who are so far inferior to us as multitudes are in their means of happiness? From how many ills are we shielded, which rain down sharp-pointed, like the hail storms of winter, upon the undefended heads of the poor and low! They, Piso, would not, I think, pray that their lot might be immortal."

"Indeed, I think not," said I. "Yet perhaps their lot is not so much more miserable than yours, as the difference in outward condition might lead one to think. Remember, the slave and the poor do not feel as you would, suddenly reduced to their state. The Arab enjoys his sleep upon his tent floor, as well as you, princess, beneath a canopy of woven gold, and his frugal meal of date or pulse tastes as sweet, as to you do dainties fetched from Rome, or fished from the Indian seas: and eating and sleeping make up much of life. Then the hearts of the great are corroded by cares and solicitudes which never visit the humble. Still, I do not deny that their condition is not far less enviable than ours. The slave who may be lashed, and tormented, and killed, at his master's pleasure, drinks from a cup of which we never so much as taste. But over the whole of life, and throughout every condition of it, there are scattered evils and sorrows which pierce every heart with pain. I look upon all conditions as in part evil, It is only by selecting circumstances, and excluding ills which are the lot of all, that I could ask to live for ever, even in the gardens of Zenobia."

"I do not think we differ much, then," said Fausta, "in what we think of human life. I hold the highest lot to be unsatisfying. You admit all are so, but have shown me that there is a nearer approach to an equality of happiness than I had supposed, though evil weighs upon all. How the mind longs and struggles to penetrate the mysteries of its being! How imperfect and without aim does life seem! Every thing beside man seems to reach its utmost perfection. Man alone appears a thing incomplete and faulty."

"And what," said I, "would make him appear to you a thing perfect and complete? What change should you suggest?"

"That which rather may be called an addition," replied Fausta, "and which, if I err not, all wise and good men desire—the assurance of immortality. Nothing is sweet; every cup is bitter; that which we are this moment drinking from, bitterest of all, without this. Of this I incessantly think and dream, and am still tossed in a sea of doubt."

"You have read Plato?" said I.

"Yes, truly," she replied; "but I found little there to satisfy me. I have enjoyed, too, the frequent con-

versation of Longinus, and yet it is the same. Would
that he were now here! The hour is serene, and the
air which comes in so gently from the west, such as he
loves."

As Fausta uttered these words, our eyes at the same
moment caught the forms of Zenobia and Longinus,
as they emerged from a walk very near, but made dark
by overhanging and embowering roses. We immediately advanced towards them, and begged them to
join us.

"We are conversing," said Julia, "upon such things
as you both love. Come and sit now with us, and let
us know what you can say upon the same themes."

"We will sit with you gladly," said the queen; "at
least for myself I may say it, for I am sure that with
you I shall find some other subjects discussed besides
perplexing affairs of state. When alone with Longinus
—as but now—our topic is ever the same."

"If the subject of our discourse, however, be ever the
same," said the Greek, "we have this satisfaction in
reflecting upon it, that it is one that in its nature is
real and tangible. The well-being of a nation is not
an undefined and shadowy topic, like so many of those
which occupy the time and thoughts of even the wise.
I too, however, shall gladly bear a part in whatever
theme may engross the thoughts of Julia, Fausta, and
Piso."

With these words, we returned to the seats we had
left, which were not within the arbour of Julia, but
were the marble steps which led to it. There we placed
ourselves, one above and one beside another as happened—Zenobia sitting between Fausta and Julia, I at
the feet of Julia, and Longinus on the same step with
myself, and next to Fausta. I could hardly believe
that Zenobia was now the same person before whom I
had in the morning, with little agitation, prostrated
myself, after the manner of the Persian ceremonial.
She seemed rather like a friend whom I both loved and
revered. The majesty of the queen was gone; there

remained only the native dignity of beauty, and goodness, and intellect, which, though it inspires reverence, yet is there nothing slavish in the feeling. It differs in degree only from that sentiment which we entertain towards the gods; it raises rather than depresses.

"We were speaking," said Julia, resuming the subject which had engaged us, "of life and of man—how unsatisfactory life is, and how imperfect and unfinished, as it were, man; and we agreed, I believe, in the opinion, that there can be no true happiness, without a certain assurance of immortality—and this we are without."

"I agree with you," said Longinus, "in all that you can have expressed concerning the unsatisfactoriness of life regarded as a finite existence, and concerning the want of harmony there is between man and the other works of God, if he is mortal; and in this also, that without the assurance of immortality, there can, to the thinking mind, be no true felicity. I only wonder that on the last point there should exist in the mind of any one of you doubts so serious as to give you much disturbance. I cannot, indeed, feel so secure of a future and then unending existence, as I am sure that I live now. What I am now, I know; concerning the future I can only believe, and belief can never possess the certainty of knowledge. Still, of a future life I entertain no doubts that distress me. My belief in it is as clear and strong as I can well conceive belief in things invisible and unexperienced to be. It is such as makes me happy in any thought or prospect of death. Without it, and life would appear to me like nothing more to be esteemed than a short, and often troubled or terrific dream."

"So I confess it seems to me," said Fausta. "How should I bless the gods, if upon my mind there could rest a conviction of immortality strong like yours! The very certainty with which you speak, seems, through the power of sympathy, to have scattered some of my doubts. But, alas! they will soon return."

"In what you have now said," replied Longinus, "and in the feeling you have expressed on this point, do I found one of the strongest arguments for the immortality of the soul."

"I do not comprehend you," said Fausta.

"Do you not, Fausta," asked Longinus, "intensely desire a life after death?"

"I do indeed. I have just expressed it."

"And do not you too, Zenobia, and Piso, and Julia?"

"Surely, and with intensity," we answered; "the question need scarcely be asked."

"I believe you," resumed Longinus. "You all earnestly desire an immortal life — you perpetually dwell upon the thought of it, and long for it. Is it not so with all who reflect at all upon themselves? Are there any such, have there ever been any, who have not been possessed by the same thoughts and desires, and who, having been greatly comforted and supported by them during life, have not at death relied upon them, and looked with some good degree of confidence towards coming forth again from death? Now I think it is far more reasonable to believe in another life, than in the delusiveness of these expectations. For I cannot suppose that this universal expectation will be disappointed, without believing in the wickedness, nay, the infinite malignity, of the Supreme Ruler, which my whole nature utterly refuses to do. For what more cruel than to create this earnest and universal longing, and not gratify it? Does it not seem so?"

We all admitted it.

"This instinctive desire," continued Longinus, "I cannot but regard as being implanted by the Being who created us. It can proceed from no other. It is an instinct, that is, a suggestion or inspiration of God. If it could be shown to be a consequence of education, we might refer for its origin to ingenious philosophers. But it exists where the light of philosophy has never shone. There have been none, of whom history has preserved even obscurest traditions, who have wanted this instinct. It is, then, the very inspiration of the Divinity, and will not be disappointed. I trust much to these tendencies of our nature. This is the best ground for our belief of a God. The arguments of the schools have never succeeded in establishing the truth, even to the conviction of a philosophical mind, much less a common one. Yet the truth is universally admitted. God, I think, has provided for so important an article of faith in the structure of our minds. He has not left it to chance, or special revelation. So, too, the determinations of the mind concerning virtue and vice, right and wrong, being for the most part so accordant throughout the whole race—these, also, I hold to be instinctive."

"I can think of nothing," said Fausta, "to urge against your argument. It adds some strength, I cannot but confess, to what belief I had before. I trust you have yet more that you can impart. Do not fear that we shall be dull listeners."

"I sit here a willing and patient learner," said Zenobia, "of any one who will pour new light into my mind. Go on, Longinus."

"To such a school," said he, "how can I refuse to speak? Let me ask you, then, if you have never been perplexed by the evils of life, such as either you have yourselves experienced, or such as you have witnessed?"

"I have, indeed," said Fausta, "and have deeply deplored them. But how are they connected with a future existence?"

"Thus," replied Longinus, "as in the last case, the benevolence of the Supreme God cannot be sustained without the admission of the reality of a future life. Nor only that, but it seems to me, direct proof may be adduced from the existence and universality of these evils to establish the blackest malignity. So that to me, belief in a future existence is in proportion to the difficulty of admitting the idea of divine malignity, and it cannot therefore be much stronger than it is."

"How can you make that clear to us?" said Fausta;

"I should truly rejoice if out of the evils which so darken the earth, any thing good or beautiful could be drawn."

"As this dark mould," rejoined the philosopher, "sends upwards, and out of its very heart, this rare Persian rose, so does hope grow out of evil, and the darker the evil the brighter the hope, as from a richer and fouler soil comes the more vigorous plant and larger flower. Take a particular evil, and consider it. You remember the sad tale concerning the Christian Probus, which Piso, in recounting the incidents of his journey from Rome to Palmyra, related to us while seated at the tables."

"Indeed, I did not hear it," said Zenobia; "so that Piso must, if he pleases, repeat it."

"We shall willingly hear it again," said Julia and Fausta.

And I then related it again.

"Now, do you wonder," resumed Longinus, when I had finished, "that Probus, when one after another four children were ravished from his arms by death, and then, as if to crown his lot with evil, his wife followed them, and he was left alone in the world, bereaved of every object to which his heart was most fondly attached—do you wonder, I say, that he turned to the heavens and cursed the gods? And can you justify the gods so that they shall not be chargeable with blackest malignity, if there be no future and immortal state? What is it to bind so the heart of a parent to a child, to give that affection a force and a tenderness which belong to no other tie, so that anxieties for its life and welfare, and cares and sacrifices for its good, constitute the very existence of the parent, what is it to foster by so many contrivances this love, and then for ever disappoint and blast it, but malignity? Yet this work is done every hour, and in almost every heart; if for children we lament not, yet we do for others as dear."

Tears to the memory of Odenatus fell fast from the eyes of Zenobia.

"Are we not, then," continued Longinus, without pausing, "are we not, then, presented with this alternative; either the Supreme God is a malignant being, whose pleasure it is to torment, or, there is an immortal state, where we shall meet again with those, who for inscrutable purposes have been torn from our arms here below? And who can hesitate in which to rest? The belief, therefore, in a future life ought to be in proportion to the difficulty of admitting the idea of divine malignity. And this idea is so repulsive, so impossible to be entertained for one moment, that the other cannot, it seems to me, rest upon a firmer foundation."

"Every word you speak," said Zenobia, "yields pleasure and instruction. It delights me, even when thickest beset by the cares of state, to pause and contemplate for a moment the prospects of futurity. It diffuses a divine calm throughout the soul. You have given me new food for my thoughts."

"I will add," said Longinus, "only one thing to what I have said, and that is, concerning the incompleteness of man as a divine work, and which has been mentioned by Fausta. Is not this an argument for a future life? Other things and beings are finished and complete—man only is left, as it were, half made up. A tree grows and bears fruit, and the end of its creation is answered. A complete circle is run. It is the same with the animals. No one expects more from a lion or a horse than is found in both. But with man it is not so. In no period of history, and among no people, has it been satisfactorily determined what man is, or what are the limits of his capacity and being. He is full of contradictions, and of incomprehensible organisation, if he is considered only in relation to this world. For while every other affection finds and rests in its appropriate object, which fully satisfies and fills it, the desire of unlimited improvement and of endless life—the strongest and best defined of any of the desires—this alone is answered by no corresponding object, which is not different from what it would be, if the gods should create a race like ours, having the same craving and necessity for food and drink, yet never provide for them the one or the other, but leave them all to die of hunger. Unless there is a future life, we all die of a worse hunger. Unless there is a future life, man is a monster in creation—compared with other things, an abortion—and in himself, and compared with himself, an enigma, a riddle, which no human wit has ever solved, or can ever hope to solve."

"This seems unanswerable," said Fausta; "yet is it no objection to all such arguments, which we ourselves construct, that the thing they establish is too great and good almost to be believed, without some divine warrant. It does to me appear almost or quite presumptuous to think, that for me there is by the gods prepared a world of never-fading light, and a never-ending joy."

"When," replied the Greek, " we look at the lower forms of man, which fall under our observation, I confess that the objection which you urge strikes me with some force. But when I think that it is for beings like you to whom I speak for whom another and fairer world is to be prepared, it loses again much of its force. And when I think of the great and good of other times, of Homer and Hesiod, of Phidias and Praxiteles, of Socrates and Plato, and of what the mind of man has in them, and in others as great and good, accomplished, the objection which you urge loses all its force. I see and feel that man has been made not altogether unworthy of a longer life and a happier lot than earth affords. And in regard to the ignorant, the low, and the almost or quite savage, we are to consider that the same powers and affections are in them as in us, and that their inferiority to us is not intrinsic and essential, but, as it were, accidental. The difference between the soul of Plato and yonder Ethiopian slave is not in any original faculty or power—the slave here equals the philosopher; but in this, that the faculties and powers of Plato were strengthened, and nurtured, and polished, by the hand of education, and the happy influences of a more civilised community, all which to the slave has been wanting. He is a diamond just as it comes from the mine; Plato like that one set in gold, which sparkles with the radiance of a star, Fausta, upon your finger. But, surely, the glory of the diamond is, that it is a diamond, not that Demetrius has polished and set it. Man has within him so much of the god, that I do not wonder he has been so often deified. The great and excellent among men, therefore, I think not unworthy of immortality, for what they are; the humble and the bad, for what they may so easily become, and might have been, under circumstances but slightly altered."

"I cannot," said Julia, as Longinus closed, "deny strength and plausibility to your arguments, but I cannot admit that they satisfy me. After the most elaborate reasoning, I am still left in darkness. No power or wit of man has ever wholly scattered the mists which rest upon life and death. I confess, with Socrates, that I want a promise or a revelation to enable me to take the voyage of life in a spirit of cheerfulness, and without the fear of fatal shipwreck. If your reasonings, Longinus, were only accompanied with authority more than that of man, if I could only believe that the Divinity inspired you, I could then rest contented and happy. One word authoritatively declaring man's immortality—a word which by infallible token I could know to be a word from the Supreme—would to me be worth infinitely more than all the conjectures, hopes, and reasonings, of all the philosophers. I fully agree with you, that the instincts of our nature all point both to a God and to immortality. But the heart longs for something more sure and clear, at least my woman's heart does. It may be that it is the woman within me which prompts the feeling, but I wish to lean upon authority in this great matter; I wish to repose calmly in a divine assurance."

"In that, princess," I could not help saying, "I am a woman too. I have long since lost all that regard for the gods in which I was so carefully nourished. I despise the popular superstitions. Yet is there nothing which I have found as yet to supply their place. I have searched the writings of Plato, of Cicero, of Seneca, in vain. I find there indeed, wisdom, and learning, and sagacity, almost more than human. But I find nothing which can be dignified by the name of religion. Their systems of morals are admirable, and sufficient perhaps to enable one to live a happy or fortunate life. But concerning the soul of man, and its destiny, they are dumb, or their words, if they utter any, are but the dark speeches of an oracle."

"I am happy that I am not alone," said Julia, "and I cannot but think that many, very many, are with me. I am sure that what most persons, perhaps, who think and feel upon these subjects, want, is some divine promise or revelation. Common minds, Longinus, cannot appreciate the subtlety of your reasonings, much less those of the Phædo. And, besides, the cares and labours of life do not allow time to engage in such inquiries, even if we supposed all men to have capacity for them. Is it not necessary that truths relating to the soul and futurity should rest upon authority, if any, or many, besides philosophers are to embrace them? And surely, if the poor and ignorant are immortal, it is as needful for them as for us to know it. It is, I conceive, on this account, that the religion of the Christians has spread so rapidly. It meets our nature. It supplies authority. It professes to bring annunciations from Heaven of man's immortality."

"It is for that reason," replied Longinus, "I cannot esteem it. The very term revelation offends. The right application of reason affects all, it seems to me, that what is called revelation can. It perfectly satisfies the philosopher, and as for common minds, instinct is an equally sufficient guide and light."

"I cannot but judge you, Longinus," said Julia, "wanting in a true fellow feeling for your kind, notwithstanding all you have said concerning the nature and powers of man. How is it, that you can desire that mankind should remain any longer under the dominion of the same gross and pernicious errors that have for so many ages oppressed them? Only consider the horrors of an idolatrous religion in Egypt and Assyria, in Greece and in Rome, and do you not desire their extermination? —and what prospect of this can there be, but through the plain authoritative language of a revelation?"

"I certainly desire with you," replied Longinus, "the extermination of error, and the overthrow of horrible and corrupting superstitions; and of nothing am I more sure than that the reason of man, in unfolding and constantly improving ages, will effect it. A plain voice from Heaven announcing important truth, might perhaps hasten the work. But this voice, as thought to be heard in Christianity, is not a plain voice, nor clearly known to be a voice from Heaven. Here is the Bishop of Antioch set upon by the Bishops of Alexandria and Cesarea, and many others, as I learn, who accuse him of wrongly receiving and falsely teaching the doctrines of Christ; and for two hundred years has there prevailed the like uncertainty about the essence of the religion."

"I look not with much hope to Christianity," said Fausta. "Yet I must first inform myself more exactly concerning it, before I judge."

"That is spoken like Fausta," said Julia; "and it is much for you to say who dislike so heartily that Paul, whom I am constantly wishing you to hear."

"Whenever he shall lay aside a little of his pomp, I may be willing to listen," replied Fausta; "but I could ill brook a discourse upon immortality from one whose soul seems so wedded to time."

"Well," said Julia, "but let us not be drawn away from our subject. I admit that there are disputes among the Christians, but, like the disputes among philosophers, they are about secondary matters. There is no dispute concerning the great and chiefly interesting part of the religion—its revelation of a future life. Christians have never divided here, nor on another great point, that Christ, the founder of the religion, was a true messenger from God. The voice of Christianity on both these points is a clear one. Thus, I think, every one will judge, who, as I have done, will read the writings in which the religion is found. And I am persuaded it is because it is so plain a voice here, that it is bidding fair to supersede every other form of religion. And that it is a voice from God, is, it seems to me, made out with as much clearness as we could look for. That Christ, the author of this religion, was a messenger from God, was shown by his miracles. How could it be shown otherwise? I can conceive of no other way in which so satisfying proof could be given of the agency and authority of God. And certainly there is evidence enough, if history is to be believed, that he wrought many and stupendous miracles."

"What is a miracle?" asked Longinus.

"It is that," replied Julia, "which being done or said, furnishes satisfactory proof of the present interposing power of God. A man who, by a word spoken, can heal sick persons, and raise to life dead ones, can be no other than a messenger of God."

"Why not of some other superior being—perhaps a bad one?"

"The character, teaching, objects, acts of Christ, make it unlikely, if not impossible, that he should have been sent by any bad intelligence. And that he came not only from a good being, but from God, we may believe on his own word."

"His goodness may have been all assumed. The whole may be a deception."

"Men do not sacrifice their lives merely to deceive, to play a child's game before the world. Christ died to show his attachment to his cause, and with him innumerable others. Would they have done this merely to impose upon mankind? And for what purpose?— for that of teaching a religion inculcating the loftiest virtue! But I do not set myself forward as a champion of this new religion," continued Julia, plainly disturbed lest she might have seemed too earnest; "would that you, Longinus, could be persuaded to search into its claims. If you would but read the books written by the founders of it, I am sure you would say this at least, that such books were never written before, nor such a character pourtrayed as that of Jesus Christ. You who profess yourself charmed with the poetry of the Jewish Scriptures, and the grandeur of the sentiments expressed in them, would not be less impressed by the gentler majesty, the mild, sweet dignity of the person and doctrine of Christ. And if the reasonings of Socrates and Plato have any power to convince you of the immortality of the soul, how must you be moved by the simple announcements of the truth by the Nazarene, and, above all, by his resurrection from the dead! Christianity boasts already powerful advocates, but I wish it could say that its character and claims had been examined by the great Longinus."

The soft yet earnest, eloquent tones of Julia's voice fell upon pleased and willing ears. The countenance of the Greek glowed with a generous satisfaction, as he listened to the reasoning of his fair pupil, poured forth in that noble tongue it had been his task and his happiness to teach her. Evidently desirous, however, not to prolong the conversation, he addressed himself to the queen.

"You are pleased," said he, "you must be, with the aptness of my scholar. Julia has not studied dialectics in vain. Before I can feel myself able to contend with her, I must study the books she has commended so—from which I must acknowledge, I have been repelled by a prejudice, I believe, rather than any thing else, or more worthy—and then, perhaps, I may agree in opinion with her."

"In truth," said Zenobia, "Julia is almost or quite a Christian. I knew not, daughter, that Paul had made such progress in his work. But all have my full consent to cherish such form of religious faith as most approves itself to their own minds. I find my highest satisfaction in Moses and the prophets. Happy shall I be if Julia find as much, or more, in Christ and his apostles. Sure am I, there is no beneficent power or charm in the religions of Greece or Rome, or Persia, or Egypt, to cause any of us to adhere to them, though our very infancy were instructed in their doctrines."

"It is not, I assure you," said Julia, "to Paul of Antioch that I owe such faith in Christ as I have, but to the Christian books themselves; or if to any human authority beside, to St Thomas, the old hermit of the mountain, to whom I would that every one should resort who would draw near to the purest living fountain of Christian knowledge."

"I trust," said I, "that at some future time, I may, with your guidance, or through your influence, gain admittance to this aged professor of the Christian faith. I confess myself now, since what I have heard, a seeker after Christian knowledge."

"Gladly shall I take you there," replied the princess, "and gladly will St Thomas receive you."

We now at the same time rose from our seats. Zenobia, taking the hand of Fausta, walked towards the palace; Longinus, with folded arms, and as if absorbed by the thoughts which were passing through his mind, began to pace to and fro beneath the thick shadows of a group of orange trees. I was left with Julia.

"Princess," said I, "it is yet early, and the beauty of the evening makes it wrong to shut ourselves up from the sight of so fair a scene: shall we follow farther some of these inviting paths?"

"Nothing can be more pleasant," said she; "these are my favourite haunts, and I never weary of them, and never did they seem to me to wear a more lovely aspect than now. Let me be your guide, and I will lead you by a winding way to Zenobia's Temple, as we call it, for the reason that it is her chosen retreat, as the arbour which we have now left is mine."

So we began to walk towards the spot of which she spake. We were for some time silent. At length the princess said, "Roman, you have now seen Zenobia, both as a queen and a woman. Has fame done her more than justice?"

"Great as her reputation is in Rome," I replied, "fame has not, to my ear at least, brought any thing that more than distantly approaches a true and faithful picture of her. We have heard much, indeed, and yet not enough, of her surpassing beauty, of the vigour of her understanding, of her vast acquirements in the Greek learning, of the wisdom and energy of her conduct as a sovereign queen, of her skill in the chase, of her bravery and martial bearing, when, at the head of her troops, she leads them to the charge. But of this union of feminine loveliness with so much of masculine power, of this womanly grace, of this winning condescension—so that it loses all the air of condescension—to those even much beneath her in every human accomplishment as well as in rank, of this I had heard nothing, and for this I was not prepared. When, in the morning, I first saw her seated in all the pride of oriental state, and found myself prostrate at her feet, it was only Zenobia that I saw, and I saw what I expected. But no sooner had she spoken, especially no sooner had she cast that look upon you, princess, when you had said a few words in reply to me, than I saw not Zenobia only, but the woman and the mother. A veil was suddenly lifted, and a new being stood before me. It seemed to me that that moment I knew her better than I know myself. I am sure that I know her. Her countenance all living with emotion, changing and working with every thought of her mind, and every feeling of her heart, reveals her with the truth of a magic mirror. She is not known at Rome."

"I am sorry for it," said Julia; "if they only knew her, they could never do her harm. You, Piso, may perhaps do much for her. I perceive, already, that she highly regards you, and values your opinion. If you are willing to do us such service, if you feel interest enough in our fate, speak to her, I pray you, with plainness, all that you think. Withhold nothing. Fear not to utter what you may deem to be most unpalatable truths. She is candid and generous, as she is ambitious. She will at least hear and weigh whatever you may advance. God grant that truth may reach her mind, and reaching, sway it!"

"I can now think of no higher satisfaction," I replied, "than to do all I may, as a Roman, in your service. I love your nation; and as a Roman and a man, I desire its welfare and permanent glory. Its existence is necessary to Rome; its ruin or decay must be, viewed aright, but so much injury to her most vital interests. Strange, how strange, that Zenobia, formed by the gods to draw her happiness from sources so much nobler than any which ambition can supply, should turn from them, and seek for it in the same shallow pool with Alexander, and Aurelian, and the hireling soldier of fortune!"

"Strange indeed," said Julia, "that she who can enter with Longinus into the deepest mysteries of philosophy, and whose mind is stored with all the learning of the schools, should still love the pomp of power better than all. And Fausta is but her second self. Fausta worships Zenobia, and Zenobia is encouraged in her opinions by the kindred sentiments of that bright spirit. All the influence, Piso, which you can exert over Fausta, will reach Zenobia."

"It seems presumptuous, princess," said I, "to seek to draw the minds of two such beings as Zenobia and Fausta to our bent. Yet surely they are in the wrong."

"It is something," quickly added the princess, "that Longinus is of our mind; but then again Zabdas and Gracchus are a host on the other part. And all the power and pride of Palmyra are with them, too. But change Zenobia, and we change all. Oh how weary am I of ambition, and how sick of greatness! Willingly would I exchange all this for an Arab's tent, or a hermit's cell."

"The gods grant that may never be," I replied; "but

that you, princess, may yet live to sit upon the throne of Zenobia!"

"I say it with sincerity, Roman, that prayer finds no echo in my bosom. I have seen enough of power, and of the honours that wait upon it. And when I say this, having had before my eyes this beautiful vision of Zenobia reigning over subjects as a mother would reign over her family, dealing justly with all, and living but to make others happy, you must believe me. I seek and love a calmer, humbler lot. This, Piso, is the temple of Zenobia. Let us enter."

We approached and entered. It was a small building, after the model of the temple of Vesta at Tivoli, constructed of the most beautiful marbles, and adorned with statues. Within, were the seats on which the queen was accustomed to recline, and an ample table, covered with her favourite authors, and the materials of writing.

"It is here," said Julia, "that, seated with my mother, we listen to the eloquence of Longinus, while he unfolds the beauties of the Greek or Roman learning; or, together with him, read the most famous works of former ages. With Homer, Thucydides, and Sophocles for our companions, we have here passed precious hours and days, and have the while happily forgotten the heavy burden of a nation's cares. I have forgotten them; not so Zenobia. They are her life, and from all we have read would she ever draw somewhat that should be of service to her in the duties of her great office."

Returning to the surrounding portico, we stood and for a time enjoyed in silence the calm beauty of the scene.

As we stood thus, Julia gazing upon the objects around us, or lost in thought, I—must I say it?—seeing scarce any thing but her, and thinking only of her; as we stood thus, shouts of merry laughter came to us, borne upon the breeze, and roused us from our reverie.

"These sounds," said I, "cannot come from the

palace; it is too far, unless these winding walks have deceived me."

"They are the voices," said Julia, "I am almost sure, of Livia and Faustula, and the young Cæsars. They seem to be engaged in some sport near the palace. Shall we join them?"

"Let us do so," said I.

So we moved towards that quarter of the gardens whence the sounds proceeded. A high wall at length separated us from those whom we sought. But reaching a gate, we passed through and entered upon a lawn covered as it seemed with children, slaves, and the various inmates of the palace. Here, mingled among the motley company, we at once perceived the queen, and Longinus and Fausta, together with many of those whom we had sat with at the banquet. The centre of attraction, and the cause of the loud shouts of laughter which continually arose, was a small white elephant with which the young princes and princesses were amusing themselves. He had evidently been trained to the part he had to perform, for nothing could be more expert than the manner in which he went through his various tricks. Sometimes he chased them, and pretended difficulty in overtaking them; then he would affect to stumble, and so fall and roll upon the ground; then springing quickly upon his feet, he would surprise some one or other lurking near him, and seizing him with his trunk would hold him fast, or first whirling him in the air, then seat him upon his back, and march gravely round the lawn, the rest following and shouting; then releasing his prisoner, he would lay himself upon the ground, while all together would fearlessly climb upon his back, till it was covered, when he would either suddenly shake his huge body, so that one after another they rolled off, or he would attempt to rise slowly upon his legs, in doing which, nearly all would slip from off his slanting back, and only two or three succeed in keeping their places. And other sportive tricks, more than it would be worth while for me to recount, did he perform for the amusement of his play-fellows. And beautiful was it to see the carefulness with which he trod and moved, lest any harm might come to those children. His especial favourite was the little flaxen-haired Faustula. He was never weary with caressing her, taking her on his trunk, and bearing her about, and when he set her down, would wait to see that she was fairly on her feet and safe, before he would return to his gambols. Her voice calling out "Sapor, Sapor," was sure to bring him to her, when, what with words and signs, he soon comprehended what was it she wanted. I myself came in unwittingly for a share of the sport. For as Faustula came bounding by me, I did as those are so apt to do who know little of children—I suddenly extended my arms and caught her. She, finding herself seized, and in the arms of one she knew not, thought, as children will think, that she was already borne a thousand leagues from her home, and screamed; whereupon, at the instant, I felt myself taken round the legs by a force greater than that of a man, and which drew them together with such violence that instinctively I dropped the child, and at the same time cried out with pain. Julia, standing next me, incontinently slapped the trunk of the elephant, for it was that twisted round me, with her hand, at which, leaving me, he wound it slightly round the waist of the princess, and held her his close prisoner. Great laughter from the children and the slaves testified their joy at seeing their elders, equally with themselves, in the power of the elephant. Milo being of the number, and in his foolish exhilaration and sportive approbation of Sapor's feats having gone up to him and patted him on his side, the beast, receiving as an affront that plebeian salutation, quickly turned upon him, and taking him by one of his feet, held him in that displeasing manner, his head hanging down, and paraded leisurely round the green, Milo making the while hideous outcry, and the whole company, especially the slaves and menials, filling the air with screams of laughter. At length Vabalathus, thinking that Milo might be injured, called out to Sapor, who thereupon released him, and he rising and adjusting his dress, was heard to affirm, that it had never happened so while he was in the service of Gallienus.

These things for the little Gallus.

Satisfied, now, with the amusements of the evening, and the pleasures of the day, we parted from one another, filled with quite different sentiments from those which had possessed us in the morning. Do members of this great human family ever meet each other in social converse, and freely open their hearts, without a new and better strength being given to the bonds which hold in their embrace the peace and happiness of society? To love each other, I think we chiefly need but to know each other. Ignorance begets suspicion, suspicion dislike or hatred, and so we live as strangers and enemies, when knowledge would have led to intimacy and friendship. Farewell!

LETTER VI.

MANY days have passed, my Curtius, since I last wrote, each bringing its own pleasures, and leaving its ineffaceable impressions upon the soul. But though all have been in many things delightful, none has equalled that day and evening at the palace of the queen. I have now mingled largely with the best society in Palmyra. The doors of the noble and the rich have been opened to me with a liberal hospitality. As the friend of Gracchus and Fausta—and now I may add, I believe, without presumption—of Zenobia also, of Julia, and Longinus, I have been received with attentions of which Aurelian himself might with reason have been proud. More and more do I love this people, more and more fervently do I beg of the Being or Beings who rule over the affairs of men, to interpose and defend them from any threatening danger. I grieve that the rumours still reaching us from Rome tend so much to confirm the belief that our emperor is making preparations for an eastern expedition. Yet I cannot bring myself to think that he aims at Zenobia. If it were so, would there be first no communication with the queen? Is it like Aurelian to plan and move so secretly? And against a woman too?—and that woman Zenobia? I'll not believe it. Your letters would not be what they are, if there were any real purpose like that which is attributed to Aurelian. But time will make its revelations. Meanwhile, let me tell you where I now am, and what pleasures I am enjoying. This will be written under various dates.

I write to you from what is called the Queen's Mountain Palace, being her summer residence, occasionally either to avoid the greater heats of the city, or that she may divert herself with athletic sports, or hunting, of which she is excessively fond, and in which she has few equals of her own or even of our sex. Roman women of the present day would be amazed, perhaps shocked, to be told what the sports and exercises are in which this great eastern queen finds her pleasures. She is not more exalted above the women of Rome by genius, and the severer studies of the closet, than she is, in my judgment, by the manner and fashion of her recreations. Let not the dear Lucilia be offended. Were she here with me, her fair and generous mind would rest, I am sure, after due comparisons, in the very same conclusions. Fausta is in these respects too, as in others, but her second self. There is not a feat of horsemanship or archery, or an enterprise in the chase, but she will dare all and do all that is dared or done by Zenobia; not in the spirit of imitation or even rivalry, but from the native impulses of a soul that reaches at all things great and difficult. And even Julia, that being who seems too ethereal for earth, and as if by some strange chance she were misplaced, being here, even Julia has been trained in the same school; and, as I shall show you, can join in the chase, and draw the bow, with scarcely less of skill and vigour, with no less courage, than either her mother or Fausta. Although I have now seen it, I still can hardly associate such excess of beauty—a beauty both of form and face so truly belonging to this soft, Syrian clime—with a strength and dexterity at every exercise that might put to shame many a Roman who wears both a beard and the manly gown. But this, I need not say, is not after Julia's heart. She loves more the gentler encounters of social intercourse, where wit, and sense, and the affections, have their full play, and the godlike that is within us asserts its supremacy.

But my purpose now is to tell you how and why it is I am here, and describe to you, as well as I can, this new Elysium: and how it is the happy spirits, whom the gods have permitted to dwell here, pass their hours.

I am here by the invitation of the queen. A few days after that which we had so highly enjoyed at the palace, she expressed her desire that Gracchus, Fausta, and myself, would accompany her, with others of her select friends, to her retreat among the hills, there to indulge in perfect repose, or engage in the rural sports of the place, according to our pleasure. I was not slow, neither were Gracchus and Fausta, to accept so agreeable an invitation. "I feared," said Fausta, "lest the troubled state of affairs would prevent the queen from taking her usual vacation, where she loves best to be. But to say the truth, Lucius, I do not think the prospect of a rupture with Rome does give her very serious thought. The vision of a trial of arms with so renowned a soldier as Aurelian, is, I doubt, not wholly displeasing to her; there being especially so good reason to believe that what befell Heraclianus might befall Aurelian. Nay, do not look so grave. Rome is not fallen—yet."

"Your tongue, Fausta, is lighter than your heart. Yet if Rome must fall, why, truly I know not at whose feet it could fall so worthily as those of Zenobia and Fausta. But I trust its destiny is never to fall. Other kingdoms as great, or almost as great, I know you will say, have fallen, and Rome must in its turn. It seems, however, I must say, to possess a principle of vitality which never before belonged to any nation. Its very vastness, too, seems to protect it. I can as soon believe that shoals of sea-carp may overcome the whale, or an army of emmets the elephant or rhinoceros, as that one nation, or many banded together, can break down the power of Rome."

"How very, very naturally and easily is that said! Who can doubt that you are a Roman, born upon the Cœlian hill! Pity but that we Palmyrenes could copy that high way you Romans have. Do you not think that strength and success lie much in confidence? Were every Roman such as you, I can believe you were then omnipotent. But then we have some like you. Here are Zenobia and I, you cannot deny that we have something of the Roman about us."

"I confess it would be a drawn battle, at least, were you a nation of Zenobias. How Fausta is at the lance, I cannot yet tell."

"That you shall see as soon as we are among the mountains. Is not this charming, now, in the queen, to bring us all together again so soon, under her own roof? And such a place, too, Lucius! We shall live there indeed; each day will, at least, be doubled. For I suppose life is to be measured, not by hours, but sensations. Are you ready for the morning start? Oh, that Solon were here! what exquisite mirth should we have! Milo is something, but Solon were more."

"Fausta, Fausta," cried Gracchus, "when will you be a woman?"

"Never, I trust," replied Fausta; "if I may then neither laugh nor cry, nor vex a Roman, nor fight for our queen. These are my vocations, and if I must renounce them, then I will be a man."

"Either sex may be proud to gain you, my noble girl," said Gracchus.

Early in the morning of the following day, all at the

house of Gracchus gave note of preparation. We were to meet the queen and her party a few miles from the walls of the city, at an appointed place, whence we were to make the rest of the journey in company. We were first at the place of meeting, which was a rising ground, shadowed by a few cedars, with their huge branching tops. We reined up our horses, and stood with our faces towards the road, over which we had just passed, looking to catch the first view of the queen. The sun was just rising above the horizon, and touching with its golden colour the higher objects of the scene, the tall cedars, the grey crags, which here jutted out into the plain, the towers, and columns, and obelisks of the still slumbering city.

"How beautiful!" exclaimed Fausta: "but look! that is more beautiful still—that moving troop of horse! See!—even at this distance you can distinguish the form and bearing of the queen. How the slant beams of this ruddy sun make her dress, and the harness of her gallant steed, to sparkle! Is it not a fair sight, Lucius?"

It was beautiful, indeed. The queen was conspicuous above all, not more for her form and bearing, than for the more than imperial magnificence of her appointments. It is thus she is always seen by her people, dazzling them equally by her beauties and her state. As she drew nearer, I felt that I had never before seen aught on earth so glorious. The fiery Arabian that bore her, knew, as well as I, who it was that sat upon him, and the pride of his carriage was visible in a thousand expressive movements. Julia was at her side, differing from her only as one sun differs from another. She, like Zenobia, seemed almost a part of the animal that bounded beneath her, so perfect was the art with which she rode.

"A fair morning to you all," cried the queen, accompanying the words with a glance that was reward enough for a life of service. "The day smiles upon our enterprise. Fausta, if you will join me, Piso will take care of Julia; as for our Zabdas and Longinus, they are sad loiterers."

Saying these things—scarcely checking her steed, and before the rest of the party had quite come up— we darted on, the queen leading the way, and, as is her wont, almost at the top of her horse's speed.

"Zenobia," said Julia, "is in fine spirits this morning, as you may judge from her beaming countenance, and the rate at which she travels. But we can hardly converse while we are going so fast."

"No bond has been signed," said I, "that we should ride like couriers. Suppose, princess, we slacken our pace."

"That will we," she replied, "and leave it to the queen to announce our approach. Here now, alas! are Zabdas and Longinus overtaking us. The queen wonders at your delay," said she, addressing them; "put spurs to your horses, and you may easily overtake her."

"Is it required?" asked the Egyptian, evidently willing to linger.

"Not so, indeed," answered Julia, "but it would be gallant; the queen, save Fausta, is alone. How can we answer it, if evil befall her? Her girth may break."

At which alarming suggestion, taking it as merrily as it was given, the two counsellors quickened their pace, and, bidding us good morning, soon, as we saw at the ascent of a little hill, overtook Zenobia.

For the rest of us, we were passing and repassing each other, mingling and separating all the remainder of the way. Our road lay through a rather rough and hilly country, but here and there sprinkled with bright spots of the richest beauty and highest cultivation. The valleys, whenever we descended into them, we found well watered and tilled, and peopled by an apparently happy peasantry. And as we saw them from first one eminence and then another, stretching away and winding among the hills, we agreed that they presented delicious retreats for those who, weary of the world, wished to taste, towards the close of life, the sweets of a repose which the world never knows. As we drew towards the end of our ride—a ride of quite twenty

Roman miles—we found ourselves forsaken by all the rest of the company, owing either to our horses not being equal to the others, or rather, perhaps, to the frequent pauses which we made at all those points where the scenery presented any thing beautiful or uncommon.

Every thing now at last indicated that we were not far from the royal demesne. All around were marks of the hand and eye of taste having been there, and of the outlay of enormous wealth. It was not, however, till we had, for a mile and more, ridden through lawns and fields covered with grains and fruits, laid out in divisions of tillage or of wood, that, emerging from a dark grove, we came within sight of the palace. We could just discern by the glittering of the sun upon the jewellery of their horses, that the last of the company were wheeling into the grounds in front of what seemed the principal part of the vast structure. That we might not be too much in the rear of all, we put spurs to our horses, which then, with the fleetness of wind, bore us to the outer gates of the palace. Passing these, we were in a moment in the midst of those who had preceded us, the grooms and slaves of the palace surrounding us, and taking charge of our horses. Zenobia was still standing in the great central portico, where she had dismounted, her face glowing with the excitement of the ride, and engaged in free discourse with the group around her. Soon as Julia reined up her horse, and quicker than any other could approach, she sprang to her daughter's side, and assisted her to dismount, holding with a strong hand the while, the fiery and restless animal she rode.

"Welcome in safety, Julia," said the queen; "and thanks, noble Piso, for your care of your charge. But perhaps we owe your safety more to the strength of your Arab's girth than to any care of Piso."

Julia's laugh rang merrily through the arches of the portico.

"Truly," said she, "I was glad to use any sudden conceit by which to gain a more solitary ride than I was like to have. It was my ambition to be Piso's companion, that I might enjoy the pleasure of pointing out to new eyes the beauties of the country. I trust I was rightly comprehended by our grave counsellors."

"Assure yourself of it," said Longinus; "and though we could not but part from you with some unwillingness, yet seeing whom we were to join, we bore the loss with such philosophy as we were able to summon on the sudden."

Zenobia now led the way to the banqueting hall, where tables loaded with meats, fruits, and wines, offered themselves most temptingly and seasonably, to those who had ridden post, as it were, twenty Roman miles.

This villa of the queen's, for its beauty and extent unrivalled in all the east, I would that I could set before you, so that you might form some conception of its greatness and variety. The palace stands at the northern extremity of a vast plain, just where the wild and mountainous region ends, and the more level and cultivated begins. To the north stretches a savage country, little inhabited, and filled with the wild animals which make the forests of Asia so terrible. This is the queen's hunting-ground. It was here that, with Odenatus, she pursued the wild boar, the tiger, or the panther, with a daring and a skill that astonished the boldest huntsmen. It was in these forests that the wretch Mœonius, insolently throwing his javelin at the game, just as he saw his uncle was about to strike, incurred that just rebuke, which, however, his revengeful nature never forgave, and was appeased only with the blood of the noble Palmyrene. Zenobia is never more herself than when she joins the chase mounted upon her fleet Arabian, and roused to all her power by the presence of a gallant company of the boldest spirits of Palmyra.

The southern view, and which my apartments overlook, presents a wide expanse of level ground, or gently undulating, offering a various prospect of cultivated fields, unbroken lawns, dense groves, of standing or flowing waters, of light bridges spanning them, of pavilions, arbours, statues, standing out in full view, or just visible through the rich foliage or brilliant flowering plants of these sunny regions. The scene is closed by the low, waving outline of the country through which we passed on the morning of our ride from Palmyra, over which there is spread a thin veil of purple haze, adding a new charm to whatever objects are dimly discerned through it. At one point only can we, when this vapour is by any cause diminished, catch a glimpse of the loftier buildings of the distant city. But the palace itself, though it be the work of man, and not of gods, is not less beautiful than all these aspects of nature. It is wholly built after the light and almost fantastic forms of the Persian architecture, which seem more suited to a residence of this kind than the heavier fashions of the Greek or Roman taste. Hadrian's villa is alone to be compared with it for vastness and magnificence, and that, compared with this, seems a huge prison, so gay and pleasing are the thoughts and sensations which this dreamlike combination of arch upon arch, of pinnacle, dome, and tower, all enriched with the most minute and costly work, inspires the mind.

Nothing has pleased me more than at times, when the sultry heats of the day forbid alike study and recreation, to choose for myself some remote and shaded spot, and lying along upon the flowery turf, soothed by the drowsy hum of the summer insects, gaze upon this gorgeous pile of oriental grandeur, and lazily drink in the draughts of a beauty (as I believe) nowhere else to be enjoyed. When at such hours Julia or Fausta is my companion, I need not say in how great degree the pleasure is heightened, nor what hues of a more rosy tint wrap all the objects of the scene. Fountains here, as every where in the eastern world, are frequent, and of such size as to exert a sensible influence upon the heated atmosphere. Huge columns of the coldest water, drawn from the recesses of the mountains, are thrown into the air, and then falling and foaming over rocks rudely piled, to resemble some natural cascade, disappear, and are led by subterranean conduits to distant and lower parts of the ground. These fountains take many and fantastic forms. In the centre of the principal court of the palace, it is an enormous elephant of stone, who disgorges from his uplifted trunk a vast but graceful shower, sometimes charged with the most exquisite perfumes, and which are diffused by the air through every part of the palace. Around this fountain, reclining upon seats constructed to allow the most easy attitudes, or else in some of the apartments immediately opening upon it, it is our custom to pass the evening hours, either conversing with each other, or listening to some tale which he who thinks he can entertain the company is at liberty to relate, or gathering at once instruction and delight, as Longinus, either from his memory or a volume, imparts to us the choicest parts of the literature of Athens or of Rome. So have I heard the Œdipus Tyrannus, and the Prometheus, as I never have heard them before. At such times, it is beautiful to see the group of listeners gathering nearer and nearer, as the philosopher reads or recites, and catching every word and accent of that divine tongue, as it falls from his lips. Zenobia, alone, of all who are there, ever presumes to interrupt the reader with either question or comment. To her voice, Longinus instantly becomes a willing listener; and well may he; for never does she speak, at such moments, without adding a new charm to whatever theme she touches. Her mind, surprisingly clear, and deeply imbued with the best spirit of ancient learning, and poetically cast, becomes of right our teacher; and commands always the profound respect, if not always the assent, of the accomplished Greek. Not unfrequently, on such casual remarks of the queen, the reading is thereupon suspended, and discussion between her and the philosopher, or conversation upon topics suggested, in which we all take part, ensues. But, however this may be, all moves on in a spirit the most liberal, frank, and free. No restraint is upon us but that which reverence for superior learning, or goodness, or beauty, imposes. I must add, that on these occasions the great Zabdas is always seen to compose himself to his slumbers, from which he often starts, uttering loud shouts, as if at the head of his troops. Our bursts of laughter wake him not, but by the strange power of sleep seem to be heard by him as if they were responsive cries of the enemy, and only cause him to send forth louder shouts than ever, "Down with the Egyptian dogs!" "Let the Nile choke with their carcasses!—The queen for ——" and then his voice dies away in inarticulate sounds.

But I should weary you, indeed, were I to go on to tell you of half the beauties and delights of this chosen spot, and cause you, perhaps, to be discontented with that quiet modest house, upon the banks of the Tiber. I leave you, therefore, to fill up with your own colours the outline which I have now set before you as I best could, and pass to other things.

Every day has seen its peculiar games and entertainments. Sometimes the queen's slaves, trained to their respective feats, have wrestled, or fought, or run, for our amusement. At other times, we ourselves have been the performers. Upon the race-course, fleet Arabians have contended for the prize, or those who have esteemed themselves skilful have tried for the mastery in two or four-horse chariots. Elephants have been put to their strength, and dromedaries to their speed. But our chief pleasure has been derived from trials of skill and of strength with the lance and the arrow, and from the chase.

It was in using the lance that Antiochus—a kinsman of the queen, whom I believe I have not before mentioned, although I have many times met him—chiefly signalised himself. This person, half Syrian and half Roman, possessing the bad qualities of both, and the good ones of neither, was made one of this party, rather, I suppose, because he could not be left out, than because he was wanted. He has few friends in Palmyra, but among wild and dissolute spirits like himself. He is famed for no quality either great or good. Violent passions and intemperate lusts are what he is chiefly noted for. But except that pride and arrogance are writ upon the lines of his countenance, you would hardly guess that his light-tinted and beardless cheeks, and soft blue eyes, belonged to one of so dark and foul a soul. His frame and his strength are those of a giant; yet is he wholly destitute of grace. His limbs seem sometimes as if they were scarcely a part of him, such difficulty does he discover in marshalling them aright. Consciousness of this embarrasses him, and sends him for refuge to his pride, which darts looks of anger and bitter revenge upon all who offend or make light of him. His ambition is, and his hope, to succeed Zenobia. You may think this strange, considering the family of the queen. But as for the sons of Zenobia, he calculates much, so it is reported, upon their weakness both of mind and body, as rendering them distasteful to the Palmyrenes, even if they should live; and as for Julia and her sisters, he has so high conceptions of his own superior merit, that he doubts not, in case of the queen's demise, that the people would by acclamation select him, in preference to them, as her successor: or in the last emergency, that it would be but to marry Julia, in order to secure the throne beyond any peradventure. These are the schemes which many do not scruple to impute to him. Whether credited or not by Zenobia, I cannot tell; but were they, I believe she would but smile at the poor lack-brain who entertains them. Intrenched as she is in the impregnable fortress of her people's heart, she might well despise the intrigues of a bolder and worthier spirit than Antiochus. For him she can spare neither words nor thoughts.

It was Fausta, who, a few days ago, as we rose from the tables, proposed that we should try our strength and skill in throwing the lance. "I promised you, Lucius," said she, "that when here, you should be permitted to judge of my abilities in that art. Are all ready for the sport?"

All sprang from their seats, like persons weary of one occupation, and grateful for the proffer of another.

Zenobia led the way to the grounds, not far from the palace, appropriated to games of this kind, and to the various athletic sports. Not all the company entered the lists, but many seated themselves, or stood around, spectators of the strife. Slaves now appeared, bearing the lances, and preparing the ground for our exercise. The feat to be performed seemed to me not difficult so much as impossible. It was to throw the lance with such unerring aim and force, as to pass through an aperture in a shield of four-fold ox-hide, of a size but slightly larger than the beam of the lance, so as not so much as to graze the sides of the perforated place. The distance, too, of the point from which the lance was to be thrown, from the shield, was such as to require great strength of arm to overcome it.

The young Cæsars advanced first to the trial. "Now," whispered Fausta, "behold the vigour of the royal arm. Were such alone our defence, well might Palmyra tremble."

Herennianus, daintily handling and brandishing his lance, in the manner prescribed at the schools, where skill in all warlike arts is taught, and having drawn all eyes upon him, at length let it fly, when, notwithstanding so much preparatory flourish, it fell short of the staff upon which the shield was reared.

"Just from the tables," said the prince, as he withdrew, angry at his so conspicuous failure; "and how can one reach what he can scarcely see?"

"Our arm has not yet recovered from its late injury," said Timolaus, as he selected his weapon; "yet will we venture a throw." His lance reached the mast, but dropped feebly at its foot. Vabalathus, saying nothing, and putting all his strength in requisition, drove his weapon into the staff, where it stood quivering a moment, and fell to the ground.

Carias, Seleucus, Otho, Gabrayas, noblemen of Palmyra, now successively tried their fortune, and all showed themselves well trained to the use of the weapon, by each fixing his lance in the body of the shield, and in the near neighbourhood of the central hole.

Zabdas now suddenly springing from his seat, which he had taken among those who apparently declined to join in the sport, seized a lance from the hands of the slave who bore them, and hurling it with the force of a tempest, the weapon, hissing along the air, struck the butt near the centre; but the wood of which it was made, unused to such violence, shivered and crumbled under the blow. Without a word, and without an emotion, so far as the face was its index, the Egyptian returned to his seat. It seemed as if he had done the whole in his sleep. It is actual war alone that can rouse the energies of Zabdas.

Zenobia, who had stood leaning upon her lance, next advanced to the trial. Knowing her admirable skill at all manly exercises, I looked with certainty to see her surpass those who had already essayed their powers. Nor was I disappointed. With a wonderful grace she quickly threw herself into the appointed position, and with but a moment's preparation, and as if it cost her but a slight effort, sent her lance, with unerring aim and incredible swiftness, through the hole. Yet was not the feat a perfect one; for, in passing through the aperture, the weapon not having been driven with quite sufficient force, did not preserve its level, so that the end grazed the shield, and the lance then consequently taking an oblique direction, plunged downwards, and buried its head in the turf.

"Now, Fausta," said the queen, "must you finish what I have but begun. Let us now see your weapon sweep on till its force shall be evenly spent."

"When Zenobia fails," said Fausta, "there must be some evil influence abroad that shall cripple the powers of others yet more. However, let me try; for I have promised to prove to our Roman friend that the women of Palmyra know the use of arms not less than the men."

So saying, she chose her lance, and with little ceremony, and almost before our eyes could trace her movements, the weapon had flown, and passing through, as it seemed, the very centre of the perforated space, swept on till its force died away in the distance, and it fell gracefully to the ground.

A burst of applause rose from the surrounding groups.

"I knew," said Zenobia, "that I could trust the fame of the women of Palmyra to you. At the harp, the needle, or the lance, our Fausta has no equal; unless," turning herself round, "in my own Julia. Now we will see what your arm can do."

Standing near the lances, I selected one eminent for its smoothness and polish, and placed it in her hand.

With a form of so much less apparent vigour than either Zenobia or Fausta, so truly Syrian in a certain soft languor that spreads itself over her, whether at rest or in motion, it was amazing to see with what easy strength she held and balanced the heavy weapon. Every movement showed that there lay concealed within her ample power for this and every manly exercise, should she please to put it forth.

"At the schools," said the princess, "Fausta and I went on ever with equal steps. Her advantage lies in being at all times mistress of her power. My arm is often treacherous, through failure of the heart."

It was not difficult to see the truth of what she said, in her varying colour, and the slightly agitated lance.

But addressing herself to the sport, and with but one instant's pause, the lance flew towards the shield, and entering the opening, but not with a perfect direction, it passed not through, but hung there by the head.

"Princess," said Zabdas, springing from his repose with more than wonted energy, "that lance was chosen, as I saw, by a Roman. Try once more with one that I shall choose, and see what the issue will be."

"Truly," said Julia, "I am ready to seize any plea under which to redeem my fame. But first give me yourself a lesson, will you not?"

The Egyptian was not deaf to the invitation, and once more essaying the feat, and with his whole soul bent to the work, the lance, quicker than sight, darted from his hand, and following in the wake of Fausta's, lighted farther than hers—being driven with more force—upon the lawn.

The princess now, with more of confidence in her air, again balanced and threw the lance which Zabdas had chosen—this time with success; for, passing through the shield, it fell side by side with Fausta's.

"Fortune still unites us," said Julia; "if for a time she leaves me a little in the rear, yet she soon repents of the wrong, and brings me up." Saying which, she placed herself at Fausta's side.

"But come, our worthy cousin," said the queen, now turning and addressing Antiochus, who stood with folded arms, dully surveying the scene, "will you not try a lance?"

"'Tis hardly worth our while," said he, "for the gods seem to have delivered all the honour and power of the cast into the hands of women."

"Yet it may not be past redemption," said Julia, "and who more likely than Hercules to achieve so great a work? Pray, begin."

That mass of a man, hardly knowing whether the princess were jesting or in earnest—for to the usual cloud that rested upon his intellect, there was now added the stupidity arising from free indulgence at the tables—slowly moved towards the lances, and selecting the longest and heaviest, took his station at the proper place. Raising then his arm, which was like a weaver's beam, and throwing his enormous body into attitudes, which showed that no child's play was going on, he let drive the lance, which, shooting with more force than exactness of aim, struck upon the outer rim of the shield, and then glancing sideways, was near spearing a poor slave, whose pleasure it was, with others, to stand in the neighbourhood of the butt, to pick up and return the weapons thrown, or withdraw them from the shield, where they might have fastened themselves.

Involuntary laughter broke forth upon this unwonted performance of the lance; upon which it was easy to see, by the mounting colour of Antiochus, that his passions were inflamed. Especially—did we afterwards suppose—was he enraged at the exclamation of one of the slaves near the shield, who was heard to say to his fellow, "Now is the reign of women at an end." Seizing, however, on the instant, another lance, he was known to exclaim, by a few who stood near him, but who did not take the meaning of his words, "With a better mark, there may be a better aim." Then resuming his position, he made at first, by a long and steady aim, as if he were going, with certainty now, to hit the shield; but, changing suddenly the direction of his lance, he launched it with fatal aim, and a giant's force, at the slave who had uttered those words. It went through him, as he had been but a sheet of papyrus, and then sung along the plain. The poor wretch gave one convulsive leap into the air, and dropped dead.

"Zenobia!" exclaimed Julia.

"Great queen!" said Fausta.

"Shameful!"—"dastardly!"—"cowardly!"—broke from one and another of the company.

"That's the mark I never miss," observed Antiochus; and at the same time regaled his nose from a box of perfume.

"'Tis his own chattel," said the queen; "he may do with it as he lists. He has trenched upon no law of the realm, but only upon those of breeding and humanity. Our presence, and that of this company, might, we think, have claimed a more gentle observance."

"Dogs!" fiercely shouted Antiochus—who, as the queen said these words, her eyes fastened indignantly upon him, had slunk sulkily to his seat—"dogs," said he, aiming suddenly to brave the matter, "off with yonder carrion!—it offends the queen."

"Would our cousin," said Zenobia, "win the hearts of Palmyra, this surely is a mistaken way. Come, let us to the palace. This spot is tainted. But that it may be sweetened as far as may be, slaves!" she cried, "bring to the gates the chariot, and other remaining chattels of Antiochus!"

Antiochus, at these words, pale with the apprehensions of a cowardly spirit, rose and strode towards the palace, from which, in a few moments, he was seen on his way to the city.

"You may judge me needlessly harsh, Piso," said the queen, as we now sauntered towards the palace, "but truly the condition of the slave is such, that seeing the laws protect him not, we must do something to enlist in his behalf the spirit of humanity. The breach of courtesy, however, was itself not to be forgiven."

"It was a merciful fate of the slave," said I, "compared with what our Roman slaves suffer. To be lashed to death, or crucified, or burned, or flayed alive, or torn by dogs, or thrown as food for fishes, is something worse than this quick exit of the thrall of Antiochus. You of these softer climes are in your natures milder than we, and are more moved by scenes like this. What would you think, queen, to see not one, but scores or hundreds of these miserable beings, upon bare suspicion of attempts against their master's life, condemned, by their absolute irresponsible possessors, to death in all its most revolting forms?—nay, even our Roman women, of highest rank, and gentlest nurture, stand by while their slaves are scourged, or themselves apply the lash! If under this torture they die, it is thought of but as of the death of vermin. War has made with us this sort of property of so cheap possession, that to destroy it is often a necessary measure of economy. By a Roman, nothing is less regarded than life. And, in truth, I see not how it can be otherwise."

"But surely," said Julia, "you do not mean to defend this condition of life. It is not like the sentiments I have heard you express."

"I defend it only thus," I replied: "so long as we have wars—and when will they cease?—there must be captives; and what can these be but slaves? To return them to their own country, were to war to no purpose. To colonise them, were to strip war of its horrors. To make them freemen of our own soil, were to fill the land with foes and traitors. Then if there must be slaves, there must be masters and owners. And the absolute master of other human beings, responsible to no one, can be no other than a tyrant. If he has, as he must have, the power to punish at will, he will exercise it, and that cruelly. If he has the power to kill, as he must have, then will he kill and kill cruelly, when his nature prompts. And this his nature will prompt, or, if not his nature absolutely, yet his educated nature. Our children grow up within the sight and sound of all the horrors and sufferings of this state of things. They use their slaves—with which, almost in infancy, they are provided—according to their pleasure —as dogs, as horses; they lash, they scourge them, long before they have the strength to kill. What wonder if the boy, who, when a boy, used a slave as his beast of burden, or his footstool, when he grows to be a man, should use him as a mark to be shot at? The youth of Antiochus was reared in Rome. I presume to say that his earliest playthings were slaves, and the children of slaves. I am not surprised at his act. And such acts are too common in Rome, for this to disturb me much. The education of Antiochus was continued and completed, I may venture also to say, at the circus. I think the result very natural. It cannot be very different, where slavery and the sports of the amphitheatre exist."

"I perceive your meaning," said Julia: "Antiochus you affirm to be the natural product of the customs and institutions which now prevail. It is certainly so, and must continue so, until some new element shall be introduced into society, that shall ultimately reform its practices, by first exalting the sentiments and the character of the individual. Such an element do I detect ——"

"In Christianity," said Fausta: "this is your panacea. May it prove all you desire; yet methinks it gives small promise, seeing it has already been at work more than two hundred years, and has accomplished no more."

"A close observer," replied Julia, "sees much of the effect of Christianity besides that which appears upon the surface. If I err not greatly, a few years more will reveal what this religion has been doing these two centuries and more. Revolutions which are acted out in a day have often been years or centuries in preparation. An eye that will see, may see the final issue, a long time foreshadowed in the tendencies and character of a preceding age."

The princess uttered this with earnestness. I have reflected upon it. And if you, my Curtius, will look around upon the state of the empire, you will find many things to startle you. But of this another time.

Assembled in the evening in the court of the elephant, we were made to forget whatever had proved disagreeable during the day, while we listened to the "Frogs," read by Julia and Longinus.

The following day was appointed for the chase, and early in the morning I was waked by the braying of trumpets, and the baying of dogs. I found the queen already mounted, and equipped for the sport, surrounded by Zabdas, Longinus, and a few of the nobles of Palmyra. We were soon joined by Julia and Fausta. In order to ensure our sport, a tiger, made fierce by being for some days deprived of food, had the preceding evening been let loose from the royal collection into the neighbouring forests. These forests, abounding in game, commence immediately, as it were, in the rear of the palace. They present a boundless continuity of crag, mountain, and wooded plain, offering every variety of ground to those who seek the pleasures of the chase. The sun had not been long above the horizon when we sallied forth from the palace gates, and from the smooth and shaven fields of the royal demesne, plunged at once into the

* * * *
* * * *

It was a moment of inexpressible horror. At the same instant, our eyes caught the form of the famished tiger, just in the act to spring from the crag upon the unconscious queen. But before we had time to alarm Zenobia—which would indeed have been useless—a shaft from an unerring arm arrested the monster in mid-air, whose body then tumbled heavily at the feet of Zenobia's Arab. The horse, rearing with affright, had nearly dashed the queen against the opposite rocks; but keeping her seat, she soon, by her powerful arm and complete horsemanship, reduced him to his obedience, though trembling like a terrified child through every part of his body. A thrust from my hunting-spear quickly dispatched the dying beast. We now gathered around the queen, * * *
 * * * *

Hardly were we arrived at the lawn in front of the palace, when a cloud of dust was observed to rise in the direction of the road to Palmyra, as if caused by a body of horse in rapid movement. "What may this mean?" said Zenobia: "orders were strict that our brief retirement should not be disturbed. This indicates an errand of some urgency."

"Some embassy from abroad, perhaps," said Julia, "that cannot brook delay. It may be from your great brother at Rome."

While we, in a sportive humour, indulged in various conjectures, an official of the palace announced the approach of a Roman herald, "who craved permission to address the queen of Palmyra." He was ordered to advance.

In a few moments, upon a horse covered with dust and foam, appeared the Roman herald. Without one moment's hesitancy, he saw in Zenobia the queen; and taking off his helmet, and bending to his saddle-bow, said, "that Caius Pétronius, and Cornelius Varro, ambassadors of Aurelian, were in waiting at the outer gates of the palace, and asked a brief audience of the queen of Palmyra, upon affairs of deepest interest, both to Zenobia and the emperor."

"It is not our custom," said Zenobia in reply, " when seeking repose, as now, from the cares of state, to allow aught to break it. But we will not be selfish nor churlish. Bid the servants of your emperor draw near, and we will hear them."

I was not unwilling that the messengers of Aurelian should see Zenobia just as she was now. Sitting upon her noble Arabian, and leaning upon her hunting-spear—her countenance glowing with a higher beauty than ever before, as it seemed to me—her head surmounted with a Parthian hunting-cap, from which drooped a single ostrich feather, springing from a diamond worth a nation's rental, her costume also Parthian, and revealing in the most perfect manner the just proportions of her form—I thought I had never seen even her, when she so filled and satisfied the eye and the mind, and, for that moment, I was almost a traitor to Aurelian. Had Julia filled her seat, I should have been quite so. As it was, I could worship her, who sat her steed with no less grace, upon the left of the queen, without being guilty of that crime. On Zenobia's right were Longinus and Zabdas, Gracchus, and the other noblemen of Palmyra. I and Fausta were near Julia. In this manner, just as we had come in from the chase, did we await the ambassadors of Aurelian.

Announced by trumpets, and followed by their train, they soon wheeled into the lawn, and advanced towards the queen. "Caius Petronius and Cornelius Varro," said Zenobia, first addressing the ambassadors, and moving towards them a few paces, "we bid you heartily welcome to Palmyra. If we receive you thus without form, you must take the blame partly to yourselves, who have sought us with such haste. We put by the customary observances, that we may cause you no delay. These whom you see, are all friends or counsellors. Speak your errand without restraint."

"We come," replied Petronius, "as you may surmise, great queen, upon no pleasing errand. Yet we cannot but persuade ourselves that the queen of Palmyra will listen to the proposals of Aurelian, and preserve the good understanding which has lasted so long between the west and the east. There have been brought already to your ears, if I have been rightly informed, rumours of dissatisfaction on the part of our emperor, with the affairs of the east, and of plans of an eastern expedition. It is my business now to say, that these rumours have been well founded. I am further to say, that the object at which Aurelian has aimed, in the preparations he has made, is not Persia, but Palmyra."

"He does us too much honour," said Zenobia, her colour rising, and her eye kindling; "and what, may I ask, are his demands, and the price of peace?"

"For a long series of years," replied the ambassador, "the wealth of Egypt, and the east, as you are aware, flowed into the Roman treasury. That stream has been diverted to Palmyra. Egypt, and Syria, and Bithynia, and Mesopotamia, were dependents upon Rome, and Roman provinces. It is needless to say what they now are. The queen of Palmyra was once but the queen of Palmyra; she is now queen of Egypt and of the East—Augusta of the Roman empire—her sons styled and arrayed as Cæsars. By whatever consent of former emperors these honours have been won or permitted, it is not, we are required to say, with the consent of Aurelian. By whatever service in behalf of Rome, they may, in the judgment of some, be thought to be deserved, in the judgment of Aurelian, the reward exceeds greatly the value of the service rendered. But while he would not be deemed insensible to those services, and while he honours the greatness and the genius of Zenobia, he would, he conceives, be unfaithful to the interests of those who have raised him to his high office, if he did not require that in the east, as in the west, the Roman empire should again be restored to the limits which bounded it in the reigns of the virtuous Antonines. This he holds essential to his own honour, and the glory of the Roman world."

"You have delivered yourself, Caius Petronius," replied the queen, in a calm and firm voice, "as it became a Roman to do, with plainness, and, as I must believe, without reserve. So far, I honour you. Now, hear me, and as you hear, so report to him who sent you. Tell Aurelian that what I am I have made myself; that the empire which hails me queen, has been moulded into what it is by Odenatus and Zenobia; it is no gift, but an inheritance—a conquest and a possession; it is held not by favour, but by right of power, and that when he will give away possessions or provinces which he claims as his or Rome's, for the asking, I will give away Egypt and the Mediterranean coast. Tell him that as I have lived a queen, so, the gods helping, I will die a queen—that the last moment of my reign and my life shall be the same. If he is ambitious, let him be told that I am ambitious too—ambitious of wider and yet wider empire—of an unsullied fame, and of my people's love. Tell him I do not speak of gratitude on the part of Rome, but that posterity will say, that the power which stood between Rome and Persia, and saved the empire in the east, which avenged the death of Valerian, and twice pursued the king of kings as far as the gates of Ctesiphon, deserved some fairer acknowledgment than the message you now bring, at the hands of a Roman emperor."

"Let the queen," quickly rejoined Petronius, but evidently moved by what he had heard, "let the queen fully take me. Aurelian purposes not to invade the fair region where I now am, and where my eyes are rejoiced by this goodly show of city, plain, and country. He hails you queen of Palmyra! He does but ask again those appendages of your greatness, which have been torn from Rome, and were once the members of her body."

"Your emperor is gracious indeed!" replied the queen, smiling; "if he may hew off my limbs, he will spare the trunk!—and what were the trunk without the limbs?"

"And is this," said Petronius, his voice significant of inward grief, "that which I must carry back to Rome? Is there no hope of a better adjustment?"

"Will not the queen of Palmyra delay for a few days her final answer?" added Varro: "I see, happily, in her train, a noble Roman, from whom, as well as from us, she may obtain all needful knowledge of both the character and purposes of Aurelian. We are at liberty to wait her pleasure."

"You have our thanks, Romans, for your courtesy, and we accept your offer; although, in what I have said, I think I have spoken the sense of my people."

"You have, indeed, great queen," interrupted Zabdas, with energy.

"Yet I owe it to my trusty counsellor, the great Longinus," continued the queen, "and who now thinks not with me, to look farther into the reasons—which, because they are his, must be strong ones—by which he supports an opposite judgment."

"Those reasons have now," said the Greek, "lost much or all of their force"—Zabdas smiled triumphantly—"yet still I would advocate delay."

"Let it be so, then," said the queen; "and in the meanwhile, let the ambassadors of Aurelian not refuse the hospitalities of the eastern queen. Our palace is yours, while it shall please you to remain."

"For the night and the morning, queen, we accept your offers; then, as strangers in this region, we would return to the city, to see better than we have yet done the objects which it presents. It seemed to us, on a hasty glance, surrounded by its luxuriant plains, like the habitations of gods. We would dwell there a space."

"It shall be as you will. Let me now conduct you to the palace."

So saying, and putting spurs to her horse, Zenobia led the way to the palace, followed by a long train of Romans and Palmyrenes. The generous hospitality of the tables closed the day and wore away the night.

LETTER VII.

You will be glad to learn, my Curtius, that the time has now come, when I may with reason look for news from Isaac, or for his return. It was his agreement to write of his progress, so soon as he should arrive at Ecbatana. But since he would consume but a very few days in the accomplishment of his task, if, the gods helping, he should be able to accomplish it at all, I may see him, even before I hear from him, and, oh day thrice happy, my brother perhaps with him! Yet am I not without solicitude, even though Calpurnius should return. For how shall I meet him?—as a Persian or a Roman?—as a friend or an enemy? As a brother, I can never cease to love him; as a public enemy of Rome, I may be obliged to condemn him.

You have indeed gratified me by what you have told me concerning the public works in which the emperor is now engaged. Would that the erection of temples and palaces might draw away his thoughts from the east. The new wall, of so much wider sweep, with which he is now enclosing the city, is well worthy the greatness of his genius. Yet do we, my Curtius, perceive in this rebuilding and strengthening of the walls of Rome, no indication of our country's decline? Were Rome vigorous and sound, as once, in her limbs, what were the need of this new defence about the heart? It is to me a confession of weakness, rather than any evidence of greatness and strength. Aurelian achieves more for Rome by the strictness of his discipline, and his restoration of the ancient simplicity and severity among the troops, than he could by a triple wall about the metropolis. Rome will then already have fallen, when a Gothic army shall have penetrated so far as even to have seen her gates. The walls of Rome are her living and moving walls of flesh. Her old and crumbling ramparts of masonry, upon which we have so often climbed in sport, rolling down into the surrounding ditch huge masses, have ever been to me, when I have thought of them, pregnant signs of security and power.

The ambassadors, Petronius and Varro, early on the morning succeeding their interview with the queen, departed for the city. They were soon followed by Zenobia, and her train of counsellors and attendants. It had been before agreed that the princess, Fausta, and myself, should remain longer at the palace, for the purpose of visiting, as had been proposed, the aged Christian hermit, whose retreat is among the fastnesses of the neighbouring mountains. I would rather have accompanied the queen, seeing it was so certain that important interviews and discussions would take place, when they should be all returned once more to the city. I suppose this was expressed in my countenance, for the queen, as she took her seat in the chariot, turned and said to me, "We shall soon see you again in the city. A few hours in the mountains will be all that Julia will require; and sure I am that the wisdom of St Thomas will more than repay you for what you may lose in Palmyra. Our topics will relate but to wordly aggrandisement—yours to more permanent interests."

How great a pity that the love of glory has so fastened upon the heart of this wonderful woman; else might she live, and reign, and die, the object of a universal idolatry. But set as her heart is upon conquest and universal empire throughout the East, and of such marvellous power to subdue every intellect, even the strongest, to her will, I can see nothing before her but a short and brilliant career indeed, ending in ruin, absolute and complete. Zenobia has not, or will not allow it to be seen that she has, any proper conception of the power of Rome. She judges of Rome by the feeble Valerian, and the unskilful Heraclianus, and by their standard measures such men as Aurelian, and Probus, and Carus. She may indeed gain a single battle, for her genius is vast, and her troops well disciplined and brave. But the loss of a battle would be to her the loss of empire, while to Rome it would be but as the sting of a summer insect. Yet this she does not, or will not see. To triumph over Aurelian, is, I believe, the vision that dazzles, deludes, and will destroy her.

No sooner had the queen and her train departed, than, mounting our horses, we took our way, Julia, Fausta, and myself, through winding valleys and over rugged hills, towards the hermit's retreat. Reaching the base of what seemed an almost inaccessible crag, we found it necessary to leave our horses in the care of attendant slaves, and pursue the remainder of the way on foot. The hill which we now had to ascend, was thickly grown over with every variety of tree and bush, with here and there a mountain stream falling from rock to rock, and forcing its way to the valley below. The sultry heat of the day compelled us frequently to pause, as we toiled up the side of the hill, seating ourselves, now beneath the dark shadows of a branching cedar or the long-lived terebinth, and now on the mossy banks of a descending brook. The mingled beauty and wildness of the scene, together with such companions, soon drove the queen, Rome, and Palmyra, from my thoughts. I could not but wish that we might lose our way to the hermit's cave, that by such means our walk might be prolonged.

"Is it, I wonder," said Fausta, "the instruction of his religion which confines this Christian saint to these distant solitudes? What a singular faith it must be which should drive all who embrace it to the woods and rocks! What would become of our dear Palmyra, were it to be changed to a Christian city? The same event, I suppose, Julia, would change it to a desert?"

"I do not think Christianity prescribes this mode of life, though I do not know but it may permit it," replied the princess. "But of this St Thomas will inform us. He may have chosen this retreat on account of his extreme age, which permits him no longer to engage in the affairs of an active life."

"I trust for the sake of Christianity it is so," added Fausta; "for I cannot conceive of a true religion inculcating, or even permitting, inactivity. What would become of the world, if it could be proved that the gods required us to pass our days in retired contemplation ?"

"Yet it cannot be denied," said Julia, "that the greatest benefactors of mankind have been those who have in solitude, and with patient labour, pursued truth till they have discovered it, and then revealed it to shed its light and heat upon the world."

"For my part," replied Fausta, "I must think that they who have sowed and reaped, have been equal benefactors. The essential truths are instinctive and universal. As for the philosophers, they have, with few exceptions, been occupied as much about mere frivolities as any Palmyrene lady at her toilet. Still, I do not deny that the contemplative race is a useful one in its way. What I say is, that a religion which enjoined a solitary life as a duty, would be a very mischievous religion. And, what is more, any such precept, fairly proved upon it, would annihilate all its claims to a divine origin. For certainly, if it were made a religious duty for one man to turn an idle, contemplative hermit, it would be equally the duty of every other, and then the arts of life by which we subsist would be forsaken. Any of the prevalent superstitions, if we may not call them religions, were better than this."

"I agree with you entirely," said Julia; "but my acquaintance with the Christian writings is not such as to enable me to say with confidence that they contain no such permission or injunction. Indeed, some of them I have not even read, and much I do not fully understand. But as I have seen and read enough to believe firmly that Christianity is a divine religion, my reason teaches me that it contains no precept such as we speak of."

We had now, in the course of our walk, reached what we found to be a broad and level ledge, about half way to the summit of the hill. It was a spot remarkable for a sort of dark and solemn beauty, being set with huge branching trees, whose tops were woven into a roof, through which only here and there the rays of the fierce sun could find their way. The turf beneath, unincumbered with any smaller growth of tree or shrub, was sprinkled with flowers that love the shade. The upper limit of this level space was bounded by precipitous rocks, up which ascent seemed impossible, and the lower by similar ones, to descend which seemed equally difficult or impossible.

"If the abode of the Christian is hereabouts," we said, "it seems well chosen, both for its security, and the exceeding beauty of the various objects which greet the eye."

"Soon as we shall have passed that tumbling rivulet," said Julia, "it will come into view."

Upon a rude bridge of fallen trunks of trees, we passed the stream as it crossed our path, and which then shooting over the edge of the precipice, was lost among the rocks and woods below. A cloud of light spray fell upon us as we stood upon the bridge, and imparted a most refreshing coolness.

"Where you see," said Julia, "that dark entrance, beneath yonder low-browed rock, is the dwelling of the aged Christian."

We moved on with slow and silent steps, our spirits partaking of the stillness and solitariness of the place. We reached the front of the grotto, without disturbing the meditations of the venerable man. A part of the rock which formed his dwelling, served him for a seat, and another part projecting after the manner of a shelf, served him for a table, upon which lay spread open a large volume. Bending over the book, his lean and shrivelled finger pointing to the words, and aiding his now dim and feeble eye, he seemed wholly wrapped in the truths he was contemplating, and heeded not our presence. We stood still for a moment, unwilling to break a repose so peaceful and profound. At length, raising his eyes from the page, they caught the form and face of the princess, who stood nearest to him. A quick and benignant smile lighted up his features; and rising slowly to his full height, he bade her welcome, with sweet and tremulous tones, to his humble roof.

"It is kind in you," said he, "so soon again to ascend these rough solitudes, to visit a now unprofitable old man; and more kind still to bring others with you. Voices from the world ring a sweet music in my ear, sweeter than any sound of bird or stream. Enter, friends, if it please you, and be rested, after the toil of your ascent."

"I bring you here, father," said Julia, "according to my sometime promise, my friend and companion, the daughter of Gracchus, and with her a noble Roman, of the house of Piso, lately come hither from the capital of the world."

"They are very, very welcome," replied the saint; "your presence breaks most gratefully the monotony of my life."

"We almost doubted," said I, "venerable father, whether it would please you to find beneath your roof those who receive not your belief, and, what is much more, belonged to a faith which has poured upon you and yours so full a flood of suffering and reproach. But your countenance assures us that we have erred."

"You have, indeed," replied the sage; "as a Christian, I see in you not pagans and unbelievers, not followers of Plato and Epicurus, not dwellers in Rome or in Alexandria, but members of the great family of man, and as such I greet you, and already love you. The design of Christianity is to unite and draw together, not divide and drive asunder. It teaches its disciples, indeed, to go out and convert the world; but if they cannot convert it, it still teaches them to love it. My days and my strength have been spent in preaching Christ to Jews and heathen, and many of those who have heard have believed. But more have not. These are not my brethren in Christ, but they are my brethren in God, and I love them as his."

"These are noble sentiments," said Fausta. "Religion has, in almost all its forms, condemned utterly all who have not received it in the form in which it has been proposed. Rome used to be mild and tolerant of every form which the religious sentiment assumed. But since the appearance of Christianity, it has wholly changed its policy. I am afraid it formerly tolerated, only because it saw nothing to fear. Fearing Christianity, it seeks to destroy it. That is scarcely generous of you, Lucius; nor very wise, either; for surely truth can neither be created nor suppressed by applications of force. Such is not the doctrine of Christianity, if I understand you right."

"Lady, most certainly not," he replied. "Christianity is offered to mankind, not forced upon them. And this supposes in them the power and the right to sit in judgment upon its truth. But were not all free judgment destroyed, and all worthy reception of it, therefore, if any penal consequences—greater or less, of one kind or another, present or future—followed upon its rejection? Rome has done wickedly, in her aim to suppress error and maintain truth by force. Is Rome a god to distinguish with certainty the one from the other? But, alas! Rome is not alone to blame in this. Christians themselves are guilty of the same folly and crime. They interpret differently the sayings of Christ—as how should they not?—and the party which is stronger in numbers already begins to oppress, with hard usage and language, the weaker party, which presumes to entertain its own opinions. The Christians of Alexandria and Rome, fond of the ancient philosophy, and desirous to recommend the doctrines of Christ, by showing their near accordance with it, have, as many think, greatly adulterated the gospel, by mixing up with its truths the fantastic dreams of Plato. Others, among whom is our Paul of Antioch, deeming this injurious and erroneous, aim to restore the Christian doctrine to the simplicity that belongs to it in the original records, and which, for the most part, it still retains among the common people. But this is not willingly allowed. On the contrary, because Paul cannot see with their eyes, and judge with their judgment, he is to be driven from his bishopric. Thus do the Christians imitate in their treatment of each other their common enemy, the Roman. They seem already ashamed of the gentleness of Christ, who would have every mind left in its own freedom to believe as its own powers enable it to believe. Our good Zenobia, though no Christian, is yet in this respect the truest Christian. All within her realm, thought is free as the air that plays among these leaves."

"But is it not," said Fausta, "a mark of imperfection in your religion, that it cannot control and bind to a perfect life its disciples? Methinks a divine religion should manifest its divinity in the superior goodness which it forms."

"Is not that just?" I added.

"A divine religion," he replied, "may indeed be expected to show its heaven-derived power in creating a higher virtue than human systems. And this, I am sure, Christianity does. I may safely challenge the world to show in human form the perfection which dwelt in Jesus, the founder of this religion. Yet his character was formed by the power of his own doctrines. Among his followers, if there have been none so perfect as he, there have been multitudes who have approached him, and have exhibited a virtue which was once thought to belong only to philosophers. The world has been accustomed to celebrate, with almost divine honours, Socrates, and chiefly because of the greatness of mind displayed by him when condemned to drink the cup of poison. I can tell you of thousands among the Christians, among common and unlearned Christians, who have met death, in forms many times more horrible than that in which the Greek encountered it, with equal calmness and serenity. This they have been enabled to do simply through the divine force of a few great truths, which they have implicitly believed. Besides this, consider the many usages of the world, which, while others hold them innocent, the Christians condemn them, and abstain from them. It is not to be denied that they are the reformers of the age. They are busy, sometimes with an indiscreet and violent zeal, in new-modelling both the opinions and practices of the world. But what then? Are they to be condemned if a single fault may be charged upon them? Must they be perfect, because their religion is divine? This might be so, if it were of the nature of religion to operate with an irresistible influence upon the mind, producing an involuntary and forced obedience. But in such an obedience, there would be nothing like what we mean by virtue, but something quite inferior in the comparison. A religion, for the reason that it is divine, will, with the more certainty, make its appeals to a free nature. It will explain the nature, and reveal the consequences of virtue and vice, but will leave the mind free to choose the one or the other. Christianity teaches, that in goodness, and faithfulness to the sense of duty, lies the chief good; in these there is a heaven of reward, not only now and on earth, but throughout an existence truly immortal. Is it not most evident, that with whatever authority this religion may propound its doctrines, men not being in a single power coerced, will not, though they may receive them, yield to them an equal observance? Hence, even among Christians, there must be, perhaps ever, much imperfection."

"Does not this appear to you, Fausta and Piso," said Julia, as the old man paused, "just and reasonable? Can it be an objection to this faith, that its disciples partake of the common weaknesses of humanity? Otherwise, religion would be a principle designed, not so much to improve and exalt our nature, as to alter it."

"We allow it readily to be both just and reasonable."

"But it seemed to us," said Fausta, "as we ascended the mountain, and were conversing, to be with certainty a proof of imperfection in your religion—pardon my freedom, we are come as learners, and they who would learn, must, without restraint, express their doubts—that it recommended or permitted a recluse and inactive life. Have your days, father, been passed in this deep solitude ? and has your religion demanded it ?"

"Your freedom pleases me," replied the venerable man, "and I wonder not at the question you propose. Not my religion, lady, but an enfeebled and decrepit frame, chains me to this solitude. I have now outlasted a century, and my powers are wasted and gone. I can do little more than sit and ponder the truths of this life-giving book, and anticipate the renewed activity of that immortal being which it promises. The Christian converts, who dwell beneath those roofs which you see gleaming in the valley below, supply the few wants which I have. When their labour is done for the day, they sometimes come up, bringing with them baskets of fresh or dried fruits, which serve me, together with the few roots and berries which I myself can gather as I walk this level space, for my food. My thirst I quench at the brook which you have just passed. Upon this simple but wholesome nutriment, and breathing this dry mountain air, my days may yet be prolonged through many years. But I do not covet them, since nature makes me a prisoner. But I submit, because my faith teaches me to receive patiently whatever the Supreme Ruler appoints. It is not my religion that prescribes this manner of life, or permits it, but as the last refuge of an imbecility like mine. Christianity denounces selfishness in all its forms, and what form of selfishness more gross than to spend the best of one's days in solitary musing and prayer, all to secure one's own salvation? The founder of this religion led an active and laborious life. He did good not only to himself by prayer and meditation; he went about doing it to others, seeking out objects whom he might benefit and bless. His life was one of active benevolence; and the record of that life is the religious code of his followers. No condemnation could be more severe than that which the Prophet of Nazareth would pronounce upon such a life as mine now is, were it a chosen, voluntary one. But it never has been voluntary. Till age dried up the sources of my strength, I toiled night and day in all countries and climates, in the face of every danger, in the service of mankind; for it is by serving others that the law of Christ is fulfilled. This disinterested labour for others constituted the greatness of Jesus Christ. This constitutes true greatness in his followers. I perceive that what I say falls upon your ear as a new and strange doctrine; but it is the doctrine of Christianity. It utterly condemns, therefore, a life of solitary devotion. It is a mischievous influence, which is now spreading outwards from the example of that Paul, who suffered so much under the persecution of the Emperor Decius, and who then, flying to the solitudes of the Egyptian Thebais, has there in the vigour of his days buried himself in a cave of the earth, that he may serve God by forsaking man. His maxim seems to be, 'The farther from man, the nearer to God,'—the reverse of the Christian maxim, 'The nearer man, the nearer God.' A disciple of Jesus has truly said, 'He who loves not his brother whom he hath seen, how shall he love God, whom he hath not seen?' This, it may be, Roman, is the first sentence you have ever heard from the Christian books."

"I am obliged to confess that it is," I replied. "I have heretofore lived in an easy indifference towards all religions. The popular religion of my country I early learned to despise. I have perused the philosophers, and examined their systems, from Pythagoras to Seneca, and am now, what I have long been, a disciple of none but Pyrrho. My researches have taught me only how the more ingeniously to doubt. Wearied at length with a vain inquiry after truth that should satisfy and fill me, I suddenly abandoned the pursuit, with the resolve never to resume it. I was not even tempted to depart from this resolution when Christianity offered itself to my notice; for I confounded it with Judaism, and for that, as a Roman, I entertained too profound a contempt to bestow upon it a single thought. I must acknowledge that the reports which I heard, and which I sometimes read, of the marvellous constancy and serenity of the Christians, under accumulated sufferings and wrongs, interested my feelings in their behalf; and the thought often arose, Must there not be truth to support such heroism? But the world went on its way, and I with it, and the Christians were forgotten. To a Christian, on my voyage across the Mediterranean, I owe much for my first knowledge of Christianity. To the princess Julia I owe a larger debt still. And now from your lips, long accustomed to declare its truths, I have heard what makes me truly desirous to hear the whole of that, which, in the little glimpses I have been able to obtain, has afforded so real a satisfaction."

"If you studied the Christian books," said the recluse, "you would be chiefly struck, perhaps, with the plainness and simplicity of the doctrines there unfolded. You would say that much which you found there, relating to the right conduct of life, you had already found scattered through the books of the Greek and Roman moralists. You would be startled by no strange or appalling truth. You would turn over their leaves in vain, in search of such dark and puzzling ingenuities as try the wits of those who resort to the pages of the Timæus. A child can understand the essential truths of Christ. And the value of Christianity consists not in this, that it puts forth a new, ingenious, and intricate system of philosophy, but that it adds to recognised and familiar truths divine authority. Some things are indeed new; and much is new, if that may be called so, which, having been neglected as insignificant by other teachers, has by Christ been singled out and announced as primal and essential. But the peculiarity of Christianity lies in this, that its voice, whether heard in republishing an old and familiar doctrine, or announcing a new one, is not the voice of man, but of God. It is a revelation. It is a word from the invisible, unapproachable, Spirit of the universe. For this Socrates would have been willing to renounce all his wisdom. Is it not this which we need? We can theorise and conjecture without end, but cannot relieve ourselves of our doubts. They will assail every work of man. We wish to repose in a divine assurance. This we have in Christianity. It is a message from God. It puts an end to doubt and conjecture. Wise men of all ages have agreed in the belief of one God; but not being able to demonstrate his being and his unity, they have had no power to change the popular belief, which has ever tended to polytheism and idolatry. Christianity teaches this truth with the authority of God himself, and already has it become the faith of millions. Philosophers have long ago taught that the only safe and happy life is a virtuous life. Christianity repeats this great truth, and adds, that it is such a life alone that conducts to immortality. Philosophers have themselves believed in the doctrine of a future life, and have died hoping to live again; and it cannot be denied that mankind generally have entertained an obscure expectation of a renewed existence after death. The advantage of Christianity consists in this, that it assures us of the reality of a future existence, on the word and authority of God himself. Jesus Christ taught that all men come forth from death, wearing a new spiritual body, and thereafter never die; and to confirm his teaching, he himself being slain, rose from the dead, and showed himself to his followers alive, and while they were yet looking upon him, ascended to some other and higher world. Surely, Roman, though Christianity announced nothing more than these great truths, yet seeing it puts them forth in the name, and with the authority of God, it is a vast accession to our knowledge."

"Indeed, it cannot be denied," I answered. "It would be a great happiness, too, to feel such an assurance, as he must who believes in your religion, of another life. Death would then lose every terror. We could approach the close of life, as calmly and cheerfully, sometimes as gladly, as we now do the close of a day of weary travel or toil. It would be but to lie down and rest, and sleep, and rise again refreshed by the slumber for the labours and enjoyments of a life which should then be without termination, and yet unattended by fatigue. I can think of no greater felicity than to be able to perceive the truth of such a religion as yours."

"This religion of the Christians," said Fausta, "seems to be full of reasonable and desirable truth—if it all be truth. But how is this great point to be determined? How are we to know whether the founder of this religion was in truth a person holding communication with God? The mind will necessarily demand a large amount of evidence, before it can believe so extraordinary a thing. I greatly fear, Julia, lest I may never be a Christian. What is the evidence, father, with which you trust to convince the mind of an inquirer? It must possess potency, for all the world seems flocking to the standard of Christ."

"I think, indeed," replied the saint, "that it possesses potency. I believe its power to be irresistible. But do you ask in sincerity, daughter of Gracchus, what to do in order to believe in Christianity."

"I do indeed," answered Fausta. "But know, that my mind is one not easy of belief."

"Christianity asks no forced or faint assent. It appeals to human reason, and it blames not the conscientious doubter or denier. When it requires you to examine, and constitutes you judge, it condemns no honest decision. The mind that approaches Christianity must be free, and ought to be fearless. Hesitate not to reject that which evidence does not substantiate. But examine, and weigh well the testimony. If then you would know whether Christianity be true, it is first of all needful that you read and ponder the Christian books. These books prove themselves. The religion of Christ is *felt* to be true, as you read the writings in which it is recorded. Just as the works of nature prove to the contemplative mind the being of a God, so do the books of the Christians prove the truth of their religion. As you read them, as your mind embraces the teaching, and above all, the character of Christ, you involuntarily exclaim, 'This must be true; the sun in the heavens does not more clearly point to a divine author, than do the contents of these books.' You find them utterly unlike any other books—differing from them just in the same infinite and essential way that the works of God differ from the works of man."

He paused, and we were for a few moments silent. At length Fausta said, "This is all very new and strange, father! Why, Julia, have you never urged me to read these books?"

"The princess," resumed the hermit, "has done wisely to leave you to the promptings of your own mind. The more every thing in religion is voluntary and free, the more worth attaches to it. Christ would not that any should be driven or urged to him, but that they should come. Nevertheless, the way must be pointed out. I have now shown you one way. Let me tell you of another. The Christian books bear the names of the persons who profess to have written them, and who declare themselves to have lived and to have recorded events which happened in the province of Judea, in the reigns of Tiberius and Nero. Now, it is by no means a difficult matter for a person desirous to arrive at the truth, to institute such inquiries as shall fully convince him that such persons lived then and there, and performed the actions ascribed to them. We are not so far removed from those times, but that by resorting to the places where the events of the Christian history took place, we can readily satisfy ourselves of their truth— if they be true—by inquiring of the descendants of those who were concerned in the very transactions recorded. This thousands and thousands have done, and they believe in the events—strange as they are—of the Christian history as implicitly as they do in the events of the Roman history, for the same period of time.

K

Listen, my children, while I rehearse my own experience as a believer in Christ.

My father, Cyprian, a native of Syria, attained, as I have attained, to an extreme old age. At the age of five score years and ten, he died within the walls of this quiet dwelling of nature's own hewing, and there, at the roots of that ancient cedar, his bones repose. He was for twenty years a contemporary of St John the evangelist—of that John, who was one of the companions of Jesus, the founder of Christianity, and who, ere he died, wrote a history of Jesus, and of his acts and doctrine. From the very lips of this holy man, did the youthful but truth-loving and truth-seeking Cyprian receive his knowledge of Christianity. He sat and listened while the aged apostle—the past rising before him with the distinctness of a picture—told of Jesus; of the mild majesty of his presence; of the power and sweetness of his discourse; of the love he bore towards all that lived; of his countenance radiant with joy, when, in using the miraculous power entrusted to show his descent from God, he gave health to the pining sick, and restored the dying and the dead to the arms of weeping friends. There was no point of the history which the apostle has recorded for the instruction of posterity, which Cyprian did not hear, with all its minuter circumstances, from his own mouth. Nay, he was himself a witness of the exercise of that same power of God which was committed without measure to Jesus, on the part of the apostle. He stood by—his spirit wrapt and wonderstruck—while at the name of Jesus the lame walked, the blind recovered their sight, and the sick leaped from their couches. When this great apostle was fallen asleep, my father, by the counsel of St John, and that his faith might yet farther be confirmed, travelled over all the scenes of the Christian history. He visited the towns and cities of Judea, where Jesus had done his marvellous works. He conversed with the children of those who had been subjects of the healing power of the Messiah. He was with those who themselves had mingled among the multitudes who encompassed him, when Lazarus was summoned from the grave, and who clung to the cross when Jesus was upon it dying, and witnessed the sudden darkness, and felt the quaking of the earth. Finding, wherever he turned his steps in Judea, from Bethlehem to Nazareth, from the Jordan to the great sea, the whole land filled with those who, as either friends or enemies, had hung upon the steps of Jesus, and seen his miracles, what was he, to doubt whether such a person as Jesus had ever lived, or had ever done these wonderful works? He doubted not; he believed, even as he would have done had he himself been present as a disciple. In addition to this, he saw, at the places where they were kept, the evangelic histories, in the writing of those who drew them up; and at Rome, at Corinth, at Phillippi, at Ephesus, he handled with his own hands the letters of Paul, which he wrote to the Christians of those places; and in those places and others, did he dwell and converse with multitudes who had seen and heard the great apostle, and had witnessed the wonders he had wrought. I, the child of Cyprian's old age, heard from him all that I have now recounted to you. I sat at his feet, as he had sat at the evangelist's, and from him I heard the various experiences of his long, laborious, and troubled life. Could I help but believe what I heard? and so could I help but be a Christian? My father was a man—and all Syria knows him to have been such an one—of a passionate love of truth. At any moment would he have cheerfully suffered torture and death, sooner than have swerved from the strictest allegiance to its very letter. Nevertheless, he would not that I should trust to him alone; but as the apostle had sent him forth, so he sent me forth, to read the evidences of the truth of this religion in the living monuments of Judea. I, too, wandered a pilgrim over the hills and plains of Galilee. I sat in the synagogue at Nazareth. I dwelt in Capernaum. I mused by the shore of the Galilean lake. I haunted the ruins of Jerusalem, and sought out the places where the Saviour of men had passed the last hours of his life. Night after night I wept and prayed upon the Mount of Olives. Whereever I went, and among whomsoever I mingled, I found witnesses eloquent and loud, and without number, to all the principal facts and events of our sacred history. Ten thousand traditions of the life and acts of Christ and his apostles, all agreeing substantially with the written records, were passing from mouth to mouth, and descending from sire to son. The whole land, in all its length and breadth, was but one vast monument to the truth of Christianity. And for this purpose it was resorted to by the lovers of truth from all parts of the world. Did doubts arise in the mind of a dweller in Rome, or Carthage, or Britain, concerning the whole or any part of the Christian story, he addressed letters to well known inhabitants of the Jewish cities, or he visited them in person, and by a few plain words from another or by the evidence of his own eyes and ears, every doubt was scattered. When I had stored my mind with knowledge from these original sources, I then betook myself to some of the living oracles of Christian wisdom, with the fame of whose learning and piety the world was filled. From the great Clement of Rome, from Dyonysius at Alexandria, from Tertullian at Carthage, from that wonder of human genius, Origen, in his school at Cæsarea, I gathered together what more was needed to arm me for the Christian warfare; and I then went forth full of faith myself to plant its divine seeds in the hearts of whosoever would receive them. In this good work my days have been spent. I have lived and taught but to unfold to others the evidences which have made me a Christian. My children," continued he, " why should you not receive my words? why should I desire to deceive you? I am an old man, trembling upon the borders of the grave. Can I have any wish to injure you? Is it conceivable that, standing thus already, as it were, before the bar of God, I could pour false and idle tales into your ears? But if I have spoken truly, can you refuse to believe? But I must not urge. Use your freedom. Inquire for yourselves. Let the leisure and the wealth which are yours carry you to read with your own eyes that wide spread volume, which you will find among the mountains and valleys of the Holy Land. Princess, my strength is spent, or there is much more I could gladly add."

"My friends," said the princess, "are, I am sure, grateful for what you have said and they have heard."

"Indeed we are," said Fausta, "and heartily do we thank you. One thing more would I ask. What think you of the prospects of the Christian faith? Are the common reports of its rapid ascendancy to be heeded? Is it making its way, as we are told, even into the palaces of kings? I know, indeed, what happens in Palmyra; but elsewhere, holy father?"

As Fausta spoke these words, the aged man seemed wrapped in thought. His venerable head sank upon his breast; his beard swept the ground. At length, slowly raising his head, and with eyes lifted upwards, he said, in deep and solemn tones, "It cannot, it cannot be difficult to read the future. It must be so. I see it as if it were already come. The throne which is red with blood, and he who sits thereon, wielding a sword dropping with blood, sinks—sinks—and disappears; and one all white, and he who sits thereon, having upon his frontlet these words, 'Peace on earth and good will towards men,' rises and fills its place. And I hear a movement as of a multitude which no man can number, coming and worshipping around the throne. God of the whole earth, arise!—visit it with thy salvation! Hasten the coming of the universal kingdom of thy Son, when all shall know thee, and love to God and love to man possess and fill every soul."

As the venerable man uttered this prayer, Julia looked steadfastly upon him, and a beauty more than of earth seemed to dwell upon her countenance.

"Father," said Fausta, "we are not now fair judges of truth. Your discourse has wrought so upon us, that we need reflection before we can tell what we ought to believe."

"That is just," said the saint; "to determine right, we must think rather than feel. And that your minds may the sooner return to the proper state, let me set before you of such as my dwelling will afford."

Saying this, he moved from the seat which till now he had retained, and closing the volume he had been reading, laid it away with care, saying as he did so, "This, children, is the Christian's book; not containing all those writings which we deem to be of authority in describing our faith, but such as are most needful. It is from reading this, and noting as you read the inward marks of honesty, and observing how easy it were, even now, by visiting Judea, to convict its authors of error and falsehood, had they been guilty of either, that your minds will be best able to judge of the truth and worth of Christianity."

"At another time, father," said Fausta, "it would give me great delight, and equally, too, I am sure, our friend from Rome, if you would read to us portions of that volume, that we may know somewhat of its contents from your lips, accompanied, too, by such comments as you might deem useful to learners. It is thus we have often heard the Greek and Roman writers from the mouth of Longinus."

"Whenever," he replied, "you shall be willing to ascend these steep and rugged paths, in pursuit of truth, I, in my turn, will stand prepared to teach. To behold such listeners before me, brings back the life of former days."

He then, with short and interrupted steps, busied himself in bringing forth his humble fare. Bread and fruits, and olives, formed our slight repast, together with ice-cold water, which Julia, seizing from his hand the hermit's pitcher, brought from a spring that gushed from a neighbouring rock.

This being ended, and with it much various and agreeable conversation, in the course of which the

Christian patriarch gave many striking anecdotes of his exposed and toilsome life, we rose, and bidding farewell, with promises to return again, betook ourselves to our horses, and mounting them, were soon at the gates of the palace.

I confess myself interested in the question of Christianity. The old religions are time-worn, and in effect dead. To the common people, when believed, they are as often injurious as useful—to others, they are the objects of open, undisguised contempt. Yet religion, in some form, the human mind must have. We feel the want of it as we do of food and drink. But, as in the case of food and drink, it must be something that we shall perceive to nourish and strengthen, not to debilitate and poison. In my searches through antiquity, I have found no system which I could rest in as complete and satisfying. They all fail in many vital points. They are frequently childish in their requisitions and their principles; their morality is faulty; their spirit narrow and exclusive; and, more than all, they are without authority. The principles which are to guide, control, and exalt our nature, it seems to me, must proceed from the author of that nature. The claim of Christianity to be a religion provided for man by the Creator of man, is the feature in it which draws me towards it. This claim I shall investigate and scan, with all the ability and learning I can bring to the work. But whatever I or you may think of it, or ultimately determine, every eye must see with what giant steps it is striding onwards—temples, religions, superstitions, and powers, crumbling and dissolving at its approach. Farewell.

LETTER VIII.

The words of that Christian recluse, my Curtius, still ring in my ear. I know not how it is, but there is a strange power in all that I have heard from any of that sect. You remember how I was struck by the manner, the countenance, and, above all, by the sentiments, of Probus, the Christian whom I encountered on his way to Carthage. A still stronger feeling possesses me, when I hear the same things from the lips of Julia. It seems as if she herself, and the religion she discourses of, must proceed from the same author. She is certainly a divine work. And there is such an alliance between her and those truths, that I am ready almost to believe that for this reason alone they must have that very divine origin which is claimed for them. Is there any thing in our Roman superstitions, or philosophy even, that is at all kindred to the spirit of a perfect woman—any thing suited to her nature? Has it ever seemed as if woman were in any respect the care of the gods? In this, Christianity differs from all former religions and philosophies. It is feminine. I do not mean by that, weak or effeminate. But in its gentleness, in the suavity of its tone, in the humanity of its doctrines, in the deep love it breathes towards all of human kind, in the high rank it assigns to the virtues which are peculiarly those of woman, in these things and many others, it is throughout for them as well as for us—almost more for them than for us. In this feature of it, so strange and new, I see marks of a wisdom beyond that of any human fabricator. A human inventor would scarcely have conceived such a system; and could he have conceived it, would not have dared to publish it. It would have been, in his judgment, to have wantonly forfeited the favour of the world. The author of Christianity, with a divine boldness, makes his perfect man, in the purity and beauty of his character, the counterpart of a perfect woman. The virtues upon which former teachers have chiefly dwelt, are by him almost unnoticed; and those soft and feminine ones, which others seem to have utterly forgotten, he has exalted to the highest place. So that, as I before said, Julia discoursing to me of Christianity is in herself, in the exact accordance between her mind and heart and that faith, the strongest argument I have yet found of its truth. I do not say that I am a believer. I am not. But I cannot say what the effect may be of a few more interviews with the hermit of the mountains, in company with the princess. His arguments, illustrated by her presence, will carry with them not a little force.

When, after our interview with the Christian, we had returned to the queen's villa, we easily persuaded ourselves that the heat of the day was too great for us to set out, till towards the close of it, for the city. So we agreed, in the absence of the queen and other guests, to pass the day after our own manner, and by ourselves. The princess proposed that we should confine ourselves to the cool retreats near the fountain of the elephant, made also more agreeable to us than any other place by the delightful hours we had sat there, listening to the melodious accents of the great Longinus. To this proposal we quickly and gladly assented. Our garments being then made to correspond to the excessive heats of the season, soothed by noise of the falling waters, and fanned by slaves who waved to and fro huge leaves of the palm tree, cut into graceful forms, and set in gold or ivory, we resigned ourselves to that sleepy but yet delicious state which we reach only a few times in all our lives, when the senses are perfectly satisfied and filled, and merely to live is bliss enough. But our luxurious ease was slightly diversified with additions and changes no ways unwelcome. Ever and anon slaves entered, bearing trays laden with every rare and curious confection which the art of the east supplies, but especially with drinks cooled by snow brought from the mountains of India. These, in the most agreeable manner, recruited our strength when exhausted by fits of merriment, or when one had become weary by reading or reciting a story for the amusement of the others, and the others as weary, or more weary, by listening. It were in vain to attempt to recall for your and Lucilia's entertainment the many pleasant things which were both said and done on this day never to be forgotten. And besides, perhaps, were they set down in order, and sent to Rome, the spicy flavour which gave life to them here, might all exhale, and leave them flat and dull. Suffice it, therefore, to say, that in our judgment many witty and learned sayings were uttered —for the learning, that must rest upon our declaration —for the wit, the slaves will bear witness to it, as they did then, by their unrestrained bursts of laughter.

It was with no little reluctance, that, as the last rays of the sun fell upon the highest jet of the fountain, we heard the princess declare that the latest hour had come, and we must fain prepare for the city. A little time sufficed for this, and we were soon upon our horses, threading the defiles among the hills, or flying over the plains. A few hours brought us within the gates of the city. Leaving Julia at the palace of the queen, we turned towards the house of Gracchus. Its noble front soon rose before us. As we passed into the court-yard, the first sound that greeted me was Milo's blundering voice: "Welcome, most noble Gallienus; welcome again to Palmyra!"

"I am not," said I, "quite an emperor yet, but notwithstanding, I am glad to be in Palmyra—more glad to be at the house of Gracchus—and glad most of all to see Gracchus himself at home, and well;" the noble Roman, as I shall call him, at that moment issuing from a door of the palace, and descending at a quick pace the steps, to assist Fausta from her horse.

"We are not," said he, "long separated; but to those who really love, the shortest separation is a long one, and the quickest return an occasion of joy." Saying so, he embraced and kissed his beautiful daughter, and grasped cordially my hand.

"Come," added he, "enter and repose. Your ride has been a sharp one, as your horses declare, and the heat is great. Let us to the banqueting-hall, as the coolest, and there sit and rest." So we were again soon within that graceful apartment, where I had first sat and tasted the hospitalities of Palmyra. The gods above were still at their feast, drinking or drunken. Below, we sat at the open windows, and with more temperance regaled ourselves with the cool air that came to us, richly laden with the fragrance of surrounding flowers, and with that social converse which is more inspiring than Falernian, or the soft Palmyrene. After talking of other things, Gracchus addressed me, saying,

"But is it not now time, Lucius, that a letter, at least, came from Isaac? I have forborne to inquire, from time to time, as I would do nothing to add to your necessary anxiety. It surely now, however, is right to consider the steps next to be taken, if he shall have failed in his enterprise."

"Isaac and Calpurnius," I replied, "are never absent from my thoughts, and I have already resolved—the gods willing and favouring—that when a period of sufficient length shall have elapsed, and the Jew does not appear—having either perished on the way or else in the capital of the great king—myself to start, as I at first designed to do, upon this expedition, and either return with my brother, or else die also, in the endeavour. Seek not, Fausta, as I perceive you are about to do, to turn me from my purpose. It will be—it ought to be—in vain. I can consent no longer to live thus in the very heart of life, while this cloud of uncertainty hangs over the fate of one so near to me. Though I should depute the service of his rescue to a thousand others, my own inactivity is insupportable, and reproaches me like a crime."

"I was not, as you supposed, Lucius," replied Fausta, "about to draw you away from your purpose, but, on the contrary, to declare my approbation of it. Were I Lucius, my thoughts would be, I am sure, what yours now are, and to-morrow's sun would light me on the way to Ecbatana. Nay, father, I would not wait a day longer. Woman though I am, I am almost ready to become our friend's companion on this pious service."

"I shall not," said Gracchus, "undertake to dissuade our friend from what seems now to be his settled purpose. Yet still, for our sakes, for the sake of the aged Portia, and all in Rome, I could wish that—supposing Isaac should fail—one more attempt might be made in the same way, ere so much is put at hazard. It needs no great penetration to see how highly prized by Persia must be the possession of such a trophy of her prowess as the head of the noble house of Piso; with what jealousy his every movement would be watched, and what danger must wait upon any attempt at his deliverance. Moreover, while a mere hireling might, if detected, have one chance among a thousand of pardon and escape, even that were wanting to you. Another Piso would be either another footstool of the Persian despot, while life should last, or else he would swing upon a Persian gibbet, and so would perish the last of a noble name."

"I cannot deny that reason is on your side," I said, in reply to this strong case of Gracchus, "but feeling is on mine, and the contest is never an equal one. Feeling is, perhaps, the essence of reason, of which no account need or can be given, and ought to prevail. But however this may be, I feel that I am right, and so I must act."

"But let us now think of nothing else," said Fausta, "than that, before another day is ended, we shall get intelligence of Isaac. Have you, Lucius, inquired, since your return, of Demetrius?"

"Milo is now absent on that very errand," I replied; ' and here he is, giving no signs of success."

Milo at the same moment entered the hall, and stated that Demetrius was himself absent from the city, but was every moment expected, and it was known that he had been seeking anxiously the preceding day for me.

While Milo was yet speaking, a messenger was announced, inquiring for me; and before I could reach the extremity of the apartment, Demetrius himself entered the room in haste, brandishing in his hand a letter, which he knew well to be from Isaac.

"'Tis his own hand," said he. "The form of his

letters is not to be mistaken. Not even the hand of Demetrius can cut with more grace the Greek character. Observe, Roman, the fashion of his touch. Isaac would have guided a rare hand at the graving tool. But these Jews shun the nicer arts. They are a strange people."

"Quickly," said I, interrupting the voluble Greek, "as you love the gods, deliver to me the letter! By and bye we will discourse of these things;" and seizing the epistle, I ran with it to another apartment, first to devour it myself.

I cannot tell you, dear friends, with what eagerness I drank in the contents of the letter, and with what ecstacy of joy I leaped and shouted at the news it brought. In one word, my brother lives, and it is possible that before this epistle to you shall be finished, he himself will sit at my side. But to put you in possession of the whole case, I shall transcribe for you the chief parts of Isaac's careful and minute account, preserving for your amusement much of what in no way whatever relates to the affair in hand, and is useful only as it will present a sort of picture of one of this strange tribe. As soon as I had filled myself with its transporting contents, I hastened to the hall where I had left Fausta and Gracchus, to whom—Demetrius having in the mean time taken his departure—I quickly communicated its intelligence, and received their hearty congratulations, and then read it to them very much as I now transcribe it for you. You will now acknowledge my obligations to this kind-hearted Jew, and will devoutly bless the gods for my accidental encounter with him on board the Mediterranean trader. Here now is the letter itself.

"*Isaac, the son of Isaac of Rome, to the most noble Lucius Manlius Piso, at Palmyra.*

THAT I am alive, Roman, after the perils of my journey, and the worse perils of this pagan city, can be ascribed to nothing else than to the protecting arm of the God of our nation. It is new evidence to me, that somewhat is yet to be achieved by my ministry, for the good of my country. That I am here in this remote and benighted region, that I should have adventured hither in the service of a Roman to save one Roman life, when, were the power mine, I would cut off every Roman life, from the babe at the breast to the silver head, and lay waste the kingdoms of the great mother of iniquity with fire and sword, is to me a thing so wonderful, that I refer it all to the pleasure of that Power who orders events according to a plan and wisdom impenetrable by us. Think not, Roman, that I have journeyed so far for the sake of thy two talents of gold—though that is considerable. And the mention of this draws my mind to a matter, overlooked in the stipulations entered into between thee and me at my dwelling in Palmyra. Singular, that so weighty a part of that transaction should have been taken no note of! Now, I must trust it wholly to thee, Piso, and feel that I may safely do so. In case of my death, the double of the recompense agreed upon was to be paid, in accordance with directions left. But what was to be done in case of thy death? Why, most thoughtful Isaac, most prudent of men, for this thou didst make no provision! And yet may not Piso die as well as Isaac? Has a Roman more lives than a Jew? Nay, how know I but thou art now dead, and no one living to do me justice! See to this, excellent Roman. Thou wouldst not have me go unrequited for all this hazard and toil. Let thy heirs be bound, by sure and legal instruments, to make good to me all thou hast bound thyself to pay. Do this, and thy gods and my God prosper thee! Forget it not. Let it be done as soon as these words are read. Demetrius will show thee one who will draw up a writing, in agreement with both the Palmyrene and Roman law. Unheard-of heedlessness! But this I thought not about till I took my pen to write.

What was I saying?—that I came not for thy gold—that is, not for that solely or chiefly. For what, and why, then? Because, as I have hinted, I felt myself driven by an invisible power to this enterprise. I wait with patience to know what its issue is to be.

Now let me inform thee of my journey and my doings. But first, in one brief word, let me relieve thy impatience by saying, *I think thy brother is to be rescued.* No more of this at present, but all in order. When I parted from thee that night, I had hardly formed my plan, though my mind, quick in all its workings, did suddenly conceive one way in which it appeared possible to me to compass the desired object. Perhaps you will deem it a piece of rashness rather than of courage so quickly to undertake your affair. I should call it so too, did I not also catch dimly in the depth of the heavens the form of the finger of God. This thou wilt not, and canst not understand. It is beyond thee. Is it not so? But, Roman, I trust the day is to come when by my mouth, if not by another's, thou shalt hear enough to understand that truth is to be found nowhere but in Moses. Avoid Probus. I fear me he is already in Palmyra. There is more cunning in him than is good. With that deep face and serene air he deceives many. All I say is, shun him. To be a Roman unbeliever is better than to be a Christian heretic. But to my journey.

The morning after I parted from thee saw me issuing at an early hour from the Persian gate, and with my single Ethiopian slave, bearing towards the desert. I took with me but a light bale of merchandise, that I might not burden my good dromedary. Than mine, there is not a fleeter in the whole east. One nearly as good, and at a huge price, did I purchase for my slave. 'Twas too suddenly bought to be cheaply bought. But I was not cozened; it proved a rare animal. I think there lives not a man in Palmyra or Damascus who could blind Isaac. I determined to travel at the greatest speed we and our beasts could bear, so we avoided as far as we could the heats of day, and rode by night. The first day being through the peopled regions of the queen's dominions, and through a cultivated country, we travelled at our ease; and not unfrequently at such places as I saw promised well, did we stop, and while our good beasts regaled themselves upon the rich herbage or richer grain, trafficked. In this surely I erred not. For, losing as I have done, by this distant and unwonted route, the trade of Ctesiphon, 'twas just, was it not, that to the extent possible, without great obstruction thrown in the way of your affairs, I should repair the evil of that loss? Truth to speak, it was only because my eye foresaw some such profitings on the way, that I made myself contented with but two gold talents of Jerusalem. Two days were passed thus, and on the third we entered upon a barren region—barren as where the prophet found no food, but such as birds from heaven brought him. But why speak of this to thee? Oh, that thou wouldst but once, only once, sit at the feet of that man of God, Simon Ben Gorah! Solomon was not more wise. His words are arrows with two heads, from a golden bow. His reasons weigh as the mountains of Lebanon. They break and crush all on whom they fall. Would, Roman, they might sometime fall on thee! The third day we were on this barren region, and the next fairly upon the desert. Now did we reap the benefit of our good beasts. The heat was like that of the furnace of Nebuchadnezzar, out of which the three children, Shadrach, Mescheck, and Abednego came, through the power of God, unscorched. And, moreover, they were soon put to an unwonted and unlooked-for burden, and in such manner as, to thy wonder, I shall relate.

It was a day the air of which was like the air of that furnace—burning, burning hot. Death was written upon the whole face of the visible earth. Where leaves had been, there were none now, or they crumbled into ashes as the hand touched them. The atmosphere, when moved by the wind, brought not, as it is used to do, a greater coolness, but a fiercer heat. It was full of flickering waves, which danced up and down with a quivering motion, and dazzled and blinded the eye that looked upon them. And often the sand was not like that which, for the most part, is met with on that desert stretching from the Mediterranean to Palmyra, and of which thou hast had some experience—heavy, and hard, and seamed with cracks, but fine and light, and raised into clouds by every breath of wind, and driven into the skin like points of needles. When the wind, as frequently it did, blew with violence, we could only stop and bury our faces in our garments, our poor beasts crying out with pain. It was on such a day, having, because there was no place of rest, been obliged to endure all the noonday heat, that, when the sun was at the highest, and when we looked eagerly every way for even a dry and leafless bush that we might crouch down beneath its shade, we saw at a distance before us the tall trunk of a cedar, bleached to ivory, and twinkling like a pharos, under the hot rays. We slowly approached it, Hadad, my Ethiopian, knowing it as one of the pillars of the desert.

"There it has stood and shone a thousand years," said he; "and but for such marks, who could cross these seas of sand, where your foot-mark is lost as soon as made?" After a few moments' pause, he again exclaimed, "And, by the beard of holy Abraham! a living human being sits at the root—or else mayhap my eyes deceive me, and I see only the twisted roots of the tree."

" 'Tis too far for my eyes to discern aught but the blasted trunk. No living creature can dwell here. 'Tis the region of death only."

A blast of the desert struck us at the moment, and well nigh buried us in its rushing whirlwind of sand. We stood still, closed our eyes, and buried our faces in the folds of our garments.

" Horrible and out of nature!" I cried—" the sun blazing without a cloud as big as a locust to dim his ray, and yet these gusts, like the raging of a tempest. The winds surely rise. Providence be our guide out of this valley of fire and death!"

L

"There is no providence here," said the slave, "nor any where; else why these savage and dreary deserts, which must be crossed, and yet we die in doing it."

"Hold thy peace, blasphemer!" I could not but rejoin, "and take heed lest thy impious tongue draw down a whirlwind of God to the destruction of us both."

"The curse of Arimanes—" began the irritated slave —when suddenly he paused, and cried out in another tone, "Look! look! Isaac, and see now for thyself: I am no Jew, if there sit not a woman at the root of yonder tree."

I looked; and now that we had drawn nearer, and the wind had subsided for an instant, I plainly beheld the form of a woman, bent over, as if in the act of holding and defending an infant. I believed it a delusion of Satan.

"It is awful," said I; "but let us hasten; if it be a reality, our coming must be as the descent of angels."

I pressed on my weary animal, and in a few moments we stood before what seemed indeed a human being, of flesh and bone—and, what was more wonderful still, a woman. Yet she stirred not, nor gave other sign of life.

"Is the breath of life yet in you?" I cried out—not doubting, however, that whoever it was, death had already released her from her misery, and at the same time laid my hand upon her shoulder. At which she started, and lifting up her head, the very ghastliness of death stamped upon every feature, she shrieked, "I drown! I drown! Hassan, save me!" and her head fell again upon her knees.

"Poor fool," said I; "thou art upon the sands of the desert, and thou dreamest: awake!—awake!—and here is water for thee—real water."

At which she waked indeed, with a convulsive start; and while with one hand she held fast her child—for a child was indeed laid away among the folds of her garments—with the other she madly grasped the small cup I held out to her, and tearing aside the covering from the face of the child, she forced open its mouth, and poured in some of the water we gave her, watching its effect. Soon as the little one gave signs of life, she drank the remainder at a draught, crying out, "More! more!" Our water, of which we had as yet good store, though hot as the wind itself, quickly restored both mother and child.

"And now, tell me, miserable woman, what direful chance has brought and left thee here!—but hasten—speak quickly as thou canst; and dost thou look for any one to come to thy relief?"

"Robbers of the desert," said she, "have either murdered or carried into slavery my husband, and destroyed and scattered the caravan of which we made a part. I am alone in the desert; and I know of no relief but such as you can give. Leave us not, if you are men, to perish in these burning sands!"

"Fear not that I will leave you," said I: "what I can spare, shall freely be thine. But time is precious, for we are yet but midway the desert, and the signs of the heavens forbode wind and whirlwind: hasten, then, and mount the dromedary of my slave, while I upon mine bear, as stronger than thou, the child."

"Isaac," here muttered Hadad, in an under tone, "art thou mad? Is thy reason wholly gone? It is scarcely to be hoped that we alone may cross in safety what remains of the desert, beset as we are by these sweeping gusts, and wilt thou oppress our fainting beasts with this new burden?"

"Thou accursed of God! wouldst thou leave these here to perish? I believed not before that out of hell there could be so black a soul. Bring down thy dromedary. One word of hesitancy, and thy own carcass shall bleach upon the sands."

I knew well who I was dealing with, that I was safe from immediate violence, though not from ultimate revenge.

Hadad then drew up his beast, which, kneeling, received the woman, while I took in my arms the child.

We then set forward at an increased pace, to reach before night, if possible, the "place of springs," where a small green spot, watered by fountains which never fail, blesses these inhospitable plains.

Not a cloud was to be seen in all the compass of the heavens, yet the winds raged. The blueness of the sky was gone, and the whole inflamed dome above us was rather of the colour of molten brass, the sun being but its brightest and hottest spot. At a distance, we saw clouds of sand whirled aloft, and driven fiercely over the boundless plain, any one of which, it seemed to us, if it should cross our path, would bury us under its moving mass. We pressed on, trembling and silent through apprehension. The blood in my veins seemed hotter than the sand, or the sun that beat upon my face. Roman, thou canst form no conception of the horrors of this day. But for my faith, I should have utterly failed. What couldst thou have done?—nay, or the Christian Probus? But I will not taunt thee. I will rather hope. The wind became more and more violent. The sand was driven before it like chaff. Sometimes the tempest immediately around us would abate, but it only served to fill us with new apprehensions, by revealing to us the tossings of this great deep in the distance. At one of these moments, as I was taking occasion to speak a word of comfort to the half dead mother, and cherish the little one whom I bore, a sound as of the roar of ocean caught my ear—more awful than aught I had yet heard, and at the same time a shriek and a shout from Hadad, "God of Israel, save us! The sand! the sand!"

I looked in the direction of the sound, and there in the south it looked—God! how terrible to behold!—as if the whole plain were risen up, and were about to fall upon us.

"'Tis vain to fly!" I screamed to Hadad, who was urging his animal to its utmost speed. "Let us perish together. Besides, observe the heaviest and thickest of the cloud is in advance of us."

The mother of the child cried out, as Hadad insanely hastened on, for her offspring, to whom I answered, "Trust the young Ishmael to me—fear me not—cleave to the dromedary."

Hardly were the words spoken, when the whirlwind struck us. We were dashed to the earth as we had been weeds. My senses were for a time lost in the confusion and horror of the scene. I only knew that I had been torn from my dromedary—borne along and buried by the sand—and that the young Ishmael was still in my arms. In the first moment of consciousness, I found myself struggling to free myself from the sand which was heaped around and over me. In this, after a time, I succeeded, and in restoring to animation the poor child, choked and blinded, yet—wonderful indeed—not dead. I then looked around for Hadad and the woman, but they were nowhere to be seen. I shouted aloud, but there was no answer. The sand had now fallen, the wind had died away, and no sound met my ear but the distant rumbling of the retreating storm. Not far from me, my own dromedary stood, partly buried in the sand, and vainly endeavouring to extricate himself. With my aid, this was quickly effected. I was soon upon his back. But I knew not which way to turn. My dependence was upon Hadad, familiar with the route. The sun, however, had declined sensibly towards the west—I knew that my general direction was toward the east and north, so that with some certainty as to the true path, I sorrowfully recommenced my journey. Have I not thy pity, Roman? Has a worse case ever come to thy ear? I will not distress thee by reciting my sufferings all the way to the "place of springs," which by the next morning, plodding on wearily through the night, I safely reached.

There one of the first objects that greeted me, was Hadad and the mother of my Ishmael. I approached them unobserved, as they sat on the border of a spring, in the midst of other travellers—some of whom I saw were comforting the wailing Hagar—and, without a

word, dropped the young child into the lap of its mother.
Who shall describe the transports of her joy? 'Twas
worth, Piso, the journey and all its hazards.

How refreshing it was to lie here on the cool soil,
beneath the shade of the grateful palm, enjoying every
moment of existence, and repairing the injuries the
journey had inflicted upon ourselves and our beasts!
Two days we passed in this manner. While here, Hadad
related what befell him after our separation. Owing to
his urging on his animal in that mad way, at the time
I called out to him, instead of stopping or retreating,
he was farther within the heart of the cloud than I,
and was more rudely handled.

"Soon as the blast fell upon us," said he, "that instant
was my reason gone. I knew nothing for I cannot tell
how long. But when I came to myself, and found that I
was not in the place of the wicked—whereat I rejoiced
and was amazed—I discovered, on looking around, that
my good dromedary, whom I could ill spare, was dead
and buried, and your Hagar, whom I could have so
well spared, alive and weeping for her lost boy. I made
her, with difficulty, comprehend that time was precious,
and that strength would be impaired by weeping and
wailing. Knowing at once in what direction to travel
—after searching in vain for thee—we set out upon a
journey, which, on foot, beneath a burning sun, and
without water, there was small hope of accomplishing.
I looked with certainty to die in the desert. But
Oromasdes was my protector. See, Isaac, the advantage of a little of many faiths. We had not travelled
far among the hillocks, or hills rather, of sand, which
we found piled up in our way, and completely altering
the face of the plain, before, to our amazement and our
joy, we discovered a camel, without rider or burden,
coming towards us. I secured him without difficulty.
At a little distance, we soon saw another; and by and
bye we found that we were passing over the graves of
a caravan, the whole, or chief part of which, had been
overwhelmed by the storm. Here was a body partly

out of the sand, there the head or leg of a dromedary or camel. Ruin and death seemed to have finished their work. But it was not quite so. For presently, on reaching the summit of a wave of sand, we discerned a remnant mounted upon the beasts that had been saved, making in the same direction, and probably to the same point, as ourselves. We joined them, and partaking of their water, were recruited, and so reached this place alive. It is now from here," he added, "a safe and easy road to Ecbatana."

So we found it. But confess now, noble Piso, if in thy judgment it would have been exorbitant if I had required of thee three talents of Jerusalem instead of two? For what wouldst thou cross that molten sea, and be buried under its fiery waves? It is none other than a miracle that I am here alive in Ecbatana. And for thee I fear that miracle would not have been wrought. Hadst thou been in my place, the sands of the desert were now thy dwelling-place. Yet have I again to tempt those horrors. Being here, I must return. The dromedary of my slave Hadad was worth an hundred aurelians. A better or a fleeter never yet was in the stables of Zenobia. And dost thou know, Roman, how curious the queen is in horses and dromedaries? There cannot a rare one of either kind enter the walls of Palmyra, but he is straightway bought up for the service of Zenobia. The swiftest in the east are hers. 'Twas my purpose, returning, to have drawn upon Hadad's beast the notice of the queen. Doubtless I should have sold it to her, and two hundred aurelians is the very least I should have asked or taken from her. To no other than Zenobia would I have parted with her for less than three hundred. But, alas! her bones are on the desert. But why, you ask, should I have so favoured Zenobia? It is no wonder you ask. And in answer, I tell thee, perhaps, a secret. Zenobia is a Jewess! Receive it or not, as thou wilt—she is a Jewess, and her heart is tender towards our tribe. I do not say, mark me, that she is one by descent, nor that she is so much as even a proselyte of the Gate, but that she believes in some sort Moses and the prophets, and reads our sacred books. These things I know well from those who have been near her. But who ever heard that she has been seen to read the books of the Christians? Probus will not dare to assert it. 'Tis not more public that Longinus himself is inclined to our faith—by my head, I doubt not that he is more than inclined—than 'tis that Zenobia is. If our Messiah should first of all gird on the sword of Palmyra, what Jew, whose sight is better than a mole's, would be surprised? My father —may his sleep be sweet!—whose beard came lower than his girdle, and whose wisdom was famous throughout the east, built much upon what he knew of the queen, and her great minister, and used to say, " That another Barchochab would arise in Palmyra, whom it would require more than another Hadrian to hinder in his way to empire; and that if horses again swam in blood, as once at Bither, 'twould be in Roman blood." Who am I, to deny truth and likelihood to the words of one in whom dwelt the wisdom of Solomon, and the meekness of Moses—the faith of Abraham, the valour of Gideon, and the patience of Job? I rather maintain their truth. And in the features of the present time, I read change and revolution—war, and uproar, and ruin—the falling of kingdoms that have outlasted centuries, and the uprising of others that shall last for other centuries. I see the queen of the East at battle with the emperor of Rome, and through her victories deliverance wrought out for Israel, and the throne of Judah once more erected within the walls of Jerusalem. Now dost thou, Piso, understand, I suppose, not one word of all this. How shouldst thou? But I trust thou wilt. Surely now you will say, "What is all this to the purpose?" Not much to any present purpose, I confess freely; and I should not marvel greatly if thou wert to throw this letter down and trample it in the dust—as Rome has done by Judea— but that thou lookest to hear of thy brother. Well, now I will tell thee of him.

When we drew near to the capital of the great king, wishing to enrage Hadad, I asked "What mud-walled village is it that we see yonder over the plain?" Thou shouldst have seen the scowl of his eye—answer he gave none. I spit upon such a city—I cast out my shoe upon it! I who have dwelt at Rome, Carthage, Antioch, and Palmyra, may be allowed to despise a place like this. There is but one thing that impresses the beholder, and that is the Palace of Sapor, and the Temple of Mithras, near it. These, truly, would be noted even in Palmyra. Not that in the building any rule or order of art is observed, but that the congregation of strange and fantastic trickery—some whereof, it cannot be gainsaid, is of rare beauty—is so vast, that one is pleased with it as he is with the remembrance of the wonderful combinations of a dream.

Soon as we entered the gates of the city, I turned to the woman whom we brought from the desert, and who rode the camel with Hadad, and said to her, " First of all, Hagar, we take thee to those who are of thy kindred, or to thy friends, and well may they bless the good providence of God that they see thee. 'Twas a foul deed of thy husband, after the manner of the patriarch, to leave thee and thy little one to perish on the burning sands of the desert."

"Good Jew," she replied, "my name is not Hagar, nor did my husband leave me willingly. I tell thee we were set upon by robbers, and Hassan, my poor husband, was either killed, or carried away no one can tell whither."

"No matter—names are of little moment. To me, thou art Hagar, and thy little one here is Ishmael— and if thou wilt, Ishmael shall be mine. I will take him and rear him as mine—he shall be rich—and thou shalt be rich, and dwell where thou wilt." The child, Roman, had wound itself all around my heart. He was of three years or more, and, feature for feature, answered to the youngest of my own, long since lost, and now in Abraham's bosom. But it was not to be as

I wished. All the mother rushed into the face of the woman.

"Good Jew," she cried, "the God of Heaven will reward thee for thy mercy shown to us; but hadst thou saved my life a thousand times, I could not pay thee with my child. I am poor, and have nought to give thee but my thanks."

"I will see thee again," said I to the widow of Hassan, as we set her down in the street where her kinsfolk dwelt, "if thou wilt allow me. Receive thy child."

The child smiled as I kissed him, and gave him again to his mother. It was the smile of Joseph. I could at that moment almost myself have become a robber of the desert, and taken what the others had left.

We here parted, and Hadad and myself bent our way to the house of Levi, a merchant well known to Hadad, and who, he assured me, would gladly receive us. His shop, as we entered it, seemed well stored with the richest goods, but the building of which it made a part promised not very ample lodgings. But the hospitable welcome of the aged Levi promised better.

"Welcome every true son of Israel," said he, as we drew near where, in a remoter part of the large apartment, he sat busy at his books of account. "Make yourselves at home beneath the roof of Levi. Follow me, and find more private quarters."

So, leaving Hadad and the camels to the care of those whom our host summoned, I followed him as desired to another part of the dwelling. It now seemed spacious enough. After winding about among narrow and dark passages, we at length came to large and well-furnished rooms, apparently quite remote from the shop, and far removed from the street. Here we seated ourselves, and I unfolded to Levi the nature of my business. He listened, wondered, smiled, shook his head, and made a thousand contrary movements and signs. When I had done, he comforted and instructed me after this manner:

"Something like a fool's errand. Yet the pay is good —that cannot be doubted. It had been better, I think, for thee to have followed thy trade in Palmyra or Ctesiphon. Yet perhaps this may turn out well. The promised sum is large. Who can tell? 'Tis worth a risk. Yet if, in taking the risk, one loses his head, it were a mad enterprise. Verily, I can say nothing but that time will disclose it, and the event prove it. A thing is not seen all at once, and the eye cannot at once reach every part of a ball. Wait with patience, and God shall show it."

I saw that nothing was to be got from this prophet. Yet perhaps he knew facts. So I asked him of Hormisdas and Sapor, and if he knew aught of the Roman Piso, held a strict prisoner in Ecbatana.

"A prisoner, say you?" he replied, beginning at the end of my question; "how can a Persian satrap be called a prisoner? He dwells in the palace of Hormisdas, and when seen abroad, rides upon a horse whose harness is jewelled like the prince's; and his dress, moreover, is of the richest stuffs, and altogether Persian. 'Tis forgotten by most that he is any other than a native Persian."

"Is he ever seen to ride alone?" I asked.

"Why the question? I know not. Who should know who rides alone and who in company? When I have seen him, it has always been in the train of others."

"I thought as much. Doubtless he goes abroad well guarded. His companions, Levi, I doubt are little better than jailors?"

Levi opened his eyes, but it was to no purpose; they can see no other thing clearly, save a Persian coin.

I found, upon further inquiry, that it was even as I had supposed and had heard. Calpurnius lives in the palace of Hormisdas, and is his chosen companion and friend, but is allowed by Sapor no liberty of movement, and wherever he goes, is attended by persons appointed to guard him. Nor have the many years that he has been here caused this vigilance in any degree to relax. All outward honour is shown him, except by the king, who, had he not, in the time of Valerian, passed his word to the prince his son, and fully surrendered Piso into his hands, would, it is believed, even now use him as he did the unhappy emperor. But he is safe in the keeping of the prince. And the guard about him, it is my present suspicion, is as much to defend him against any sudden freak of the king or his satellites, as it is to prevent his escape. The least that could happen to any Roman falling into Sapor's power, would be to be flayed alive. My safety will lie in my being known only as a Jew, not as a dweller in Rome.

And now, Roman, thou desirest to know in what manner I mean to accomplish the deliverance of thy brother. It is thus. Commend the cunning of it. My Ethiopian slave is then—I must tell thee to thine amazement—no Ethiopian and no slave! He is one of my own tribe whom I have many times employed in difficult affairs, and having often conferred upon him the most essential favours, have bound him to my will. Him I am to leave in Ecbatana, being first cleansed of the deep dye with which by my art—and what art is it. I am not familiar with?—I have stained his skin to the darkest hue of the African, and then in his place, and stained to the same hue, am I to take thy brother, and so with security, and in broad day, walk through the gates of Ecbatana. Is it to be thought of that I should fail? All will rest with Calpurnius. If, in the first place, he shall be willing to return, and, then, in the next place, shall consent to submit to this momentary and only apparent degradation, the issue is as certain to be happy, as the means shall be tried. My head never sat with a sense of more security upon my shoulders, than now, while planning and putting into execution this Carthaginian plot.

It was first of all necessary that I should become acquainted with the city, with the situation and structure of the palace of Hormisdas, and become known in the streets as one of those way-side merchants whom all abuse, yet whom all are glad to trade with. So, with my slave bending under the burden of those articles of use or luxury which I thought would be most attractive, we set forth into the midst of the busy streets, seeking a market for our commodities. Several days were passed in this manner, returning each night to lodge in the house of the rich and foolish, but hospitable Levi.

While thus employed, I frequently saw Calpurnius, in company with the prince or other nobles, either riding in state through the streets of the city, or else setting out upon excursions of pleasure beyond the walls. But my chief object was to observe well the palace of the prince, and learn the particular part of it inhabited by the Roman, and how and where it was his custom to pass his time. This it was not difficult to do. The palace of the prince I found to occupy a square of the city not far from that of the king his father. It is of vast extent, but of a desolate aspect, from the fewness of its inhabitants and the jealousy with which the prince and all his movements are watched by the wicked and now superannuated Sapor. Every day I diligently paced the streets upon which it stands. I at first went without Hadad, that I might observe with the more leisure. I at length discovered the apartments used by Calpurnius, and learned that it was his custom, when not absent from the palace upon some enterprise of pleasure, to refresh himself by breathing the air, and pacing to and fro upon a gallery of light Persian architecture, and which bordered immediately upon one of the four streets which bounded the palace. This gallery was not so high above the street but what the voice could easily reach those who were walking there, and that without greatly increasing its natural tone. From pillar to pillar there ran along a low latticework of fanciful device, upon which it was the usage of Calpurnius, and those who were with him, often to lean, and idly watch the movements of the passengers below. Here, I found, must be my place of audience. Here I must draw his attention, and make myself known to him. For an opportunity to do this, I saw at once I might be obliged to wait long, for scarce ever was Calpurnius there but Hormisdas, or some one of the nobles, was with him; or if he was alone, yet the street was so thronged that it must be difficult to obtain a hearing.

Having learned these things, I then came forth, with Hadad bearing my merchandise, I myself going before him as owner and crier. Many times did I pass and repass the gallery of Calpurnius, to no purpose—he either not being there, or attended closely by others, or wrapped in thought so that my cries could not arouse him. It was clear to me that I must make some bold attempt. He was one day standing at the lattice-work already named, alone, and looking at the passers by. Seeing him there as I entered the street, I made directly towards the spot, crying in the loudest tone my goods; and notwithstanding the numbers who were on their way along the street, I addressed myself boldly to him, purposely mistaking him for Hormisdas. "Prince," said I, " buy a little, if it please you, of a poor Jew, who has lately traversed the desert to serve you. I have in these panniers wonders from all parts of the world. There is not a city famous for its art in any rare and curious work, that is not represented here. Kings, queens, and princes, have not disdained to purchase of me. The great Sapor at Ctesiphon has of me procured some of his largest diamonds. I have sold to Claudius, and Zenobia, and half the nobility of Palmyra. Dost thou see, prince, the glory of this assortment of diamonds? Look! How would they become thy finger, thy hunting-cap, or thy sandals?"

Thy brother listened to me with unmoved countenance and folded arms, receiving passively whatever I was pleased to say. When I paused, he said, in a tone of sadness, though of affected pleasantry,

"Jew, I am the worst subject for thee in all Ecbatana. I am a man without wants. I do nothing but live, and I have nothing to do to live."

"Now," I replied, "is it time for me to die, having seen the chief wonder of the world—a man without wants."

"There is a greater yet," said he smiling; "thou must live on."

"And what is that?"

"A woman."

"Thou hast me. But I can easily compound with life. I have many wants, yet I love it. I was but a day or two since buried alive under the burning sands of the desert, and lost there a dromedary, worth—if a farthing—four hundred aurelians, for which thou mayest have him. Yet I love to live, and take the chances of the world as they turn up. Here now have I all the way consoled myself with the thought of what I might sell to the great Prince Hormisdas, and thou seest my reward. Still, I cry my goods with the same zeal. But surely thou wantest something! I have jewels from Rome of the latest fashion."

"I want nothing from Rome."

Seeing no one was near, and lowering my voice, I said, "Thou wantest nothing from Rome? What wouldst thou give, Roman, for news from Rome?"

"News from Rome! Not an obolus. How knowest thou me to be a Roman? But now, I was the Prince Hormisdas!"

"I have seen thee many times, and know thee well as the Roman Piso. I have news for thee."

"The prince approaches!" said Piso, in a hurried manner. "Begone, but come again at the hour of dusk, and I shall be alone, and will have thee admitted within the gates of the palace."

The fates ordering it so, I was obliged to depart, and trust again to the future for such chances of renewing my conversation with him as it might have to offer. Here let me tell thee, Lucius Piso, that not having seen thy brother, thou hast never seen a man. He is one with every mark of the noblest manhood. His air is that of a born prince, of the highest bearing, yet free and unrestrained. The beauty of his countenance is beyond that of any other I have yet seen, yet is it a manly beauty. A line of dark short hair covers his upper lip. His eyes are large, dark, and soft in their general expression. He seems of a melancholy and thoughtful temper, and sometimes in his words there is an inexpressible bitterness. Yet it has appeared to me, that his nature is gentle, and that the other character is one accidental or assumed. If I should compare him with any one for beauty, it would be, Roman, not with thee—though I see him and thee to be of the same stock—but with the Princess Julia. Were her beauty only made masculine, she would then be Calpurnius; or were his made feminine, he would then be Julia. But this fancy might not strike others. His features and air are not so much Roman as oriental—thine are purely Roman. It may be that costume alone imparts this eastern aspect to the countenance and the form, for his dress is wholly that of a Persian.

As I passed into the dwelling of my host, entering it as at first by the way of the shop, its owner was holding a conversation of business with some of his customers. How does money seem native to the palm of some men! They have but to open it, and straight it is lined with gold. If they blunder, it is into more wealth. With wit scarce sufficient to make it clear to another that they are properly men, do they manage to make themselves the very chief of all, by reason of the riches they heap up—which ever have claimed and received, and ever will, the homage of the world. Levi is of this sort. The meanness of his understanding words cannot express—or no words but his own. He was talking after this manner as I entered, to one who seemed to hold him in utmost reverence:

"The thing is so—the thing is so. If 'twere otherwise, 'tis most clear it would not be the same. Ha! The price may change. Who can say? The world is full of change. But it cannot be less, and leave a gain to the seller—unless indeed, circumstances altering, the profit should still be the same. But who can understand the future? An hour is more than I can comprehend. He that deals well with the present, is it not he, holy Abraham! who best secures the passing time? It cannot be denied."

As the oracle ended, the Persian bowed low, saying, "The wisdom of it is clearer than the light. I shall so report to the prince." Seeing me, he, in his friendly way, inquired after my success, shaking his head at what he is pleased to regard my mad enterprise. "Better not meddle nor make in such matters. With thy pack upon thy back, and exercising diligence, thou wouldst become rich here in the streets of Ecbatana. And for what else shouldst thou care? 'Tis only money that remains the same in the midst of change. All agree in the value they place upon this, while they agree in nothing else. Who can remember a difference here? Leave thy project, Isaac, which thou must have undertaken half for love, and I will make thee a great man in Ecbatana." Little does he know of Isaac, and thou I believe as little.

No sooner had the god of these idolators gone down to his rest, and the friendly twilight come, than I set forth for the palace of Hormisdas. Upon coming beneath the gallery, I waited not long before thy brother appeared, and pointed out the way in which, through a low and private entrance at a remote spot, I might reach an apartment in which I should find him. Following his directions, I was received, accompanied by Hadad, at the specified place, by a slave of the palace, who conducted me to Piso's presence. It was in one of his more private apartments, but still sumptuously set out with every article of Persian luxury, in which I found myself once more in company with thy brother, and where I ordered Hadad to display for his entertainment the most curious and costly of the contents of his pack.

"I marvel chiefly, Roman," I began by saying, "at the ease with which I obtain an entrance into the palace,

and into thine own apartment. I had thought this to
have been attended with both difficulty and danger."

"It is not without danger," he replied; "thou mayest
lose thy head for this adventure. But this risk I suppose thee to have weighed. Every one in Ecbatana
knows Sapor and me—with what jealousy I am guarded
—and that the king will not flinch to keep his word,
and take off any head that meddles. But fear not. The
king is old and weak, and though cruel as ever, forgets
me, as every thing else. Besides, it is found that I am
so good a Persian, that all strictness in the watch has
long since ceased. Half Ecbatana believe me more a
Persian than a Roman—and in truth they are right."

"Thou hast not, Roman, forgotten thy country!
Surely thou hast not, though suffering captivity, ceased
to love and long for thy native land. The Jew never
forgets his. He lives indeed in every corner and hole
of the earth, but in the hope—'tis this that keeps his
life—either himself or through his children to dwell once
more within the walls of Jerusalem, or among the hills
and valleys of Judea."

"Where we are not loved or remembered, we cannot love," he bitterly replied. "I loved Rome once,
more than I loved parent or kindred. The greatness
and glory of Rome were to me infinitely more than my
own. For her, in my beardless youth, I was ready to
lay down my life at any moment. Nay, when the trial
came, and the good Valerian set forth to redeem the
east from the encroaching power of Persia, I was not
found wanting, but abandoned a home, than which there
was not a prouder or happier within the walls of Rome,
to take my chance with the emperor and my noble
father. The issue thou knowest. How has Rome
remembered me, and the brave legions that with me
fell into the hands of these fierce barbarians? Even
as Gallienus, the son, seemed to rejoice in the captivity
of his parent, so has Rome, the mother, seemed to rejoice in the captivity of her children. Not an arm has
she lifted, not a finger has she moved, to lighten the

chains of our bondage, or rescue us from this thraldom. Rome is no longer my country."

"Consider, Roman," I replied, "in extenuation of thy country's fault, who it was that succeeded the good Valerian—then the brief reign of virtuous Claudius, who died ere a single purpose had time to ripen—and the hard task that has tied the hands of Aurelian, on the borders of Gaul and Germany. Have patience."

"Dost thou not blush, old man," he said, "with that long grey beard of thine, and thy back bent with years, to stand there the apologist of crime? If ingratitude and heartlessness are to be defended, and numbered among the virtues, the reign of Arimanes has indeed begun. Such is not the lesson, Jew, thy sacred books have taught thee. But a truce with this! Thy last words this morning were, that thou hadst news for me. For Roman news I care not, nor will hear. If thou canst tell me aught of family and friends, say on, although—oh gods, that it should be so!—even they seem to share the guilt of all. How many messengers have I bribed with gold, more than thou hast ever seen, Jew, to bear my letters to Rome, and never a word has been returned of good or evil. Canst thou tell me anything of Portia, my mother, or of Lucius Piso, my brother? Live they?"

"Do I not know them well?" I replied: "who that dwells in Rome knows not the noble Portia? She lives yet, and long may she live, the friend of all! To Jew, and even to Nazarene, she is good, even as to her own. Never did age, or want, or helplessness, ask of her in vain. Years have not stopped the fountains of her tears, nor chilled a single affection of her heart; and dost thou think that while she remembers the outcast Jew, and the despised Nazarene, she forgets her own offspring? Where is thy heart, Roman, to suppose it? Have I not heard her many a time, when I have been to solicit alms for some poor unfortunate of my tribe, run back upon the line of years, and speak of the wars of Valerian, of the day when she parted from her great husband and her two sons, and of that dark day, too, when the news came that they were all fast in the clutch of that foul barbarian, Sapor—and stood a silent and astonished witness of a love such as I never saw in any other, and which seemed so great as to be a necessary seed of death to her frail and shattered frame? Of thee, especially, have I heard her descant as mothers will, and tell one after another of all thy beauties, nay and of the virtues, which bound her to thee so, and of her trust, so long cherished, that thou, more than either of her other sons, wouldst live to sustain, and even bear up higher, the name of Piso.''

"My noble mother! Was it so, indeed?"

"How should it be otherwise? Is it any thing, that thou hast not heard from her? Was she to tempt herself the horrors of a Persian journey? Was she, in her age, to seek thee over the sands of Asia? or thy brother? Especially when it was held in Rome not more certain that Valerian was dead, than that thy father and thou wert also. The same messengers related both events. No other news ever came from Ctesiphon. Was not one event as likely as the other? Did not both rest upon the same authority? In the same commemorative acts of the senate were thy name, thy father's, thy brother's, and the emperor's, with others who were also believed to have perished. Was Portia, alone, of all Rome to give the lie to universal fame? As for thy messengers, art thou so foolish as to believe that one ever crossed the desert, or escaped the meshes set for him by the jealous and malignant Sapor?"

"It is enough, Jew—say no more."

"But I have much more to say, or else be false to those who sent me."

"Sent thee! who sent thee? Speak! do Portia, then, and Lucius, know that I live? And art thou here, a messenger from them?"

"It is even so."

Thy brother was greatly moved. At first he made as though he would have embraced me, but turned and paced the room with quick and agitated steps.

I then related to him how we had in Rome first heard through that soldier a rumour of his being yet alive—but at the same time, that he had renounced his country, and become a Persian satrap. I told him of thy faith in him, and of Portia's, that he would never prove a recreant to his country—of thy instant journey to Palmyra, with purpose to cross the desert thyself, and risk all the dangers of Ecbatana to accomplish his deliverance, and of the counsel of Gracchus, which caused thee to make me a substitute.

"Lucius, then," he at length said, approaching me, "is in Palmyra? Is it so?"

"It is," I said; "at least I left him there. He was to remain there, and learn the issue of my attempt. If I perished, or failed in the endeavour to obtain thy freedom, then was it his purpose himself to try—unless in the meantime he should learn through me, or otherwise, that thou wert too wedded to Persia, and to Persian customs, to consent to change them for Rome and Roman ways."

"Jew, thou seest that now I hesitate. Thou hast roused all the son, the brother, and something of the Roman, within me. I am drawn many ways. To Rome I will never return. Towards her a resentment burns deep within, which I know will close only with life itself. But towards Palmyra my heart yearns. 'Twas Zenobia alone, of all the world, that ever moved for the rescue of Valerian: 'twas she alone, of all the world, who pitied our sorrows, and, though she could not heal, revenged them. Her image has been a dear source of consolation in this long captivity. I have eagerly sought for all that could be obtained concerning her character, her acts, her policy, and the state of her affairs. And often have I thought to slip my bonds, and throw myself at her feet, to serve with her, if need should be, either against Rome or Persia. But habit has prevailed, and the generous friendship of Hormisdas, to keep me here. And why should I change this not unpleasing certainty for the doubtful future that must await me in Palmyra? Here, I am in the very lap of luxury. I am, as I have said to thee, a man without wants. All countries, and climates, and seas, and arts, minister to my pleasure. The learning of ancient and of modern times, you see there piled upon shelves, to entertain my leisure, or task my hours of study. I am without care—without the necessity of toil—with a palace, its slaves, and, I may add, its prince, at my command. And beyond all this present reality, there is the prospect of every thing else that Persia contains, upon the death of Sapor, which, in the course of nature, cannot be far off, if violence do not anticipate that hour. Yet what thou now tellest me, renews my desire of change. Lucius is in Palmyra—perhaps he would dwell there. 'Tis the home, I learn, of many noble Romans. Who can say that Portia might not come and complete our happiness?"

And saying these things, he began to muse. He again paced, with folded arms, the long apartment. I saw that he was still distracted by doubts. I knew of but one thing more to say, by which to work upon his passionate nature. I resolved to do it, though I know not what thou wilt say to it, nor what the event may be. There was, thou knowest, ere I left Palmyra, rumour of war between Palmyra and Rome. Barely to name this, it seemed to me, would be on the instant to fix his wavering mind. I could not withstand the temptation. But, Piso once in Palmyra, and sure I am I shall be forgiven. I began again thus:

"Gracchus, too, Roman, dost thou not remember the family of Gracchus! He, also, is in Palmyra."

"Ay, I remember him well. A man of true nobility—now one of the queen's chief advisers, and head of the senate. He had a daughter too, who, her mother dying young, was committed to the care of Portia, and was as a sister. Does she live?—and dwells she in Palmyra?"

"She lives, and beneath her father's roof. Fame speaks loudly of her beauty and her wit, and more loudly still, of her young wisdom, and influence with the queen. Her spirit is the counterpart of Zenobia's. She is, notwithstanding her long Roman nurture, a Palmyrene of the truest stamp. And ever since there have been these rumours of a war with Rome ——"

"What sayst thou! What is that! War with Rome! Did I hear aright?"

"Verily thou didst. 'Twas the current report when I left Palmyra. It came both by the way of Antioch and Alexandria. Nothing was talked of else, ever since, I say."

"Why hast thou not said this before? How shall I believe thee?"

"I said it not before, simply because I thought not of it. How was I to know what thou most desired to hear? I can give thee no other ground of belief than common rumour. If my own opinion will weigh aught, I may add, that for myself I have not a doubt that the report springs from truth. When at Rome, it was commonly spoken of, and by those, too, whom I knew to be near the emperor, that Aurelian felt himself aggrieved and insulted, that a woman should hold under her dominion territories that once belonged to Rome, and who had wrested them from Rome by defeat of Roman generals—and had sworn to restore the empire in the east as well as west, to its ancient bounds. At Palmyra, too, I found those who were of deep intelligence in the politics of the times, who felt sure of nothing more than that, what with the pride of Zenobia and the ambition of Aurelian, war was inevitable. I tell thee these things as they fell upon my ear. Before this, as I think, it is most likely that war may have broken out between the two nations."

"Thou hast now spoken, Jew," said Calpurnius. "Hadst thou said these things at first, thou hadst spared me much tormenting doubt. My mind is now bent and determined upon flight. This it will not be difficult, I think, to accomplish. But what is thy plan? for I suppose, coming upon this errand, thou hast one well digested. But remember, now, as I have already warned thee, that thy head will answer for any failure: detection will be death."

"Death is little to a Jew, who in dying dies for his country. And such would be my death. Whether I live or die, 'tis for Jerusalem. Thy brother rewards me largely for this journey, and these dangers I encounter; and if I perish, the double of the whole sum agreed upon is to be paid according to certain directions left with him. I would rather live; but I shall not shrink from death. But, Piso, detection shall not ensue. I have not lived to this age, to writhe upon a Persian spear, or grin from over a Persian gateway. What I have devised is this. Thou seest my slave Hadad?"

"I see him—an Ethiopian."

"So he seems to thee. But his skin is white as thine. By an art, known only to me, it has been changed to this ebon hue."

"What follows?"

"This follows. Thou art to take his place, thy skin being first made to resemble his, while he is cleansed, and remains in Ecbatana. We then, thou bearing my packages of merchandise, take our way, quietly and in broad daylight, through the gates of Ecbatana. How sayst thou?"

"The invention is perfect. I cannot fear the result. Soon, then, as I shall have made some few preparations, for which to-morrow will suffice, I shall be ready for the desert."

I heard these words with joy. I now called to Hadad to open his cases of jewels, from which I took a seal, having upon it the head of Zenobia, and offered it to Calpurnius. He seized it with eagerness, having never before seen even so much as a drawing of the great queen. I then drew forth thine own ring and gave it him, with that locket containing the hair of Portia, and thy letter. He received them with emotion; and as I engaged myself in repacking my goods, my quick ear caught tears falling upon the sheet as he read.

I then returned to the house of Levi.

Thus have I accomplished, successfully so far, my errand. I write these things to thee, because a caravan leaves Ecbatana in the morning, and may reach Palmyra before ourselves, though it is quite possible that we may overtake and join it. But we may also be delayed for many days. So that it is right, in that case, thou shouldst hear."

* * * *

In these words, my Curtius, you have, for the most part, the letter of Isaac. I have omitted many things which at another time you shall see. They are such as relate chiefly to himself and his faith—abounding in cautions against that heretic, Probus, who haunts his imagination as if he were the very genius of evil.

How can I believe it, that within a few hours I may embrace a brother, separated so long, and so long numbered with the dead? Yet how mixed the pleasure! He returns a brother, but not a Roman. Nay, 'tis the expectation of war with Rome that has gained him. I am perplexed and sad, at the same time that I leap for joy. Fausta cannot conceal her satisfaction, yet she pities me. Gracchus tells us to moderate our feelings and expectations, as the full cup is often spilled. No more now, except this, that you fail not at once to send this letter to Portia. Farewell!

LETTER IX.

SEVERAL days have elapsed since I last wrote, yet Calpurnius is not arrived. I am filled with apprehensions. I fear lest he may have thought too lightly of the difficulties of an escape, and of the strictness with which he is watched; for while he seems to have held it an easy matter to elude the vigilance of his keepers, common opinion at Ecbatana appears to have judged very differently. Yet, after all, I cannot but rely with much confidence upon the discretion and the cunning of Isaac. I must now relate what has happened in the mean time.

It was the morning after Isaac's letter had been received and read, that Milo presented himself, with a countenance and manner indicative of some inward disturbance.

"And what," I asked, "may be the matter?"

"Enough is the matter, both for yourself and me," he replied. "Here now has been a wretch of an Arab, a fellow of no appearance, a mere camel-driver, desiring to see you. I told him flatly that you were not to be seen by scum such as he. I advised him to be gone, before he might have to complain of a broken head; and what do you suppose was the burden of his errand? Why, truly, to ask of the most noble Piso concerning his wife and child! I begged him to consider whether, supposing you did know aught concerning them, you would deign to communicate with a sun-baked beggar of the desert like he? Whereupon, he raised a lance longer than a mast, and would have run me through, but for the expertness with which I seized and wrested it from him, and then broke it over his head. 'Twas the same scowling knave whose camels choked the street the first day we entered the city, and who sent his curse after us. Hassan is his name. His eye left a mark on me that's not out yet. A hyena's is nothing to it."

Thus did he run on. I could have speared him as willingly as Hassan. It was plain that the husband of the woman found in the desert by Isaac, hearing a rumour of intelligence received by me, had been to obtain such information as possibly I might possess of his wife and child. Upon asking my slave where the camel-driver now was, he replied, that "Truly he did not know; he had been driven from the courtyard with blows, and it was a mercy that his life was left to him. He had been taught how again to curse Romans."

It was in vain that I assured him once and again that he was no longer in the service of an emperor, and that it was unnecessary to treat me with quite so much deference; his only regret was that the robber had got off so easily. As the only reparation in my power for such stupidity and inhumanity, I ordered Milo instantly to set forth in search of Hassan, in the quarter of the city which the Arabs chiefly frequent, and, finding him, to bring him to the house of Gracchus, for I had news for him. This was little relished by Milo, and I could see, by the change of his countenance, that his cowardly soul was ill inclined to an encounter with the insulted Arab, in the remote parts of the city, and unaccompanied by any of the slaves of the palace. Nevertheless, he started upon his mission—but, as I afterwards learned, bribed Hannibal to act as life-guard.

Thinking that I might possibly fall in with him myself, and desirous, moreover, of an occupation that should cause me to forget Calpurnius and my anxieties for a season, I went forth also, taking the paths that first offered themselves. A sort of instinct drew me, as it almost always does, to one of the principal streets of the city, denominated, from the size and beauty of the trees which adorn it, the Street of Palms. This is an avenue which traverses the city in its whole length; and at equal distances from its centre, and also running its whole length, there shoots up a double row of palms, which, far above the roofs of the highest buildings, spread out their broad and massy tufts of leaves, and perfectly protect the throngs below from the rays of the blazing sun. Thus a deep shadow is cast upon the floor of the street, while, at the same time, it is unencumbered by the low branches, which on every other kind of tree stretch out in all directions, and obstruct the view, taking away a greater beauty and advantage than they give. This palm is not the date-bearing species, but of another sort, attaining a loftier growth, and adorned with a larger leaf. A pity, truly, it is, that Rome cannot crown itself with this princely diadem; but even though the bitter blasts from the Appenines did not prevent, a want of taste for what is beautiful would. The Roman is a coarse form of humanity, Curtius, compared with either the Greek or the Palmyrene.

Romans will best conquer the world, or defend it, but its adorning should be left to others. Their hands are rude, and they but spoil what they touch. Since the days of Cicero, and the death of the republic, what has Rome done to advance any cause, save that of slavery and licentiousness? A moral Hercules is needed to sweep it clean of corruptions, which it is amazing have not ere this drawn down the thunder of the gods. Julia would say that Christ is that Hercules. May it be so!

Along the street which I had thus entered, I slowly sauntered, observing the people who thronged it, and the shops with their varieties which lined it. I could easily gather, from the conversation which now and then fell upon my ear—sometimes as I mingled with those who were observing a fine piece of sculpture, or a new picture, exposed for sale, or examining the articles which some hawker, with much vociferation, thrust upon the attention of those who were passing along, or waiting at a fountain, while slaves in attendance served round in vessels of glass, water cooled with snow, and flavoured with the juice of fruits peculiar to the east—that the arrival of the ambassadors had caused a great excitement among the people, and had turned all thoughts into one channel. Frequently were they gathered together in groups, around some of the larger trees, or at the corners of the streets, or at the entrance of some conspicuous shop, to listen to the news which one had to tell, or to arguments upon the all-engrossing theme with which another sought to bring over those who would listen to one or another side of the great question. But I must confess, that but in a very few instances the question was no question at all, and had but one side. Those whom I heard, and who were listened to by any numbers, and with any patience, were zealous patriots, inveighing bitterly against the ambition and tyranny of Rome, and prognosticating national degradation, and ruin, and slavery, if once the policy of concession to her demands was adopted.

"Palmyra," they said, "with Zenobia and Longinus

at her head, the deserts around her, and Persia to back her, might fearlessly stand against Rome and the world. Empire began in the east: it had only wandered for a while to the west—losing its way. The east was its native seat, and there it would return. Why should not Palmyra be what Assyria and Persia once were? What kingdom of the world, and what age, could ever boast a general like Zabdas, a minister like Longinus, a queen like the great Zenobia?" At such flights, the air would resound with the plaudits of the listening crowd, who would then disperse and pursue their affairs, or presently gather around some new declaimer.

I was greatly moved, on several of these occasions, to make a few statements in reply to some of the orators, and which might possibly have let a little light upon minds willing to know the truth; but I doubted whether even the proverbially good-natured and courteous Palmyrenes might not take umbrage at it. As I turned from one of these little knots of politicians, I encountered Otho, a nobleman of Palmyra, and one of the queen's council. "I was just asking myself," said I, saluting him, "whether the temper of your people, even and forbearing as it is, would allow a Roman in their own city to harangue them, who should not so much advocate a side as aim to impart truth."

"Genuine Palmyrenes," he answered, "would listen with patience and civility. But in a crowded street one can never answer for his audience. You see here not only Palmyrenes, but strangers from all parts of the east—people from our conquered provinces and dependencies, who feel politically with the Palmyrene, but yet have not the manners of the Palmyrene. There is an Armenian, there a Saracen, there an Arab, there a Cappadocian, there a Jew, and there an Egyptian—all politically, perhaps, with us, but otherwise, a part of us not more than the Ethiopian or Scythian. The senate of Palmyra would hear all you might say, or the queen's council—but not the street, I fear. Nay, one of these idle boys, but whose patriotism is ever boiling over, might, in his zeal and his ignorance, do that which should bring disgrace upon our good city. I should rather pray you to forbear. But if you will extend your walk to the Portico which I have just left, you will there find a more select crowd than jostles us where we stand, and perhaps, ears ready to hear you. All that you may say to divert the heart of the nation from this mad enterprise, I shall be most grateful for. But any words which you may speak, or which a present god might utter, would avail no more against the reigning phrensy, than would a palm leaf against a whirlwind of the desert."

As he uttered these words, with a voice somewhat elevated, several had gathered about us, listening with eagerness to what the noble and respected Otho had to say. They heard him attentively, shook their heads, and turned away, some saying, "He is a good man, but timid." Others scrupled not to impute to him a "Roman bearing." When he had ended, seeing that a number had pressed around, he hastily wished me a happy day, and moved down the street. I bent my way towards the Portico, ruminating the while upon the fates of empire.

I soon reached that magnificent structure, with its endless lines of columns. More than the usual crowd of talkers, idlers, strangers, buyers and sellers, thronged its ample pavements. One portion of it seems to be appropriated, at least abandoned, to those who have aught that is rare and beautiful to dispose of. Around one column stands a Jew with antiquities raked from the ruins of Babylon or Thebes—displaying their coins, their mutilated statuary, or half legible inscriptions. At another, you see a Greek with some masterpiece of Zeuxis—nobody less—which he swears is genuine, and to his oaths added a parchment containing its history, with names of men in Athens, Antioch, and Alexandria, who attest it all. At the foot of another, sits a dealer in manuscripts, remarkable either as being the complete works of distinguished authors, or for the perfection of the art of the copyist, or for their great antiquity. Here were Manetho and Sanchoniathon to be had, perfect and complete! Not far from these stood others, who offered statuary ancient and modern—vases of every beautiful form, from those of Egypt and Etruria, to the freshly-wrought ones of our own Demetrius—and jewellery of the most rare and costly kind. There is scarce an article of taste, or valuable of any sort whatever, but may be found here, brought from all parts of the world. In Persian, Indian, and Chinese rarities—and which in Rome are rarities indeed—I have dealt largely, and shall return with much to show you.

When, with some toil, I had won a passage through this busy mart, I mingled with a different crowd. I passed from buyers and sellers among those who were, like myself, brought there merely for the purpose of seeing others, of passing the time, and observing the beautiful effects of this interminable Portico, with its moving and changing crowds, robed in a thousand varieties of the richest costume. It was indeed a spectacle of beauty, such as I never had seen before, or elsewhere. I chose out point after point, and stood a silent and rapt observer of the scene. Of the view from one of these points, I have purchased a painting, done with exquisite skill, which I shall send to you, and which will set before you almost the living reality.

To this part of the Portico those resort who wish to hear the opinions of the day upon subjects of politics or literature, or philosophy, or to disseminate their own. He who cherishes a darling theory upon any branch of knowledge, and would promulgate it, let him come here, and he will find hearers at least. As I walked along, I was attracted by a voice declaiming with much earnestness to a crowd of hearers, and who seemed as I drew near to listen with attention, some being seated upon low blocks of marble, arranged among the columns of the Portico for this purpose, others leaning against the columns themselves, and others standing on the outside of the circle. The philosopher—for such I perceived him at once to be—was evidently a Greek. He was arrayed in a fashionable garb, with a robe much like our toga, thrown over his shoulders, and which he made great use of in his gesticulations. A heavy chain of gold wound around his neck, and then, crossing several times his breast, hung down in artificially arranged festoons. A general air of effeminacy produced in the hearer at once a state of mind not very favourably disposed to receive his opinions. The first words I caught were these: " In this manner," said he, " did that wonderful genius interpret the universe. 'Tis not credible that any but children and slaves should judge differently. Was there once nothing? Then were there nothing now. But there is something now. We see it. The world is. Then it has always been. It is an eternal Being. It is infinite. Ha! can you escape me now? Say, can there be two infinites? Then where are your gods? The fabled creator or creators —be they many or one—of the universe? Vanished, I fancy at the touch of my intellectual wand, into thin air. Congratulate yourselves upon your freedom. The Egyptians had gods, and you know what they were. The Greeks had gods, and you know what they were. Those nations grovelled and writhed under their partly childish, partly terrific, and partly disgusting, superstitions. Happy that the reality of divine natures can, so easily as I have now done it, be disproved! The superincumbent gloom is dispersed. Light has broken through. And so, too, touching the immortality of the soul. Immortality of the soul! Did any one of you ever see a soul? I should like to have that question answered;"—he swung defyingly his robe and paused —" did any one ever see a soul! Yes, and that it was immortal, too! You see a body, and therefore you believe in it. You see that it is mortal, and therefore you believe in its mortality. You do not see the soul —therefore you believe in one. Is that your reasoning? How plain the argument is! When the god or gods—

suppose their being—shall send down and impart to me the astounding fact that I am not one, as I seem, but two—am not mortal as I seem, but immortal—do not melt into dust at death, but rise in spirit—then will I believe such things, not otherwise. Have we knowledge of any other existences—elemental existences—than corporeal atoms? None. These constitute the human being. Death is their separation, and that separation means the end of the being they did once constitute. But it may all be summed up in a word. When you can see and touch your own soul, as you do see and touch your body, believe in it. Deny and reject this principle, and the world will continue to suffer from its belief in gorgons, demons, spectres, gods, and monsters —in Tartarean regions and torments of damned spirits. Adopt it, and life flows undisturbed by visionary fears, and death comes as a long and welcome sleep, upon which no terrors and no dreams intrude."

Such was the doctrine, and such nearly the language, of the follower of Epicurus. You will easily judge how far he misrepresented the opinions of that philosopher. As I turned away from this mischievous dealer in Cimmerian darkness, I inquired of one who stood near me, who this great man might be?

"What!" said he in reply, "do you not know Critias, the Epicurean? You must be a stranger in Palmyra. Do you not see, by the quality of his audience, that he leads away with him all the fine spirits of the city? Observe how the greater number of those who hang upon his lips resemble in their dress and air, the philosopher."

"I see it is so. It seems as if all the profligates and young rakes of Palmyra, of the nobler sort, were assembled here to receive some new lessons in the art of self-destruction."

"Many a philosopher of old would, I believe," he rejoined, "have prayed that his system might perish with himself, could he have looked forward into futurity, and known how it would be interpreted and set forth by his followers. The temperate and virtuous Epicurus little thought that his name and doctrine would in after times be the rallying point for the licentious and dissolute. His philosophy was crude enough, and mischievous, I grant, in its principles and tendencies. But it was promulgated, I am sure, with honest intentions, and he himself was not aware of its extreme liability to misapprehension and perversion. How would his ears tingle at what we have now heard!"

"And would, after all, deserve it," I replied. "For he, it seems to me, is too ignorant of human nature, to venture upon the office of teacher of mankind, who believes that the reality of a superintending providence can be denied, with safety to the world. A glance at history, and the slightest penetration into human character, would have shown him, that atheism, in any of its forms, is incompatible with the existence of a social state."

"What you say is very true," replied the Palmyrene; "I defend only the intentions and personal character of Epicurus, not his real fitness for his office. This Critias, were it not for the odiousness of any interference with men's opinions, I should like to see driven from our city back to his native Athens. Listen, now, as he lays down the method of a happy life. See how these young idlers drink in the nectarean stream. But enough. I leave them in their own stye. Farewell! Pray invite the philosopher to visit you at Rome. We can spare him."

Saying this, he turned upon his heel, and went his way. I also passed on. Continuing my walk up the Portico, I perceived at a little distance, another dark mass of persons, apparently listening with profound attention to one who was addressing them. Hoping to hear some one discoursing upon the condition of the country and its prospects, I joined the circle. But I was disappointed. The orator was a follower of Plato, and a teacher of his philosophy. His aim seemed to be to darken the minds of his hearers by unintelligible refinements, at least such I thought the effect must be. He clothed his thoughts—if thoughts there really were any—in such a many-coloured cloud of poetic diction, that the mind, while it was undoubtedly excited, received not a single clear idea, but was left in a pleasing, half bewildered, state, with visions of beautiful divine truth floating before it, which it in vain attempted to arrest, and convert to reality. All was obscure, shadowy, impalpable. Yet was he heard with every testimony of reverence, on the part of his audience. They evidently thought him original and profound, in proportion as he was incomprehensible. I could not help calling to mind the remark of the Palmyrene who had just parted from me. It is difficult to believe that Plato himself laboured to be obscure, though some affirm it. I would rather believe that his great mind, always searching after truth at the greatest heights and lowest depths, often but partially seized it, being defeated by its very vastness; yet, ambitious to reveal it to mankind, he hesitated not to exhibit it in the form, and with the completeness, he best could. It was necessary, therefore, that what he but half knew himself, should be imperfectly and darkly stated, and dimly comprehended by others. For this reason, his writings are obscure—obscure, not because of truths for their vastness beyond the reach of our minds, but because they abound in conceptions but half formed—in inconsequential reasonings—in logic overlaid and buried beneath a poetic phraseology. They will always be obscure, in spite of the labours of the commentators; or, a commentary can make them plain, only by substituting the sense of the critic for the no-sense of the original. But Plato did not aim at darkness. And could his spirit have listened to the jargon which I had just heard proclaimed as Platonism, consisting of common-place thoughts, laboriously tortured and involved, till their true semblance was lost, and instead of them a wordy mist—glowing indeed, oftentimes, with rainbow-colours—was presented to the mind of the hearer, for him to feed upon, he would at the moment have as heartily despised, as he had formerly gloried in, the name and office of philosopher.

I waited not to learn the results at which this great master of wisdom would arrive, but quickly turned away, and advanced still farther towards the upper termination of the Portico. The numbers of those who frequented this vast pile diminished sensibly at this part of it. Nevertheless, many were still like myself wandering listlessly around. Quite at the extremity of the building, I observed, however, a larger collection than I had noticed before; and, as it appeared to me, deeply absorbed by what they heard. I cared not to make one of them, having had enough of philosophy for the day. But as I stood not far from them, idly watching the labours of the workmen who were carrying up the column of Aurelian—noting how one laid the stone which another brought, and how another bore along and up the dizzy ladders the mortar which others tempered, and how the larger masses of marble were raised to their places by machines worked by elephants, and how all went on in an exact order—while I stood thus, the voice of the speaker frequently fell upon my ear, and at last, by its peculiarity, and especially by the unwonted earnestness of the tone, drew me away to a position nearer the listening crowd. By the words which I now distinctly caught, I discovered that it was a Christian who was speaking. I joined the outer circle of hearers, but the preacher—for so the Christians term those who declare their doctrines in public—was concealed from me by a column. I could hear him distinctly, and I could see the faces, with their expressions, of those whom he addressed. The greater part manifested the deepest interest and sympathy with him who addressed them, but upon the countenances of some sat scorn and contempt—ridicule, doubt, and disbelief. As the voice fell upon my ear, in this my nearer position, I was startled. "Surely," I said, "I have heard it before, and yet as surely I never before heard a Christian preach." The thought of Probus flashed across my mind; and suddenly changing my place—and by passing round the assembly, coming in front of the preacher—I at once recognised the pale and melancholy features of the afflicted Christian. I was surprised and delighted. He had convinced me, at the few interviews I had had with him, that he was no common man, and I had determined to obtain from him, if I should ever meet him again, all necessary knowledge of the Christian institutions and doctrine. Although I had learned much, in the mean time, from both Julia and the hermit, still there was much left which I felt I could obtain, probably in a more exact manner, from Probus. I was rejoiced to see him. He was evidently drawing to the close of his address. The words which I first caught were nearly these.

"Thus have I declared to you, Palmyrenes, Romans, and whoever are here, how Christianity seeks the happiness of man, by securing his virtue. Its object is your greater well-being through the truths it publishes and enforces. It comes to your understandings, not to darken and confound them, by words without meaning, but to shed light upon them, by a revelation of those few sublime doctrines of which I have now discoursed to you. Has the Greek, the Roman, or the Persian philosophy, furnished your minds with truths like these? Has life a great object, or death an issue of certainty and joy, under either of those systems of faith? Systems of faith! I blush to term them so. I am a Roman, the son of a priest of the temple of Jupiter. Shall I reveal to you the greater and the lesser mysteries of that worship? I see by most expressive signs that it cannot be needful. Why, then, if ye yourselves know and despise the popular worship, why will you not consider the claims of Jesus of Nazareth?"

"I despise it not," cried a voice from the throng; "I honour it."

"In every nation," continued the preacher, "and

among all worshippers, are there those whom God will accept. The sincere offering of the heart will never be refused. Socrates, toiling and dying in the cause of truth—though that truth, in the light of the gospel, were error—is beloved of God. But if God has in these latter days announced new truth, if he has sent a special messenger to teach it, or if it be asserted by persons of intelligence and apparent honesty, that he has, ought not every sincere lover of truth and of God, or the gods, to inquire diligently whether it be so or not? Socrates would have done so. Search, men of Palmyra, into the certainty of these things. These many years has the word of Christ been preached in your streets, yet how few followers can as yet be counted of him who came to bless you! Sleep no longer. Close not the ear against the parent voice of the gospel. Fear not that the religion of Jesus comes to reign over aught but your hearts. It asks no dominion over your temporal affairs. It cares not for thrones, or the sword, or princely revenues, or seats of honour. It would serve you, not rule over you. And the ministers of Christ are your servants in spiritual things, seeking not yours, but you."

"Paul! Paul of Antioch!" shouted several voices at once.

"I defend not Paul of Antioch," cried Probus, no ways disconcerted. "Judge Christianity, I pray you, not by me, or by Paul, but by itself. Because a fool lectures upon the philosophy of Plato, you do not therefore condemn Plato for a fool. Because a disciple of Zeno lives luxuriously, you do not, for that, take up a judgment against the philosopher himself. Paul of Samosata, not in his doctrine, but in his life, is an alien, a foreigner, an adversary, and no friend or servant of Jesus. Listen, citizens of Palmyra, while I read to you what the founder of Christianity himself says touching this matter;" and he drew from beneath his robe a small parchment roll, and turning to the page he sought, read in a loud voice words of Jesus such as these: "'He that is greatest among you shall be your servant. Whosoever shall exalt himself shall be abased, and he that shall humble himself shall be exalted.' This is the doctrine of Christ. According to Jesus, 'he among his disciples is greatest, who performs for others the most essential service.'" He then turned to another part of the book, and read a long, and, as it struck me, beautiful passage, in which the author of Christianity was represented as stooping and washing the feet of his disciples, to enforce, in a more lively way, his doctrine of humility and philanthropy. When he had finished it, a deep silence had fallen upon those who listened. It was broken by the voice of Probus once more saying, in low and sorrowful tones, "I confess—with grief and shame, I confess—that pride, and arrogance, and the lust of power, are already among the ministers of Jesus. They are sundering themselves from their master, and thrusting a sword into the life of his gospel. And if this faith of Christ should ever—as a prophetic eye sees it is sure to do—fill the throne of the world, and sit in Cæsar's place, may the God who gave it appear for it, that it perish not through the encumbering weight of earthly glory. Through tribulation and persecution it has held on its way without swerving. Prosperity begins already to weaken and defile ——"

What more Probus would have added, I know not; but at this point, an unusual disturbance arose in the streets. Trumpets sent forth their long peal, and a troop of out-riders, as accompanying some great personage, rode rapidly along, followed by the crowd of idle lookers-on. And immediately a chariot appeared, with a single individual seated in it, and who seemed to take great pleasure in his own state. No sooner had the pageant arrived over against that part of the Portico where we stood, than one and another of Probus's hearers exclaimed,

"Ha! Paul! Paul of Antioch! Behold a Christian servant!" And the whole throng turned away in confusion, to watch the spectacle.

"An unhappy commentary upon the doctrine," said a Palmyrene to me, as he turned sneeringly away.

"What say you to this?" asked another of Probus himself, as he descended from his rostrum, and stood gazing with the rest, but with a burning cheek and downcast eye.

"I say," he replied, "what I have said before, that yonder bishop, however christianised his head may be, is a misbeliever in his heart. He is a true anti-Christ."

"I am disposed to trust you," rejoined the other. "I have heard you not without emotion. We have had among us many who have declared the doctrine of Christ, but I have heeded them not. It is different with me now. I am desirous to know what this doctrine of Christ is. I have been impressed by what you recited from the writings of Jesus. How, Christian, shall I apply myself, and where, to learn more than I know now?"

"If thou wilt learn of so humble a teacher as I am —who yet know somewhat of what Christianity really is—come and hear me at the place of Christian worship in the street that runs behind the great Persian Inn. There, this evening, when the sun is down, shall I preach again the truth in Christ."

"I shall not fail to be there," said the other, and moved away.

"Nor shall I, Probus," said I, heartily saluting him.

"Noble Piso!" he cried, his countenance suddenly growing bright as the sun, "I am glad to meet you at length. And have you, too, heard a Christian preach? —a senator of Rome?"

"I have, and shall gladly hear more. I am not however a Christian, Probus; I profess to be but a seeker after truth, if perhaps it may be found in your faith, having failed to discover it among dead or living philosophers. I shall hear you to-night."

After many mutual inquiries concerning each other's welfare, we separated.

Upon returning to the house of Gracchus, and finding

myself again in the company of Fausta and her father, I said, "I go to-night to hear a Christian—the Christian Probus—discourse concerning the Christian doctrine. Will you accompany me, Fausta?"

"Not now, Lucius," she replied; "my head and heart are too full of the interests and cares of Zenobia, to allow me to think of aught else. No other reason, I assure you, prevents. I have no fears of the opinions of others to hinder me. When our public affairs are once more in a settled state, I shall not be slow to learn more of the religion of which you speak. Julia's attachment to it, of itself, has almost made a convert of me already, so full of sympathy in all things is a true affection. But the heart is a poor logician. It darts to its object, overleaping all reasons, and may as well rest in error as truth. Whatever the purity of Julia and the honesty and vigour of Zenobia accept and worship, I believe I should, without further investigation, though they were the fooleries and gods of Egypt. Did you succeed in your search of the Arab?"

"No; but perhaps Milo has. To tell the truth, I was soon diverted from that object, first by the excitement I found prevailing among the people on the affairs of the kingdom, and afterwards by the spectacles of the Portico, and the preaching of Probus, whom I encountered there."

In the evening, soon as the sun was set, I wound my way to the Christians' place of worship.

It was in a part of the city remote and obscure, indicating, very plainly, that whatever Christianity may be destined to accomplish in this city, it has done little as yet. Indeed, I do not as yet perceive what principle of strength or power it possesses, sufficient to force its way through the world, and into the hearts of men. It allows not the use of the sword; it resorts not to the civil arm; it is devoid of all that should win upon the senses of the multitude, being, beyond all other forms of faith, remarkable for its simplicity, for its spiritual and intellectual character. Moreover, it is stern and uncompromising in its morality, requiring the strictest purity of life, and making virtue to consist not in the outward act, but in the secret motive which prompts the act. It is at open and unintermitting war with all the vain and vicious inclinations of the heart. It insists upon an undivided sovereignty over the whole character and life of the individual. And in return for such surrender, it bestows no other reward than an inward consciousness of right action, and of the approbation of God, with the hope of immortality. It seems thus to have man's whole nature, and all the institutions of the world, especially of other existing religions, to contend with. If it prevail against such odds, and with such means as it alone employs, it surely will carry along with it its own demonstration of its divinity. But how it shall have power to achieve such conquests, I now cannot see, nor conjecture.

Arriving at the place designated by Probus, I found a low building of stone, which seemed to have been diverted from former uses of a different kind, to serve its present purpose as a temple of religious worship. Passing through a door, of height scarce sufficient to admit a person of ordinary stature, I reached a vestibule, from which, by a descent of a few steps, I entered a large circular apartment, low but not inelegant, with a vaulted ceiling, supported by chaste Ionic columns. The assembly was already seated, but the worship not begun. The service consisted of prayers to God, offered in the name of Christ—of reading a portion of the sacred books of the Christians, of preaching, of music sung to religious words, and voluntary offerings of money, or other gifts, for the poor.

I cannot doubt that you are repelled, my Curtius, by this account of a worship of such simplicity as to amount almost to poverty. But I must tell you that never have I been so overwhelmed by emotions of the noblest kind, as when sitting in the midst of these despised Nazarenes, and joining in their devotions; for to sit neuter in such a scene, it was not in my nature to do, nor would it have been in yours, much as you affect to despise this " superstitious race." This was indeed worship. It was a true communion of the creature with the Creator. Never before had I heard a prayer. How different from the loud and declamatory harangues of our priests! The full and rich tones of the voice of Probus, expressive of deepest reverence of the Being he addressed, and of profoundest humility on the part of the worshipper, seeming, too, as if uttered in no part by the usual organs of speech, but as if pronounced by the very heart itself, fell upon the charmed ear like notes from another world. There was a new and strange union, both in the manner of the Christian, and in the sentiments he expressed, of an awe such as I never before witnessed in man towards the gods, and a familiarity and child-like confidence, that made me feel as if the God to whom he prayed was a father and a friend, in a much higher sense than we are accustomed to regard the Creator of the universe. It was a child soliciting mercies from a kind and considerate parent—conscious of much frailty and ill desert, but relying, too, with a perfect trust, both upon the equity and benignity of the God of his faith. I received an impression, too, from the quiet and breathless silence of the apartment, from the low and but just audible voice of the preacher, of the near neighbourhood of gods and men—of the universal presence of the infinite spirit of the Deity—which certainly I had never received before. I could hardly divest myself of the feeling that the God addressed, was, in truth, in the midst of the temple; and I found my eye turning to the ceiling, as if there must be some visible manifestation of his presence. I wish you could have been there. I am sure that after witnessing such devotions, contempt or ridicule would be the last emotions you would ever entertain towards this people. Neither could you any longer apply to them the terms fanatic, enthusiast, or superstitious. You would have seen a calmness, a sobriety, a decency, so remarkable; you would have heard sentiments so rational, so instructive, so exalted, that you would have felt your prejudices breaking away and disappearing, without any volition or act of your own. Nay, against your will, they would have fallen; and nothing would have been left but the naked question—not is this faith beautiful and worthy, but is this religion true or false?

When the worship had been begun by prayer to God, in the name of Christ, then one of the officiating priests opened the book of the Christians, the gospels, and read from the Greek in which they are written—changing it into the Palmyrene dialect, as he read—divers passages, some relating to the life of Jesus, and others being extracts of letters written by apostles of his to individuals or churches, to which I listened with attention and pleasure. When this was over, Probus rose, standing upon a low platform, like the rostrums from which our lawyers plead, and first reading a sentence from the sayings of Paul, an apostle of Jesus, of which this was the substance, " Jesus came into the world, bringing life and immortality to light," he delivered, with a most winning and persuasive beauty, a discourse, or oration, the purpose of which was to show, that Jesus was sent into the world to bring to light or make plain the true character and end of the life on earth, and also the reality and true nature of a future existence. In doing this, he exposed—but in a manner so full of the most earnest humanity, that no one could be offended—the errors of many of the philosophers concerning a happy life, and compared, with the greatest force, their requisitions with those of the gospel, as he termed his religion; showing what unworthy and inadequate conceptions had prevailed, as to what constitutes a man truly great, and good, and happy. Then he went on to show, that it was such a life only as he had described, that could make a being like man worthy of immortality —that although Jesus had proved the reality of a future and immortal existence, yet he had, with even more importunity, and earnestness, and frequency, laid down his precepts touching a virtuous life on earth. He finally went into the Christian argument in proof of a future existence, and exhorted those who heard him, and who desired to inhabit the Christian's heaven, to live the life which Christ had brought to light, and himself had exemplified, on earth, labouring to impress their minds with the fact, that it was a superior goodness which made Jesus what he was, and that it must be by a similar goodness that his followers could fit themselves for the immortality he had revealed. All this was with frequent reference to existing opinions and practices, and with large illustrations drawn from ancient and modern religious history.

What struck me most, after having listened to the discourse of Probus to the end, was the practical aim and character of the religion he preached. It was no fanciful speculation or airy dream. It was not a plaything of the imagination he had been holding up to our contemplation, but a series of truths and doctrines, bearing with eminent directness, and with a perfect adaptation, upon human life, the effect and issue of which, widely and cordially received, must be to give birth to a condition of humanity not now any where to be found on the earth. I was startled by no confounding and overwhelming mysteries; neither my faith nor my reason was burdened or offended; but I was shown, as by a light from heaven, how truly the path which leads to the possession and enjoyment of a future existence, coincides with that which conducts to the best happiness of earth. It was a religion addressed to the reason and the affections; and evidence enough was afforded in the representations given of its more important truths, that it was furnished with ample power to convince and exalt the reason, to satisfy and fill the affections. No sooner shall I have returned to the leisure of my home, to my study and my books, than I shall seriously undertake an examination of the Christian argument. It surely becomes those who fill the place in the social state which I do, to make up an intelligent judgment upon questions like this, so that I may stand prepared to defend it, and urge it upon my countrymen, if I am convinced of its truth, and of its advantage to my country, or assail and oppose it, if I shall determine it to be, what it is so frequently termed, a pernicious and hateful superstition.

When the discourse was ended, of the power and various beauty of which I cannot pretend properly to acquaint you, another prayer, longer and more general, was offered, to parts of which there were responses by the hearers. Then, as a regular part of the service, voluntary offerings and gifts were made by those present for the poor. More than once, as a part of the worship, hymns were sung to some plain and simple air, in which all the assembly joined. Sometimes, to the services which I witnessed, Probus informed me there is added a further ceremony, called the "Lord's Supper," being a social service, during which bread and wine are partaken of, in memory of Jesus Christ. This was the occasion, in former times, of heavy charges against the Christians, of rioting and intemperance, and even of more serious crimes. But Probus assures me that they were even then utterly groundless, and that now nothing can be more blameless than this simple spiritual repast.

The worship being ended, and Probus having descended from his seat, I accosted him, giving him what I am certain were very sincere thanks for the information I had obtained from his oration, concerning the primary articles of the Christian faith.

"It has been," said he in reply, "with utmost satisfaction, that I beheld a person of your rank and intelligence among my hearers. The change of the popular belief throughout the Roman empire, which must come, will be a less tumultuous one, in proportion as we can obtain even so much as a hearing from those who sit at the head of society in rank and intelligence. Let me make a sincere convert of a Roman emperor, and in a few years the temples of paganism would lie even with the ground. Believe me, Christianity has penetrated deeper and farther than you in the seats of power dream of. While you are satisfied with things as they are, and are content to live on and enjoy the leisure and honours the gods crown you with, the classes below you, less absorbed by the things of the world, because perhaps having fewer of them, give their thoughts to religion, and the prospects which it holds out of a happier existence after the present. Having little here, they are less tied to the world than others, and more solicitous concerning the more, and the better, of which Christianity speaks."

"I am not insensible," I replied, "to the truth of what you say. The cruelties, moreover, exercised by the emperors towards the Christians, the countless examples of those who have died in torments for the truth of this religion, have drawn largely and deeply upon the sympathy of the general heart, and disposed it favourably towards belief. In Rome, surrounded by ancient associations, embosomed in a family remarkable for its attachment to the ancient order of things—friends of power, of letters, and philosophy, I hardly was conscious of the existence of such a thing as Christianity. The name was never heard where I moved. Portia, my noble mother, with a heart beating warm for every thing human, instinctively religious beyond any whom I have ever seen or known of the Christian or any other faith, living but to increase the happiness of all around her, was yet—shall I say it?—a bigot to the institutions of her country. The government and the religion under which all the Pisos had lived and flourished, which had protected the rights and nursed the virtues of her great husband and his family, were good enough for her, for her children, and for all. Her ear was closed against the sound of Christianity, as naturally as an adder's against all sound. She could not, and never did hear it. From her I received my principles and first impressions. Not even the history, nor so much as a word, of the sufferings of the Christians, ever fell on my car. I grew up in all things a Piso—the true child of my mother—in all save her divine virtues. And it was not till a few years since I broke loose from domestic and Roman life, and travelled to Greece and Egypt, and now to the east, that I became practically aware of the existence of such a people as the Christians—and my own is, I suppose, but a specimen of the history of my order. I now perceive, that while we have slept, truth has been advancing its posts, till the very citadel of the world is about to be scaled. The leaven of Christianity is cast into the lump, and will work its necessary end. It now, I apprehend, will matter but little what part the noble and the learned shall take, or even the men in power. The people have taken theirs, and the rest must follow, at least submit. Do I over-estimate the inroads of the religion upon the mind and heart of the world?"

"I am persuaded you do not," replied the Christian. "Give me, as I said before, one Roman emperor for a convert, and I will ensure the immediate and final triumph of Christianity. But in the meantime, another Nero, another Domitian, another Decius, may arise, and the bloody acts of other persecutions stain the annals of our guilty empire."

"The gods forbid!" said I; "yet who shall say it may not be! Much as I honour Aurelian for his many virtues, I feel not sure that in the right hands he might not be roused to as dark deeds as any before him—darker they would be—inasmuch as his nature for sternness and severity has not, I think, been equalled. If the mild and just Valerian could be so wrought upon by the malignant Macrianus, what security have we in the case of Aurelian? He is naturally superstitious."

"Oh that in Aurelian," said the Christian, "were lodged the woman's heart of Zenobia!—we then could trust the morrow as well as enjoy to-day. Here no laws seal the lips of the Christian: he may tell his tale to as many as choose to hear. I learn, since my arrival, that the Princess Julia is favourably inclined towards the Christian cause. Dost thou know what the truth may be?"

"It is certain that she admires greatly the character and the doctrine of Christ, and I should think, believes —but she does not as yet openly confess herself a follower of the Nazarene. She is perhaps as much a Christian as Zenobia is a Jewess."

"I may well rejoice in that," replied the Christian— "yes, and do."—The lights of the apartment were now extinguished, and we parted.

If I am ever again in Rome, my Curtius, it shall be my care to bring to your acquaintance and Lucilia's, the Christian Probus. Farewell!

LETTER X.

As I returned from the worship of the Christians to the house of Gracchus, my thoughts wandered from the subjects which had just occupied my mind, to the condition of the country, and the prospect, now growing more and more portentous, of an immediate rupture with Rome. On my way I passed through streets of more than Roman magnificence, exhibiting all the signs of wealth, taste, refinement, and luxury. The happy, light-hearted populace were moving through them, enjoying at their leisure the calm beauty of the evening, or hastening to or from some place of festivity. The earnest tone of conversation, the loud laugh, the witty retort, the merry jest, fell upon my ear from one and another as I passed along. From the windows of the palaces of the merchants and nobles, the rays of innumerable lights streamed across my path, giving to the streets almost the brilliancy of day; and the sound of music, either of martial instruments, or of the harp accompanied by the voice, at every turn arrested my attention, and made me pause to listen.

A deep melancholy overcame me. It seemed to me that the days of this people were numbered, and that

the gods, intending their ruin, had first made them mad.
Their gaiety appeared to me no other than madness.
They were like the gladiators of our circuses, who,
doomed to death, pass the last days of life in a delirium
of forced and frantic joy. Many of the inhabitants I
could not but suppose utterly insensible to the dangers
which impend, or ignorant of them; but more I believe
are cheerful, and even gay, through a mad contempt
of them. They look back upon their long and uninterrupted prosperity—they call to mind their late glorious
achievements under Odenatus and their queen—they
think of the wide extent of their empire—they remember
that Longinus is their minister, and Zenobia still their
queen—and give their fears to the winds. A contest
with Rome, they approach as they would the games of
the amphitheatre.

The situation of their city, defended as it is by the
wide-stretching deserts, is, indeed, enough of itself to
inspire the people with a belief that it is impregnable.
It requires an effort, I am aware, to admit the likelihood of an army from the far west first overcoming the
dangers of the desert, and then levelling the walls of
the city, which seem more like ramparts of nature's
making, so massy are they, than any work of man. And
the Palmyrenes have certainly also some excuse in the
wretched management of our generals, ever since the
expedition of Valerian, and in the brilliancy of their own
achievements, for thinking well of themselves, and anticipating, without much apprehension for the issue, a
war with us. But these and the like apologies, however
they may serve for the common people, surely are of
no force in their application to the intelligent, and such
as fill the high places of the kingdom. They know that
although, upon some mere question of honour or of
boundary, it might be very proper and politic to fight a
single battle rather than tamely submit to an encroachment, it is quite another thing when the only aim of the
war is to see which is the stronger of the two—which
is to be master. This last, what is it but madness?—the

madness of pride and ambition in the queen—in the people the madness of a love and a devotion to her, unparalleled since the world began ? A blindness as of death has seized them all.

Thinking of these things, and full of saddest forebodings as to the fate of this most interesting and polished people, I reached the gate of the palace of Gracchus. The inmates, Gracchus and Fausta, I learned from Milo, were at the palace of the queen, whither I was instructed by them to resort at the request of Zenobia herself. The chariot of my host soon bore me there. It was with pleasure that I greeted this unexpected good fortune. I had not even seen the queen since the day passed at her villa, and I was not a little desirous, before the ambassadors should receive their final answer, to have one more opportunity of conversing with her.

The moment I entered the apartment where the queen was with her guests, I perceived that all state was laid aside, and that we were to enjoy each other with the same social ease as when in the country, or as on that first evening in the gardens of the palace. There was on this occasion no prostration, and no slave crouched at her feet; and all the various Persian ceremonial in which this proud woman so delights, was dispensed with. The room in which we met was vast, and opening on two of its sides upon those lofty Corinthian porticoes, which add so greatly to the magnificence of this palace. Light was so dispersed as to shed a soft and moon-like radiance, which, without dazzling, perfectly revealed every person and object, even to the minutest beauties of the paintings upon the walls, or the statuary that offered to the eye the masterpieces of ancient and modern sculpture. The company was scattered; some being seated together in conversation, others observing the works of art, others pacing the marble floors of the porticoes, their forms crossing and recrossing the ample arched door-ways which opened upon them.

"We feared," said the queen, advancing towards me, as I entered, "that we were not to be so happy as to see you. My other friends have already passed a precious hour with me. But every sacrifice to the affections, be it ever so slight, is a virtue, and therefore you are still an object of praise rather than of censure."

I said in reply that an affair of consequence had detained me, or I should have been earlier at the house of Gracchus, so as to have accompanied Fausta.

Fausta, who had been sitting with the queen, now came forward, Julia leaning on her arm, and said, "And what do you imagine to be the affair of consequence that has deprived us of Piso's company?"

"I cannot tell, indeed," replied Zenobia.

"Julia at least," said Fausta, "will applaud him, when she hears that he has just come from an assembly of Christians. May I ask, Lucius, what new truth you have learned with which to enlighten us? But your countenance tells me I must not jest. There—let me smooth that brow and make my peace. But in seriousness, I hope your Mediterranean friend rewarded you for the hour you have given him, and deprived us of."

"I wish," I could not but reply, "that but one out of every thousand hours of my life had been as well rewarded, and it would not have been so worthless. The princess may believe me when I say that not even the Bishop of Antioch could have done better justice to the Christian argument. I have heard this evening a Christian of the name of Probus, whose history I related—and which you may remember—at the tables, within a few days after my arrival in Palmyra. He is in my opinion a follower of Paul, so I am informed, though not—you, Julia, will be glad to learn it—in his manner of life. What the differences are which separate the Christians from one another in their belief, I know not. I only know that truth cannot take a more winning shape than that in which it came from the lips of Probus, and it was largely supported by the words of the founder of the religion. I think you may justly congratulate your city and your subjects," I continued, addressing Zenobia, " upon the labours and teaching of a man like Probus. The sentiments which he utters are such as must tend to the strength of any government which relies for its support, in any sense, upon the social and personal virtues of the people. In implanting the virtues of justice, temperance, and piety, and in binding each heart to every other, by the bonds of a love which this religion makes itself almost to consist in, it does all that either philosophy or religion can do for the harmony and order of society, the safety of governments, and the peace of the world."

" You speak with the earnestness of a deep persuasion, Roman," replied the queen, " and I shall not forget the name and office of the person whom you have now named to me. I hear with pleasure of the arrival of any teacher of truth in my kingdom. I have derived so much myself from the influences of letters and philosophy, that it is no far-off conclusion for me to arrive at, that my people must be proportionally benefited by an easy access to the same life-giving fountains. Whatever helps to quicken thought, and create or confirm habits of reflection, is so much direct service to the cause of humanity. I truly believe that there is no obstacle but ignorance, to prevent the world from attaining a felicity and a virtue such as we now hardly dream of—ignorance respecting the first principles of philosophy and religion. Knowledge is not less essential to the increase and elevation of virtue, than it is to the further advances of truth, and the detection of error. Prove the truth, and mankind will always prefer it to falsehood. So, too, demonstrate wherein goodness consists, and the road that leads to it, and mankind will prefer it to vice. Vice is a mistake, as well as a fault; I do not say as often. I fear that the Christian teachers are occupying themselves and their disciples too much about mere speculative and fanciful distinctions, while they give too little heed to that which alone is of any consequence, virtue. In this, Longinus," turning towards the philosopher, who had now joined us, "I think they affect to imitate the commentators and living expositors of the great Plato. I have heard from Paul of Samosata accounts of differences among Christians, where the points were quite too subtle for my understanding to appreciate. They reminded me of the refinements of some of the young adventurers from Athens, who occasionally have resorted here for the purpose of elucidating the doctrines of your great master—pseudo-philosophers and tyros, I perceive you are waiting to term them. Is it so that you denominate Polemo, the Athenian, who, as I learn, is now here with the benevolent design of enlightening my people?"

"He is a man," replied Longinus, "hardly worthy to be named in this connection and this presence at all. I have neither met him nor heard him, nor do I desire to do so. It is through the mischievous intermeddling of such as he that the honourable name and office of philosopher are brought into contempt. It requires more intellect than ever enlightens the soul of Polemo, to comprehend the lofty truth of Plato. I trust that when it has been my pleasure to unfold the sense of that great teacher, it has not been found to be either unprofitable or unintelligible."

Zenobia smiled and said, "I must confess that at times, as I have ever frankly stated, my mind has been a little tasked. There has been but an approach to a perfect idea. But I do not say that a perfect conception has not been presented. So that when this has happened, Longinus being the teacher, and Zenobia and Julia the pupils, I cannot doubt that when the task is entrusted to less cultivated minds—the task both of teaching and learning—it must frequently end in what it might be rash to term light or knowledge."

"I grieve, oh queen," replied Longinus, smiling in his turn, "that both you and the princess should have possessed so little affinity for the soul-purifying and elevating doctrines of the immortal Plato—that you, queen, should have even preferred the dark annals of

Egyptian and Assyrian history and politics, and the Greek learning; and you, princess, should have fixed your affections upon this, not new-found philosophy, but new-invented religion, of the Christians. I still anticipate the happiness to lead you both into the groves of the Academy, and detain you there, where, and where only, are seats that well become you."

"But is it not," I ventured here to suggest, "some objection to the philosophy of Plato as the guide of life, that it requires minds of the very highest order to receive it? Philosophy, methinks, should be something of such potency, yet, at the same time, of such simplicity, that it should not so much require a lofty and elevated intellect to admit it, as tend, being received readily and easily by minds of a humbler order, to raise them up to itself. Now, this, so far as I understand it, is the character of the Christian philosophy—for philosophy I must think it deservedly called. It is admitted into the mind with ease. But once being there, its operation is continually to exalt and refine it, leading it upwards for ever to some higher point than it has hitherto arrived at. I do not deny an elevating power to your philosophy when once an inmate of the soul; I only assert the difficulty of receiving it on the part of the common mind."

"And the common mind has nothing to do," replied the Greek, "with Plato or his wisdom. They are for minds of a higher order. Why should the man who makes my sandals and my cloak be at the same time a philosopher? Would he be the happier? In my opinion, it would but increase his discontent. Every stitch that he set would be accompanied by the reflection, 'What a poor employment is this for a soul like mine, imbued with the best wisdom of Greece!' and if this did not make him miserable at his task, it would make him contemptible when he should forsake it to do the work of some Polemo—who, it may safely be presumed, has made some such exchange of occupation. No. Philosophy is not for the many, but the few. Parts there are of it which may descend and become a common inheritance. Other parts there are, and it is of these I speak, which may not."

"Therein," I rejoined, "I discern its inferiority to Christianity, which appeals to all and is suited to all, to lowest as well as highest, to highest as well as lowest."

"But I remember to have been told," said the Greek in reply, "that Christian teachers too have their mysteries—their doctrines for the common people, and their refinements for the initiated."

"I have heard not of it," I answered; "if it be so, I should lament it. It would detract from its value greatly in my judgment."

"Where your information fails, Piso, mine perhaps may serve," said Julia, as I paused at fault. "It is indeed true, as has been hinted by Longinus, that some of the Christian doctors, through their weak and mistaken ambition to assimilate their faith the nearest possible to the Greek philosophy, have magnified the points in which the least resemblance could be traced between them; and through the force of a lively imagination, have discovered resemblances which exist only in their fancies. These they make their boast of, as showing that if Platonism be to be esteemed for its most striking peculiarities, the very same, or ones nearly corresponding, exist also in Christianity. Thus they hope to recommend their faith to the lovers of philosophy. Many have by these means been drawn over to it, and have not afterwards altered any of their modes of life, and scarce any of their opinions—still wearing the philosopher's robe and teaching their former doctrines, slightly modified by a tincture of Christianity. However the motive for such accommodation may be justified, it has already resulted, and must do so more and more, to the corruption and injury of Christianity. This religion, or philosophy, whichever it should be called, ought, however," continued the princess, addressing particularly the Greek, "certainly to be judged on its own merits, and not by the conduct or opinions of injudicious, weak, or dishonest advocates. You are not willing that Plato should be judged by the criticisms of a Polemo, but insist that the student should go to the pages of the philosopher himself, or else to some living expositor worthy of him. So the Christian may say of Christianity. I have been a reader of the Christian records, and I can say, that such secret and mysterious doctrines as you allude to, are not to be found there. Moreover, I can refer you, for the same opinion, to Paul of Antioch—I wish he were here— who, however he may depart from the simplicity of the Christian life, maintains the simplicity of its doctrine."

"You have well shown, my fair pupil," replied the philosopher, "that the imputation upon Christianity, of a secret and interior doctrine for the initiated alone is unjust, but therein have you deprived it of the very feature that would commend it to the studious and inquisitive. It may present itself as a useful moral guide to the common mind, but scarcely can it hope to obtain that enthusiastic homage of souls imbued with the love of letters and of a refined speculation, which binds in such true-hearted devotion every follower of Plato to the doctrine of his divine master."

At this moment Zabdas and Otho entered the apartment, and drawing near to our group to salute the queen, our conversation was broken off. I took occasion, while this ceremony was going through, to turn aside and survey the various beauty and magnificence of the room, with its rare works of art. In this I was joined by Longinus, who, with a taste and a power which I have seen in no other, descanted upon the more remarkable of the pictures and statues, not in the manner of a lecturer, but with a fine perception and observance of that nice line which separates the learned philosopher from the polite man of the world. He was both at once. He never veiled his learning or his genius, and yet never, by the display of either, jarred the sensibilities of the most refined and cultivated taste.

When we had in this way passed through the apartment, and were standing looking towards where Zenobia sat engaged in earnest conversation with Gracchus and Zabdas, Longinus said,

"Do you observe the restlessness of the queen, and that flush upon her cheek? She is thinking of to-morrow, and of the departure of the ambassadors. And so, too, is it with every other here. We speak of other things, but the mind dwells but upon one. I trust the queen will not lose this fair occasion to gather once more the opinions of those who most love and honour her. Piso, you have seen something of the attachment of this people to their queen. But you know not the one half of the truth. There is not a living man in Palmyra, save only Antiochus, who would not lay down his life for Zenobia. I except not myself. This attachment is founded in part upon great and admirable qualities. But it is to be fully explained only when I name the fascinations of a manner and a beauty such as poets have feigned in former ages, but which have never been realised till now. I acknowledge it—we are slaves yoked to her car, and ask no higher felicity or glory."

"I wonder not," said I; "though a Roman, I have hardly myself escaped the common fate; you need not be surprised to see me drawn, by and bye, within the charmed circle, and binding upon my own neck the silken chains and the golden yoke. But see, the queen asks our audience."

We accordingly moved towards the seat which Zenobia now occupied, surrounded by her friends, some being seated, and others standing, without order around her.

"Good friends," she said, "I believe one thought fills every mind present here. Is it not better that we give it utterance? I need the sympathy and the counsel of those who love me. But I ask not only for the opinions of those who agree with me, but as sincerely for those of such as may differ from me. You know me well in this, that I refuse not to hearken to reasons, the strongest that can be devised, although they oppose my own settled judgment. Upon an occasion like this it would ill become the head of a great empire, to shut out the slenderest ray of light, that from any quarter might be directed upon the questions which so deeply interest and agitate us. I believe that the great heart of my people goes with me in the resolution I have taken, and am supported in by my council; but I am well aware, that minds not inferior to any in strength, and hearts that beat not less warmly towards their country and towards me than any others, are opposed to that resolution, and anticipate nought but disaster and ruin from a conflict with the masters of the world. Let us freely open our minds to each other, and let no one fear to offend me, but by withholding his full and free opinion."

"We who know our queen so well," said Gracchus, "hardly need these assurances. Were I as bitterly opposed to the measures proposed as I am decidedly in favour of them, I should none the less fearlessly and frankly declare the reasons of my dissent. I am sure that every one here experiences the freedom you enjoin. But who will need to use it? For are we not of one mind? I see, indeed, one or two who oppose the general mind. But for the rest, one spirit animates all, and, what is more, to the farthest limits of the kingdom am I persuaded the same spirit spreads, and possesses, and fills every soul. The attempt of Aurelian to control us in our affairs, to dictate to us concerning the limits of our empire so far removed, is felt to be a wanton freak of despotic power, which, if it be not withstood in its first encroachment, may proceed to other acts less tolerable still, and which may leave us scarcely our name as a distinct people, and that covered with shame. Although a Roman by descent, I advocate not Roman intolerance. I can see and denounce injustice in Aurelian as well as another. Palmyra is my country and Zenobia my queen, and when I seek not their honour, may my own fall blasted and ruined. I stand ready to pledge for them in this emergency, what every other man of Palmyra holds it his privilege to offer, my property and

my life, and if I have any possession dearer than these,
I am ready to bring and lay it upon the same altar."

The eyes of Zenobia filled at the generous enthusiasm
of her faithful councillor—and for Fausta, it was only
a look and sign of the queen that held her to her seat.

Longinus then, as seemed to be his place, entered at
length into the merits of the question. He did not
hesitate to say that at the first outbreak of these difficulties he had been in favour of such concessions to the
pride of Rome, as would, perhaps, have appeased her,
and cast no indignity upon Palmyra. He did not
scruple to add that he had deeply disapproved and
honestly censured that rash act of the young princes in
assuming the garb and state of Cæsars. He would
rather leave to Rome her own titles and empire, and
stand here upon a new and independent footing. It
was a mad and useless affront, deeply wounding to the
pride of Aurelian, and the more rankling as it was of
the nature of a personal as well as national affront. He
withheld not blame, too, from that towering ambition
that, as he said, coveted the world because the gods had
indeed imparted a genius capable to rule the world. He
had exerted all his powers to moderate and restrain it,
by infusing a love of other than warlike pursuits. "But,"
said he, "the gods weave the texture of our souls, not
ourselves; and the web is too intensely wove, and
drenched in too deep a dye, for us to undo or greatly
change. The eagle cannot be tamed down to the softness of a dove, and no art of the husbandman can send
into the gnarled and knotted oak the juices that shall
smooth and melt its stiffness into the yielding pliancy
of the willow. I wage no war with the work of the
gods. Besides, the demands of Rome have now grown
to such a size that they swallow up our very existence
as a free and sovereign state. They leave us but this
single city and province out of an empire that now
stretches from the Nile to the Bosphorus—an empire
obtained by what cost of blood and treasure I need not
say, any more than by what consummate skill in that

art which boasts the loftiest minds of all ages." He went on to say, that Palmyra owed a duty not only to herself in this matter, but to the whole east especially, and even to the world. For what part of the civilised world had not been trampled into the dust by the despotism of almighty Rome. It was needful to the well-being of nations that some power should boldly stand forth and check an insolence that suffered no city or kingdom to rest in peace. No single people ought to obtain universal empire. A powerful nation was the more observant of the eternal principles of honour and justice for being watched by another, its equal. Individual character needs such supervision—and national as much. Palmyra was now an imposing object in the eye of the whole world. It was the second power. All he wished was, that for the sake of the world's peace, it should retain this position. He deprecated conquest. However another might aspire to victory over Aurelian, to new additions from the Roman territory, he had no such aspirations. On the other hand, he should deplore any success beyond the maintenance of a just and honourable independence. "This was our right," he said, "by inheritance, and as much also by conquest, and for this he was ready, with the noble Gracchus, to offer to his sovereign his properties, his powers, and his life. If my poor life," he closed with saying, "could prolong by a single year the reign of one who, with virtues so eminent and a genius so vast, fills the throne of this fair kingdom, I would lay it at her feet with joy, and think it a service well done for our own and the world's happiness."

No sooner had Longinus ended, than Otho, a man of whom I have more than once spoken to you, begged to say a few words.

"My opinions are well known," he began with saying, "and it may be needless that I should again, and especially here, declare them, seeing that they will jar so rudely with those entertained by you, my friends around me. But sure I am, that no one has advocated

the cause and the sentiments which Zenobia cherishes
so fondly, with a truer, deeper affection for her, with a
sincerer love of her glory, than I rise to oppose them
with." "We know it, we know it, Otho," interrupted the
queen. "Thanks, noble queen, for the fresh assurance of
it. It is because I love, that I resist you. It is because I
glory in your reign, in your renown, in your virtues, that
I oppose an enterprise that I see with a prophet's vision
will tarnish them all. Were I your enemy, I could not do
better than to repeat the arguments that have just fallen
from the lips of the head of our councils, set off with
every trick of eloquence that would send them with a yet
more resistless power into the minds not only of those
who are assembled here, but of those your subjects,
wherever over these large dominions they are scattered.
To press this war is to undermine the foundations of
the fairest kingdom the sun shines upon, and unseat the
most beloved ruler that ever swayed a sceptre over the
hearts of a devoted people. It can have no other issue.
And this is not, oh noble queen, to throw discredit upon
former achievements, or to express a doubt of powers
which have received the homage of the world. It is
only, with open eyes, to acknowledge what all but the
blind must see and confess, the overwhelming superiority in power of every kind of the other party. With
a feeble man upon the Roman throne, and I grant that
upon the outskirts of her empire, a brave and determined opposition might obtain great advantages, and
conquer or re-conquer provinces and cities, and bring
disgrace upon Roman generals. But this must be a
transitory glory—the mere shooting of an evening star
—ending in deeper gloom. For what is Rome? Is it
the commander of a legion, or the resident governor of
a dependent kingdom, or even Cæsar himself? And have
you dealt with Rome when you have dealt with Balista,
or Heraclianus, or Probus? Alas! no. Rome still
stands omnipotent and secure. The lion has been but
chafed, and is still a lion, with more than his former
fury—one hair has been drawn—his teeth, his limbs,

his massy weight, his untouched energies, remain. Rome has been asleep for thirteen long years. Any empire but Rome, which is immortal, would have slept the sleep of death under the dastardly, besotted, Gallienus. But Rome has but slumbered, and has now awaked with renovated powers, under the auspices of a man whose name alone has carried terror and dismay to the farthest tribes of the German forests. Against Aurelian, with all the world at his back, and what can any resistance of ours avail? We may gain a single victory—to that, genius and courage are equal, and we possess them in more than even Roman measure—but that very victory may be our undoing, or it will but embitter the temper of the enemy, call forth a new display of unexhausted and inexhaustible resources, while our very good success itself will have nearly annihilated our armies, and what can happen then but ruin, absolute and complete. Roman magnanimity may spare our city and our name. But it is more likely that Roman vengeance may blot them both out from the map of the world, and leave us nought but the fame of our queen, and the crumbling ruins of this once flourishing city, by which to be remembered by posterity.

These are not the counsels of fear—of a tame and cowardly spirit. I may rebut that imputation without vanity, by referring to the siege of Ctesiphon and the reduction of Egypt. The generous Zabdas will do me justice—nay, you all will—why am I apprehensive? Bear with me a moment more." "Say on, say on, noble Otho," said the queen, and many other voices at the same time. "The great Longinus has said," continued he, "that it is needful that there be one empire, at least, in the world to stand between Rome and universal dominion. I believe it. And that Palmyra may be, or continue to be that kingdom, I counsel peace—I counsel delay—temporary concession—negotiation—any thing but war. A Roman emperor lives not for ever; and let us once ward off the jealousy of Aurelian, by yielding to some of his demands, and resigning pretensions

which are nothing in reality, but exist as names and
shadows only, and long years of peace and prosperity
may again arise, when our now infant kingdom may
shoot up into the strong bone and muscle of a more
vigorous manhood, and with reason assert rights,
which now it seems but madness, essential madness, to
do. Listen, great queen, to the counsels of a time-
worn soldier, whose whole soul is bound up in most
true-hearted devotion to your greatness and glory. I
quarrel not with your ambition, or your love of warlike fame. I would only direct them to fields where
they may pluck fresh laurels, and divert them from
those where waits—pardon me, my royal mistress—
inevitable shame."

Soon as Otho had given a single sign of pause, Zabdas,
like a war-horse, sprang upon his feet. "Were not the
words," said he, "which we have just heard, the words
of Otho, I should cry out Treason! treason! But Otho
—is Otho. What nation would ever, oh queen, out-
grow its infancy, were a policy like this now descanted
upon to guide its councils? The general who risks
nothing can win nothing. And the nation that should
wait till absolutely sure of victory before unsheathing
the sword, would never draw it, or only in some poor
skirmish, where victory would be as disgraceful as
defeat. Besides, although such a nation were to rise
by such victories, if victories those may be called, won
by a thousand over an hundred, who would not blush
to own himself a citizen of it? Greatness lies not in
pounds' weight of flesh, but in skill, courage, warlike
genius, energy, and an indomitable will. A great heart
will scatter a multitude. The love of freedom in a few
brave spirits overthrows kingdoms. It was not, if I
rightly remember, numbers by which the Persian hosts
were beaten upon the plains of Greece. It was there
something like three hundred to a million—the million
weighed more than the three hundred, yet the three
hundred were the heavier. The arm of one Spartan fell
like a tempest upon the degenerate Persians, crushing

its thousands at a single sweep. It was a great heart and a trusting spirit, that made it weigh so against mere human flesh. Are we to wait till Palmyra be as multitudinous as Rome, ere we risk a battle? Perhaps Rome will grow as fast as Palmyra—and how long must we then wait? I care not though Aurelian bring half Europe at his back, there sits a throned spirit—whether of earth or not I cannot tell, but as I think more than half divine—who will drive him back shattered and bleeding, the jest and ridicule of the observing world. She who, by the force of pure intellect, has out of this speck in the desert made a large empire, who has humbled Persia, and entered her capital in triumph, has defeated three Roman armies, and wrested more provinces than time will allow me to number, from the firm grasp of the self-styled mistress of the world, this more than Semiramis is to be daunted, forsooth, because a Roman soldier of fortune sends his hirelings here, and asks of her the surrender of three fourths of her kingdom—she is to kneel and cry him mercy—and humbly lay at his royal feet the laurels won by so much precious blood and treasure. May the sands of the desert bury Palmyra and her queen, sooner than one humiliating word shall pass those lips, or one act of concession blast a fame, to this hour spotless as the snows of Ararat, and bright as the Persian god. Shame upon the man who, after the lessons of the past, wants faith in his sovereign. Great queen, believe me, the nation is with you. Palmyra, as one man, will pour out treasure to the last and least dust of gold, and blood to the last drop, that you may still sit secure upon that throne, and stretch your sceptre over a yet wider and undishonoured empire."

"Let not the queen," resumed Otho, as Zabdas ceased, "let not the queen doubt my faith——"

"I doubt it not, good Otho," she replied; "heed not the sharp words of the impetuous Zabdas; in his zeal for the art he only loves, and for his queen, he has thrust his lance hither and thither at all adventures, but, as in the sports of the field, he means no injury."

"Zabdas intends no wrong, I am well assured," rejoined Otho. "I would only add a word, to show upon what I ground my doubt of good success, should Aurelian muster all his strength. It cannot be thought that I have lost my faith in the military genius and prowess of either Zenobia or Zabdas, with both of whom, side by side, I have fought so many times, and by their conduct mounted up to victory. Neither do I doubt the courage of our native Palmyrenes, or their devotion to the interests of their country. They will war to the death. But should a second army be to be raised—should the chosen troops of the city and its neighbouring territories be once cut off, upon whom are we then to rely? Where are the auxiliaries whom we can trust? What reliance can be placed upon Arabs, the Armenians, the Saracens, the Cappadocians, the Syrians? Is our empire so old, and so well moulded into one mass, so single in interest and affection, that these scattered tribes, formerly hostile to each other and to us, many, most of them, at different times subject to Rome, may be depended upon as our own people? Have we legions already drawn from their numbers, disciplined, and accustomed to our modes of warfare? Truly, this war with Rome seems to be approached much as if it were but some passing show of arms, some holiday pastime. But the gods grant that none of my forebodings turn true."

The words of the sober-minded and honest Otho found no echo in the bosoms of those who heard him, and he ceased when I believe he would willingly have gone on to a closer and sharper opposition. Others followed him, each one present eagerly pressing forward, to utter were it but one word, to show his loyalty, and his zeal in the service of the queen.

When all, or nearly all, had in this manner manifested their attachment and declared their opinions, the queen turned to me, saying, that as I had there heard so much of what I could not approve, and perhaps had power to disprove, it was right that if I wished, I should also express my opinions—nay, it would be esteemed as a favour by herself, and she was sure also by all her friends, if I would freely impart any knowledge I might possess, by which any error might be corrected, or false impressions dissipated.

Being thus invited, I not unwillingly entered into the questions that had been agitated; and with earnestness and sincerity, and with all the power I could bring to bear, laboured to expose the imminent hazard to the very existence of the kingdom, which was run by this rash encounter with the countless hosts of Rome. I revealed a true picture of the resources of our country, and sketched, as I could so well do in their proper colours, the character of the fierce Aurelian; and, in a word, did all that a Roman could do for Rome, and a Palmyrene for Palmyra. I remembered what Otho had told me of the courtesy and willingness with which any company of genuine Palmyrenes would listen to me, and shrunk not from any statement however harsh and grating to their national vanity, but which seemed to me to convey wholesome truth. It appeared to me, indeed, too late to work any change in minds so pledged already to an adopted opinion, but I resolved to leave nothing untried, however unlikely to turn them from a bent that must end in irretrievable ruin. I was encouraged, too, and urged on to more than a common effort, by the imploring countenance of the Princess Julia, who, in that expressive manner, begged me to use all frankness and boldness in my communications. Otho had, it is true, with great power and unshrinking fidelity, advocated the cause of peace, and laid bare the true motives to the war, but still it appeared to me that much might be said by a Roman and a stranger, that would carry with it more weight than as coming from a citizen, however loved and respected. To you, my friend, I need enter into no detail—you will easily imagine what it was, as a Roman, I should urge upon such an occasion, and in such a presence. I shall always remember with satisfaction I am sure, whatever the issue of this difference may be, my efforts to preserve peace between two nations, whose best interests must be advanced not by enmity and war, but by the closest alliance of friendly intercourse.

I was heard with attention and respect, and afterwards with sincerity thanked, not only by the opposers of the present measures, but by their advocates also—they were glad to know the worst that could be said against the cause they had espoused. A brief silence ensued as I ended, and the eyes of all were instinctively turned upon Zenobia, the ruling spirit—the maker of the kingdom—its soul—its life-blood—its head, and bright, peerless crown.

"It was my wish," said Zenobia, answering the general expectation, "before the final decision of the senate and the council, to receive from my friends, in social confidence, a full expression of their feelings, their opinions, their hopes, and their fears, concerning the present posture of our affairs. My wish has been gratified, and I truly thank you all, and not least those my friends—as a philosopher, should I not term them my best friends?—who, with a generous trust in me and in you who are on my part, have not shrunk from the duty, always a hard one, of exposing the errors and the faults of those they love. After such exposure—and which at more length and with more specification will, I trust, be repeated in the hearing of the senate and the council—it cannot be said that I blindly rushed upon danger and ruin—if these await us—or weakly blundered upon a wider renown, if that, as I doubt not, is to be the event of the impending contest. I would neither gain nor lose, but as the effect of a wise calculation and a careful choice of means. Withhold not now your confidence, which before you have never refused me. Believe that now, as ever before, I discern with a clear eye the path which is to conduct us to a yet higher pitch of glory. I have long anticipated the emergency that has arisen. I was not so ignorant of the history and character of the Roman people, as to suppose that they would suffer an empire like this, founded, too, and governed by a woman, to divide long with them the homage of the world. With the death of the ignoble son of Valerian, I believed would close our undisputed reign over most of these eastern provinces. Had Claudius lived, good as he was, he was too Roman in his mould not to have done what Aurelian now attempts. I prepared then for the crisis which has come not till now. I am ready now. My armies are in complete discipline—the city itself so fortified with every art and muniment of war as safely to defy any power that any nation may array before its walls. But were this not so, did the embassy of Aurelian take us by surprise and unprepared, should a people that respects itself, and would win or keep the good opinion of mankind, tamely submit to requisitions like these? Are we to dismember our country at the behest of a stranger, of a foreigner, and a Roman? Do you feel that without a struggle first for freedom and independence, you could sink down into a mean tributary of all-engulfing Rome, and lose the name of Palmyrene? I see by the most expressive of all language, that you would rather die. Happy are you, my friends, that this is not your case —you are ready for the enemy—you shall not lose your name or your renown—and you shall not die. I and my brave soldiers will at a distance breast the coming storm—your ears shall not so much as hear its thunder —and at the worst, by the sacrifice of our lives, yours and your country's life shall be preserved.

I am advised to avert this evil by negotiation, by delay. Does any one believe that delay on our part will change the time-engendered character of Rome? If I cease to oppose, will Rome cease to be ambitious? Will fair words turn aside the fierce spirit of Aurelian from his settled purpose? Will he, so truly painted by the Roman Piso, who looks to build an undying name, by bringing back the empire to the bounds that compassed it under the great Antonines, let slip the glory for a few cities now in hand, and others promised!

or for the purple robe humbly pulled from our young Cæsars' shoulders? Believe it not. The storm that threatens might be so warded off perhaps for a day, a month, a year, a reign, but after that it would come, and, in all reasonable calculation, with tenfold fury. I would rather meet the danger at its first menace, and thereby keep both our good name (which otherwise should we not sully or lose?) and find it less, too, than a few years more would make it.

I am charged with pride and ambition. The charge is true, and I glory in its truth. Who ever achieved any thing great in letters, arts, or arms, who was not ambitious? Cæsar was not more ambitious than Cicero. It was but in another way. All greatness is born of ambition. Let the ambition be a noble one, and who shall blame it? I confess I did once aspire to be queen not only of Palmyra, but of the east. That I am. I now aspire to remain so. Is it not an honourable ambition? Does it not become a descendant of the Ptolemys and of Cleopatra? I am applauded by you all for what I have already done. You would not it should have been less. But why pause here? Is so much ambition praiseworthy, and more criminal? Is it fixed in nature that the limits of this empire should be Egypt on the one hand, the Hellespont and the Euxine on the other? Were not Suez and Armenia more natural limits? Or hath empire no natural limit, but is broad as the genius that can devise, and the power that can win. Rome has the west. Let Palmyra possess the east. Not that nature prescribes this and no more. The gods prospering, and I swear not that the Mediterranean shall hem me in upon the west, or Persia on the east. Longinus is right—I would that the world were mine. I feel within the will and the power to bless it, were it so.

Are not my people happy? I look upon the past and the present, upon my nearer and remoter subjects, and ask nor fear the answer—whom have I wronged? what province have I oppressed? what city pillaged?

what region drained with taxes? whose life have I unjustly taken, or estates coveted or robbed? whose honour have I wantonly assailed? whose rights, though of the weakest and poorest, have I trenched upon? I dwell where I would ever dwell, in the hearts of my people. It is writ in your faces, that I reign not more over you than within you. The foundation of my throne is not more power than love. Suppose, now, my ambition add another province to our realm? Is it an evil? The kingdoms already bound to us by the joint acts of ourself and the late royal Odenatus, we found discordant and at war. They are now united and at peace. One harmonious whole has grown out of hostile and sundered parts. At my hands they receive a common justice and equal benefits. The channels of their commerce have I opened, and dug them deep and sure. Prosperity and plenty are in all their borders. The streets of our capital bear testimony to the distant and various industry which here seeks its market. This is no vain boasting—receive it not so, good friends—it is but truth. He who traduces himself sins with him who traduces another. He who is unjust to himself, or less than just, breaks a law as well as he who hurts his neighbour. I tell you what I am, and what I have done, that your trust for the future may not rest upon ignorant grounds. If I am more than just to myself, rebuke me. If I have overstepped the modesty that became me, I am open to your censure, and will bear it. But I have spoken, that you may know your queen, not only by her acts, but by her admitted principles. I tell you, then, that I am ambitious, that I crave dominion, and while I live will reign. Sprung from a line of kings, a throne is my natural seat. I love it. But I strive, too—you can bear me witness that I do— that it shall be, while I sit upon it, an honoured, unpolluted seat. If I can, I will hang a yet brighter glory around it.

And as to pride—what if my woman's nature, that nature the gods implanted, and I have received from royal ancestors, loves the pomp and show of power? What if the pride which dwells in all high natures, gratifies itself in me by planting its feet upon an Indian princess, as its only fitting footstool, who ——." Suddenly at this point of her discourse the queen broke off, and advancing from where she stood—she had risen from her seat in the ardour of her address—greeted with native courtesy and grace the Roman ambassadors, who, in company with others of their train, we now saw to enter the apartments.

The company, upon this, again resolved itself into many separate groups, and returned to such private topics as each one liked, Zenobia devoting herself to Varro and Petronius.

By and bye, at the striking up of music, we moved to another apartment, the banqueting hall—the same Egyptian room in which I had before partaken the hospitalities of the eastern queen, where tables, set out with the most lavish magnificence, and bending beneath the most tempting burdens, awaited our approach. A flood of light was poured from the ceiling, and reflected back again from the jewelled wine-cups and embossed gold of Demetrius.

But I cannot pretend to describe this sumptuous feast. I will only say, that the queen, seated between the Roman ambassadors, gave the evening to them. And what with the frequent cups in which she pledged them, and the fascinating charms of her beauty and her conversation, I fear there was but little of the Roman in them when they rose to depart. In this more peaceful way has Zenobia won provinces and cities, as well as at the head of her armies. Farewell!

LETTER XI.

FROM my late letters to Portia, and which, without doubt, you have before this read, you have learned with certainty, what I am sure the eye of Lucilia must before have clearly discerned, my love of the princess Julia. I have there related all that it can import my friends to know. The greatest event of my life—the issues of which, whether they are to crown me with a felicity the gods might envy, or plunge me in afflictions divine compassions could not assuage—I have there described with that careful concern for your fullest information, touching all that befalls me, by which, you will bear me testimony, I have been actuated during my residence in this eastern capital.

You will not be surprised to learn that my passion is opposed by the queen. It was in the same apartment of the palace where I first saw this wonderful woman, that at a late interview with her, at her command I was enjoined to think no more of an alliance with her house.

I was, as you may easily imagine, not a little disturbed in anticipation of an interview with such a person, on such an occasion. Fausta assured me that I might rely upon the queen's generosity, and could look to receive only the most courteous reception, whatever her decision might be on my suit. "I fear greatly for your success," said she, "but pray the gods both for your and the princess's sake my fears may not come true. Julia lives in her affections—she cannot, like me, become part of the world abroad, and doubly live in its various action. She loves Zenobia indeed with the truest affection, but she has given her heart to you, Lucius, and disappointment here would feed upon her very life. She ought not to be denied. She cannot bear it. Yet Zenobia, devoured by ambition, and holding so little sympathy with human hearts in their mutual loves—all the world to them—may deny her, nor ever half conceive the misery she will inflict upon a being she loves and even reveres. Press your cause, Lucius, with a manly boldness. The gods succeed you."

The queen received me graciously, but with a fixed and almost severe countenance. She expressed herself obliged to me for the early knowledge of what otherwise she had not so much as suspected. "Living myself," said she, "far above any dependence upon love for my happiness, I am not prone to see the affection in others. The love which fastens upon objects because they are worthy, I can understand and honour. But that mad and blind passion, which loves only because it will love, which can render no reason for its existence but a hot and capricious fancy, I have had no experience of in my own heart; and where I see it, I have no feeling for it but one of disapprobation or contempt. If it be but the beauty of Julia which has bewitched thy fancy, Roman, amuse thyself with a brief tour of pleasure, either to Antioch or Alexandria, and other objects will greet thee, and soon drive her from thy thoughts."

I assured her that my regard was not only of this kind; that, indeed, her transcendant beauty had first won me, but that other qualities retained me; that the bond which held me was as much friendship as love, and, I might say, as much reverence as friendship.

"The greater the pity, Roman," rejoined the queen, in a voice somewhat stern, but yet melancholy, "the greater the pity. In truth, I had hoped yours was but the love of the painted image, and might, without pain, be transferred to another, painted but as well. Yet had I reflected upon the sentiments I had heard from thee, I might have judged thee nobler. But, Piso, this must not be. Were I to look only to myself and Julia, I might well be pleased with a tie that bound us to one whom I have so weighty reasons to respect and honour. But to do this I have no right. I am not my own, but the state's. Julia is no daughter of mine, but the property of Palmyra. Marriage is one of the chief bonds of nations as of families. Were it not a crime in me, with selfish regard to my own or my daughter's pleasure, to bestow her upon a private citizen, of whatever worth, when, espousing her to some foreign prince, a province or a kingdom may be won or saved?"

"But," I ventured to remark, "are the hearts of princes and princesses to be bartered away for power or territory? are the affections to be bought and sold? Is the question of happiness to be no question in their case?"

"By no means the principal one. It is not necessarily a sacrifice, but if necessary the sacrifice must be made. The world envies the lot of those who sit upon thrones; but the seat is not without its thorns. It seems all summer with them; but upon whom burst more storms, or charged with redder fury? They seem to the unreflecting mind to be the only independent—while they are the slaves of all. The prosperous citizen may link himself and his children when and with whom he likes, and none may gainsay him. He has but to look to himself and his merest whim. The royal family must go and ask his leave. My children are more his than mine. And if it be his pleasure and preference that my daughters ally themselves to an Indian or a Roman prince, their will is done, not mine—theirs is the gain, mine the loss. Were it just that when joining hands though not hearts, two nations could be knit together in amity, the royal house should refuse the sacrifice? Roman, I live for Palmyra. I have asked of the gods my children, not for my own pleasure, but for Palmyra's sake. I should give the lie to my whole life, to every sentiment I have harboured since that day I gave myself to the royal Odenatus, were I now to bestow upon a private citizen, her, through whom we have so long looked to ally ourselves, by a new and stronger bond, to some neighbouring kingdom. Julia, Roman—you have seen her, you know her, you can appreciate her more than human qualities—Julia is the destined bride of Hormisdas. By her, on Sapor's death, do we hope to bind together, by chains never to be afterwards sundered, Persia and Palmyra, who, then leagued by interest and affection, may as one kingdom stand up with the more hope against the overwhelming force of Rome. Were I justified to forego this advantage for any private reason? Can you doubt, were I not constrained to act otherwise, whether I should prefer some nobleman of Palmyra, or thee—that so I might ever dwell within the charmed influence of one, from whom to part will be like the pang of death?"

"But the princess," I again urged.

"That is scarcely a question," she rejoined. "She may be a sacrifice, but it will be upon her country's altar. How many of our brave soldiers, how many of our great officers, with devoted patriotism throw away their lives for their country! You will not say that this is done for the paltry recompense, which at best scarce shields the body from the icy winds of winter, or the scorching rays of summer. And shall not a daughter of the royal house stand ready to encounter the hardships of a throne, the dangers of a Persian court, and the terrors of a royal husband, especially when by doing so, fierce and bloody wars may be stayed, and nations brought into closer unity? I know but little of Hormisdas; report speaks well of him. But were it much less that I know, and were report yet less favourable, it were not enough to turn me from my purpose. Palmyra married to Persia, through Julia married to Hormisdas, is that upon which I and my people dwell."

"Better a thousand times," I then said, "to be born to the lot of the humblest peasant—a slave's is no worse."

"Upon love's calendar," said the queen, "so it is. But have I not freely admitted, Roman, the dependency, nay, slavery of a royal house? It would grieve my mother's heart, I need scarce assure thee, were Julia unhappy. But grief to me might bring joy to two kingdoms."

I then could not but urge the claims of my own family, and that by a more powerful and honoured one she could not ally herself to Rome—and might not national interest be as well promoted by such a bond, as one with the remoter east? I was the friend, too, of Aurelian, much in his confidence and regard.

Zenobia paused, and was for a few moments buried in thought. A faint smile for the first time played over her features as she said in reply, "I wish for your sake and Julia's it could be so. But it is too late. Rome is resolved upon the ruin of Palmyra—she cannot be turned aside. Aurelian for worlds would not lose the glory of subduing the east. The greater need of haste in seeking a union with Persia. Were Sapor dead to-day, to-morrow an embassy should start for Ecbatana. But think not, Piso, I harbour ill will towards you, or hold your offer in contempt. A queen of the east might not disdain to join herself to a family whose ancestors were like yours. That Piso who was once the rival, and in power—not indeed in virtue—the equal of the great Germanicus, and looked, not without show of reason, to the seat of Tiberius; and he who so many years and with such honour reigned over the city its unequalled governor; and thou the descendant and companion of princes—an alliance with such might well be an object of ambition with even crowned heads. And it may well be, seeing the steps by which many an emperor of Rome has climbed upon his precarious seat, that the coming years may behold thee in the place which Aurelian fills, and were I to pleasure thee in thy request, Julia empress of the world! The vision dazzles! But it cannot be. It would be sad recreancy to my most sacred duty, were I, falling in love with a dream, to forsake a great reality."

"I may not, then——" I began.

"No, Piso, you may not even hope. I have reasoned with you because I honour you; but think not that I hesitate or waver. Julia can never be yours. She is the daughter of the state, and to a state must be espoused. Seek not, therefore, any more to deepen the place which you hold in her affections. Canst thou not be a friend, and leave the lover out? Friendship is a sentiment worthy godlike natures, and is the true sweetener of the cup of life. Love is at best but a bitter sweet; and when sweetest, it is the friendship mingled with it that makes it so, and it wastes away with years. Friendship is eternal. It rests upon qualities that are a part of the soul. The witchery of the outward image helps not to make it, nor being lost as it is with age, can dissolve it. Friendship agrees, too, with ambition, while love is its most dreaded rival. Need I point to Antony? If, Piso, thou wouldst live the worthy heir of thy great name—if thou wouldst build for thyself a throne in the esteem of mankind—admit friendship, but bar out love. And I trust to hear that thou art great in Rome—greater even than thine ancestor Galba's adopted son. Aim at even the highest, and the arrow, if it reach it not, will hit the nearer. When thou art Cæsar, send me an embassy. Then, perhaps ——"

She closed with that radiant smile that subdues all to her will, her manner, at the same time, giving me to understand that the conversation was ended, her own sentence being left playfully unfinished.

I urged not many things which you may well suppose it came into my mind to do, for I neither wished, nor did I feel as if I had a right, at an hour of so much public inquietude, to say aught to add to the burden already weighing upon her. Besides, it occurred to me, that when within so short a time great public changes may take place, and the relations of parties be so essentially altered, it was not worth while to give utterance to sentiments which the lapse of a brief period might show to have been unnecessary and unwise. I may also add, that the presence of this great woman is so imposing, she seems in the very nature and form the gods have given her, to move so far above the rest of her kind, that I found it impossible both to say what I had intended to say, and to express what I did say with ease and propriety, which are common to me on ordinary or other extraordinary occasions. They are few, I believe, who possess themselves fully in her presence. Even Longinus confesses a constraint.

"It is even as I apprehended," said Fausta, as I communicated to her the result of my interview with the queen. "I know her heart to have been set upon a foreign alliance by marriage with Julia, and that she has been looking forward with impatience to the time when her daughters should be of an age, to add in this way new strength to her kingdom. I rather hoped than had faith that she would listen to your proposals. I thought that, perhaps, the earnestness of the princess, with the queen's strong affection for her, together with the weight of your family and name, might prevail. But, then, I have asked myself, if it were reasonable to indulge such a hope. The queen is right, in stating as she did, her dependence, in some sort, upon the people. It is they, as well as she, who are looking forward to this Persian marriage. I know not what discontents would break out were Hormisdas postponed to Piso, Persia to Rome. My position, Lucius, I think a sadder one than Zenobia's. I love Julia as dearly as Zenobia, and you a great deal more than Zenobia does, and would fain see you happy, and yet I love Palmyra I dare not say how much; nor that, if by such an act good might come to my country, I could almost wish that Julia should live in Persia."

I have within me a better ground of hope, than is guessed either by the queen or Fausta, but yet can name it not. I mention this to you, and pass to other things.

The city has to-day been greatly moved, owing to the expected audience of our ambassadors before the council, and their final answer. The streets are thronged with multitudes not engaged in the active affairs of traffic, but standing in larger or smaller crowds talking, and hearing or telling news, as it arrives from the palace, or from abroad.

The die is cast. The ambassadors are dismissed. The decision of the council has been confirmed by the senate, and Varro and Petronius have, with their train, departed from the city. War, therefore, is begun. For it was the distinct language of the embassy, that no other terms need be proposed, or would be accepted, besides those offered by them. None others have been offered on the part of Palmyra. And the ambassadors have been delayed, rather to avoid the charge of unreasonable precipitancy, than in the belief that the public mind would incline to, or permit any reply more moderate than that which they have borne back to the emperor.

It is understood that Aurelian, with an army perfectly equipped, stands waiting, ready to start for Asia on the arrival of the ambassadors, or the couriers. From your last letters I gather as much. How, again I ask—as I have often asked both myself and the principal persons here—how is it possible there should be but one issue to this contest? Yet from language which I heard in the senate, as well as in the private apartments of the queen, there is a mad confidence, that after a battle or two on the outskirts of the kingdom, in which they shall conquer as always heretofore, an advantageous peace will end the contest. In the senate, scarce a voice was raised for concession; its mere mention was enough to bring down the most bitter charges of a want of patriotism, a Roman bearing, a sordid regard to the interests of commerce over those of honour, a poor and low-minded spirit. Such as had courage to lift up a warning voice, were soon silenced by the universal clamour of the opposite party; and although the war was opposed by some of the ablest men in the kingdom, men inferior to none of those who have come more especially within my notice, and whom I have named to you, yet it is termed an unanimous decision, and so will be reported at Rome.

The simple truth is, however, that with the exception of these very few, there is no independent judgment in Palmyra, on great national questions. The queen is all in all. She is queen, council, and senate. Here are the forms of a republican deliberation with the reality of a despotic will. Not that Zenobia is a despotic prince, in any bad sense of the term, but being of so exalted a character, ruling with such equity and wisdom, moreover, having created the kingdom with her own unrivalled energies and genius, it has become the habit of the people to defer to her in all things; their confidence and love are so deep and fervent, that they have no will nor power now, I believe, to oppose her in any measure she might propose. The city and country of Palmyra proper are her property, in as real a sense as my five hundred slaves, on my Tiburtine farm, are mine. Nor is it very much otherwise with many of the nearer allied provinces. The same enthusiasm pervades them. Her watchfulness over their interests, her impartiality, her personal oversight of them, by means of the frequent passages she makes among them, have all contributed to knit them to her by the closest ties. With the more remote portions of the empire it is very different, and it would require the operation of but slight causes to divide from their allegiance Egypt, Armenia, and the provinces of Asia Minor.

How is not this rashness, this folly, to be deplored! Could the early counsels of Longinus have been but heeded, all had been well. But he is now as much devoted to the will and interests of Zenobia as any in the kingdom, and lends all the energies of his great mind to the promotion of her cause. He said truly, that he, like others, is but a slave yoked to her car. His opinion now is, that no concessions would avail to preserve the independent existence of Palmyra. The question lies between war and a voluntary descent to the condition of a Roman province. Nothing less than that will satisfy the ambition and the pride of Rome. The first step may be such as that proposed by Varro—the lopping off of the late conquered provinces, leaving Zenobia the city, circumjacent territory, and Syria. But a second step would soon follow the first, and the foot of Aurelian would plant itself upon the neck of Zenobia herself. This he felt assured of, from observation upon the Roman character and history, upon the personal character of Aurelian, and from private advices from Rome. He is now, accordingly, the moving spirit of the enterprise, going with all his heart and mind into every measure of the queen.

I am just returned from a singular adventure. My

hand trembles as I write. I had laid down my pen and gone forth upon my Arab, accompained by Milo, to refresh and invigorate my frame after our late carousal—shall I term it?—at the palace. I took my way, as I often do, to the Long Portico, that I might again look upon its faultless beauty and watch the changing crowds. Turning from that, I then amused my vacant mind by posting myself where I could overlook, as if I were indeed the builder or superintendent, the labourers upon the column of Aurelian. I became at length particularly interested in the efforts of a huge elephant, who was employed in dragging up to the foundations of the column, so that they might be fastened to machines to be then hoisted to their place, enormous blocks of marble. He was a noble animal, and, as it seemed to me, of far more than common size and strength. Yet did not his utmost endeavours appear to satisfy the demands of those who drove him, and who plied without mercy the barbed scourges which they bore. His temper at length gave way. He was chained to a mass of rock, which it was evidently beyond his power to move. It required the united strength of two at least. But this was nothing to his inhuman masters. They ceased not to urge him with cries and blows. One of them, at length transported by that insane fury which seizes the vulgar when their will is not done by the brute creation, laid hold upon a long lance, terminated with a sharp iron goad, long as my sword, and rushing upon the beast, drove it into his hinder part. At that very moment the chariot of the queen, containing Zenobia herself, Julia, and the other princesses, came suddenly against the column, on its way to the palace. I made every possible sign to the charioteer to turn and fly. But it was too late. The infuriated monster snapped the chains that held him to the stone at a single bound, as the iron entered him, and, trampling to death one of his drivers, dashed forward to wreak his vengeance upon the first object that should come in his way. That, to the universal terror and distraction of the gathered but now scattered and flying crowds, was the chariot of the queen. Her mounted guards, at the first onset of the maddened animal, put spurs to their horses, and by quick leaps escaped. The horses attached to the chariot, springing forward to do the same, urged by the lash of the charioteer, were met by the elephant with straightened trunk and tail, who, in the twinkling of an eye, wreathed his proboscis around the neck of the first he encountered, and wrenching him from his harness, whirled him aloft and dashed him to the ground. This I saw was the moment to save the life of the queen, if it was indeed to be saved. Snatching from a flying soldier his long spear, and knowing well the temper of my horse, I put him to his speed, and running upon the monster as he disengaged his trunk from the crushed and dying Arabian, for a new assault, I drove it with unerring aim into his eye, and through that opening on into the brain. He fell as if a bolt from heaven had struck him. The terrified and struggling horses of the chariot were secured by the now returning crowds, and the queen with the princesses relieved from the peril that seemed so imminent, and had blanched with terror every cheek but Zenobia's. She had stood the while, I was told—there being no exertion which she could make—watching with eager and intense gaze my movements, upon which she felt that their safety, perhaps their lives, depended.

It all passed in a moment. Soon as I drew out my spear from the dying animal, the air was rent with the shouts of the surrounding populace. Surely, at that moment I was the greatest, at least the most fortunate, man in Palmyra. These approving shouts, but still more the few words uttered by Zenobia and Julia, were more than recompense enough for the small service I had performed; especially, however, the invitation of the queen:—

"But come, noble Piso, leave not the work half done; we need now a protector for the remainder of the way. Ascend, if you will do us such pleasure, and join us to the palace."

I needed no repeated urging, but taking the offered seat—whereupon new acclamations went up from the now augmented throngs—I was driven, as I conceived, in a sort of triumph to the palace, where passing an hour, which, it seems to me, held more than all the rest of my life, I have now returned to my apartment, and relate what has happened for your entertainment. You will not wonder that for many reasons my hand trembles, and my letters are not formed with their accustomed exactness.

Again I am interrupted. What can be the meaning of the noise and running to and fro which I hear? Some one, with a quick, light foot, approaches.

It is now night. The palace is asleep; but I take again my pen to tell you of the accomplishment of the dear object for which I have wandered to this distant spot. Calpurnius is arrived.

The quick, light foot by which I was disturbed was Fausta's. I knew it, and sprang to the door. She met me with her bright and glowing countenance bursting with expression; "Calpurnius," said she, "your brother, is here!"—and seizing my hand, drew me to the apartment where he sat by the side of Gracchus—Isaac, with his inseparable pack, standing near.

I need not, as I cannot, describe our meeting. It was the meeting of brothers, yet of strangers, and a confusion of wonder, curiosity, vague expectation, and doubt, possessed the soul of each. I trust and believe, that notwithstanding the different political bias which sways each, the ancient ties which bound us together as brothers will again unite us. The countenance of Calpurnius, though dark and almost stern in its general expression, yet unbends and relaxes frequently and suddenly, in a manner that impresses you forcibly with an inward humanity as the presiding though often concealed quality of his nature. I can trace faintly the features which have been stamped upon my memory—and the form too—chiefly by the recollected scene of that bright morning, when he, with our elder brother and venerable parent, gave us each a last embrace, as they started for the tents of Valerian. A warmer climate has deepened the olive of his complexion, and at the same time added brilliancy to an eye, by nature soft as a woman's. His Persian dress increases greatly the effect of his rare beauty, yet I heartily wish it off, as it contributes more, I believe, than the lapse of so many years, to separate us. He will not seem and feel as a brother, till he returns to the costume of his native land. How great this power of mere dress is upon our affections and our regard, you can yourself bear witness, when those who parted from you to travel in foreign countries, have returned metamorphosed into Greeks, Egyptians, or Persians, according to the fashions that have struck their foolish fancies. The assumed and foreign air chills the untravelled heart as it greets them. They are no longer the same. However the reason may strive to overcome what seems the mere prejudice of a wayward nature, we strive in vain—nature will be uppermost—and many, many times have I seen the former friendships break away and perish.

I could not but be alive to the general justness of the comparison instituted by Isaac, between Calpurnius and Julia. There are many points of resemblance. The very same likeness in kind that we so often observe between a brother and a sister—such as we have often remarked in your nephew and niece, Drusus and Lavinia—whose dress being changed, and they are changed.

No sooner had I greeted and welcomed my brother, than I turned to Isaac and saluted him, I am persuaded with scarcely less cordiality.

"I sincerely bless the gods," said I, "that you have escaped the perils of two such passages through the desert, and are safe in Palmyra. May every wish of your heart, concerning your beloved Jerusalem, be accomplished. In the keeping of Demetrius will you find not only the single talent agreed upon in case you returned, but the two which were to be paid had you perished. One such tempest upon the desert escaped, is more and worse than death itself, met softly upon one's bed."

"Now, Jehovah be praised," ejaculated Isaac, "who himself has moved thy heart to this grace. Israel will feel this bounty through every limb; it will be to her as the oil of life."

"And my debt," said Calpurnius, "is greater yet, and should in reason be more largely paid. Through the hands of Demetrius I will discharge it."

"We are all bound to you," said Fausta, "more than words can tell or money pay."

"You owe more than you are perhaps aware of to the rhetoric of Isaac," added Calpurnius. "Had it not been for the faithful zeal and cunning of your messenger, in his arguments not less than his contrivances, I had hardly now been sitting within the walls of Palmyra."

"But then again, noble Roman," said Isaac, "to be honest, I ought to say what I said not—for it had not then occurred—in my letter to thy brother, how, by my indiscretion, I had nearly brought upon myself the wrath, even unto death, of a foul Persian mob, and so sealed thy fate, together with my own. Ye have heard, doubtless, of Manes the Persian, who deems himself some great one, and sent of God. It was noised abroad ere I left Palmyra, that for failing in a much-boasted attempt to work a cure by miracle upon the Prince Hormisdas, he had been strangled by order of Sapor. Had he done so, his love of death-doing had at length fallen upon a proper object, a true child of Satan. But as I can testify, his end was not such, and is not yet. He still walks the earth, poisoning the air he breathes, and deluding the souls of men. Him I encountered one day, the very day I had dispatched thy letter, in the streets of Ecbatana, dogged at the heels by his twelve ragged apostles, dragging along their thin and bloodless limbs, that seemed each step ready to give way beneath the weight—little as it was—they had to bear. Their master, puffed up with the pride of a reformer—as, forsooth, he holds himself—stalked by at their head, drawing the admiration of the besotted people by his great show of sanctity, and the wise saws which every now and then he let drop for the edification of such as heard. Some of these sayings fell upon my ear, and who was I to hear them and not speak? Ye may know that this false prophet has made it his aim to bring into one the Magian and Christian superstitions, so that by such incongruous and deadly mixture, he might feed the disciples of those two widely-sundered religions, retaining—as he foolishly hoped—enough of the faith of each to satisfy all who should receive the compound. In doing this he hath cast dirt upon the religion of the Jew, blasphemously teaching that our sacred books are the work of the author of evil, while those of Christ are by the author of good. With more zeal, it must be confessed, than wisdom, seeing where I was, and why I was there, I resisted this father of lies, and withstood him to his face. 'Who art thou, bold blasphemer,' I said, 'that takest away the Godhead, breaking into twain that which is infinite and indivisible? Who art thou, to tread into the dust the faith of Abraham, and Moses, and the prophets, imputing their words, uttered by the spirit of Jehovah, to the great enemy of mankind? I wonder, people of Ecbatana, that the thunders of God sleep and strike him not to the earth as a rebel —nay, that the earth cleaveth not beneath him and swalloweth him not up, as once before the rebels Korah, Dathan, and Abiram,' and much more in the same mad way, till while I was yet speaking, those lean and hungry followers of his set upon me with violence, crying out against me as a Jew, and stirring up the people, who were nothing unwilling, but fell upon me, and throwing me down, dragged me to a gate of the city, and casting me out as I had been a dead dog, returned themselves, like dogs to their vomit—that accursed dish of Manichean garbage. I believed myself for a long while surely dead; and in my half conscious state, took to myself, as I was bound to do, shame for meddling in the affairs of pagan misbelievers—putting thy safety at risk. Through the compassion of an Arab woman, dwelling without the walls, I was restored and healed —for whose sake I shall ever bless the Ishmaelite. I doubt not, Roman, while I lay at the hut of that good woman, thou thoughtest me a false man."

"I could not but think so," said Calpurnius, "and after the strong desire of escape which you had at length kindled, I assure you I heaped curses upon you in no stinted measure."

"But all has ended well, and so all is well," said Fausta, "and it was perhaps too much to expect, Isaac, that you should stand quietly by and hear the religion of your fathers traduced. You are well rewarded for what you did and suffered, by the light in which your tribe will now regard you—as an almost martyr, and owing to no want of will or endeavour on your part, that almost did not end in quite. Hannibal, good Isaac, will now see to your entertainment."

"One word if it please you," said Isaac, "before I depart. The Gentile despises the Jew. He charges upon him usury and extortion. He accuses him of avarice. He believes him to subsist upon the very life-blood of whomsoever he can draw into his meshes. I have known those who have firm faith that the Jew feeds but upon the flesh and blood of pagan and Christian infants, whom, by necromantic power, he beguiles from their homes. He is held as the common enemy of man, a universal robber, whom all are bound to hate and oppress. Reward me now with your belief, better than even the two gold talents I have earned, that all are not such. This is the charity, and all that I would beg; and I beg it of you, for that I love you all, and would have your esteem. Believe that in the Jew there is a heart of flesh as well as in a dog. Believe that some noble ambition visits his mind as well as yours. Credit it not—it is against nature—that any tribe of man is what you make the Jew. Look upon me, and behold the emblem of my tribe. What do you see? A man bent with years and toil; this ragged tunic his richest garb; his face worn with the storms of all climates; a wanderer over the earth; my home, Piso, thou hast seen it—a single room, with my good dromedary's furniture for my bed at night, and my seat by day; this pack, my only apparent wealth. Yet here have I now received two gold talents of Jerusalem! what most would say were wealth enough, and this is not the tithe of that which I possess. What then? Is it for that I love obscurity, slavery, and a beggar's raiment, that I live and labour thus, when my wealth would raise me to a prince's state? Or is it that I love to sit and count my hoarded gains? Good friends, for such you are, believe it not. You have found me faithful and true to my engagements; believe my word also. You have heard of Jerusalem, once the chief city of the east, where stood the great temple of our faith, and which was the very heart of our nation, and you know how it was beleaguered by the Romans, and its very foundations rooted up, and her inhabitants driven abroad as outcasts, to wander over the face of the earth, with every where a country, but no where a home. And does the Jew, think you, sit down quietly under these wrongs? Trajan's reign may answer that. Is there no patriotism yet alive in the bosom of a Jew? Will every other toil and die for his country, and not the Jew? Believe me, again, the prayers which go up morning, noon, and night, for the restoration of Jerusalem, are not fewer than those which go up for Rome or Palmyra. And their deeds are not less; for every prayer there are two acts. It is for Jerusalem that you behold me thus in rags, and yet rich. It is for her glory that I am the servant of all and the scorn of all, that I am now pinched by the winters of Byzantium, now scorched by the heats of Asia, and buried beneath the sands of the desert. All that I have and am is for Jerusalem. And in telling you of myself, I have told you of my tribe. What we do and are is not for ourselves, but for our country. Friends, the hour of our redemption draweth nigh. The Messiah treads in the steps of Zenobia! And when the east shall behold the disasters of Aurelian, as it will, it will behold the restoration of that empire, which is destined in the lapse of ages to gather to itself the glory and dominion of the whole earth."

Saying these words, during which he seemed no longer Isaac the Jew, but the very prince of the captivity himself, he turned and took his departure.

Long and earnest conversation now ensued, in which we received from Calpurnius the most exact accounts of his whole manner of life during his captivity; of his early sufferings and disgraces, and his late honours and elevation, and gave, in return, similar details concerning the history of our family and of Rome, during the same period of time. I will not pretend to set down the narrative of Calpurnius. It was delivered with a grace which I can by no means transfer to these pages. I trust you may one day hear it from his own lips. Neither can I tell you how beautiful it was to see Fausta hanging upon his words, with an attention that made her insensible to all else; her varying colour and changing expression showing how deeply she sympathised with the narrator. When he had ended, and we had become weary of the excitement of this first interview, Fausta proposed that we should separate to meet again at supper. To this we agreed.

According to the proposal of Fausta, we were again, soon as evening had come, assembled around the table of the princely Gracchus.

When we had partaken of the luxuries of the feast, and various lighter discourse had caused the time to pass by in an agreeable manner, I said thus, turning to my brother:

"I would, Calpurnius, that the temper of one's mind could as easily be changed as one's garments. You now seem to me, having put off your Persian robes, far more like Piso than before. Your dress, though but in part Roman and part Palmyrene, still brings you nearer. Were it wholly Roman, it were better. Is nothing of the Persian really put off, and nothing of the Roman put on, by this change?"

"Whatever of the Persian there was about me," replied Calpurnius, " I am free to say I have laid aside with my Persian attire. I was a Persian not by choice and preference, I need scarcely assure you, but by a sort of necessity, just as it was with my costume. I could not procure Roman clothes if I would. I could not help, too, putting off the Roman, seeing how I was dealt by, and putting on the Persian. Yet I part with whatever of the Persian has cleaved to me without reluctance—would it were so that I could again assume the Roman—but that can never be. But Isaac has already told you all."

"Isaac has indeed informed me, in his letter from Ecbatana, that you had renounced your country, and that it was the expectation of war with Rome that alone had power to draw you from your captivity. But I have not believed that you would stand by that determination. The days of republican patriotism, I know, are passed, but even now, under the empire, our country has claims, and her children owe her duties."

"The figure is a common one," Calpurnius answered, "by which our country is termed a parent, and we her children. Allow it just. Do I owe obedience to an unjust or tyrannical parent—to one who has abandoned me in helplessness, or exposed me in infancy? Are not the natural ties then sundered?"

"I think not," I replied; "no provocation or injury can justify a parricidal blow. Our parent is our creator, in some sense a god to us. The tie that binds us to him is like no other tie; to do it violence, is not only a wrong, but an impiety."

"I cannot think so," he rejoined. "A parent is our creator, not so much for our good as his own pleasure. In the case of the gods, this is reversed. They have given us being for our advantage, not theirs. We lie under obligation to a parent, then, only as he fulfils the proper duties of one. When he ceases to be virtuous, the child must cease to respect. When he ceases to be just, or careful, or kind, the child must cease to love. And from whomsoever else, then, the child receives the treatment becoming a parent, that person is to him the true parent. It is idle to be governed by names rather than things; it is more, it is mischievous and injurious."

"I still am of opinion," I replied, "that nature has ordained, what I have asserted to be an everlasting and universal truth, by the instincts which she has implanted. All men, of all tribes, have united in expressions of horror against him who does violence to his parents. And have not the poets truly painted, when they have set before us the parricide, for ever after the guilty act, pursued by the furies, and delivered over to their judicial torments."

"All instincts," he replied, "are not to be defended. Some animals devour their own young as soon as born. Vice is instinctive. If it be instinctive to honour, and love, and obey, a vicious parent, to be unresisting under the most galling oppression, then, I say, the sooner reason usurps the place of instinct, the safer for mankind. No error can be more gross or hurtful than to respect vice because of the person in whom it is embodied, even though that person be a parent. Vice is vice, injustice is injustice, wrong is wrong, wheresoever they are found, and are to be detested and withstood. But I might admit that I am in an error here; and still maintain my cause, by denying the justice of the figure by which our country is made our parent, and our obligations to her made to rest on the same ground. It is mere fancy—it is a nullity—unless it be true, as I think it is, that it has been the source of great mischiefs to the world, in which case it cannot be termed a nullity, but something positively pernicious. What age of the world can be named when an insane devotion to one's country has not been the mother of war upon war, evil upon evil, beyond the power of memory to recount. Patriotism, standing for this instinctive slavery of the will, has cursed as much as it has blessed mankind. Men have not reasoned, they have only felt. They have not inquired, Is the cause of my country just? but, Is it her cause? That has ever been the cry in Rome. 'Our country!—our country!—right or wrong!—our country!' It is a maxim good for conquest and despotism, bad for peace and justice. It has made Rome mistress of the world, and at the same time the scourge of the world, and trodden down into their own blood-stained soil the people of many a clime, who had else dwelt in freedom. I am no Roman in this sense, and ought never to have been. Admit that I am not justified in raising my hand against the life of a parent—though, if I could defend myself against violence no otherwise, I should raise that hand—I will never allow that I am to approve and second with my best blood all the acts of my country, but when she errs am bound, on the other hand, to blame, and, if need be, oppose! Why not? What is this country? Men like myself. Who enact the decrees by which I am to be thus bound? Senators, no more profoundly wise, perhaps, and no more irreproachably virtuous, than myself. And do I owe their judgments a dearer allegiance—and which I esteem false—than I do to my own, which I esteem right and true. Never. Such patriotism is a degradation and a vice. Rome, Lucius, I think to have dealt by me and the miserable men who with me fell into the hands of Sapor, after the manner of a selfish, cold-hearted, unnatural parent, and I renounce her, and allegiance to her. I am from this hour a Palmyrene—Zenobia is my mother, Palmyra my country."

"But," I could not but still urge, "should no distinction be made between your country and her emperor? Is the country to rest under the imputation which is justly, perhaps, cast upon its men? That were hardly right. To renounce Gallienus, were he now emperor, were a defensible act. But why Rome or Aurelian?"

"I freely grant, that had a just emperor been upon

the throne—a man with human feelings—the people, had he projected our rescue or revenge, would have gone with him. But how is their conduct to be defended during the long reign of the son of Valerian? Was such a people as the people of Rome to conform their minds and acts to a monster like him? Was that the part of a great nation? Is it credible that the senate and the people together had no power to compel Gallienus to the performance of his duties to his own father, and the brave legions who fell with him? Alas! they, too, wanted the will."

"Oh, not so, Calpurnius," I rejoined; "Gallienus wished the death or the captivity of his father, that he might reign. To release him was the last act that wretch could have been urged to do. And could he, then, have been made to interpose for the others? He might have been assassinated; but all the power of Rome could not have compelled him to a war, the issue of which might have been, by the rescue of Valerian, to lose him his throne."

"Then he should have been assassinated. Rome owed herself a greater duty than allegiance to a beast in human form."

"But, Calpurnius, you are now at liberty. Why consider so curiously whence it comes? Besides, you have, while in Persia, dwelt in comfort, and at last even in magnificence. The prince himself has been your companion and friend."

"What was it," he replied, "what was it, when I reflected upon myself, but so much deeper degradation, to find that, in spite of myself, I was every day sinking deeper and deeper in Persian effeminacy? What was it but the worst wretchedness of all to feel as I did, that I, a Roman and a Piso, was losing my nature as I had lost my country? If any thing seemed to turn my blood into one hot current of bitterness and revenge, it was this. It will never cool till I find myself, sword in hand, under the banners of Zenobia. Urge me no more. It were as hopeful an endeavour to stem the current of the Euphrates, as to turn me from my purpose. I have reasoned with you because you are a brother, not because you are a Roman."

"And I," I replied, "can still love you—because you are a brother, nor less because you are also a Palmyrene. I greet you as the head of our house, the elder heir of an illustrious name. I still will hope, that when these troubles cease, Rome may claim you as her own."

"No emperor," he answered, "unless he were a Piso, I fear, would permit a renegade of such rank ever to dwell within the walls of Rome. Let me rather hope, that when this war is ended, Portia may exchange Rome for Palmyra, and that here, upon this fair and neutral ground, the Pisos may once more dwell beneath the same roof."

"May it be so," said Gracchus; "and let not the heats of political opposition change the kindly current of your blood, or inflame it. You, Lucius Piso, are to remember the provocations of Calpurnius, and are to feel that there was a nobleness in that sensibility to a declension into Persian effeminacy, that, to say the least, reflects quite as much honour upon the name of Piso, and even Roman, as any loyalty to an emperor like Gallienus, or that senate, filled with his creatures. And you, Calpurnius Piso, are to allow for that instinctive veneration for every thing Roman which grows up with the Roman, and, even in spite of his better reason, ripens into a bigotry that deserves the name of a crime rather than a virtue; and are to consider, that while in you the growth of this false sentiment has been checked by causes, in respect to which you were the sport of fortune, so in Lucius it has been quickened by other causes over which he also was powerless. But to utter my belief, Lucius, I think, is now more than half Palmyrene, and I trust yet, if committed, as he has been, to the further tuition of our patriot Fausta, will be not only in part, but altogether, of our side."

"In the meantime, let us rejoice," said Fausta, "that the noble Calpurnius joins our cause. If we may judge by the eye, the soft life of a Persian satrap has not yet quite exhausted the native Roman vigour."

"I have never intermitted," replied Calpurnius, "martial exercises. Especially have I studied the whole art of horsemanship, so far as the chase and military discipline can teach it. It is in her cavalry, as I learn, that Zenobia places her strength. I shall there, I trust, do her good service."

"In the morning," said Fausta, "it shall be my office to bring you before our queen."

"And now, Fausta," said Gracchus, "bring your harp, and let music perfect the harmony which reason and philosophy have already so well begun—music, which for its power over our souls, may rather be held an influence of the gods, a divine breathing, than any thing of mortal birth."

"I fear," said Fausta, as she touched the instrument —the Greek, and not the Jewish harp—"I shall still further task your philosophy; for I can sing nothing else than the war-song, which is already heard all through the streets of Palmyra, and whose author, it is said, is no less than our chief spirit, Longinus. Lucius, you must close your ears."

"Never while your voice sounds, though bloody treason were the only burden."

"You are a gentle Roman."

Then, after a brief but fiery prelude, which of itself, struck by her fingers, was enough to send life into stones, she broke forth into a strain, abrupt and impassioned, of wild Pindaric energy, that seemed the very war-cry of a people striking and dying for liberty. Her voice, inspired by soul too large for mortal form, rang like a trumpet through the apartment, and seemed to startle the gods themselves at their feast. As the hymn moved on to its perfect close, and the voice of Fausta swelled with the waxing theme, Calpurnius seemed like one entranced—unconsciously he had left his seat, and there, in the midst of the room, stood before the divine girl, converted to a statue. As she ceased, the eyes of Calpurnius fell quickly upon me, with an expression which I instantly interpreted, and should have instantly returned, but that we were all alike roused out of ourselves by the loud shouts of a multitude without the palace, who apparently had been drawn together by the far-reaching tones of Fausta's voice, and who, as soon as the last strings of the harp were touched, testified their delight by reiterated and enthusiastic cries.

"When Zabdas and Zenobia fail," said Calpurnius, "you, daughter of Gracchus, may lead the armies of your country by your harp and voice—they would inspire not less than the fame of Cæsar or Aurelian."

"But be it known to you, Piso," said Gracchus, "that this slight girl can wield a lance or a sword, while, centaur-like, she grows to the animal she rides, as well as sweep these idle strings."

"I will learn of her in either art," replied my brother. "As I acknowledge no instinct which is to bind me to an unjust parent, but will give honour only where there is virtue, so on the field of war I will enlist under any leader in whom I behold the genius of a warrior, be that leader man or woman, boy or girl."

"I shall be satisfied," said Fausta, "to become your teacher in music, that is, if you can learn through the force of example alone. Take now another lesson. Zenobia shall teach you the art of war."

With these words she again passed her fingers over her harp; and after strains of melting sweetness, prolonged till our souls were wholly subdued to the sway of the gentler emotions, she sang, in words of Sappho, the praise of love and peace, twin-sisters. And then, as we urged, or named to her Greek or Roman airs which we wished to hear, did she sing and play till every sense was satisfied and filled.

It needs not so much sagacity as I possess to perceive the effect upon my brother of the beauty and powers of Fausta. He speaks with difficulty when he addresses her, and while arguing or conversing with me or Grac-

chus, his eye seeks her countenance, and then falls as
it encounters hers, as if he had committed some crime.
Fausta, I am sure, is not insensible to the many rare
and striking qualities of Calpurnius. But her affections
can be given only where there is a soul of very uncommon elevation. Whether Calpurnius is throughout
that which he seems to be, and whether he is worthy
the love of a being like Fausta, I know not yet, though
I am strong in faith that it is so. In the mean time, a
mutual affection is springing up and growing upon the
thin soil of the fancy, and may reach a quick and rank
luxuriance before it shall be discovered that there is
nothing more substantial beneath. But why indulge a
single doubt? only, I suppose, because I would rather
Rome should fall than that any harm come to the heart
of Fausta.

It was a little after the noon of this day that the ambassadors, Petronius and Varro, passed from out the
gates of Palmyra, bearing with them a virtual declaration of war.

The greatest excitement prevails. The streets are
already filled with sights and sounds admonitory of the
scenes which are soon to be disclosed. There is the
utmost enthusiasm in every quarter, and upon every
face you behold the confidence and pride of those, who,
accustomed to conquest, are about to extend their dominion over new territories, and to whom war is a game
of pleasure rather than a dark hazard, that may end in
utter desolation and ruin. Intrenched within these
massy walls, the people of this gay capital cannot realise
war. Its sounds are afar off—it has ever been so—
beyond the wide sweep of the deserts, and will be so
—so they judge now, and they are scarcely turned for
a moment, or by the least remove, from their accustomed cares or pleasures.

LETTER XII.

I LAMENT to hear of the disturbances among your slaves, and of the severity with which you have thought it necessary to proceed against them. You will bear me witness, that I have often warned you that the cruelty with which Tiro exercised his authority, would lead to difficulties, if not to violence and murder. I am not surprised to learn his fate. I am, indeed, very free to say that I rejoice at it. I rejoice not that you are troubled in your affairs, but that such an inhuman overseer as Tiro, a man wholly unworthy the kindness and indulgence with which you have treated him, should at length be overtaken by a just retribution. That the poison took effect upon his wife and children I sincerely regret, and wish that some other mode of destruction had been chosen, and whose effects could have been safely directed and limited, for I do not believe that the least ill will existed towards Claudia and her little ones. But rest satisfied, I beseech you, with the punishments already inflicted. Enough have been scourged, put to the torture, and crucified. Let the rest escape. Remember your disposition—now indulgent, now tyrannical—and lay a restraint upon your passions, if you would save yourself from lasting regrets. It is some proof that you are looking to yourself more than formerly, that so many have been imprisoned to wait a further deliberation, and that you are willing first to ask my opinion. Be assured that further crucifixions would serve only to exasperate those who survive, and totally alienate them from you, so that your own life, instead of being the more safe, would be much less so. They will be driven to despair, and say that they may as well terminate their wretched lives in one way as another, and so end all at once by an assault upon yourself and Lucilia, which, while it destroyed you, and so glutted their revenge, could do no more than destroy them—a fate which they dread now, but which at all times, owing to their miseries, they dread much less than we suppose, and so are more willing than we imagine to take the lives of their masters or governors, not caring for death themselves. A well-timed lenity would now be an act of policy as well as of virtue. Those whom you have reprieved, being pardoned, will be bound to you by a sort of gratitude—those of them at least who put a value upon their lives; and now that Tiro is fairly out of the way, and his scourgings at an end, they will all value their lives at a higher rate than before.

But let me especially intercede for Laco and Cælia, with their children. It was they who, when I have been at your farm, have chiefly attended upon me; they have done me many acts of kindness beyond the mere duties of their office, and have ever manifested dispositions so gentle, and so much above their condition, that I feel sure they cannot be guilty of taking any part in the crime. They have been always too happy to put their all at risk by such an attempt. Be assured they are innocent; and they are too good to be sacrificed merely for the effect. There are others—wretches in all respects—who will serve for this, if enough have not already suffered.

When will sentiments of justice assert their supremacy in the human mind? When will our laws and institutions recognise the rights inherent in every man, as man, and compel their observance. When I reflect that I myself possess, upon one only of my estates, five hundred slaves, over whom I wield despotic power, and that each one of these differs not from myself, except in the position into which fortune and our laws have cast him, I look with a sort of horror upon myself, the laws, and my country which enacts and maintains them. But if we cannot at once new-model our institutions and laws, we can do something. By a strict justice, and by merciful treatment, we can mitigate the evils of their lot who are within our own power. We can exercise the authority and temper of fathers, and lay aside, in a greater degree than we do, the air and manner of tyrant.

When upon the fields of every farm, as I ride through our interior, I hear the lash of the task-master, and behold the cross rearing aloft its victim, to poison the air with fœtid exhalations, and strike terror into all who toil within their reach, I hate my country and my nature, and long for some power to reveal itself, I care not of what kind nor in what quarter, capable to reform a state of society rotten as this is to its very heart.

You, yourself, advocate as you are for the existing order of things, would be agitated alternately by horror and compassion, were I to relate to you the scenes described to me by Milo, as having a thousand times been witnessed by him when in the service of Gallienus. To torture and destroy his slaves, by the most ingenious devices of cruelty, was his daily pastime. They were purchased for this very end. When I see you again, I will give to you instances with which I could not soil these pages. Antiochus, were he in Rome, would be a monster of the same stamp. But all this is, as I have often mentioned, a necessary accompaniment of such power as the laws confer upon the owner.

And now that war has actually broken out between Palmyra and Rome, you will wish to know what part I intend to take. Your letters imply, that in such an event you would expect my immediate return. But this pleasure must, for the present at least, be deferred. I am too deeply interested in too many here, to allow me to forsake them in a time of so much anxiety, and, as I think, of peril too. Zenobia's full consent I have already obtained. Indeed, she is now desirous that I should remain. The services that I have accidentally rendered her, have increased the regard with which she treats me. I confess, too, that I am less unwilling to remain than I was, out of a rooted disapprobation of the violent course of Aurelian. I cannot, as Calpurnius has done, renounce my country, but I can blame our emperor. His purposes are without a colour of justice. Nor are they only unjust and iniquitous—they are impolitic. I can enter fully into and defend the feelings and arguments of Palmyra in this direction. Her cause is in the main a just one. She has done somewhat, indeed, to provoke a sensitive and jealous mind, but nothing to warrant the step which Aurelian is taking. And when I counsel peace, and by concessions too, I do it not because I hold it right that such concessions should be made, but because I deem it frantic on the part of Zenobia to encounter the combined power of Rome, under such a soldier as Aurelian. My sympathies are accordingly enlisted in behalf of this people as a people, my heart is closely bound to both the house of Gracchus and of Zenobia, and therefore I cannot leave them. I shall not bear arms against my country—I think I would sooner die—but in any case of extremity, I shall not wear a sword in vain, if by using it I can save the life or honour of persons dear to me. I am firm in the belief, that no such extremity will ever present itself; but should it come, I am ready for it. I cannot but hope that a battle, one or more, upon the outskirts of the empire, will satisfy the pride of Aurelian, and convince the queen, that to contend for empire with him, and Rome at his back, is vain, and that negotiation will therefore end what passion has begun. I shall expect no other issue than this. Then, having done all here, I shall return to Italy, if the queen relents not, to pass an unhappy life upon the Tiburtine farm.

Preparations of every kind for the approaching contest are going forward with activity. The camp of the queen is forming without the walls, upon a wide and beautiful plain, stretching towards the south. One army will be formed here, chiefly consisting of cavalry, in which lies the strength of the queen, and another in the vicinity of Antioch, where a junction will be effected, and whence the whole will move either towards the Bosphorus or Egypt, according to the route which it shall be learned Aurelian intends to pursue.

During these few days that have elapsed since the departure of the ambassadors, the stir and confusion incident to such a time have continually increased. In the streets, I meet scarce any who are not engaged in some service connected with the army. Troops of soldiers are forming, exercising at their arms, and passing from the city as they are severally equipped to join the camp. The shops of the armourers resound with the blows of an innumerable body of artisans, manufacturing or repairing those brilliant suits of steel, for which the cavalry of Zenobia are distinguished. Immense repositories of all the various weapons of our modern warfare, prepared by the queen against seasons of emergency, furnish forth arms of the most perfect workmanship and metal, to all who offer themselves for the expedition. Without the walls, in every direction, the eye beholds clouds of dust raised by different bodies of the queen's forces, as they pour in from their various encampments to one central point. Trains of sumptuary elephants and camels, making a part of every legion as it comes up, and stretching their long lines from the verge of the plain to the very walls, contribute a fresh beauty and interest to the scene.

Within the camp, whatever the tumult and confusion may be without, every thing is conducted with the most admirable order, and with the observance of a discipline as exact, if not as severe, as that of Vespasian, or Aurelian himself. Here are to be séen the commanders of the chief divisions of the army, inspecting the arms and equipments of each individual soldier, and not with less diligence inquiring into the mettle and points of the horse he rides. Every horse, pronounced in any way defective, is rejected from the service, and another procured. The queen's stable has been exhausted in providing in this manner substitutes for such as have been set aside as unworthy.

Zenobia herself is the most active and laborious of all. She is in every place, seeing with her own eyes that every arrangement and provision ordered to be made is completed, and that in the most perfect manner. All the duties of a general are performed by her, with a freedom, a power, and a boldness, that fills one with astonishment who is acquainted with those opposite qualities which render her, as a woman, the most lovely and fascinating of her sex. She is seen sometimes driving rapidly through the streets in an open chariot, of the antique form; but more frequently on horseback, with a small body of attendants, who have quite enough to do to keep pace with her, so as to catch from her the orders which she rapidly issues, and then execute them in every part of the camp and city. She inspires all who behold her with her own spirit. In every soldier and leader you behold something of the same alertness and impetuosity of movement which are so remarkable in her. She is the universal model, and the confidence in the resources of her genius is universal and boundless. "Let our courage and conduct," they say, "be only in some good proportion to our queen's, and we may defy Rome and the world." As the idea of nought but conquest ever crosses their minds, the animation and even gaiety that prevail in the camp, and throughout the ranks, is scarcely to be believed, as it is, I doubt not, unparalleled in the history of war. Were she a goddess, and omnipotent, the trust in her could not be more unwavering.

I have just encountered Calpurnius returning from the palace of the queen, whither he has been to offer his services during the war, in any capacity in which it might please her to employ him.

"What was your reception?" said I.

"Such as Fausta had assured me of. She gives me a hearty welcome to her camp, and assigns me a legion of horse. And, in addition, one more charge, dearer, and yet more anxious a thousand fold."

"May I know it?" said I, but readily surmising the nature of it.

"It is," he replied, with visible emotion, "it is Fausta herself."

"It is fixed, then, that she accompanies the queen?"

"She entreats, and the queen consents."

"Would that she could be turned from this purpose; but I suppose the united power of the east could not do it. To be near Zenobia, and if evil should befall her, to share it, or to throw herself as a shield between the queen and death, is what she pants for more than for renown, though it should be double that of Semiramis."

"Lucius, have you urged every reason, and used all the power you possess over her, to dissuade her?"

"I have done all I have dared to do. The decisions of some minds, you know, with the motives which sway them, we too much revere to oppose to them our own. Girl though Fausta be, yet when I see by the lofty expression of her countenance, her firm and steadfast eye, that she has taken her part, I have no assurance sufficient to question the rectitude of her determination, or essay to change it. I have more faith in her than in myself."

"Yet it must never be," said my brother with earnestness; "she could never support the fatigues of such a campaign, and it must not be permitted that she should encounter the dangers and horrors of actual combat. I have learned that at the palace, which, while it has dismissed the most painful apprehensions of one sort, has filled me with others more tolerable, but yet intolerable. How, Lucius, has it happened that your heart, soft in most of its parts, on one side has been adamant."

"The way of the heart," I said, "like the way of Providence, is mysterious. I know not. Perhaps it was that I knew her longer in Rome and more closely than you, and the sentiment always uppermost towards her has been that of a brother's love. Hers towards me has never been other than the free, unrestrained affection of a sister. But you have not seen the princess?"

"I have not."

"That will complete the explanation. The queen rejects me; but I do not despair. But to return to Fausta. As no force could withhold her from the army,

I thank the gods that in you she will find a companion and defender, and that to you the queen has committed her. Fail her not, Calpurnius, in the hour of need. You do not know, for your eye has but taken in her outward form, what a jewel, richer than eastern monarch ever knew, is entrusted to your care. Keep it as you would your own life—nay, your life will be well given for its safety. Forgive me, if in this I seem to charge you as an elder. Remember that you I do not know, Fausta I do. Of you I scarcely know more than that you are a Piso, and that the very soul of honour ought to dwell within you. The queen's ready confidence in you, lays you under obligations heavy as injunctions from the gods to fidelity. If, as you journey on towards Antioch, the opportunities of the way throw you together, and your heart is won by your nearer knowledge of her sweet qualities as well as great ones, as your eye has already been, ask not, seek not for hers, but after a close questioning of yourself, whether you are worthy of her. Of your life and the true lineaments of your soul you know every thing—she knows nothing; but she is more free and unsuspicious than a child, and without looking further than the show and colour of honesty and truth, will surrender up her heart where her fancy leads, trusting to find according to her faith—and to receive all that she gives. Brother though you be, I here invoke the curses of the gods upon your head, if the faintest purpose of dishonest or deceptive dealing have place within you."

"Your words," said Calpurnius in reply—a wholesome and natural expression of indignation spreading over his countenance, which inspired more confidence than any thing he could say—" your words, Lucius, are earnest and something sharp. But I hear them without complaint, for the sake of the cause in which you have used them. I blame you not. It is true, I am a stranger both to yourself and Fausta, and it were monstrous to ask confidence before time has proved me. Leave it all to time. My conduct under this trust shall be my trial. Not till our return from Antioch will I aim at more than the happiness to be her companion and guard. The noble Otho will be near us, to whom you may commit us both."

"Brother," I rejoined, "I doubt you not; but where our treasure is great, we are tormented by imaginary fears, and we guard it by a thousand superfluous cares. What I have said has implied the existence of doubts and apprehensions. But in sober truth they were forced into existence. My nature from the first, has been full of trust in you; but this very promptness to confide, my anxious fears converted to a fault, and urged suspicion as a duty. Your countenance and your words have now inspired me with an assurance, not, I am certain, to be ever shaken in your virtues. It shall be my joy to impart the same to Gracchus. Fausta shall be left free to the workings of her own mind and heart."

I should not have been justified, it seems to me, in saying less than this, though I said it with apprehensions, many and grave, of a breach between us, which perhaps time might never heal. It has ended in a deep and settled conviction that the character of Calpurnius is what it at first appears to be. Persian duplicity has made no lodgment within him, of that I am sure. And where you feel sure of sincerity, almost any other fault may be borne.

The army has taken up its march, and the city is deprived of its best and bravest spirits—Zenobia and Fausta, those kindred souls, are gone. How desolate is this vast palace! The loss of Gracchus and Fausta seems the loss of all. A hundred attendant slaves leave it still empty.

A period of the most active preparation has been closed to-day, by the departure of as well-appointed an army as ever issued from the Prætorian camps. It was a spectacle as beautiful as my eyes ever beheld, and as sad. Let me set before you the events of the day. As I descended to the apartment where we take together our morning meal, and which we were now

for the last time to partake in each other's company, I
found Fausta already there, and surveying with sparkling eyes and a flushed cheek, a suit of the most brilliant armour, which having been made by the queen's
workmen, and by her order, had just now been brought
and delivered to her.

"I asked the honour," said the person with whom
she was conversing, "to bring it myself, who have made
it with the same care as the queen's, of the same materials, and after the same fashion. So it was her order
to do. It will sit, lady, believe me, as easy as a riding
dress, though it be all of the most impenetrable steel.
The polish, too, is such, that neither arrow nor javelin
need be feared; they can but touch and glance. Hercules could not indent this surface. Let me reveal to
you divers secret and perfect springs and clasps, the
use of which you should be well acquainted with. Yet
it differs not so much from that in which you have performed your exercises, but what you will readily comprehend the manner of its adjustment."

He then went through with his demonstrations, and
departed.

"This is beautiful indeed," I said, as I surveyed and
handled parts of the armour; "the eye can hardly bear
it when the rays of the sun fall upon it. But I wish
it was fairly back again in the shop of the armourer."

"That would be," said Fausta, "only to condemn me
to an older and worse one; and if you should wish that
away too, it would be only to send me into the ranks
defenceless. Surely that you would not do?"

"The gods forbid. I only mean that I would rather
these walls, Fausta, should be your defence. You were
not made, whatever you may think, to brave the dangers
of the desert, and the horrors of a war. Do you remember, at the amphitheatre you hid your eyes from
the cruel sights of the arena? I doubt not your courage.
But it is not after your heart."

"From the useless barbarities of the circus I might
indeed turn away my eyes, and yet, I think, with per-

fect consistency, strike my lance into the heart of a man who came against my country or my queen, nor even blench. But do not suppose that it is with any light or childish joy that I resolve to follow in the steps of Zenobia, even to the field of slaughter. I would far rather sit here in the midst of security and peace, making mimic war upon my embroidery, or tuning my voice and harp, with Gracchus and you to listen and applaud. But there is that within me that forbids my stay. I am urged from within by a voice which seems as the voice of a god, to do according to my strength, for what may be the last struggle of our country against the encroachments and ambition of Rome. You may deem it little that a woman can do."

"I confess I am of opinion that many a substitute could do Palmyra a better service than even the arm of Fausta. A woman may do much and bravely, but a man may do more."

"Therein, Lucius, am I persuaded you err. If it were only that in the language of Zabdas, I added so many pounds' weight of bone and flesh, by adding myself to the queen's troops, I would stay at home. There are heavier arms than mine—for mine are slight; and sturdier limbs—for mine, in spite of the sports of the field, are still a woman's. But you know nothing of Palmyra if you know not this, that her victories have been won, not by the arm, but by the presence of Zenobia; to be led to the onset by a woman, and that woman Zenobia—it is this that has infused a spirit and an enthusiasm into our soldiery, that has rendered them irresistible. Were it a thousand against ten thousand, not a native Palmyrene would shrink from the trial, with Zenobia at their head. I am not Zenobia, Lucius, but what she can do for an army, I can do for a legion. Mark the sensation, when this morning Zenobia presents herself to the army, and even when Fausta wheels into the ranks, and acknowledge that I have uttered a truth."

"There must be truth in what you say, for were I

in your train, I can feel how far I should follow you, and when forsake you. But what you say only fills me with new apprehensions, and renders me the more anxious to detain you. What but certain death awaits you if you are to lead the way?"

"And why should not I die as well as another? And is it of more consequence that Fausta, the daughter of Gracchus, should die upon a bed of down, and beneath silken canopies, than that the common soldier should, who falls at her side? How could I die better than at the head of a legion, whom, as I fell, I saw sweeping on like a tempest, to emulate and revenge my death?"

"But Gracchus—has he another Fausta, or another child?"

Her eyes were bent to the ground, and for a few moments she was buried in thought. They were filled with tears as she raised them, and said,

"You may well suppose, Lucius, having witnessed, as you have, what the love is which I bear Gracchus, and how his life is bound up in mine, that this has been my heaviest thought. But it has not prevailed with me to change my purpose, and ought not to do so. Could I look into futurity, and know that while I fell upon the plains of Antioch, or on the sands of the desert, he returned to these walls to wear out, childless and in solitude, the remnant of his days, my weakness, I believe, would yield, and I should prefer my parent to my country. But the future is all dark. And it may as well be, that either we shall both fall, or both return; or that he may fall, and I survive. It is unworthy of me, is it not, then, to consider so anxiously such chances! The only thing certain and of certain advantage is this—I can do my country, as I deem it, a signal service, by joining her forces in this hour of peril. To this I cleave, and leave the rest to the disposal of the gods. But come, urge me no more, Lucius; my mind is finally resolved, and it but serves to darken the remaining hours. See, Gracchus and Calpurnius are come; let us to the tables."

This last meal was eaten in silence, save the few required words of courtesy.

Soon as it was over, Fausta, springing from her seat, disappeared, hastening to her apartments. She returned in a few moments, her dress changed and prepared for her armour.

"Now, Lucius," she exclaimed, "your hour of duty has come, which is to fit upon me this queenly apparel. Show your dexterity, and prove that you, too, have seen the wars, by the grace with which you shall do your service."

"These pieces differ not greatly," I said, "from those which I have worn in Gaul and Germany; and were they to be fastened upon my own limbs, or a comrade's, the task were an easy one. I fear lest I may use too rough a hand in binding on this heavy iron."

"Oh, never fear—there, that is well. The queen's armourer has said truly; this is easy as a robe of silk. Now, these clasps—are they not well made? will they not catch?"

"The clasps are perfect, Fausta, but my eye is dim. Here—clasp them yourself," and I turned away.

"Lucius, Lucius, are you a Roman, with eyes so melting? Julia were a better handmaid. But one thing remains, and that must be done by no other hand than yours—crown me now with this helmet."

I took it from her, and placed it upon her head, saying, as I did it, "The gods shield you from danger, dear Fausta, and when you have either triumphed or suffered defeat, return you again to this happy roof. Now, for my services allow me this reward"—and for the first time since she was a girl, I kissed her forehead.

She was now a beautiful vision to behold as ever lighted upon the earth. Her armour revealed with exactness the perfection of her form, and to her uncommon beauty added its own, being of the most brilliant steel, and frequently studded with jewels of dazzling lustre. Her sex was revealed only by her hair, which, parting over her forehead, fell towards either eye, and then was drawn up and buried in her helmet. The ease with which she moved showed how well she had accustomed herself, by frequent exercises, to the cumbrous load she bore. I could hardly believe, as she paced the apartment, issuing her final orders to her slaves and attendants who pressed around, that I was looking upon a woman reared in all the luxury of the east. Much as I had been accustomed to the sight of Zenobia, performing the part of an emperor, I found it difficult to persuade myself, that when I looked upon Fausta, changing so completely her sex, it was any thing more than an illusion.

Gracchus and Calpurnius now joined us, each, like Fausta, arrayed in the armour of the queen's cavalry.

"Fausta," said Gracchus, hastily, "the hour is come that we were at the camp; our horses wait us in the courtyard—let us mount. Farewell, Lucius Piso," continued he, as we moved towards the rear of the palace, "would you were to make one of our company; but as that cannot be, I bequeath to you my place, my honours, and my house. Be ready to receive us with large hospitality and a philosophic composure, when we return loaded with the laurels of victory, and the spoils of your countrymen. It is fortunate, that as we lose you we have Calpurnius, who seems of the true warrior breed. Never, Lucius, has my eye lighted upon a nobler pair than this. Observe them. The queen, careful of our Fausta, has given her in special charge to your brother. I thank her. By his greater activity, and my more prudent counsel, I trust to bring her again to Palmyra with a fame not less than Zenobia's."

"I can spare the fame," I replied, "so I see her once more in Palmyra, herself unharmed, and her country at peace."

"Palmyra would no longer be itself without her," rejoined the fond father.

We were now in the courtyard, where we found the horses, fully caparisoned, awaiting their riders. Fausta's was her favourite Arab, of a jet black colour, and of a fierce and fiery temper, hardly to be managed by the Saracen, whose sole office it was to attend upon him, while in the hands of Fausta, though still spirited almost to wildness, he was yet docile and obedient. Soon as her feet were in the stirrups, although before it had been difficult to hold him, he became quiet and calm.

"See the power of woman," said Gracchus; "were Antiochus here, he would look upon this as but another proof that the gods are abandoning Palmyra to the sway of women."

"It is," said Fausta, "simply the power of gentleness. My Saracen operates through fear, and I through love. My hand laid softly upon his neck, gains more a thousand fold than the lash laid hardly upon his back."

Mounting my horse, which Milo stood holding for me, we then sallied out of the courtyard gate towards the camp.

The city itself was all pouring forth upon the plains in its vicinity. The crowds choked the streets as they passed out, so that our progress was slow. Arriving at length, we turned towards the pavilion of the queen, pitched over against the centre of the army. There we stood, joined by others, awaiting her arrival; for she had not yet left the palace. We had not stood long, before the braying of trumpets, and other warlike instruments, announced her approach. We turned; and looking towards the gate of the city, through which we had but now passed, saw Zenobia, having on either side Longinus and Zabdas, and preceded and followed by a select troop of horse, advancing at her usual speed towards the pavilion. She was mounted upon her far-famed white Numidian, for power an elephant, for endurance a dromedary, for fleetness a very Nicœan, and who had been her companion in all the battles by which she had gained her renown and her empire.

Calpurnius was beside himself; he had not before seen her when assuming all her state. "Did eye ever look upon aught so like a celestial apparition? It is a descent from other regions; I can swear 'tis no mortal, still less a woman. Fausta, this puts to shame your eulogies, swollen as I termed them."

I did not wonder at his amazement, for I myself shared it, though I had seen her so often. The object that approached us truly seemed rather a moving blaze of light than an armed woman, which the eye and the reason declared it to be, with such gorgeous magnificence was she arrayed. The whole art of the armourer had been exhausted in her appointments. The caparison of her steed, sheathed with burnished gold, and thick studded with precious stones of every various hue, reflected an almost intolerable splendour as the rays of a hot morning sun fell upon it. She, too, herself being clothed in armour of polished steel, whose own fiery brightness was doubled by the diamonds—that was the only jewel she wore—sown with profusion all over its more prominent parts, could be gazed upon scarcely with more ease than the sun himself, whose beams were given back from it with undiminished glory. In her right hand she held the long slender lance of the cavalry; over her shoulders hung a quiver, well loaded with arrows; while at her side depended a heavy Damascus blade. Her head was surmounted by a steel helmet, which left her face wholly uncovered, and showed her forehead, like Fausta's, shaded by the dark hair, which, while it was the only circumstance that revealed the woman, added to the effect of a countenance unequalled for a marvellous union of feminine beauty, queenly dignity, and masculine power. Sometimes it has been her usage, upon such occasions, to appear with arms bare, and gloved hands; they were now cased, like the rest of the body, in plates of steel.

"Calpurnius," said Fausta, "saw you ever in Persia such horsemanship? See now, as she draws nearer, with what grace and power she moves! Blame you the enthusiasm of this people?"

"I more than share it," he replied; "it is reward enough for my long captivity, at last to follow such a leader. Many a time, as Zenobia has in years past visited my dreams, and I almost fancied myself in her train, I little thought that the happiness I now experience was to become a reality. But, hark! how the shout of welcome goes up from this innumerable host."

No sooner was the queen arrived where we stood, and the whole extended lines became aware of her presence, than the air was filled with the clang of trumpets, and the enthusiastic cries of the soldiery, who waved aloft their arms, and made a thousand expressive signs of most joyful greeting. When this hearty salutation, commencing at the centre, had died away along the wings, stretching one way to the walls of the city, and the other towards the desert, Zenobia rode up nearer the lines, and being there surrounded by the ranks which were in front, and by a crowd of the great officers of the army, spoke to them, in accordance with her custom. Stretching out her hand, as if she would ask the attention of the multitude, a deep silence ensued, and in a voice clear and strong, she thus addressed them—" Men and soldiers of Palmyra! Is this the last time that you are to gather together in this glittering array, and go forth as lords of the whole east? Conquerors in so many wars, are you now about to make an offering of yourselves and your homes to the emperor of Rome? Am I, who have twice led you to the gates of Ctesiphon, now to be your leader to the footstool of Aurelian? Are you thinking of any thing but victory? Is there one in all these ranks, who doubts whether the same fate that once befell Probus, shall now befall Aurelian? If there be, let him stand forth! Let him go and entrench himself within the walls of Palmyra. We want him not. (The soldiers brandished and clashed their arms.) Victory, soldiers, belongs to those who believe. Believe that you can do so, and we will return with a Roman army captive at our chariot wheels. Who should put trust in themselves, if not the men and soldiers of Palmyra? Whose memory is long enough to reach backward to a defeat? What was the reign of Odenatus but an unbroken triumph? Are you now, for the first time, to fly or fall before an enemy? And who the enemy? Forget it not—Rome! and Aurelian!—the greatest empire and the greatest soldier of the world. Never before was so large a prize within your reach. Never before fought you on a stage with the whole world for spectators. Forget not, too, that defeat will be not only defeat, but ruin! The loss of a battle will be not only so many dead and wounded, but the loss of empire! For Rome resolves upon our subjugation. We must conquer or we must perish, and for ever lose our city, our throne, and our name. Are you ready to write yourselves subjects and slaves of Rome—citizens of a Roman province—and forfeit the proud name of Palmyrene? (Loud and indignant cries rose from the surrounding ranks.) If not, you have only to remember the plains of Egypt and of Persia; and the spirit that burned within your bosoms then will save you now, and bring you back to these walls, your brows bound about with the garlands of victory. Soldiers! strike your tents, and away to the desert!"

Shouts long and loud, mingled with the clash of arms, followed these few words of the queen. Her own name was heard above all. "Long live the great Zenobia!" ran along the ranks from the centre to the extremes, and from the extremes back again to the centre. It seemed as if, when her name had once been uttered, they could not cease, through the operation of some charm, to repeat it again and again, coupled, too, with a thousand phrases of loyalty and affection.

The queen, as she ended, turned towards the pavilion, where dismounting, she entered, and together with her, her councillors, the great officers of the army and empire, her family and friends. Here was passed an hour, in the interchange of the words and signs of affection, between those who were about to depart upon this uncertain enterprise, and those who were to remain. The queen would fain inspire all with her light, bold, and confident spirit, but it could not prevail to banish the fears and sorrows that filled many hearts. Julia's eyes never moved from her mother's face, or only to rest on Fausta's, whose hand she held clasped in her own. Zenobia often turned towards her with a look, in which the melting tenderness of the mother contended but too successfully with the calm dignity of the queen, and bore testimony to the strong affection working at the heart. She would then, saying a word or two, turn away again, and mingle with those who made less demand upon her sympathies. Livia was there too, and the flaxen-haired Faustula—Livia, gay even, through excess of life—Faustula sad and almost terrified at the scene, and clinging to Julia as to her haven of safety. The Cæsars were also there, insignificant as always, but the youngest, Vabalathus, armed for the war; the others are not to be drawn away from the luxuries and pleasures of the city. Antiochus, sullen and silent, was of the number too—stalking with folded arms apart from the company, or else arm in arm with one of his own colour, and seeming to be there rather because he feared to be absent, than because he derived any pleasure from the scene. It was with an effort, and with reluctance, that he came forward from his hiding-place, and with supreme awkwardness, yet with an air of haughtiness and pride, paid his court to the queen. As he retreated from his audience, the queen's eye sought me, and approaching me, she said, "Piso, I am not prone to suspicion, and fear is a stranger to my heart. But I am told to distrust Antiochus. I have been warned to observe him. I cannot now do it, for I depart while he remains in Palmyra. It has been thrown out that he has designs of a treasonable nature, and that the princess Julia is connected with them. He is an object too contemptible to deserve my thought, and I have not been willing so much as to name the circumstance to any of the council. He may prove an amusing and interesting subject for your contemplation while we are gone."

This was said in a partly serious, partly trifling vein.

I answered her, saying, "that I could not but fear lest there might be more foundation for the warnings that had been given her than she was disposed to allow. He was indeed insignificant and contemptible in character, but he was malignant and restless. Many an insect, otherwise every way despicable, is yet armed with a deadly sting. A swarm may conquer even the monarch of the forest. Antiochus, mean as he is, may yet inflict a secret and fatal wound; and he is not alone. There are those who affect him. I believe you have imposed no task, which, as a Roman, I may not innocently perform. Rest assured, that if watchfulness of mine may avert the shadow of an evil from your head, it shall not be wanting. I would that you yourself could look more seriously upon this information, but I perceive you to be utterly incredulous."

"It is so indeed," she replied. "It were better for me perhaps were it otherwise. Had I heeded the rumours which reached me of the base Mæonius, Odenatus had now perhaps been alive and at my side. But it is against the grain of my nature. I can neither doubt nor fear."

Sounds from without now indicated that the camp was broken up, and the army in motion. The moment of separation had come. The queen hastily approached her daughters, and impressing a mother's kisses upon them, turned quickly away, and springing upon her horse, was soon lost to sight, as she made her way through the ranks, to assume her place at their head. Fausta lingered long in the embraces of Julia, who, to part with her, seemed as if about to lose as much more as she had just lost in Zenobia.

"These our friends being now gone, let us," said the princess, "who remain, together ascend the walls of the city, and from the towers of the gate observe the progress of the army so long as it shall remain in sight."

Saying this, we returned to the city, and from the highest part of the walls watched the departing glories of the most magnificent military array I had ever beheld. It was long after noon before the last of the train of loaded elephants sank below the horizon. I have seen larger armies upon the Danube, and in Gaul; but never have I seen one that in all its appointments presented so imposing a spectacle. This was partly owing to the greater proportion of cavalry, and to the admixture of the long lines of elephants with their burdens, their towers, and litters; but more, perhaps, to the perfectness with which each individual, be he on horse or foot, be he servant, slave, or master, is furnished, respecting arms, armour, and apparel. Julia beheld it if with sorrow, with pride also.

"Between an army like this," she said, " so appointed, and so led and inflamed, and another like that of Rome coming up under a leader like Aurelian, how sharp and deadly must be the encounter! What a multitude of this and that living host, now glorious in the blaze of arms, and burning with desires of conquest, will fall and perish, pierced by weapons or crushed by elephants, nor ever hear the shout of victory! a horrid death, winding up a feverish dream. And of that number how likely to be Fausta and Zenobia!"

"Why, sister," said Faustula, whom I held, and in pointing out to whom the most remarkable objects of the strange scene I had been occupied, "why does our mother love to go away and kill the Romans? I am sure she would not like to kill you," looking up in my face; " and are not you a Roman? She will not let me hurt even a little fly or ant, but tells me they feel as much to be killed, as if Sapor were to put his great foot on me, and tread me into the sand."

" But the Romans," said Julia, " are coming to take away our city from us, and perhaps do us a great deal of harm, and must they not be hindered?"

" But," replied Faustula, " would they do it if Zenobia asked them not to do it? Did you ever know any body who could help doing as she asked them? I wish Aurelian could only have come here and heard her speak, and seen her smile, and I know he would not have wanted to hurt her. If I were a queen, I would never fight."

"I do not believe you would," said I, "you do not seem as if you could hurt any body or any thing."

"And, now, is not Zenobia better than I? I think perhaps she is only going to frighten the Romans, and then coming home again."

"Oh no; do not think so," said Livia; "has not Zenobia fought a great many battles before this? If she did not fight battles, we should have no city to live in."

"If it is so good to fight battles, why does she prevent me from quarrelling, or even speaking unkindly? I think she ought to teach me to fight. I do not believe that men or women ought to fight, any more than children; and, I dare say, if they first saw and talked with one another before they fought, as I am told to do, they never would do it. I find, that if I talk and tell what I think, then I do not want to quarrel. See, is that Zenobia? How bright she shines! I wish she would come back."

"Wait a little while, and she will come again," said Livia, "and bring Aurelian perhaps with her? Should you not like to see Aurelian?"

"No; I am sure I should not. I do not want to see any one that does not love Zenobia."

So the little child ran on, often uttering truths, too obviously truths for mankind to be governed by, yet containing the best philosophy of life. Truth and happiness are both within easy reach. We miss them, in fact, because they are so near. We look over them, and grasp at distant and more imposing objects, wrapped in the false charms which distance lends.

During the absence of the queen and Fausta, we have, in agreement with the promise we made, repeated our visit, more than once, to the retreat of the Christian hermit—from whom I have drawn almost all that remains to be known concerning the truths of his religion. Both Julia and Livia have been my companions,

Of the conversations at these visits, I shall hope at some future time to furnish you with full accounts.

In the meanwhile, farewell.

LETTER XIII.

THESE few days having passed in the manner I have described, our impatience has been relieved by news from the west. We learn that Aurelian, having appointed Illyricum as the central point for assembling his forces, has, marching thence through Thrace, and giving battle on the way to the Goths, at length reached Byzantium, whence, crossing the Bosphorus, it is his purpose to subdue the Asiatic provinces, and afterwards advance towards Palmyra. The army of the queen, judging by the last accounts received by her messengers, must now have reached the neighbourhood of Antioch, and there already perhaps have encountered the forces of the emperor.

The citizens begin at length to put on the appearance of those who feel that something of value is at stake. The Portico is forsaken, or frequented only by such as hope to hear news by going there. The streets are become silent and solitary. I myself partake of the general gloom. I am often at the palace and at the house of Longinus. The dwelling, or rather—should I not term it?—the spacious palace of the minister, affords me delightful hours of relaxation and instruction, as I sit and converse with its accomplished lord, or wander among the compartments of his vast library, or feast the senses and imagination upon the choice specimens of sculpture and painting, both ancient and modern, which adorn the walls, the ceilings, the stairways, and, indeed, every part of the extensive interior. Here I succeed in forgetting the world and all its useless troubles, and am fairly transported into those regions of the fancy, where the airs are always soft and the skies serene, where want is unknown, and solicitations to vice come not, where men are just, and true, and kind, and women the goddesses we make them in our dreams, and the whole of existence is a calm summer's day, without storm of the inward or outward world. And when upon these delicious moments the philosopher himself breaks in, the dream is not dissolved, but stands rather converted to an absolute reality, for it then shines with the actual presence of a god. It is with unwillingness that I acknowledge my real state, and consent to return to this living world of anxieties and apprehensions in which I now dwell.

I am just returned from the palace and the princess Julia. While there seated in conversation with her, Longinus, and Livia, a courier was suddenly announced from Zenobia. He entered, woe stamped upon his features, and delivered letters into the hands of Longinus. Alas, alas, for Palmyra! The intelligence is of disaster and defeat. The countenance of the Greek grew pale as he read. He placed the dispatches in silence in the hands of Julia, having finished them, and hastily withdrew.

The sum of the news is this. A battle has been fought before Antioch, and the forces of the queen completely routed. It appears, that upon the approach of Aurelian, the several provinces of Asia Minor, which by negotiation and conquest had by Zenobia been connected with her kingdom, immediately returned to their former allegiance. The cities opened their gates, and admitted the armies of the conqueror. Tyana alone of all the queen's dominions in that quarter, opposed the progress of the emperor, and this stronghold was soon by treachery delivered into his power. Thence he pressed on without pause to Antioch, where he found the queen awaiting him. A battle immediately ensued. At first, the queen's forces obtained decided advantages, and victory seemed ready to declare for her as always before, when the gods decreed otherwise, and the day was lost —but lost, in the indignant language of the queen, "not in fair and honourable fight, but through the baseness of a stratagem rather to have been expected from a Carthaginian than the great Aurelian." "Our troops," she writes, " had driven the enemy from his ground at every point. Notwithstanding the presence of Aurelian, and the prodigies of valour by which he distinguished himself anew, and animated his soldiers, our cavalry, led by the incomparable Zabdas, bore him and his legions backwards, till, apparently discomfited by the violence of the onset, the Roman horse gave way and fled in all directions. The shout of victory arose from our ranks, which now dissolved, and in the disorder of a flushed and conquering army, scattered in hot pursuit of the flying foe. Now, when too late, we saw the treachery of the enemy. Our horse, heavy armed, as you know, were led on by the retreating Romans into a broken and marshy ground, where their movements were in every way impeded, and thousands were suddenly fixed immoveable in the deep morass. At this moment, the enemy, by preconcerted signals, with inconceivable rapidity—being light-armed—formed; and, returning upon our now scattered and broken forces, made horrible slaughter of all who had pushed farthest from the main body of the army. Dismay seized our soldiers—the panic spread—increased by the belief that a fresh army had come up and was entering the field, and our whole duty centered upon forming and covering our retreat. This, chiefly through the conduct of Calpurnius Piso, was safely effected; the Romans being kept at bay while we drew together, and then, under cover of the approaching night, fell back to a new and strong position.

I attempt not, Longinus, to make that better which is bad. I reveal the whole truth, not softening or withholding a single feature of it, that your mind may be possessed of the exact state of our affairs, and know how to form its judgments. Make that which I write public, to the extent and in the manner that shall seem best to you.

After mature deliberation, we have determined to

retreat farther yet, and take up our position under the walls of Emesa. Here, I trust in the gods, we shall redeem that which we have lost."

In a letter to Julia, the queen says, "Fausta has escaped the dangers of the battle; selfishly, perhaps, dividing her from Piso, she has shared my tent and my fortunes, and has proved herself worthy of every confidence that has been reposed in her. She is my inseparable companion in the tent, in the field, and on the road, by night and by day. Give not way to despondency, dear Julia. Fortune, which has so long smiled upon me, is not now about to forsake me. There is no day so long and bright, that clouds do not sail by and cast their little shadows. But the sun is behind them. Our army is still great, and in good heart. The soldiers receive me, whenever I appear, with their customary acclamations. Fausta shares this enthusiasm. Wait without anxiety or fear for news from Emesa."

When we had perused and reperused the dispatches of the queen, and were brooding in no little despondency over their contents, Longinus, re-entering, said to me,

"And what, Piso, may I ask, is your judgment of the course which Aurelian will now pursue? I see not that I can offend in asking, or you in answering. I have heretofore inclined to the belief that Rome, having atoned her injured honour by a battle, would then prefer to convert Palmyra into a useful ally, by the proposal of terms which she could accept—terms which would leave her an independent existence as formerly —in friendly alliance with, though in no sense subject to, Rome. But neither preceding the battle at Antioch, nor since, does it appear that terms have been so much as proposed or discussed. I can hardly believe that Aurelian, even if victory should continue to sit upon his eagles, would desire to drive the queen to extremities, and convert this whole people into a united and infuriated enemy. If he be willing to do this, he little understands the best interests of Rome, and proves only this, that though he may be a good soldier, he is a bad sovereign, and really betrays his country while achieving the most brilliant victories."

"I am obliged to say," I replied, "that I have wavered in my judgment. Sometimes, when I have thought of policy, of the past services of Palmyra, and of Persia, I have deemed it hardly possible that Aurelian should have had any other purpose in this expedition than to negotiate with Zenobia, under the advantages of an army at his back—that at the most and worst a single battle would suffice, and the differences which exist be then easily adjusted. But, then, when again I have thought of the character of Aurelian, I have doubted these conclusions, and believed that conquest alone will satisfy him, and that he will never turn back till he can call Palmyra a Roman province. From what has now transpired at Antioch, and especially from what has not transpired, I am strengthened in this last opinion. One or the other must fall. I believe it has come to this."

"One or the other may fall at Emesa," said Livia, "but no power can ever force the walls of Palmyra."

"I am ready to believe with you, princess," said Longinus, "but I trust never to see a Roman army before them. Yet if your last judgment of Aurelian be the true one, Piso, it may happen. We are not a power to pour forth the hordes of Rome or Germany. We have valour, but not numbers."

"Ought not," said Julia, "every provision to be made, even though there be but the remotest possibility of the city sustaining a siege?"

"The most fruitful imagination," replied Longinus, "could hardly suggest a single addition to what is already done, to render Palmyra impregnable. And long before the food now within the walls could be exhausted, any army, save one of Arabs of the desert, lying before them, must itself perish. But these things the council and senate will maturely weigh."

Longinus departed.

At the same moment that he left the apartment, that

Indian slave, whom I have often seen sitting at the feet of the queen, entered where we were, and addressing a few words to the princess Julia, again retreated. I could not but remark again what I had remarked before, her graceful beauty, and especially the symmetry of her form and elasticity of her step. There was now also an expression in the countenance which, notwithstanding its dark beauty, I liked not, as I had often before liked it not, when I had seen her in the presence of Zenobia.

"Princess," said I, "is the slave who has just departed sincere in her attachment to Zenobia?"

"I cannot doubt it," she replied; "at least I have observed nothing to cause me to doubt it. Thinking herself injured and degraded by Zenobia, she may perhaps feel towards her as the captive feels towards the conqueror. But if this be so, the lip breathes it not. To the queen she is, as far as the eye may judge, fondly attached, and faithful to the trusts reposed in her."

"But why," I asked, "thinks she herself injured and degraded? Is she not what she seems to be—a slave?"

"She is a slave by the chances of fortune and war, not by descent or purchase. She was of the household of Sapor, when his tents, wives, and slaves, fell into the hands of Odenatus, and by him, as we learned, had been taken in his wars with an Indian nation. In her own country she was a princess, and were she now there, were queen. Zenobia's pride is gratified by using her for the purposes she does, nor has it availed to intercede in her behalf. Yet has it always seemed, as if a strong attachment drew the fair slave to our mother, and sure I am that Zenobia greatly esteems her, and, save in one respect, maintains and holds her rather as an equal than inferior. We all love her. Others besides yourself have questioned her truth, but we have heeded them not. Upon what, may I ask, have you founded a doubt of her sincerity?"

"I can scarcely say," I rejoined, "that I have ground

to doubt her sincerity. Indeed, I know nothing of her but what you have now rehearsed, except, that a few days since, as I retired from the palace, I observed her near the eastern gate, in earnest conversation with Antiochus. Soon as her eye caught me, although at a great distance, she hastily withdrew into the palace, while Antiochus turned towards the neighbouring street."

Julia smiled. "Ah!" said she, "our cousin Antiochus, were he to lose all hope of me, would hasten to throw himself at the feet of the beautiful Sindarina. When at the palace, his eyes can hardly be drawn from her face. I have been told he exalts her above her great mistress. Were Antiochus king, I can hardly doubt that Sindarina were queen. His visit to the palace must have been to her alone. Livia, have you received him since the departure of Zenobia?"

Her sister had not seen him. I said no more. But never have I read aright the human countenance, if in her there be not hidden design of evil. I knew not before this interview her history. This supplies a motive for a treacherous turn, if by it her freedom or her fortune might be achieved. I have mentioned my suspicions to Longinus, but he sees nothing in them.

The intelligence thus received has effectually sobered the giddy citizens of Palmyra. They are now of opinion that war really exists, and that they are a party concerned. The merchants, who are the princes of the place, perceiving their traffic to decline or cease, begin to interest themselves in the affairs of the state. So long as wealth flowed in as ever, and the traders from India and Persia saw no obstruction in the state of things to a safe transaction of their various businesses and transportation of their valuable commodities, the merchants left the state to take care of itself, and whatever opinions they held, expressed them only in their own circles, thinking but of accumulation by day, and of ostentatious expenditure by night. I have often heard, that their general voice, had it been raised,

would have been hostile to the policy that has prevailed.
But it was not raised; and now, when too late, and
these mercenary and selfish beings are driven to some
action by the loss of their accustomed gains, a large
and violent party is forming among them, who loudly
condemn the conduct of the queen and her ministers,
and advocate immediate submission to whatever terms
Aurelian may impose. This party, however, powerful
though it may be through wealth, is weak in numbers.
The people are opposed to them, and go enthusiastically
with the queen, and do not scruple to exult in the distresses of the merchants. Their present impotence is
but a just retribution upon them for their criminal
apathy during the early stages of the difficulty. Then
had they taken a part, as they ought to have done, in
the public deliberations, the rupture which has ensued
might, it is quite likely, have been prevented. Their
voice would have been a loud and strong one, and
would have been heard. They deserve to lose their
liberties, who will not spare time from selfish pursuits
to guard them. Where a government is popular, even
to no greater extent than this, it behoves every individual, if he values the power delegated to him, and
would retain it, to use it, otherwise it is by degrees
and insensibly lost; and once absorbed into the hands
of the few, it is not easy, if at all, to be recovered.

Nothing can exceed the activity displayed on all hands
in every preparation which the emergency demands.
New levies of men are making, and a camp again forming to reinforce the queen, at Emesa, or in its neighbourhood, if she should not be compelled to retire upon
Palmyra. In the mean time, we wait with beating
hearts for the next arrival of couriers.

After an anxious suspense of several days, all my
worst apprehensions are realised. Messengers have
arrived, announcing the defeat of Zenobia before the
walls of Emesa, and with them fugitives from the conquered army are pouring in. Every hour now do we
expect the approach of the queen, with the remnant of

her forces. Our intelligence is in the hand of Zenobia herself. She has written thus to her minister:

"*Septimia Zenobia to Dyonysius Longinus.*

I am again defeated. Our cavalry were at first victorious, as before at Antioch. The Roman horse were routed. But the infantry of Aurelian, in number greatly superior to ours, falling upon our ranks when deprived of the support of the cavalry, obtained an easy victory; while their horse, rallying, and increased by reinforcements from Antioch, drove us in turn at all points, penetrating even to our camp, and completed the disaster of the day. I have now no power with which to cope with Aurelian. It remains but to retreat upon Palmyra, there placing our reliance upon the strength of our walls, and upon our Armenian, Saracen, and Persian allies. I do not despair, although the favour of the gods seems withdrawn. Farewell."

The city is in the utmost consternation. All power seems paralysed. The citizens stand together in knots at the corners of the streets, like persons struck dumb, and without command of either their bodies or their minds. The first feeling was, and it was freely expressed, "to contend further is hopeless. The army is destroyed; another cannot now be recruited; and if it could, before it were effected Aurelian would be at the gates with his countless legions, and the city necessarily surrender. We must now make the best terms we can, and receive passively conditions which we can no longer oppose."

But soon other sentiments took the place of these; and being urged by those who entertained them with zeal, they have prevailed.

"Why," they have urged, "should we yield before that becomes the only alternative? At present we are secure within the walls of our city, which may well defy all the power of a besieging army. Those most skilled in such matters, and who have visited the places in the world deemed most impregnable, assert that the defences of Palmyra are perfect, and surpassed by none; and that any army, whether a Roman or any other, must perish before it would be possible either to force our gates or reduce us by hunger. Besides, what could we expect by submitting to the conqueror, but national extinction? Our city would be pillaged—our principal citizens murdered; perhaps a general slaughter made of the inhabitants, without regard to age or sex. The mercies of Rome have ever been cruel; and Aurelian we know to be famed for the severity of his temper. No commander of modern times has instituted so terrible a discipline in his army, and Rome itself has felt the might of his iron hand; it is always on his sword. What can strangers, foreigners, enemies, and rebels, as he regards us, expect? And are the people of Palmyra ready to abandon their queen, to whom we owe all this great prosperity—this wide renown—this extended empire? But for Zenobia we were now what we so many ages were, a petty trading village—a community of money-makers, hucksters, and barterers, without arts, without science, without fame, destitute of all that adorns and elevates a people. Zenobia has raised us to empire; it is Zenobia who has made us the conquerors of Persia, and the rival of Rome. Shame to those who will desert her! Shame to those who will distrust a genius that has hitherto shone with greater lustre, in proportion to the difficulties that have opposed it. Who can doubt that by lending her all our energies and means, she will yet triumph. Shame and death to the enemies of the queen and the state!"

Sentiments like these are now every where heard, and the courage and enthusiasm of the people are rising again. Those who are for war and resistance are always the popular party. There is an instinctive love of liberty and power, and a horror at the thought of losing them, that come to the aid of the weak, and often cause them to resist, under circumstances absolutely desperate. Palmyra is not weak, but to one who contemplates both parties, and compares their relative strength, it is little short of madness to hope to hold out with ultimate success against the power of Rome. But such is the determination of the great body of the people. And the queen, when she shall approach with her broken, and diminished, and defeated army, will meet the welcome of a conqueror. Never before in the history of the world, was there so true-hearted a devotion of a whole people to the glory, interests, and happiness of one—and never was such devotion so deserved.

The princess Julia possesses herself like one armed for such adversities, not by nature, but by reflection and philosophy. She was designed for scenes of calmness and peace; but she has made herself equal to times of difficulty, tumult, and danger. She shrinks not from the duties which her station now imposes upon her, but seems like one who possesses resolution enough to reign with the vigour and power of Zenobia. Her two brothers who have remained in the city, Herennianus and Timolaus, leave all affairs of state to her and the council; they preferring the base pleasures of sensuality, in which they wallow day and night, in company with Antiochus and his crew. If a deep depression is sometimes seen to rest upon her spirit, it comes rather when she thinks of her mother, than of herself. She experiences already, through her lively sympathies, the grief that will rage in the soul of Zenobia, should fortune deprive her of her crown.

"Zenobia," she has said to me, "Zenobia cannot descend from a throne, without suffering such as common souls cannot conceive. A goddess driven from heaven and the company of the gods, could not endure more. To possess and to exercise power is to her heaven; to be despoiled of it, Tartarus and death. She was born for a throne, though not on one; and how she graces it, you and the world have seen. She will display fortitude under adversity and defeat, I am sure; and to the common eye, the same soul, and vigorous with all its energies, will appear to preside over her. But the prospect or expectation of a fall from her high place will rack with torments such as no mortal can hope to assuage. To witness her grief, without the power to relieve, I cannot bear to think of it."

In Livia there is more of the mother. She is proud, imperious, and ambitious, in a greater measure even than Zenobia. Young as she is, she believes herself of a different nature from others; she born to rule, others to serve. It is not the idea of her country and its renown that fills and sways her, but of a throne and its attendant glories. So she could reign a queen, with a queen's state and homage, it would matter little to her whether it were in Persia or Palmyra. Yet with those who are her equals is she free, and even sportive, light of heart, and overflowing with excess of life. Her eye burns with the bright lustre of a star, and her step is that of the mistress of a world. She is not terrified at the prospect before her, for her confident and buoyant spirit looks down all opposition, and predicts a safe egress from the surrounding peril, and an ascent, through this very calamity itself, to a position more illustrious still.

"Julia," said she, on one occasion of late, while I sat a listener, "supposing that the people of Palmyra should set aside our renowned brothers, and again prefer a woman's sway, would not you renounce your elder right in favour of me? I do not think you would care to be a queen?"

"That is true," replied Julia, "I should not care to be a queen; and yet, I believe, I should reign that you might not. Though I covet not the exercise of power, I believe I should use it more wisely than you would, who do."

"I am sure," said Livia, "I feel within me that very superiority to others which constitutes the royal character, and would fit me eminently to reign. He cannot be a proper slave who has not the soul of a slave. Neither can he reign well who has not the soul of a monarch. I am suited to a throne, just as others are, by the providence of the gods, suited to uphold the throne, and be the slaves of it."

"Were you queen, Livia, it would be for your own sake; to enjoy the pleasures which, as you imagine, accompany that state, and exercise over others the powers with which you were clothed, and receive the homage of dependent subjects. Your own magnificence and luxurious state would be your principal thought. Is that being suited to a throne?"

"But," said Livia, "I should not be guilty of intentional wrong towards any. So long as my people obeyed my laws and supported my government, there would be no causes of difficulty. But surely, if there were resistance, and any either insulted or opposed my authority, it would be a proper occasion for violent measures. For there must be some to govern as well as others to obey. All cannot rule. Government is founded in necessity. Kings and queens are of nature's making. It would be right, then, to use utmost severity towards such as ceased to obey, as the slave his master. How could the master obtain the service of the slave, if there were not reposed in him power to punish? Shall the master of millions have less?"

"Dear Livia, your principles are suited only to some Persian despotism. You very soberly imagine, unless you jest, that governments exist for the sake of those who govern—that kings and queens are the objects for which governments are instituted."

"Truly, it is very much so. Otherwise what would the king or queen of an empire be but a poor official, maintained in a sort of state by the people, and paid by them for the discharge of a certain set of duties which must be performed by some one—but who possesses, in fact, no will or power of his own—rather the servant of the people than their master."

"I think," replied Julia, "you have given a very just definition of the imperial office. A king, queen, or emperor, is indeed the servant of the people. He exists not for his own pleasure or glory, but for their good. Else he is a tyrant, a despot—not a sovereign."

"It is, then," said Livia, "only a tyrant or a despot that I would consent to be—not in any bad meaning of the terms, for you know, Julia, that I could not be cruel or unjust. But unless I could reign as one independent of my people, and irresponsible to them—not in name only, but in reality above them—receiving the homage due to the queenly character and office—I would not reign at all. To sit upon a throne, a mere painted puppet, shaken by the breath of every conceited or discontented citizen, a butt for every shaft to fly at, a mere hireling, a slave in a queen's robe, the mouthpiece for others to speak by, and proclaim their laws, with no will or power of my own—no, no. It is not such that Zenobia is."

"She is more than that, indeed," replied Julia; "she is in some sense a despot; her will is sovereign in the state; she is an absolute prince in fact; but it is through the force of her own character and virtues, not by the consent and expressed allowance of her subjects. Her genius, her goodness, her justice, and her services, have united to confer upon her this dangerous pre-eminence. But who else, with power such as hers, would reign as she has reigned? An absolute will, guided by perfect wisdom and goodness, constitutes, I indeed believe, the simplest and best form of human government. It is a copy of that of the universe, under the providence of the gods. But an absolute will, moved only or chiefly by the selfish love of regal state and homage, or by a very defective wisdom and goodness, is, on the other hand, the very worst form of human government. You would make an unequalled queen, Livia, if to act the queen were all—if you were but to sit and receive the worship of the slaves, your subjects. As you sit now, I can almost believe you queen of the east. Juno's air was not more imperial, nor the beauty of Venus more enslaving. Piso will not dissent from what I began with, or now end with."

"I think you have delivered a true doctrine," I replied, "but which few who have once tasted of power will admit. Liberty would be in great danger were Livia queen. Her subjects would be too willing to forget their rights, through a voluntary homage to her queenly character and state. Their chains would, however, be none the less chains, that they were voluntarily assumed. That, indeed, is the most dangerous slavery which men impose upon themselves, for it does not bear the name of slavery, but some other; yet as it is real, the character of the slave is silently and unconsciously formed, and then unconsciously transmitted."

"I perceive," said Livia, "if what you philosophers urge be true, that I am rather meant by nature for a Persian or a Roman throne than any other. I would be absolute, though it were over but a village. A divided and imperfect power I would not accept, though it were over the world. But the gods grant it long ere any one be called in Palmyra to fill the place of Zenobia."

"Happy were it for mankind," said Julia, "could she live and reign for ever."

Thus do all differences cease and run into harmony at the name of Zenobia.

Every hour do we look for the arrival of the army.

As I sit writing at my open window, overlooking the street and spacious courts of the Temple of Justice, I am conscious of an unusual disturbance—the people at a distance are running in one direction—the clamour approaches—and now I hear the cries of the multitude, "The queen, the queen!"

I fly to the walls.

I resume my pen. The alarm was a true one. Upon gaining the streets, I found the populace all pouring towards the gate of the desert, in which direction, it was affirmed, the queen was making her approach. Upon reaching it, and ascending one of its lofty towers, I beheld from the verge of the horizon to within a mile of the walls, the whole plain filled with the scattered forces of Zenobia, a cloud of dust resting over the whole, and marking out the extent of ground they covered.

As the advanced detachments drew near, how different a spectacle did they present from that bright morning, when, glittering in steel, and full of the fire of expected victory, they proudly took their way towards the places from which they now were returning, a conquered, spoiled, and dispirited remnant, covered with the dust of a long march, and wearily dragging their limbs beneath the rays of a burning sun! Yet was there order and military discipline preserved, even under circumstances so depressing, and which usually are an excuse for their total relaxation. It was the silent, dismal march of a funeral train, rather than the hurried flight of a routed and discomfited army. There was the stiff and formal military array, but the life and spirit of an elevated and proud soldiery were gone. They moved with method to the sound of clanging instruments, and the long, shrill blast of the trumpet, but they moved as mourners. They seemed as if they came to bury their queen.

Yet the scene changed to a brighter aspect, as the army drew nearer and nearer to the walls, and the city throwing open her gates, the populace burst forth, and with loud and prolonged shouts welcomed them home. These shouts sent new life into the hearts of the desponding ranks, and with brightened faces and a changed air, they waved their arms and banners, and returned shout for shout. As they passed through the gates to the ample quarters provided within the walls, a thousand phrases of hearty greeting were showered down upon them, from those who lined the walls, the towers, and the way-side, which seemed, from the effects produced in those on whom they fell, a more quickening restorative than could have been any medicine or food that had ministered only to the body.

The impatience of the multitude to behold and receive the queen, was hardly to be restrained from breaking forth in some violent way. They were ready to rush upon the great avenue, bearing aside the troops, that they might the sooner greet her. When, at length, the centre of the army approached, and the armed chariot appeared in which Zenobia sat, the enthusiasm of the people knew no bounds. They broke through all restraint, and with cries that filled the heavens, pressed towards her—the soldiers catching the phrensy and joining them—and quickly detaching the horses from her carriage, themselves drew her into the city just as if she had returned victor, with Aurelian in her train. There was no language of devotion and loyalty that did not meet her ear, nor any sign of affection that could be made from any distance, from the plains, the walls, the gates, the higher buildings of the city, the roofs of which were thronged, that did not meet her eye. It was a testimony of love so spontaneous and universal, a demonstration of confidence and unshaken attachment so hearty and sincere, that Zenobia was more than moved by it, she was subdued—and she, who by her people had never before been seen to weep, bent her head, and buried her face in her hands.

With what an agony of expectation, while this scene was passing, did I await the appearance of Fausta, and Gracchus, and Calpurnius—if, indeed, I were destined ever to see them again. I waited long, and with pain, but, the gods be praised, not in vain, nor to meet with disappointment only. Not far in the rear of Zenobia, at the head of a squadron of cavalry, rode, as my eye distinctly informed me, those whom I sought. No sooner did they in turn approach the gates, than almost the same welcome that had been lavished upon Zenobia, was repeated for Fausta, Gracchus, and Calpurnius. The names of Calpurnius and Fausta—of Calpurnius, as he who had saved the army at Antioch, of Fausta as the intrepid and fast friend of the queen, were especially heard from a thousand lips, joined with every title of honour. My voice was not wanting in the loud acclaim. It reached the ears of Fausta, who, starting and looking upwards, caught my eye just as she passed beneath the arch of the vast gateway. I then descended from my tower of observation, and joined the crowds who thronged the close ranks, as they filed along the streets of the city. I pressed upon the steps of my friends, never being able to keep my eyes from the forms of those I loved so well, whom I had so feared to lose, and so rejoiced to behold returned alive and unhurt.

All day the army has continued pouring into the city, and beside the army, greater crowds still of the inhabitants of the suburbs, who, knowing that before another day shall end, the Romans may encamp before the walls, are scattering in all directions—multitudes taking refuge in the city, but greater numbers still mounted upon elephants, camels, dromedaries, and horses, flying into the country to the north. The whole region, as far as the eye can reach, seems in commotion, as if society were dissolved, and breaking up from its foundations. The noble and the rich, whose means are ample, gather together their valuables, and with their children and friends, seek the nearest parts of Mesopotamia, where they will remain in safety till the siege shall be raised. The poor, and such as cannot reach the Euphrates, flock into the city, bringing with them what little of provisions or money they may possess, and are quartered upon the inhabitants, or take up a temporary abode in the open squares, or in the courts and porticoes of palaces and temples—the softness and serenity of the climate rendering even so much as the shelter of a tent superfluous. But by this vast influx the population of the city cannot be less than doubled; and I should tremble for the means of subsistence for so large a multitude, did I not know the inexhaustible magazines of corn, laid up by the prudent foresight of the queen, in anticipation of the possible occurrence of the emergency which has now arrived. A long time—longer than he himself would be able to subsist his army—must Aurelian lie before Palmyra, ere he can hope to reduce it by famine. What impression his engines may be able to make upon the walls, remains to be seen. Periander pronounces the city impregnable. My own judgment, formed upon a comparison of it with the cities most famous in the world for the strength of their defences, would agree with his.

Following on in the wake of the squadron to which Fausta was attached, I wished to reach the camp at the same time with herself and Gracchus and my brother; but owing to the press in the streets, arising from the causes just specified, I was soon separated from, and lost sight of it. Desirous, however, to meet them, I urged my way along with much labour till I reached the quarter of the city assigned to the troops, and where I found the tents and the open ground already occupied. I sought in vain for Fausta. While I waited, hoping still to see her, I stood leaning upon a pile of shields, which the soldiers, throwing off their arms, had just made, and watching them as they were, some disencumbering themselves of their armour, others unclasping the harness of their horses, others arranging their weapons into regular forms, and others, having gone through their first tasks, were stretching themselves at rest beneath the shadow of their tents, or of some branching tree. Near me sat a soldier, who, apparently too fatigued to rid himself of his heavy armour, had thrown himself upon the ground, and was just taking off his helmet, and wiping the dust and sweat from his face, while a little boy, observing his wants, ran to a neighbouring fountain, and filling a vessel with water, returned and held it to him, saying, "Drink, soldier, this will make you stronger than your armour." "You little traitor," said the soldier, "art not ashamed to bring drink to me, who have helped to betray the city! Beware, or a sharp sword will cut you in two."

"I thought," replied the child, nothing daunted, "that you were a soldier of Palmyra, who had been to fight the Romans. But whoever you may be, I am sure you need the water."

"But," rejoined the soldier, swallowing at long draughts, as if it had been nectar, the cooling drink, "do I deserve water, or any of these cowards here, who have been beaten by the Romans, and so broken the heart of our good queen, and possibly lost her her throne? Answer me that."

"You have done what you could, I know," replied the boy, "because you are a Palmyrene; and who can do more? I carry round the streets of the city in this palm-leaf basket, date cakes, which I sell to those who love them. But does my mother blame me because I do not always come home with an empty basket? I sell what I can. Should I be punished for doing what I can not?"

"Get you gone, you little rogue," replied the soldier, "you talk like a Christian boy, and they have a new way of returning good for evil. But here, if you have cakes in your basket, give me one, and I will give you a penny, all the way from Antioch. See! there is the head of Aurelian on it. Take care he don't eat you up—or at least your cakes. But hark you, little boy: do you see yonder that old man with a bald head, leaning against his shield—go to him with your cakes."

The boy ran off.

"Friend," said I, addressing him, "your march has not lost you your spirits—you can jest yet."

"Truly I can; if the power to do that were gone, then were all lost. A good jest in a time of misfortune, is food and drink. It is strength to the arm, digestion to the stomach, courage to the heart. It is better than wisdom or wine. A prosperous man may afford to be melancholy, but if the miserable are so, they are worse than dead—but it is sure to kill them. Near me I had a comrade whose wit it was alone that kept life in me upon the desert. All the way from Emesa, had it not been for the tears of laughter, those of sorrow and shame would have killed me."

"But, in the words of the little cake urchin, you did what you could. The fates were opposed to you."

"If all had done as much and as well as some, we would have had the fates in our own keeping. Had it not been for that artifice of the Romans at Antioch, we would have now been rather in Rome than here; and it was a woman—or girl rather, as I am told—the daughter of Gracchus, who first detected the cheat, and strove to save the army, but it was too late."

" Were you near her?"

" Was I not? Not the great Zabdas himself put more mettle into the troops than did that fiery spirit and her black horse. And beyond doubt, she would have perished through an insane daring, had not the queen in time called her from the field, and afterwards kept her within her sight and reach. Her companion, a Roman turned Palmyrene as I heard, was like one palsied when she was gone, till when he had been the very Mars of the field. As it was, he was the true hero of the day. He brought to my mind Odenatus. 'Twas so he looked that day we entered Ctesiphon. I could wish, and hope, too, that he might share the throne of Zenobia, but that all the world knows what a man-hater she is. But were you not there?"

" No; it could not be. I remained in the city."

" Ten thousand more of such men as you, and we would not have fallen back upon Emesa, nor left Antioch without the head of Aurelian. But, alas for it, the men of Palmyra are men of silk, and love their pleasures too well to be free. I should call them women, but for Zenobia and the daughter of Gracchus."

" Do not take me for one of them. I am a Roman, and could not fight against my country."

" A Roman! and what make you here? Suppose I were to run you through with this spear."

" Give me another, and you are welcome to try."

" Am I so? Then will I not do it. Give a man his will, and he no longer cares for it. Besides, having escaped with hazard from the clutches of one Roman, I will not encounter another. Dost thou know that demon Aurelian? Half who fell, fell by his hand. His sword made no more of a man in steel armour, than mine would of a naked slave. Many a tall Palmyrene did he split to the saddle, falling both ways. The ranks broke and fled wherever he appeared. Death could not keep pace with him. The Roman Piso—of our side—sought him over the field, to try his fortune with him, but the gods protected him, and he found him not. Otherwise his body were now food for hyenas. No arm of mortal mould can cope with him. Mine is not despicable. There is not its match in Palmyra. But I would not encounter Aurelian, unless I were in love with death."

"It is as you say, I well know. He is reputed in our army to have killed more with his single arm in battle, than any known in Roman history. Our camp resounds with songs which celebrate his deeds of blood. His slain are counted by thousands, nothing less."

"The gods blast him, ere he be seen before the walls of Palmyra; our chance were better against double the number of legions under another general. The general makes the soldier. The Roman infantry are so many Aurelians. Yet to-morrow's sun will see him here. I am free to say, I tremble for Palmyra. A war ill begun, will, if auguries are aught, end worse. Last night the sky was full of angry flashes, both white and red. While the army slept overwrought upon the desert, and the silence of death was around, the watches heard sounds as of the raging of a battle, distinct and clear, dying away in groans as of a host perishing under the sword and battle-axe. These horrid sounds at length settled over the sleeping men, till it seemed as if they proceeded from them. The sentinels—at first struck dumb with terror and amazement—called out to one another to know what it should mean, but they could only confirm to each other what had been heard, and together ask the protection of the gods. But what strikes deeper yet, is what you have heard, that the queen's far-famed Numidian, just as we came in sight of the walls of the city, stumbled, and where he stumbled, fell, and died. What these things forebode, if not disaster and ruin, 'tis hard to say. I need no one to read them to me."

Saying thus, he rose, and began to divest himself of the remainder of his heavy armour, saying, as he did it, "It was this heavy armour that lost us the day at Antioch—lighter, and we could have escaped the meshes. Now, let me lie and sleep."

Returning, hardly had I arrived at the house of Gracchus, when it was announced in loud shouts by the slaves of the palace, that Gracchus himself, Fausta, and Calpurnius, were approaching. I hastened to the portico overlooking the courtyard, and was there just in season to assist Fausta to dismount. It was a joyful moment, I need scarce assure you. Fausta returns wholly unhurt. Gracchus is wounded upon his left, and Calpurnius upon his right arm, but will not long suffer from the injury.

It was an unspeakable joy, once more to hear the cheerful voice of Gracchus resounding in the walls of his own dwelling, and to see Fausta eased of her unnatural load of iron, again moving in her accustomed sphere in that graceful costume, partly Roman and partly Persian, and which now hides and now betrays the form, so as to reveal its beauty in the most perfect manner. A deep sadness, deeper than ever, sits upon her countenance, whenever her own thoughts occupy her. But surrounded by her friends, and her native spirit, too elastic to be subdued, breaks forth, and she seems her former self again.

Our evening meal was sad, but not silent.

Gracchus instructed me, by giving a minute narrative of the march to Antioch, of the two battles and the retreat. Calpurnius related with equal exactness the part which he took, and the services which Fausta, by her penetrating observation, had been able to render to the army. They united in bestowing the highest encomiums upon Zenobia, who herself planned the battle, and disposed the forces, and with such consummate judgment, that Zabdas himself found nothing to disapprove or alter.

"The day was clearly ours," said Fausta, "but for

the artifice of Aurelian—allowable, I know, by all the rules of war—by which we were led on blindfold to our ruin. But flushed as we were by the early and complete success of the day, is it to be severely condemned that our brave men followed up their advantages with too much confidence, and broke from that close order, in which till then they had fought, and by doing so, lost the command of themselves and their own strength? Oh, the dulness of our spirits, that we did not sooner detect the rank insincerity of that sudden, unexpected retreat of the Roman horse."

"The gods rather be praised," said Gracchus, "that your watchful eye detected so soon, what was too well concerted and acted to be perceived at all, and as the fruit of it we sit here alive, and Zenobia holds her throne, and so many of our brave soldiers are now locked in sleep beneath their quiet tents."

"That, I think," said Calpurnius, "is rather the sentiment that should possess us. You will hardly believe, Lucius, that it was owing to the military genius of your ancient playmate, that we escaped the certain destruction that had been prepared for us?"

"I can believe any thing good in that quarter, and upon slighter testimony. I have already heard from the lips of a soldier of your legion, that which you have now related. Part of the praise was by him bestowed upon one Piso, a Roman turned Palmyrene, as he termed him, who, he reported, fought at the side of the daughter of Gracchus."

"He could not have said too much of that same Piso," said Gracchus. "Palmyra owes him a large debt of gratitude, which I am sure she will not be slow to pay. But let us think rather of the future than of the past, which, however we may have conducted, speaks only of disaster."

I thank you for your assurances concerning Laco and Cælia. Your conscience will never reproach you for this lenity.

LETTER XIV.

The last days of this so lately favoured empire draw near—at least such is my judgment. After a brief day of glory, its light will set in a long night of utter darkness and ruin.

Close upon the rear guard of the queen's forces followed the light troops of Aurelian, and early this morning it was proclaimed that the armies of Rome were in sight, and fast approaching the city. These armies were considered too numerous to hazard another battle; therefore the gates were shut, and we are now beleaguered by a power too mighty to contend with, and which the Arabs, the climate, and want, must be trusted to subdue. The circumjacent plains are filled with the legions of Rome. Exhausted by the march across the desert, they have but pitched their tents, and now repose.

The queen displays more than ever her accustomed activity and energy. She examines in person every part of the vast extent of wall, and every engine planted upon them for their defence. By her frequent presence in every part of the city, she inspires her soldiers with the same spirit which possesses herself; and for herself, to behold her careering through the streets of the city, reviewing, and often addressing, the different divisions of the army, and issuing her commands, she seems rather like one who is now queen of the east, and is soon to be of the world, than one whose dominion is already narrowed down to the compass of a single city, and may shortly be deprived even of that. The lofty dignity of her air has assumed a more imposing greatness still. The imperial magnificence of her state is noways diminished, but rather increased, so that, by a sort of delusion of the senses, she seems more a queen than ever. By her native vigour and goodness, and by the addition of a most consummate art, by which she manages as she will a people whom she perfectly comprehends, she is at this moment more deeply intrenched within the affections of her subjects, and more completely the object of their idolatrous homage, than ever before. Yet in her secret soul there is a deep depression, and a loss of confidence in her cause, which amounts not yet to a loss of hope, but approaches it. This is seen by those who can observe her in her more quiet hours, when the glare of public action and station is off, and her mind is left to its own workings. But, like those who play at dice, she has staked all—her kingdom, her crown, her life, perhaps—upon a single throw; and having wound herself up to the desperate act, all the entreaty or argument of the whole earth could not move her to unclasp the hand that wields the fatal box. She will abide the throw.

There are still those who use both entreaty and argument to persuade her, even at this late hour, to make the best terms she may with Rome. Otho, though perfectly loyal and true, ceases not to press upon her, both in public and in private, those considerations which may have any weight with her to induce a change of measures. But it has thus far been to no purpose. Others there are, who, as the danger increases, become more and more restless, and scruple not to let their voice be heard in loud complaint and discontent, but they are too few in proportion to the whole, to make them objects of apprehension. It will, however, be strange if, as the siege is prolonged, they do not receive such accessions of strength as to render them dangerous.

The emperor has commenced his attacks upon the city, in a manner that shows him unacquainted with its strength. The battle has raged fiercely all day, with great loss, we infer, to the Romans, with none, we know, to the Palmyrenes.

Early on the morning of the second day, it was evident that a general assault was to be made upon the walls. The Roman army completely surrounding the city, at the same signal approached, and under cover of their shields attempted both to undermine and scale them.

But their attempts were met with such vigour, and with such advantage of action by the besieged, that although repeated many times during the day, they have resulted in only loss and death to the assailants. It is incredible the variety and ingenuity of the contrivances by which the queen's forces beat off and rendered ineffectual all the successive movements of the enemy, in their attempts to surmount the walls. Not only from every part of the wall were showers of arrows discharged from the bows of experienced archers, but from engines also, by which they were driven to a much greater distance, and with great increase of force.

This soon rendered every attack of this nature useless and worse, and their efforts were then concentrated upon the several gates, which simultaneously were attempted to be broken in, fired, or undermined. But here again, as often as these attempts were renewed, were they defeated, and great destruction made of those engaged in them. The troops approached, as is usual, covered completely, or buried rather, beneath their shields. They were suffered to form directly under the walls, and actually commence their work of destruction, when suddenly from the towers of the gates, and through channels constructed for the purpose in every part of the masonry, torrents of liquid fire were poured upon the iron roof, beneath which the soldiers worked. This at first they endured. The melted substances ran off from the polished surface of the shields, and the stones which were dashed upon them from engines, after rattling and bounding over their heads, rolled harmless to the ground. But there was in reserve a foe which they could not encounter. When it was found that the fiery streams flowed down the slanting sides of the shell, penetrating scarcely at all through the crevices of the well-joined shields, it was suggested, by the ingenious Periander, that there should first be thrown down a quantity of pitch in a half-melted state, by which the whole surface of the roof should be completely covered, and which should then, by a fresh discharge of fire, be set in a blaze, the effect of which must be to heat the shields to such a degree, that they could neither be held, nor the heat beneath endured by the miners. This was immediately resorted to at all the gates, and the success was complete. For no sooner was the cold pitch set on fire and constantly fed by fresh quantities from above, than the heat became insupportable to those below, who suddenly letting go their hold, and breaking away from their compacted form, in hope to escape from the stifling heat, the burning substance then poured in upon them, and vast numbers perished miserably upon the spot, or ran burning, and howling with pain, towards the camp. The slaughter made was very great, and very terrible to behold.

Nevertheless, the next day the same attempts were renewed, in the hope, we supposed, that the queen's missiles might be expended, but were defeated again in the same manner and with like success.

These things being so, and Aurelian being apparently convinced that the city cannot be taken by storm, the enemy are now employed in surrounding it with a double ditch and rampart, as defences both against us and our allies, between which the army is to be safely encamped—an immense labour, to which I believe a Roman army is alone competent. While this has been doing, the Palmyrenes have made frequent sallies from the gates, greatly interrupting the progress of the work, and inflicting severe losses. These attacks have usually been made at night, when the soldiers have been wearied by the exhausting toil of the day, and only a small proportion of the whole have been in a condition to ward off the blows.

The Roman works are at length completed. Every lofty palm tree, every cedar, every terebinth, has disappeared from the surrounding plains, to be converted into battering rams, or wrought into immense towers, planted upon wheels, by which the walls are to be approached and surmounted. Houses and palaces have been demolished, that the ready hewed timber might be detached and applied to various warlike purposes. The once beautiful environs already begin to put on the appearance of desolation and ruin.

The citizens have awaited these preparations with watchful anxiety. The queen has expressed every where and to all, her conviction that all these vast and various preparations are futile—that the bravery of her soldiers and the completeness of her counter provisions, will be sufficient for the protection and deliverance of the city.

Another day of fierce and bloody war. At four different points have the vast towers been pushed to the walls, filled with soldiers, and defended against the fires of the besieged by a casing of skins and every incombustible substance, and provided with a store of water to quench whatever part might by chance kindle. It was fearful to behold these huge structures, urged along by a concealed force, partly of men and partly of animals, and drawing nigh the walls. If they should once approach so near that they could be fastened to the walls, and so made secure, then could the enemy pour their legions upon the ramparts, and the battle would be transferred to the city itself. But in this case, as in the assaults upon the gates, the fire of the besieged has proved irresistible.

It was the direction of Periander, to whose unequalled sagacity this part of the defence was entrusted, that so soon as the towers should approach within reach of the most powerful engines, they should be fired, if possible, by means of well-barbed arrows and javelins, to which were attached sacs and balls of inflammable and explosive substances. These, fastening themselves upon every part of the tower, could not fail to set fire to them while yet at some distance, and in extinguishing which the water, and other means provided for that purpose, would be nearly or quite exhausted, before they had reached the walls. Then, as they came within easier reach, the engines were to belch forth those rivers of oil, fire, and burning pitch, which he was sure no structure, unless of solid iron, could withstand.

These directions were carefully observed, and their success to every point such as Periander had predicted. At the gate of the desert the most formidable preparations were made, under the directions of the emperor himself, who, at a distance, could plainly be discerned directing the work and encouraging the soldiers. Two towers of enormous size were here constructed, and driven towards the walls. Upon both, as they came within the play of the engines, were showered the fiery javelins and arrows, which it required all the activity of the occupants to ward off or extinguish, where they had succeeded in fastening themselves. One was soon in flames. The other, owing either to its being of a better construction, or to a less vigorous discharge of fire on the part of the defenders of the walls, not only escaped the more distant storm of blazing missiles, but succeeded in quenching the floods of burning pitch and oil, which, as it drew nearer and nearer, were poured upon it in fiery streams. On it moved, propelled by its invisible and protected power, and had now reached the wall—the bridge was in the very act of being thrown and grappled to the ramparts—Aurelian was seen pressing forward the legions, who, as soon as it should be fastened, were to pour up its flights of steps and out upon the walls—when to the horror of all, not less of the besiegers than of the besieged, its foundations upon one side, being laid over the moat, suddenly gave way, and the towering and enormous mass, with all its living burden, fell thundering to the plain. A shout, as of a delivered and conquering army, went up from the walls, while upon the legions below such as had not been crushed by the tumbling ruin, and who endeavoured to save themselves by flight, a sudden storm of stones, rocks, burning pitch, and missiles of a thousand kinds, was directed, that left few to escape to tell the tale of death to their comrades. Aurelian, in his fury, or his desire to aid the fallen, approaching too near the walls, was himself struck by a well-directed shaft, wounded, and borne from the field.

At the other gates, where similar assaults had been made, the same success attended the Palmyrenes. The towers were in each instance set on fire and destroyed.

The city has greatly exulted at the issue of these repeated contests. Every sound and sign of triumph has been made upon the walls. Banners have been waved to and fro, trumpets have been blown, and, in bold defiance of their power, parties of horse have sallied out from the gates, and after careering in sight of the enemy, have returned again within the walls. The enemy are evidently dispirited, and already weary of the work they have undertaken.

The queen and her ministers are confident of success, so far as active resistance of the attacks upon the walls is concerned — and, perhaps, with reason. For not even the walls of Rome, as they are now rebuilding, can be of greater strength than these—and never were the defences of a besieged city so complete at all points. But with equal reason are they despondent in the prospect of Aurelian's reducing them by want. If he shall succeed in procuring supplies for his army, and if he shall defeat the allies of the queen, who are now every day looked for, captivity and ruin are sure. But the queen and the citizens entertain themselves with the hope, that Aurelian's fiery temper will never endure the slow and almost disgraceful process of starving them into a surrender; and that, finding his army constantly diminishing through the effects of such extraordinary exertions in a climate like this, he will at length propose such terms as they, without dishonour, can accept.

Many days have passed in inactivity on both sides— except that nothing can exceed the strictness with which all approaches to the city are watched, and the possibility of supplies reaching it cut off.

That which has been expected has come to pass. The emperor has offered terms of surrender to the queen—

but such terms, and so expressed, that their acceptance was not so much as debated. The queen was in council with her advisers, when it was announced that a herald from the Roman camp was seen approaching the walls. The gates were ordered to be opened, and the messenger admitted. He was conducted to the presence of the queen, surrounded by her ministers.

"I come," said he, as he advanced towards Zenobia, "bearing a letter from the emperor of Rome to the queen of Palmyra. Here it is."

"I receive it gladly," replied the queen, "and hope that it may open a way to an honourable composition of the difficulties which now divide us. Nichomachus, break the seals and read its contents."

The secretary took the epistle from the hands of the herald, and opening, read that which follows:—

"*Aurelian, Emperor of Rome and Conqueror of the East, to Zenobia and her companions in arms.*

You ought of your own accord long since to have done what now by this letter I enjoin and command. And what I now enjoin and command is this, an immediate surrender of the city, but with assurance of life to yourself and your friends—you, oh queen! with your friends, to pass your days where the senate, in its sovereign will, shall please to appoint. The rights of every citizen shall be respected, upon condition that all precious stones, silver, gold, silk, horses, and camels, be delivered into the hands of the Romans."

As the secretary finished these words, the queen broke forth:

"What think you, good friends"—her mounting colour and curled lip showing the storm that raged within—"what think you? Is it a man or a god who has written thus? Can it be a mortal, who speaks in such terms to another? By the soul of Odenatus, but I think it must be the god of war himself. Slave, what sayest thou?"

"I am but the chosen bearer," the herald replied,

"of what I took from the hands of the emperor. But between him and the god just named, there is, as I deem, but small difference."

"That's well said," replied the queen; "there's something of the old Roman in thee. Friends," she continued, turning to her councillors, "what answer shall we send to this lordly command? What is your advice?"

"Mine is," said Zabdas, "that the queen set her foot upon the accursed scrawl, and that yonder wretch that bore it be pitched headlong from the highest tower upon the walls, and let the wind from his rotting carcass bear back our only answer."

"Nay, nay, brave Zabdas," said the queen, the fury of her general having the effect to restore her own self-possession, "thou wouldst not counsel so. War then doubles its woe and guilt, when cruelty and injustice bear sway. Otho, what sayest thou?"

"Answer it in its own vein. You smile, queen, as if incredulous. But I repeat—in its own vein! I confess an inward disappointment and an inward change. I hoped much from terms which a wise man might at this point propose, and soil neither his own nor his country's honour. But Aurelian—I now see—is not such a one. He is but the spoiled child of fortune. He has grown too quickly great to grow well. Wisdom has had no time to ripen."

Others concurring, Zenobia seized a pen, and wrote that which I transcribe.

"*Zenobia, Queen of the East, to Aurelian Augustus.*

No one before you ever thought to make a letter serve instead of a battle. But let me tell you, whatever is won in war, is won by bravery, not by letters. You ask me to surrender—as if ignorant that Cleopatra chose rather to die, than, surrendering, to live in the enjoyment of every honour. Our Persian allies will not fail me. I look for them every hour. The Saracens are with me—the Armenians are with me. The Syrian robbers have already done you no little damage.

What, then, can you expect, when these allied armies are upon you? You will lay aside, I think, a little of that presumption with which you now command me to surrender, as if you were already conqueror of the whole world."

The letter being written and approved by those who were present, it was placed by Nichomachus in the hands of the herald.

No one can marvel, my Curtius, that a letter in the terms of Aurelian's should be rejected, nor that it should provoke such an answer as Zenobia's. It has served merely to exasperate passions which were already enough excited. It was entirely in the power of the emperor to have terminated the contest, by the proposal of conditions which Palmyra would have gladly accepted, and by which Rome would have been more profited and honoured than it can be by the reduction and ruin of a city and kingdom like this. But it is too true, that Aurelian is rather a soldier than an emperor. A victory got by blood, is sweeter far to him, I fear, than tenfold wider conquests won by peaceful negotiations.

The effect of the taunting and scornful answer of the queen, has been immediately visible in the increased activity and stir in the camp of Aurelian. Preparations are going on for renewed assaults upon the walls, upon a much larger scale than before.

On the evening of the day on which the letter of Aurelian was received and answered, I resorted, according to my custom during the siege, to a part of the walls not far from the house of Gracchus, whence an extended view is had of the Roman works and camp. Fausta, as often before, accompanied me. She delights thus, at the close of these weary, melancholy days, to walk forth, breathe the reviving air, observe the condition of the city, and, from the towers upon the walls, watch the movements and labours of the enemy. The night was without moon or stars. Low and heavy clouds hung, but did not move, over our heads. The air was still, nay, rather dead, so deep was its repose.

"How oppressive is this gloom!" said Fausta, as we came forth upon the ramparts, and took our seat where the eye could wander unobstructed over the plain, "and yet how gaily illuminated is this darkness by yonder belt of moving lights! It seems like the gorgeous preparation for a funeral. Above us and behind it is silent, dark, and sad. These show like the torches of the approaching mourners. The gods grant there be no omen in this."

"I know not," I replied. "It may be so. To-day has, I confess it, destroyed the last hope in my mind that there might come a happy termination to this unwise and unnecessary contest. It can end now only in the utter defeat and ruin of one of the parties—and which that shall be I cannot doubt. Listen, Fausta, to the confused murmur that comes from the camp of the Roman army, bearing witness to its numbers, and to those sounds of the hammer, the axe, and the saw, plied by ten thousand arms, bearing witness to the activity and exhaustless resources of the enemy, and you cannot but feel, that at last—it may be long first, but that at last—Palmyra must give way. From what has been observed to-day, there is not a doubt that Aurelian has provided, by means of regular caravans to Antioch, for a constant supply of whatever his army requires. Reinforcements, too, both of horse and foot, are seen daily arriving, in such numbers as more than to make good those who have been lost under the walls, or by the excessive heats of the climate."

"I hear so," said Fausta, "but I will not despair. If I have one absorbing love, it is for Palmyra. It is the land of my birth, of my affections. I cannot tell you with what pride I have watched its growth, and its daily advancement in arts and letters, and have dwelt in fancy upon that future, when it should rival Rome, and surpass the traditional glories of Babylon and Nineveh. Oh, Lucius, to see now a black pall descending—these swollen clouds are an emblem of it—and settling upon the prospect and veiling it for ever in death—I cannot believe it. It cannot have come to this. It is treason to give way to such fears. Where Zenobia is, final ruin cannot come."

"It ought not, I wish it could not," I replied, "but my fears are that it will, and my fears now are convictions. Where, now, my dear Fausta, are the so certainly expected reliefs from Armenia, from Persia?— Fausta, Palmyra must fall."

"Lucius Piso, Palmyra shall not fall—I say it, and every Palmyrene says it—and what all say is decreed. If we are true in our loyalty and zeal, the Romans will be wearied out. Lucius, could I but reach the tent of Aurelian, my single arm should rid Palmyra of her foe, and achieve her freedom."

"No, Fausta, you could not do it."

"Indeed, I would and could. I would consent to draw infamy upon my head as a woman, if by putting off my sex and my nature too, I could by such an act give life to a dying nation, and what is as much, preserve Zenobia her throne."

"Think not in that vein, Fausta. I would not that your mind should be injured even by the thought."

"I do not feel it to be an injury," she rejoined; "it would be a sacrifice for my country, and the dearer, in that I should lose my good name in making it. I should be sure of one thing, that I should do it in no respect for my own glory. But let us talk no more of it. I often end, Lucius, in thinking of our calamities, and of a fatal termination of these contests to us, with dwelling upon one bright vision. Misfortune to us will bring you nearer to Julia."

"The gods forbid that my happiness should be bought at such a price."

"It will only come as an accidental consequence, and cannot disturb you. If Palmyra falls, the pride of Zenobia will no longer separate you."

"But," I replied, "the prospect is not at all so bright. Captive princes are, by the usages of Rome, often sacrificed, and Aurelian, if sometimes generous, is often cruel. Fears would possess me in the event of a capitulation or conquest, which I cannot endure to entertain."

"Oh, Lucius, you rate Aurelian too low, if you believe he could revenge himself upon a woman—and such a woman as Zenobia. I cannot believe it possible. No. If Palmyra falls, it will give you Julia, and it will be some consolation, even in the fall of a kingdom, that it brings happiness to two whom friendship binds closer to me than any others."

As Fausta said these words, we became conscious of the presence of a person at no great distance from us, leaning against the parapet of the wall, the upper part of the form just discernible.

"Who stands yonder?" said Fausta. "It has not the form of a sentinel—besides, the sentinel paces by us to and fro without pausing. It may be Calpurnius. His legion is in this quarter. Let us move towards him."

"No. He moves himself and comes towards us. How dark the night! I can make nothing of the form."

The figure passed us, and unchallenged by the sentinel whom it met. After a brief absence, it returned, and stopping as it came before us,

"Fausta!" said a voice, once heard not to be mistaken.

"Zenobia!" said Fausta, and forgetting dignity, embraced her as a friend.

"What makes you here?" inquired Fausta; "are there none in Palmyra to do your bidding, but you must be abroad at such an hour, and such a place?"

"'Tis not so fearful quite," replied the queen, "as a battle field, and there you trust me."

"Never willingly."

"Then you do not love my honour?" said the queen, taking Fausta's hand as she spoke.

"I love your safety better; no—no—what have I said! —not better than your honour; and yet to what end is honour, if we lose the life in which it resides. I sometimes think we purchase human glory too dearly, at the sacrifice of quiet, peace, and security."

"But you do not think so long. What is a life of indulgence and sloth. Life is worthy only in what it achieves. Should I have done better to have sat over my embroidery, in the midst of my slaves, all my days, than to have spent them in building up a kingdom?"

"Oh no, no!—you have done right. Slaves can embroider. Zenobia cannot. This hand was made for other weapon than the needle."

"I am weary," said the queen; "let us sit;" and saying so, she placed herself upon the low stone block upon which we had been sitting, and drawing Fausta near her, she threw her left arm round her, retaining the hand she held clasped in her own.

"I am weary," she continued, "for I have walked nearly the circuit of the walls. You asked what makes me here? No night passes but I visit these towers and battlements. If the governor of the ship sleeps, the men at the watch sleep. Besides, I love Palmyra too well to sleep while others wait and watch. I would do my share. How beautiful is this! The city girded by these strange fires!—its ears filled with this busy music! Piso, it seems hard to believe an enemy, and such an enemy is there, and that these sights and sounds are all of death."

"Would it were not so, noble queen! Would it were not yet too late to move in the cause of peace! If even at the risk of life, I ——"

"Forbear, Piso," quickly rejoined the queen; "it is to no purpose. You have my thanks, but your emperor has closed the door of peace for ever. It is now war unto death. He may prove victor. It is quite possible. But I draw not back—no word of supplication goes from me. And every citizen of Palmyra, save a few sottish souls, is with me. It were worth my throne and my life the bare suggestion of an embassy now to Aurelian. But let us not speak of this, but of things more agreeable. The day for trouble, the night for rest. Fausta, where is the quarter of Calpurnius? methinks it is hereabouts."

"It is," replied Fausta, "just beyond the towers of the gate next to us; were it not for this thick night, we could see where at this time he is usually to be found doing, like yourself, an unnecessary task."

"He is a good soldier and a faithful—may he prove as true to you, my noble girl, as he has to me! Albeit I am myself a sceptic in love, I cannot but be made happier when I see hearts worthy of each other united by that bond. I trust that bright days are coming, when I may do you the honour I would. Piso, I am largely a debtor to your brother, and Palmyra as much. Singular fortune!—that while Rome thus oppresses me, to Romans I should owe so much—to one twice my life, to another my army. But where, Lucius Piso, was your heart, that it fell not into the snare that caught Calpurnius?"

"My heart," I replied, "has always been Fausta's; from childhood ——"

"Our attachment," said Fausta, interrupting me, "is not less than love, but greater. It is the sacred tie of nature, if I may say so—of brother to sister; it is friendship."

"You say well," replied the queen. "I like the sentiment. It is not less than love, but greater. Love is a delirium, a dream, a disease. It is full of disturbance. It is unequal, capricious, unjust; its felicity, when at the highest, is then nearest to deepest misery; a step, and it is into unfathomable gulfs of woe. While the object loved is as yet unattained, life is darker than darkest night. When it is attained, it is then oftener like the ocean heaving and tossing from its foundations, than the calm peaceful lake which mirrors friendship. And when lost, all is lost; the universe is nothing. Who will deny it the name of madness? Will love find entrance into elysium? Will heaven know more than friendship? I trust not. It were an element of discord there where harmony should reign perpetual."

After a pause, in which she seemed buried in thought, she added musingly—"What darkness rests upon the future. Life, like love, is itself but a dream—often a brief or a prolonged madness. Its light burns sometimes brightly, oftener obscurely, and with a flickering ray, and then goes out in smoke and darkness. How strange, that creatures so exquisitely wrought as we are, capable of such thoughts and acts, rising by science, and art, and letters, almost to the level of gods, should be fixed here for so short a time, running our race with the unintelligent brute—living not so long as some, dying like all. Could I have ever looked out of this life into the possession of any other beyond it, I believe my aims would have been different. I should not so easily have been satisfied with glory and power. At least I think so; for who knows himself? I should then, I think, have reached after higher kinds of excellence, such, for example, as, existing more in the mind itself, could be of avail after death—could be carried out of the world, which power, riches, glory, cannot. The greatest service which any philosopher could perform for the human race, would be to demonstrate the certainty of a future existence, in the same satisfactory manner that Euclid demonstrates the truths of geometry. We cannot help believing Euclid if we would, and the truths he has established concerning lines and angles influence us whether we will or not. Whenever the immortality of the soul shall be proved in like manner, so that men cannot help believing it, so that they shall draw it in with the first elements of all knowledge, then will mankind become a quite different race of beings. Men will be more virtuous and more happy. How is it possible to be either in a very exalted degree, dwelling as we do in the deep obscure, uncertain whether we are mere earth and water, or parts of the divinity; whether we are worms or immortals, men or gods; spending all our days in, at best, miserable perplexity and doubt. Do you remember, Fausta and Piso, the discourse of Longinus in the garden, concerning the probability of a future life?"

"We do, very distinctly,"

"And how did it impress you?"

"It seemed to possess much likelihood," replied Fausta, "but that was all."

"Yes," responded the queen, sighing deeply, "that was indeed all. Philosophy, in this part of it, is a mere guess. Even Longinus can but conjecture. And what to his great and piercing intellect stands but in the strength of probability, to ours will, of necessity, address itself in the very weakness of fiction. As it is, I value life only for the brightest and best it can give now, and these to my mind are power and a throne. When these are lost, I would fall unregarded into darkness and death."

"But," I ventured to suggest, "you derive great pleasure and large profit from study—from the researches of philosophy, from the knowledge of history, from contemplation of the beauties of art, and the magnificence of nature. Are not these things that give worth to life? If you reasoned aright, and probed the soul well, would you not find that from these, as from hidden springs, a great deal of all the best felicity you have tasted, has welled up? Then, still more, in acts of good and just government—in promoting the happiness of your subjects—from private friendship—from affections resting upon objects worthy to be loved—has no happiness come worth living for? And besides all this, from an inward consciousness of rectitude? Most of all this may still be yours, though you no longer sat upon a throne, and men held their lives but in your breath."

"From such sources," replied Zenobia, "some streams have issued, it may be, that have added to what I have enjoyed, but of themselves they would have been nothing. The lot of earth, being of the low and common herd, is a lot too low and sordid to be taken if proffered. I thank the gods mine has been better. It has been a throne, glory, renown, pomp, and power, and I have been happy. Stripped of these, and without the prospect of immortality, and I would not live."

With these words, she rose quickly from her seat, saying, that she had a further duty to perform. Fausta entreated to be used as an agent or messenger, but could not prevail. Zenobia, darting from our side, was in a moment lost in the surrounding darkness. We returned to the house of Gracchus.

In a few days, the vast preparations of the Romans being complete, a general assault was made by the whole army upon every part of the walls. Every engine known to our modern methods of attacking walled cities, was brought to bear. Towers constructed in the former manner were wheeled up to the walls. Battering-rams of enormous size, those who worked them being protected by sheds of hide, thundered on all sides at the gates and walls. Language fails to convey an idea of the energy, the fury, the madness, of the onset. The Roman army seemed as if but one being, with such equal courage and contempt of danger and of death, was the dreadful work performed. But the queen's defences have again proved superior to all the power of Aurelian. Her engines have dealt death and ruin in awful measure among the assailants. The moat and the surrounding plain are filled and covered with the bodies of the slain. As night came on, after a long day of uninterrupted conflict, the troops of Aurelian, baffled and defeated at every point, withdrew to their tents, and left the city to repose.

The temples of the gods have resounded with songs of thanksgiving for this new deliverance, garlands have been hung around their images, and gifts laid upon their altars. Jews and Christians, Persians and Egyptians, after the manner of their worship, have added their voices to the general chorus.

Again there has been a pause. The Romans have rested, after the late fierce assault, to recover strength, and the city has breathed free. Many are filled with new courage and hope, and the discontented spirits are silenced. The praises of Zenobia, next to those of the gods, fill every mouth. The streets ring with songs composed in her honour.

Another day of excited expectations and bitter disappointment. It was early reported that forces were seen approaching from the east, on the very skirts of the plain, and that they could be no other than the long looked-for Persian army. Before its approach was indicated to those upon the highest towers of the gates, by the clouds of dust hovering over it, it was evident, from the extraordinary commotion in the Roman intrenchments, that somewhat unusual had taken place. Their scouts must have brought in early intelligence of the advancing foe. Soon as the news spread through the city, the most extravagant demonstrations of joy broke forth on all sides. Even the most moderate and sedate could not but give way to expressions of heartfelt satisfaction. The multitudes poured to the walls to witness a combat upon which the existence of the city seemed suspended.

"Father," said Fausta, after Gracchus had communicated the happy tidings, "I cannot sit here; let us hasten to the towers of the Persian gate, whence we may behold the encounter."

"I will not oppose you," replied Gracchus, "but the sight may cost you naught but tears and pain. Persia's good-will, I fear, will not be much, nor manifested by large contributions to our cause. If it be what I suspect—but a paltry subdivision of her army, sent here rather to be cut in pieces than aught else—it will but needlessly afflict and irritate."

"Father, I would turn away from no evil that threatens Palmyra. Besides, I should suffer more from imagined, than from real disaster. Let us hasten to the walls."

We flew to the Persian gate.

"But why," asked Fausta, addressing Gracchus on the way, "are you not come more elated? What suspicion do you entertain of Sapor? Will he not be sincerely desirous to aid us?"

"I fear not," replied Gracchus. "If we are to be the conquering party in this war, he will send such an army as would afterwards make it plain that he had intended an act of friendship, and done the duty of an ally. If we are to be beaten, he will lose little in losing such an army, and will easily, by placing the matter in certain lights, convince the Romans that their interests had been consulted, rather than ours. We can expect no act of true friendship from Sapor. Yet he dares not abandon us. Were Hormisdas upon the throne, our prospects were brighter."

"I pray the gods that ancient wretch may quickly perish, then," cried Fausta, "if such might be the consequences to us. Why is he suffered longer to darken Persia and the earth with his cruel despotism?"

"His throne shakes beneath him," replied Gracchus; "a breath may throw it down."

As we issued forth upon the walls, and then mounted to the battlements of the highest tower, whence the eye took in the environs of the city, and even the farthest verge of the plain, and overlooked, like one's own courtyard, the camp and intrenchments of the Romans, we beheld with distinctness the Persian forces within less than two Roman miles. They had halted and formed, and there apparently awaited the enemy.

No sooner had Gracchus surveyed well the scene, than he exclaimed, "The gods be praised. I have done Sapor injustice. Yonder forces are such as may well call forth all the strength of the Roman army. In that case there will be much for us to do. I must descend and to the post of duty."

So saying, he left us.

"I suppose," said Fausta, "in case the enemy be such as to draw off the larger part of the Roman army, sorties will be made from the gates upon their camp."

"Yes," I rejoined, "if the Romans should suffer themselves to be drawn to a distance, and their forces divided, a great chance would fall into the hands of the city. But that they will not do. You perceive the Romans move not, but keep their station just where they are. They will oblige the Persians to commence the assault upon them in their present position, or there will be no battle."

"I perceive their policy now," said Fausta. "And the battle being fought so near the walls, they are still as strongly beleagured as ever—at least half their strength seems to remain within their intrenchments. See, see—the Persian army is on the march. It moves towards the city. Now again it halts."

"It hopes to entice Aurelian from his position, so as to put power into our hands. But they will fail in their object."

"Yes, I fear they will," replied Fausta. "The Romans remain fixed as statues in their place."

"Is it not plain to you, Fausta," said I, "that the Persians conceive not the full strength of the Roman army? Your eye can now measure their respective power."

"It is too plain, alas!" said Fausta. "If the Persians should defeat the army now formed, there is another within the trenches to be defeated afterwards. Now they move again. Righteous gods, interpose in our behalf!"

At this moment, indeed, the whole Persian army put itself into quick and decisive motion, as if determined to dare all and achieve all for their ally, if fate should so decree. It was a sight beautiful to behold, but of an interest too painful almost to be endured. The very existence of a city and an empire seemed to hang upon its issues; and here, looking on and awaiting the decisive moment, was as it were the empire itself assembled upon the walls of its capital, with which, if it should fall, the kingdom would also fall, and the same ruin cover both. The queen herself was there to animate and encourage by her presence, not only the hearts of all around, but even the distant forces of the Persians, who, from their position, might easily behold the whole extent of the walls and towers, covered with an innumerable multitude of the besieged inhabitants, who, by waving their hands, and by every conceivable demonstration, gave them to feel more deeply than they could otherwise have done, how much was depending upon their skill and bravery.

Soon after the last movement of the Persians, the light troops of either army encountered, and by a discharge of arrows and javelins, commenced the attack. Then in a few moments, it being apparently impossible to restrain the impatient soldiery, the battle became general. The cry of the onset, and the clash of arms, fell distinctly upon our ears. Long, long were the opposing armies mingled together in one undistinguishable mass, waging an equal fight. Now it would sway towards the one side, and now towards the other, heaving and bending as a field of ripe grain to the fitful breeze. Fausta sat with clenched hands, and straining eye, watching the doubtful fight, and waiting the issue in speechless agony. A deep silence, as of night and death, held the whole swarming multitude of the citizens, who hardly seemed as if they dared breathe while what seemed the final scene was in the act of being performed.

Suddenly a new scene, and more terrific because nearer, burst upon our sight. At a signal given by Zenobia, from the high tower which she occupied, the gates below us flew open, and Zabdas, at the head of all the flower of the Palmyra cavalry, poured forth, followed closely from this and the other gates by the infantry. The battle now raged between the walls and the Roman entrenchments, as well as beyond. The whole plain was one field of battle and slaughter. Despair lent vigour and swiftness to the horse and foot of Palmyra—rage at the long-continued contest, revenge for all they had lost and endured, nerved the Roman arm, and gave a double edge to its sword. Never before, my Curtius, had I beheld a fight in which every blow seemed so to carry with it the whole soul, boiling with wrath, of him who gave it. Death sat upon every arm.

"Lucius!" cried Fausta. I started, for it had been long that she had uttered not a word. "Lucius! unless my eye grows dim and lies, which the gods grant, the Persians! look! they give way—is it not so? Immortal gods, forsake not my country!"

"The battle may yet turn," I said, turning my eyes where she pointed, and seeing it was so. "Despair not, dear Fausta. If the Persians yield—see, Zabdas has mounted the Roman intrenchments."

"Yes—they fly," screamed Fausta, and would madly have sprung over the battlements, but that I seized and held her. At the same moment a cry arose that Zabdas was slain—her eye caught his noble form as it fell backwards from his horse; and with a faint exclamation "Palmyra is lost!" she fell lifeless into my arms.

While I devoted myself to her recovery, cries of distress and despair fell from all quarters upon my ear. And when I had succeeded in restoring her to consciousness, the fate of the day was decided—the Persians were routed—the Palmyrenes were hurrying in wild confusion before the pursuing Romans, and pressing into the gates.

"Lucius," said Fausta, "I am sorry for this weakness. But to sit, as it were, chained here, the witness of such disaster, is too much for mere mortal force. Could I but have mingled in that fight! Ah, how cruel the slaughter of those flying troops! Why do they not turn, and at least die with their faces towards the enemy? Let us now go and seek Calpurnius and Gracchus."

"We cannot yet, Fausta, for the streets are thronged with this flying multitude."

"It is hard to remain here, the ears rent, and the heart torn by these shrieks of the wounded and dying. How horrible this tumult! It seems as if the world were expiring. There—the gates are swinging upon their hinges. They are shut. Let us descend."

We forced our way as well as we could through the streets, crowded now with soldiers and citizens—the soldiers scattered and in disorder, the citizens weeping and alarmed—some hardly able to drag along themselves, others sinking beneath the weight of the wounded whom they bore upon their shoulders, or upon lances as upon a litter. The way was all along obstructed by the bodies of men and horses who had there fallen and died, their wounds allowing them to proceed no farther, or who had been run down and trampled to death in the tumult and hurry of the entrance.

After a long and weary struggle, we reached the house of Gracchus—still solitary, for neither he nor Calpurnius had returned. The slaves gathered around us to know the certainty and extent of the evil. When they had learned it, their sorrow for their mistress, whom they loved for her own sake, and whom they saw overwhelmed with grief, made them almost forget that they only were suffering these things who had inflicted a worse injury upon themselves. I could not but admire a virtue which seemed of double lustre from the circumstances in which it was manifested.

Calpurnius had been in the thickest of the fight, but had escaped unhurt. He was near Zabdas when he fell, and avenged his death by hewing down the soldier who had pierced him with his lance.

"Zabdas," said Calpurnius, when in the evening we recalled the sad events of the day, "was not instantly killed by the thrust of the spear, but falling backwards from his horse, found strength and life enough remaining to raise himself upon his knee, and cheer me on, as I flew to avenge his death upon the retreating Roman. As I returned to him, having completed my task, he had sunk upon the ground, but was still living, and his eye bright with its wonted fire. I raised him in my arms, and lifting him upon my horse, moved towards the gate, intending to bring him within the walls. But he presently entreated me to desist.

'I die,' said he; 'it is all in vain, noble Piso. Lay me at the root of this tree, and that shall be my bed, and its shaft my monument.'

I took him from the horse as he desired.

'Place me,' said he, 'with my back against the tree, and my face towards the intrenchments, that while I live I may see the battle. Piso, tell the queen that to the last hour I am true to her. It has been my glory in life to live but for her, and my death is a happiness, dying for her. Her image swims before me now, and over her hovers a winged victory. The Romans fly—I knew it would be so—the dogs cannot stand before the cavalry of Palmyra—they never could—they fled at Antioch. Hark!—there are the shouts of triumph—bring me my horse—Zenobia! live and reign for ever!'

With these words his head fell upon his bosom, and he died. I returned to the conflict; but it had become a rout, and I was borne along with the rushing throng towards the gates."

After a night of repose and quiet, there has come another day of adversity. The hopes of the city have again been raised, only again to be disappointed. The joyful cry was heard from the walls in the morning, that the Saracens and Armenians, with united forces, were in the field. Coming so soon upon the fatiguing duty of the last day, and the Roman army not having received reinforcements from the west, it was believed that the enemy could not sustain another onset as fierce as that of the Persians. I hastened once more to the walls—Fausta being compelled by Gracchus to remain within the palace, to witness, as I believed, another battle.

The report I found true. The allied forces of those nations were in sight—the Romans were already drawn from their encampment to encounter them. The same policy was pursued on their part as before. They awaited the approach of the new enemy just on the outer side of their works. The walls and towers, as far as the eye could reach, were again swarming with the population of Palmyra.

For a long time neither army seemed disposed to move.

"They seem not very ready to try the fortune of another day," said a citizen to me standing by my side; "nor do I wonder. The Persians gave them rough handling. A few thousands more on their side, and the event would not have been as it was. Think you not the sally under Zabdas was too long deferred?"

"It is easy afterwards," I replied, "to say how an action should have been performed. It requires the knowledge and wisdom of a god never to err. There were different judgments, I know, but for myself I believe the queen was right; that is, whether Zabdas had left the gates earlier or later, the event would have been the same."

"What means that?" suddenly exclaimed my companion; "see you yonder herald bearing a flag of truce, and proceeding from the Roman ranks? It bodes no good to Palmyra. What think you the purpose is?"

"It may be but to ask a forbearance of arms for a few hours, or a day perhaps. Yet it is not the custom of Rome. I cannot guess."

"That can I," exclaimed another citizen on my other side. "Neither in the Armenians, nor yet the Saracens, can so much trust be reposed as in a Christian or a Jew. They are for the strongest. Think you they have come to fight? Not if they can treat to better purpose. The Romans, who know by heart the people of the whole earth, know them. Mark me, they will draw never a sword. As the chances are now, they will judge the Romans winners, and a little gold will buy them."

"The gods forbid," cried the other, "that it should be so—they are the last hope of Palmyra. If they fail us, we must e'en throw open our gates, and take our fate at the mercy of Aurelian."

"Never, while I have an arm that can wield a sword, shall a gate of Palmyra swing upon its hinge to let in an enemy."

"Food already grows short," said the first; "better yield than starve."

"Thou, friend, art in no danger for many a day, if, as is fabled of certain animals, thou canst live on thine own fat. Or if it came to extremities, thou wouldst make a capital stew or roast for others."

At which the surrounding crowd laughed heartily, while the fat man, turning pale, slunk away and disappeared.

"That man," said one, "would betray a city for a full meal."

"I know him well," said another; "he is the earliest at the markets, where you may always see him feeling out with his fat finger the parts of meats that are kindred to himself. His soul, could it be seen, would be of the form of a fat kidney. His riches he values only as they can be changed into food. Were all Palmyra starved, he, were he sought, would be found in some deep down vault, bedded in the choicest meats, enough to stand a year's siege, and leave his paunch as far about as 'tis to-day. See, the queen betrays anxiety. The gods shield her from harm."

Zenobia occupied the same post of observation as before. She paced to and fro with a hasty and troubled step the narrow summit of the tower, where she had placed herself.

After no long interval of time, the Roman herald was seen returning from the camp of the Armenians. Again he sallied forth from the tent of Aurelian, on the same errand. It was too clear now that negotiations were going on which might end fatally for Palmyra. Doubt, fear, anxiety, intense expectation, kept the multitude around me in breathless silence, standing at fixed gaze, like so many figures of stone.

They stood not long in this deep and agonising suspense, for no sooner did the Roman herald reach the tents of the allied armies, and hold brief parley with their chiefs, than he again turned towards the Roman intrenchments at a quick pace, and at the same moment the tents of the other party were struck; and while a part commenced a retreat, another and larger part moved as auxiliaries to join the camp of Aurelian.

Cries of indignation, rage, grief, and despair, then burst from the miserable crowds, as with slow and melancholy steps they turned from the walls to seek again their homes. Zenobia was seen once to clasp her hands, turning her face towards the heavens. As she emerged from the tower and ascended her chariot, the enthusiastic throngs failed not to testify their unshaken confidence and determined spirit of devotion to her and her throne, by acclamations that seemed to shake the very walls themselves.

This last has proved a heavier blow to Palmyra than the former. It shows that their cause is regarded by the neighbouring powers as a losing one, or already lost, and that hope, so far as it rested upon their friendly interposition, must be abandoned. The city is silent and sad. Almost all the forms of industry having ceased, the inhabitants are doubly wretched through their necessary idleness; they can do little but sit and brood over their present deprivations, and utter their dark bodings touching the future. All sounds of gaiety have ceased. They who obtained their subsistence by ministering to the pleasures of others, are now the first to suffer, for there are none to employ their services. Streets, which but a little while ago resounded with notes of music, and the loud laughter of those who lived to pleasure, are now dull and deserted. The brilliant shops are closed, the fountains forsaken, the Portico solitary—or they are frequented by a few who resort to them chiefly to while away some of the melancholy hours that hang upon their hands. And those who are abroad seem not like the same people. Their step is now measured and slow, the head bent, no salutation greets the passing stranger or acquaintance, or only a few cold words of inquiry, which pass from cold lips into ears as cold. Apathy, lethargy, stupor, seem fast settling over all.

They would, indeed, bury all, I believe, were it not that the parties of the discontented increase in number and power, which compels the friends of the queen to keep upon the alert. The question of surrender is now openly discussed. "It is useless," it is said, "to hold out longer. Better make the best terms we can. If we save the city, by an early capitulation, from destruction, coming off with our lives and a portion of our goods, it is more than we shall get if the act be much longer postponed. Every day of delay adds to our weakness, while it adds also to the vexation and rage of the enemy, who, the more and longer he suffers, will be less inclined to treat us with indulgence."

These may be said to have reason on their side, but the other party are inflamed with national pride and devotion to Zenobia, and no power of earth is sufficient to bend them. They are the principal party for numbers—much more, for rank and political power. They will hold out till the very last moment—till it is reduced to a choice between death and capitulation; and on the part of the queen and the great spirits of Palmyra, death would be their unhesitating choice, were it not for the destruction of so many with them. They will, therefore, until the last loaf of bread is divided, keep the gates shut; then throw them open, and meet the terms, whatever they may be, which the power of the conqueror may impose.

A formidable conspiracy has been detected, and the supposed chiefs of it seized and executed. The design was to secure the person of the queen, obtain, by a violent assault, one of the gates, and, sallying out, deliver her into the hands of the Romans, who, with her in their power, could immediately put an end to the contest. There is little doubt that Antiochus was privy to it, although those who suffered betrayed him not, if that were the fact. But it has been urged, with some force, in his favour, that none who suffered would have felt regard enough for him to have hesitated to sacrifice him, if by doing so they could have saved their own lives or others.

Zenobia displayed her usual dauntless courage, her clemency, and her severity. The attack was made upon her, surrounded by her small body guard, as she was returning, towards evening, from her customary visit of observation to the walls. It was sudden, violent, desperate; but the loyalty and bravery of the guards was more than a match for the assassins, aided, too, by the powerful arm of the queen herself, who was no idle spectator of the fray. It was a well-laid plot; and but for an accidental addition which was made at the walls to the queen's guard, might have succeeded; for the attack was made just at the Persian gate, and the keeper of the gate had been gained over. Had the guard been overpowered but for a moment, they would have shut the gate too quickly for the citizens to have roused to her rescue. Such of the conspirators as were not slain upon the spot were secured. Upon examination, they denied the participation of others than themselves in the attempt, and died—such of them as were executed —involving none in their ruin. The queen would not permit a general slaughter of them, though urged to do so. "The ends of justice and the safety of the city," she said, "would be sufficiently secured, if an example were made of such as seemed manifestly the chief movers. But there should be no indulgence of the spirit of revenge." Those, accordingly, were beheaded, the others imprisoned.

While these long and weary days are passing away, Gracchus, Fausta, Calpurnius, and myself, are often at the palace of Zenobia. The queen is gracious, as she ever is, but labouring under an anxiety and an inward sorrow, that imprint themselves deeply upon her countenance, and reveal themselves in a greater reserve of manner. While she is not engaged in some active service, she is buried in thought, and seems like one revolving difficult and perplexing questions. Sometimes she breaks from these moments of reverie with some sudden question to one or another of those around her, from which we can obscurely conjecture the subjects of her meditations. With Longinus, Otho, and Gracchus, she passes many of her hours in deep deliberation. At times, when apparently nature cries out for relief, she will join us, as we sit diverting our minds by conversation upon subjects as far removed as possible from the present distresses, and will, as formerly, shed the light of her penetrating judgment upon whatever it is we discuss. But she soon falls back into herself again, and remains silent and abstracted, or leaves us, and retreats to her private apartments.

Suddenly the queen has announced a project, which fills the city with astonishment at its boldness, and once more lights up hope within the bosoms of the most desponding.

Soon as her own mind had conceived and matured it, her friends and councillors were summoned to receive it from her, and pronounce their judgment. Would that I could set before you, my Curtius, this wonderful woman, as she stood before us at this interview. Never before did she seem so great, or of such transcendant beauty—if under such circumstances such a thought may be expressed. Whatever of melancholy had for so long a time shed its gloom over her features, was now gone. The native fire of her eye was restored and doubled, as it seemed, by the thoughts which she was waiting to express. A spirit greater than even her own appeared to animate her, and to breathe an unwonted majesty into her form, and over the countenance.

She greeted all with the warmth of a friend, and besought them to hear her while she presented a view of the present condition of their affairs, and then proposed what she could not but believe might still prove a means of final deliverance—at least, it might deserve their careful consideration. After having gone over the course that had been pursued, and defended it as that alone which became the dignity and honour of a sovereign and independent power, she proceeded thus:

"We are now, it is obvious to all, at the last extremity. If no new outlet be opened from the difficulties which environ us, a few days will determine our fate. We must open our gates, and take such mercy as our conquerors may bestow. The provision laid up in the public granaries is nearly exhausted. Already has it been found necessary greatly to diminish the amount of the daily distribution. Hope, in any power of our own, seems utterly extinct. If any remain, it rests upon foreign interposition; and of this I do not despair. I still rely upon Persia. I look with confidence to Sapor, for further and yet larger succours. In the former instance, it was apprehended by many—I confess I shared the apprehension—that there would be on the part of Persia but a parade of friendship, with nothing of reality. But you well know it was far otherwise. There was a sincere and vigorous demonstration in our behalf. Persia never fought a better field, and with slightly larger numbers would have accomplished our rescue. My proposition is, that we sue again at the court of Sapor—no, not again, for the first was a free-will offering—and that we fail not, I would go myself my own ambassador and solicit; what so solicited, my life upon it will not be refused. You well know that I can bear with me jewels, gathered during a long reign, of such value as to plead eloquently in my cause, since the tithe of them would well repay the Persian for all his kingdom might suffer for our sakes."

"What you propose, great queen," said Longinus, as Zenobia paused, "agrees with your whole life. But how can we, who hold you as we do, sit in our places, and allow you alone to encounter the dangers of such an enterprise? for without danger it cannot be—from the robber of the desert—from the Roman—from the Persian. In disguise and upon the road, you may suffer the common fate of those who travel where, as now, marauders of all nations swarm—Sapor may, in his capricious policy, detain you prisoner—Aurelian may intercept. Let your servants prevail with you to dismiss this thought from your mind. You can name no one of all this company who will not plead to be your substitute."

There was not one present who did not spring upon his feet, and express his readiness to undertake the charge.

"I thank you all," said the queen, "but claim, in this, perhaps, the last act of my reign, to be set free in your indulgence to hold an unobstructed course. If, in your honest judgments, you confess that of all who could appear at the court of Sapor, I should appear there as the most powerful pleader for Palmyra, it is all I ask you to determine. Is such your judgment?"

"It is," they all responded; "without doubt it is."

"Then am I resolved. And the enterprise itself you judge wise and of probable success?"

"We do. The reasons are just upon which it is founded. It is greatly conceived, and the gods giving you safe conduct to Sapor, we doubt not a happy result."

"Then all that remains is, to contrive the manner of escape from the city and through the Roman camp."

"There is, first, one thing more," said the princess Julia, suddenly rising from her mother's side, but with a forced and trembling courage, "which remains for me to do. If there appear any want of maidenly reserve in what I say, let the cause, good friends, for which I speak and act, be my excuse. It is well known to you, who are familiar with the councils of the state, that not many months past Persia sought through me an alliance with Palmyra. But in me you have hitherto found an uncomplying daughter, and you a self-willed princess. I now seek what before I have shunned. Although I know not the prince Hormisdas, report speaks worthily of him; but of him I think not: yet if, by the offer of myself I could now help the cause of my country, the victim is ready for the altar. Let Zenobia bear with her not only the stones torn from her crown, but this which she so often has termed her living jewel; and if the others, first proffered, fail to reach the Persian's heart, then, but not till then, add the other to the scale. If it weigh to buy deliverance and prosperity to Palmyra, though I can never be happy, yet I shall be happy if the cause of happiness to you."

"My noble child!" said Zenobia, "I cannot have so startled the chiefs of Palmyra by a new and unthought-of project, as I am now amazed in my turn. I dreamed not of this. But I cannot hinder you in your purpose. It ensures success to your country; and to be the instrument of that, will be a rich compensation for even the largest sacrifice of private affections."

The councillors and senators who were present expressed a great, and, I doubt not, sincere unwillingness that so dangerous a service should be undertaken by those whom they so loved, and whom, beyond all others, they would shield with their lives from the very shadow of harm. But they were overcome by the determined spirit both of the queen and Julia, and by their own secret conviction that it was the only act in the power of mortals by which the existence of the empire and city could be preserved.

At this point of the interview, Calpurnius, whom we had missed, entered, and learning what had passed, announced, that by a channel not to be mistrusted, he had received intelligence of a sudden rising in Persia—of the assassination of Sapor, and the elevation of Hormisdas to the throne of his father. This imparted to all the liveliest pleasure, and seemed to take away from the project of the queen every remaining source of disquietude and doubt. Calpurnius, at the same moment, was besought and offered himself to serve as the queen's companion and guide; the chosen friend of Hormisdas, and whose friendship he had not forfeited by his flight, no one could so well as he advocate her cause with the new king.

"But how is it," inquired Longinus, "that you obtain foreign intelligence, the city thus beset?"

"It may well be asked," replied Calpurnius. "It is through the intelligence and cunning of a Jew well known in Palmyra, and throughout the world I believe, called Isaac. By him was I rescued from Persian captivity, and through him have I received letters thence ever since the city has been besieged. He is acquainted with a subterranean passage—in the time of Trajan, he has informed me, a public conduit, but long since much choked and dry—by which one may pass from the city under and beyond the lines of the Roman intrenchments, emerging into a deep ravine or fissure, grown

thickly over with vines and olives. Once it was of size
sufficient to admit an elephant with his rider, now, he
says, has it become so obstructed, and in some places
fallen in, that it is with difficulty that a dromedary of
but the common size can force his way through."

"Through this, then, the queen may effect her escape,"
said Longinus.

"With perfect ease and security," rejoined Calpurnius. "At the outlet, Isaac shall be in waiting with the
fleetest dromedaries of the royal stables."

"We are satisfied," said Longinus; "let it be as you
say. The gods prosper the pious service."

So ended the conversation.

Of the ancient aqueduct or conduit, you have already
heard from me; it is the same by which Isaac has
transmitted my late letters to Portia—which I trust
you have received and read. To Portia alone—be not
offended—do I pour out my whole soul. From her
learn more of what relates to the princess.

I returned from the palace of Zenobia overwhelmed
with a thousand painful sensations. But this I need
not say.

Fausta, upon learning of the determination of the
queen, which had been communicated not even to her,
exclaimed, "There, Lucius, I have always told you
Palmyra brought forth WOMEN! Where in the wide
world shall two be found to match Zenobia and Julia?
But when is the time fixed for the flight?"

"To-morrow night."

"I will to the palace. These may be the last hours
permitted by the gods to our friendship. I must not
lose one of them."

I went not there again.

Late on the evening of the following day, Fausta returned, her countenance betraying what she had suffered
in parting from those two, her bosom friends. It was
long ere she could possess herself so far as to give to
Gracchus and myself a narrative of what had occurred.
To do it, asked but few words.

"We have passed the time," she said at length, "as you might suppose those would about to be separated—for ever; yes, I feel that I have seen them for the last time. It is like a conviction inspired by the gods. We did nought till the hour of attiring for the flight arrived, but sit, look upon each other, embrace, and weep. Not that Zenobia, always great, lost the true command of herself, or omitted aught that should be done, but that she was a woman, and a mother, and a friend, as well as a queen and a divinity. But I can say no more."

"Yet one thing," she suddenly resumed, "alas! I had well nigh forgotten it—it should have been said first—what think you? The Indian slave, Sindarina, was to accompany the queen, but at the hour of departing she was missing. Her chamber was empty—the Arabian disguise, in which all were to be arrayed, lying on her bed—she herself to be found neither there nor any where within the palace. Another of the queen's women was chosen in her place. What make you of it?"

"Treason!—treachery!" cried Gracchus, and springing from his seat, shouted for a horse.

"The gods forgive me," cried the afflicted Gracchus, that this has been forgotten. Why, why did I not lay to heart the hints which you dropped?"

"In very truth," I replied, "they were almost too slight to build even a suspicion upon. The queen heeded them not, and I myself had dismissed them from my mind not less than yourself."

"Not a moment is to be lost," said Gracchus; "the slave must be found, and all whom we suspect seized."

The night was spent in a laborious search, both of the slave and Antiochus. The whole city was abroad in a common cause. All the loose companions of Antiochus and the young princes were taken and imprisoned—the suspected leaders in the affair, after a scrutinising search, and public proclamation, could not be found. The inference was clear, agonising as clear, that the queen's flight had been betrayed.

Another day has revealed the whole. Isaac, who acted as a guide through the conduit, and was to serve in the same capacity till the party were secure within a Persian fortress, not far from the banks of the Euphrates, has, by a messenger—a servant of the palace—found means to convey a relation of what befell after leaving Palmyra.

"Soon," he says, "as the shades of evening fell, the queen, the princess Julia, Nichomachus, a slave, and Calpurnius, arrayed in the garb of Arabs of the desert, together with a guard of ten soldiers, selected for their bravery and strength, met by different routes at the mouth of the old conduit. So noble a company had I never before the charge of. Thou wouldst never have guessed the queen through the veil of her outlandish garment. She became it well. Not one was more a man than she. For the princess, a dull eye would have seen through her. Entering a little way in utter darkness, I then bade them stand while I lighted torches. The queen was near me the while, and asked me the length of the passage, and whether the walls were of that thickness as to prevent the voice from being heard above.

'Till we reach one particular spot, where the arch is partly fallen in,' I said, 'we may use our tongues as freely and as loud as we please—at that place there will be need of special caution, as it is directly beneath the Roman intrenchments. Of our approach thereto I will give timely warning.'

I took occasion to say, that I was sorry the queen of Palmyra should be compelled to pass through so gloomy a cavern, but doubtless he who was with Deborah and Judith, would not forsake her who was so fast a friend to his people, and who, if rumour might be believed, was even herself one of them. This, Roman, you will doubtless think bold, but how could one who was full refrain? I even added, 'Fear not: he who watches over Judah and Israel, will not fail to appear for one by whose arm their glories are to be restored.'

The queen at that smiled, and if a countenance may be read, which I hold it can, as well as a book, it spoke favourable things for Jerusalem.

When our torches were kindled, we went on our way —a narrow way and dark. We went in silence too, for I quickly discerned that minds and hearts were too busy with themselves and their own sorrows and fears to choose to be disturbed. Ah, Roman, how many times harder the lot of the high than the low! When we drew nigh to the fissure in the arch, the torches were again extinguished, and we proceeded at a snail's pace and with a hyena's foot, while we were passing within a few feet of the then, as I doubted not, sleeping Romans. As we came beneath the broken and open part, I was startled by the sound of voices. Soldiers were above conversing. As we paused through apprehension, a few words were distinctly heard.

'The times will not bear it,' muttered one. ''Tis a vain attempt.'

'His severity is cruelty,' said another. 'Gods! when before was it heard of, that a soldier, and such a one, for what every one does whom chance favours, should be torn limb from limb? The trees that wrenched Stilcho asunder, ere they grow too stiff, may serve a turn on "Hand to his sword himself." He will fatten on these starved citizens when he climbs over their walls.'

'Oh no, by Jupiter!' said the first; 'it is far likelier he will let them off, as he did at Tyana, and we lose our sport. It is his own soldiers' blood he loves.'

'He may yet learn,' replied the other, 'that soldiers wear weapons for one purpose as well as another. Hark! what noise was that?'

'It is but some rat at work within this old arch. Come, let us to bed.'

They moved away, and we, breathing again, passed along, and soon relighted our torches.

After walking a weary distance from this point, and encountering many obstacles, we at length reached the long-desired termination. The dromedaries were in readiness; and mounting them without delay, we ascended the steep sides of the ravine, and then at a rapid pace sought the open plains. When they were attained, I considered that we were out of all danger from the Romans, and had only to apprehend the ordinary dangers of this route during a time of war, when freebooters of all the neighbouring tribes are apt to abound. 'Here,' I said to the queen, 'we will put our animals to their utmost speed, as the way is plain and smooth, having regard only, I added, to yours and the princess's strength.' 'On, on, in the name of the gods,' said they both; 'we can follow as fast as you shall lead.' And on we flew with the speed of the wind. The queen's animals were like spirits of the air, with such amazing fleetness and sureness of foot did they shoot over the surface of the earth. The way was wholly our own. We met none—we saw none. Thrice we paused to relieve those not accustomed to such speed, or to the peculiar motion of this animal. But at each resting-place, the queen, with impatience, hastened us away, saying, that 'rest could be better had at once when we had crossed the river—and once upon the other bank, and we were safe.'

The first flush of morning was upon the sky as we came within sight of the valley of the Euphrates. The river was itself seen faintly gleaming as we wound down the side of a gentle hill. The country here was broken, as it had been for many of the last miles we had ridden, divided by low ridges, deep ravines, and stretches of wood and bush; so that to those approaching the banks in the same general direction, many distinct paths offered themselves. It was here, oh Piso, just as we reached the foot of this little hill, riding more slowly by reason of the winding road, that my quick ear caught at a distance the sounds of other hoofs upon the ground besides our own. My heart sank within me—a sudden faintness spread over my limbs. But at the instant I gave the alarm to our troop, and at greatest risk of life and limb, we put our beasts to their extreme speed, and dashed towards the river. I still, as we rode, turning my ear in the direction of the sound, heard with distinctness the clatter of horses' hoofs. Our beasts were dromedaries—in that lay my hope. Two boats awaited us among the rushes on the river's bank, in the keeping of those who had been sent forward for that purpose, and off against them, upon the other side of the stream, lay a small Persian village and fortress. Once off in the boats but ever so short a distance, and we were safe. On we flew, and on, I was each moment conscious, came pursuers, whoever they might be. We reached the river's edge. 'Quick, for your lives!' I cried. 'The queen, the princess, and four men, in this boat. The packages in the other.' In a moment, and less than that, we were in our boat, a troop of horse at the same instant sweeping like a blast of the desert, down the bank of the river. We shot into the stream, but ere the other could gain the water, the Romans, as we now too plainly saw them to be, were upon them. A brief but desperate strife ensued. The Romans were five for one of the others, and quickly putting them to the sword, sprang into their boat.

'Pull! pull!' cried the queen, the first words she had uttered, 'for your lives and Palmyra.' They gained upon us. We had six oars; they eight. But the strength of three seemed to nerve the arm of Calpurnius.

'Immortal gods!' cried he, in inexpressible agony, 'they near us;' and straining with redoubled energy, his oar snapped, and the boat whirled from her course.

'All is lost!' ejaculated Zenobia.

A Roman voice was now heard, 'Yield you, and your lives are safe.'

'Never!' cried Calpurnius; and as the Roman boat struck against ours, he raised his broken oar, and aiming at him who had spoken, lost his balance and plunged headlong into the stream.

'Save him—save him!' cried the queen, but they

heeded her not. 'It is vain to contend,' she cried out again; 'we yield, but save the life of him who has fallen.'

The light was yet not sufficient to see but to a little distance. Nothing was visible upon the smooth surface of the water, nor any sound heard.

'His own rash fury has destroyed him,' said the Roman, who, we now could discern, bore the rank of centurion.

'We seek,' said he, turning towards where the queen sat, 'we seek Zenobia, queen of Palmyra.'

'I am Zenobia,' said the queen.

'The gods be praised therefor,' rejoined the centurion; 'our commands are to bear you to the tent of Aurelian.'

'Do with me as you list,' replied the queen; 'I am in your power.'

'To the shore,' exclaimed the Roman, and our boat, fastened to the other, was soon at the place whence but a moment before it had parted.

'Who are these?' asked the centurion, as we reached the shore, pointing to the princess, and the slave and secretary their attendants. 'Our orders extend only to the person of the queen.'

'Divide them not,' I said, willing to spare the queen the bandying of words with a Roman soldier; 'they are of the queen's family. They are a part of herself. If thou takest one, take all to thy emperor.'

'So be it; and now to your horses, and once more over the plain. It shall go hard, but that what we carry with us will make our fortune with Aurelian.'

Saying this, the whole troop formed, placing Zenobia and Julia in the midst, and, winding up the banks of the river, disappeared.

Such, oh unhappy Piso! was this disastrous night. Surely all was done on our part to secure a successful issue. I can discern no defect or fault. We could not have been more fleet. Swifter beasts never trod the sands of Arabia. What then? Hath there not been, think you, foul play? Whence got the Romans knowledge, not only of our flight, but of the very spot to which we aimed? I doubt not there has been treachery —and that of the very colour of hell. Look to it, and let not the guilty go free.

One word touching thy brother. Despond not. I cannot think he is lost. We were but a furlong from the shore. My belief is, that seeing the capture of the queen was certain, and that to him, if taken with her in arms against his country, death was inevitable, he, when he fell, rose again at a safe distance, and will yet be found.

These things I send in haste by a returning servant of the palace, I remaining both to secure the dromedaries, now wandering at will along the banks of the river, and to search diligently for Calpurnius, whom I trust to bear back with me to Palmyra."

Here, my Curtius, was food for meditation and grief —the renowned queen of this brilliant capital and kingdom, so late filling a throne that drew the admiration of the world, sitting there in a proud magnificence that cast into shade Persia itself, is in one short night shorn of all her power, a captive at the mercy of a cruel foe —Julia also a captive—my brother, so late redeemed, as I cannot but suppose, dead. I need not, nor can I tell you, with what emotions I read the fatal letter. The same messenger who delivered it to me had spread through the city the news of the queen's captivity. What related to Calpurnius I determined to conceal from Fausta, since it was at least possible by communicating it, I might cause a useless suffering.

Fausta, upon learning the horrors of the night, which she first did from the outcries and lamentations in the streets, seemed more like one dead than alive. She could not weep—the evil was too great for tears. And there being no other way in which to give vent to the grief that wrung her soul in every feeling and affection, I trembled lest reason should be hurled from its seat. She wandered from room to room, her face of the hue of death, but indicating life enough in its intense expression of inward pain—and speechless, save that at intervals, in a low tone, "Zenobia! Palmyra!" fell from her scarcely moving lips. To Gracchus and myself, essaying to divert her from thoughts that seemed to prey upon her very life, she said, "Leave me to wrestle alone with my grief—it is the way to strength. I do not doubt that I shall find it."

"She is right," said Gracchus; "to overcome, she must fight her own battle. Our aid but ministers to her weakness."

It was not long before she rejoined us, tears having brought relief to her overburdened heart.

Her first inquiry now was for Calpurnius. "I have feared to ask, for if he too is captive, I know that he is lost. Now I can hear and bear all. How is it, Lucius?"

I answered, "that he was not a captive, so much was known; but where he now was, or what had befallen him, was not known. I had reason to believe that he would find his way back, through the guidance of Isaac, to the city."

"Alas! I read in your words his fate. But I will not urge you further. I will live upon all the hope that I can keep alive. Yet it is not the death of Calpurnius—nor yet of Zenobia—or Julia, that wrings the soul and saps its life, like this bitter, bitter disappointment—this base treason of Antiochus. To be so near the summit of our best hopes, only to be cast down into this deep abyss—that is the sting in our calamity that shoots deepest, and for which there is no cure. Is there no other way, father, in which we can explain the capture of the queen? Accident—could it not be accident that threw the troop of Aurelian in their way?"

"I fear not," said Gracchus. "When we add what rumour has heretofore reported of the aims of Antiochus, but which we have all too much contemned him to believe him capable of, to what has now occurred, I think we cannot doubt that he is the author of the evil, seducing into his plot the queen's slave, through whom he received intelligence of every plan and movement.

"Ah, cruel treachery! How can one join together the sweet innocent face of Sindarina and such deep hypocrisy? Antiochus surely must have perverted her by magic arts. Of that I am sure. But what fruit can Antiochus hope his treason shall bear for him? Can he think that Palmyra will endure his rule?"

"That," replied Gracchus, "must be his hope. The party of the discontented we well know to be large; upon them he feels that he may rely. Then his treason recommending him to Aurelian, he builds upon his power to establish him upon the throne, and sustain him there till his own strength shall have grown, so that he can stand alone. That the city will surrender upon the news of the queen's captivity, he doubtless calculates upon as certain."

"May his every hope," cried Fausta, "be blasted, and a little of the misery he has poured without stint into our hearts wring his own! and when he cries for mercy, may he find none!"

"One hope," I said here, "if I know aught of the nature of Aurelian, and upon which he must chiefly found his project, will sink under him to his shame and ruin."

"What mean you?" said Fausta eagerly.

"His belief that Aurelian will reward baseness though to an enemy. He never did it yet, and he cannot do it. Were there within the thick skull of Antiochus the brains of a foolish ostrich, he would have read in the fate of Heraclammon, the rich traitor of Tyana, his own. If I err not, he has indiscreetly enough thrust himself into a lion's den. If Aurelian is fierce, his is the grand and terrific ferocity of the lion."

"May it be so!" said Fausta. "There were no providence in the gods, did such villany escape punishment, still more, did it grow great. But if Aurelian is such as you describe him, oh then, is there not reason in the belief that he will do gently by her? Were it compatible with greatness, or generosity—and these, you say, belong to the emperor—to take revenge upon an enemy, thrown by such means into his power—and such an enemy—and that, too, a woman—Julia, too! Oh immortal gods, how bitter past drinking is this cup!"

"Yet must you—must we—not lean too confidently upon the dispositions of Aurelian. He is subject, though supreme, to the state, nay, and in some sense to the army, and what he might gladly do of his own free and generous nature, policy, and the contrary wishes, and sometimes requisitions, of his troops, or of the people, compel him to forbear. The usage of Rome towards captive princes has been, and is, cruel. Yet the emperor does much to modify it, giving it, according to his own temper, a more or less savage character. And Aurelian has displayed great independence in his acts, both of people and soldiers. There is much ground for hope, but it must not pass into confident expectation."

"You, Lucius, in former days, have known Aurelian well before fortune raised him to this high eminence. You say you were his friend. Could you not ——"

"No. I fear with scarce any hope of doing good. My residence here during all these troubles will, I doubt not, raise suspicions in the mind of Aurelian which it will not be easy to allay. But whenever I shall have it in my power to present myself before him, I shall not fail to press upon him arguments, which, if he shall act freely, cannot, I think, but weigh with him."

"Ought not the city now," said Fausta, addressing Gracchus, "to surrender, and, if it can do no better, throw itself upon the mercy of Aurelian? I see not now what can be gained by longer resistance; and would not a still protracted refusal to capitulate, and when it must be without the faintest expectation of ultimate success, tend merely and with certainty to exasperate Aurelian, and perhaps embitter him towards the queen?"

"I can scarcely doubt that it would," replied Gracchus. "The city ought to surrender. Soon as the first flood of grief has spent itself, must we hasten to accomplish it if possible. Longinus, to whom will now be entrusted the chief power, will advocate it, I am sure—so will Otho, Seleucus, Gabrayas; but the army will, I fear, be opposed to it, and will, more through a certain pride of their order, than from any principle, incline to hold out. It is time I sought Longinus."

He departed in search of the Greek. I went forth into the streets to learn the opinions and observe the behaviour of the people.

The shades of night are around me—the palace is still—the city sleeps. I resume my pen to add a few words to this epistle, already long—but they are words that convey so much, that I cannot but add them for my own pleasure, not less than yours. They are in brief these: Calpurnius is alive, and once again returned to us. The conjecture of Isaac was a description of the truth. My brother, knowing well that if apprehended his death were certain, had in the outset resolved, if attacked, rather to provoke his death, and insure it in the violence of a conflict, than be reserved for the axe of the Roman executioner. But in the short moment in which he fell headlong into the river, it flashed across his mind—"The darkness favours my escape—I can reach the shore;" so, swimming a short distance below the surface, and falling down with the stream and softly rising, concealed himself among the reeds upon the margin of the stream. Finding the field in a short time wholly in possession of Isaac, he revealed himself and joined him, returning to the city as soon as the darkness of the night permitted. Here is a little gleam of light breaking through Fausta's almost solid gloom. A smile has once more played over her features. In the evening after Calpurnius's return, she tried her harp, but the sounds it gave out only seemed to increase her sorrow, and she threw it from her. "Music," said Gracchus, "is in its nature melancholy, and how, my child, can you think to forget or stifle grief, by waking the strings of your harp, whose tones, of all other instruments, are the most melancholy? And yet, sometimes, sadness seeks sadness, and finds in it its best relief. But now, Fausta, rather let sleep be your minister and nurse."

So we parted. Farewell.

LETTER XV.

It were a vain endeavour, my Curtius, to attempt to describe the fever of indignation, and rage, and grief, that burned in the bosoms of this unhappy people, as soon as it was known that their queen was a captive in the hands of the Romans. Those imprisoned upon suspicion of having been concerned in her betrayal, would have been torn from their confinement, and sacrificed to the wrath of the citizens, in the first hours of their excitement, but for the formidable guard by which the prisons were defended. The whole population seemed in the streets and public places, giving and receiving with eagerness such intelligence as could be obtained. Their affliction is such as it would be, had each one lost a parent or a friend. The men rave, or sit, or wander about listless and sad; the women weep; children catch the infection, and lament as for the greatest misfortune that could have overtaken them. The soldiers, at first dumb with amazement at so unlooked-for and unaccountable a catastrophe, afterwards, upon learning that it fell out through the treason of Antiochus, bound themselves by oaths never to acknowledge or submit to his authority, though Aurelian himself should impose him upon them, nay, to sacrifice him to the violated honour of the empire, if ever he should fall into their power.

Yet all are not such. The numbers are not contemptible of those who, openly or secretly, favour the cause and approve the act of Antiochus. He has not committed so great a crime without some prospect of advantage from it, nor without the assurance that a large party of the citizens, though not the largest, is with him, and will adhere to his fortunes. These are they who think, and justly think, that the queen has sacrificed the country to her insane ambition and pride. They cleave to Antiochus, not from personal regard towards him, but because he seems more available for their present purposes than any other, principally through his fool-hardy ambition; and, on the other hand, they abandon the queen, not for want of a personal affection, equal perhaps to what exists in any others, but because they conceive that the power of Rome is too mighty to contend with, and that their best interests rather than any extravagant notions of national honour, ought to prompt their measures.

The city will now give itself up, it is probable, upon the first summons of Aurelian. The council and the senate have determined that to hold out longer than a few days more is impossible. The provisions of the public granaries are exhausted, and the people are already beginning to be pinched with hunger. The rich, and all who have been enabled to subsist upon their own stores, are now engaged in distributing what remains among the poorer sort, and who are now thrown upon their compassions. May it not be, that I am to be a witness of a people dying of hunger? Gracchus and Fausta are busily employed in relieving the wants of the suffering.

We have waited impatiently to hear the fate of the queen. Many reports have prevailed, founded upon what has been observed from the walls. At one time, it has been said that she had perished under the hands of the executioner—at another, that the whole Roman camp had been seen to be thrown into wild tumult, and that she had doubtless fallen a sacrifice to the ungovernable fury of the licentious soldiery. I cannot think either report probable. Aurelian, if he avenged himself by her death, would reserve her for execution on the day of his triumph. But he would never tarnish his glory by such an act. And for the soldiers—I am sure of nothing more than that they are under too rigid a discipline, and hold Aurelian in too great terror, to dare to commit a violence like that which has been imputed to them.

At length—for hours are months in such suspense—we are relieved. Letters have come from Nichomachus to both Longinus and Livia.

First, their sum is, the queen lives!

I shall give you what I gather from them.

"When we had parted," writes the secretary, "from the river's edge, we were led at a rapid pace over the same path we had just come, to the neighbourhood of the Roman camp. I learned, from what I overheard of the conversation of the centurion, with his companion at his side, that the flight of the queen had been betrayed. But beyond that, nothing.

We were taken not at once to the presence of Aurelian, but lodged in one of the abandoned palaces in the outskirts of the city—that of Seleucus, if I err not—where the queen being assigned the apartments needful for her and her effects, a guard was set around the building.

Here we had remained not long, yet long enough for the queen to exchange her disguise for her usual robes, when it was announced by the centurion that we must proceed to the tent of the emperor. The queen and the princess were placed in a close litter, and conveyed secretly there, out of fear of the soldiers, 'who,' said the centurion, ' if made aware of whom we carry, would in their rage tear to fragments and scatter to the winds both the litter and its burden.'

We were in this manner borne through the camp to the tent of Aurelian. As we entered, the emperor stood at its upper end, surrounded by the chief persons of his army. He advanced to meet the queen; and in his changing countenance and disturbed manner might it be plainly seen how even an emperor, and he the emperor of the world, felt the presence of a majesty such as Zenobia's. And never did our great mistress seem more a queen than now—not through that commanding pride, which, when upon her throne, has impressed all who have approached her with a feeling of inferiority, but through a certain dark and solemn grandeur that struck with awe, as if some superior being, those who looked upon her. There was no sign of grief upon her countenance, but many of a deep and rooted sadness, such as might never pass away. No one could behold her, and not lament the fortune that had brought her to such a pass. Whoever had thought to enjoy the triumph of exulting over the royal captive, was rebuked by that air of calm dignity and profound melancholy, which, even against the will, touched the hearts of all, and forced their homage.

'It is a happy day for Rome,' said Aurelian, approaching and saluting her, 'that sees you, lately queen of Palmyra and of the east, a captive in the tent of Aurelian.'

'And a dark one for my afflicted country,' replied the queen.

'It might have been darker,' rejoined the emperor, 'had not the good providence of the gods delivered you into my hands.'

'The gods preside not over treachery. And it must have been by treason among those in whom I have placed my most familiar trust, that I am now where and what I am. I can but darkly surmise by whose baseness the act has been committed. It had been a nobler triumph to you, Roman, and a lighter fall to me, had the field of battle decided the fate of my kingdom, and led me a prisoner to your tent.'

'Doubtless it had been so,' replied Aurelian; 'yet was it for me to cast away what chance threw into my power? A war is now happily ended, which, had your boat reached the farther bank of the Euphrates, might yet have raged—and but to the mutual harm of two great nations. Yet it was both a bold and sagacious device, and agrees well with what was done by you at Antioch, Emesa, and now in the defence of your city. A more determined, a better appointed, or more desperate foe, I never yet have contended with.'

'It were strange, indeed,' replied the queen, 'if you met not with a determined foe, when life and liberty were to be defended. Had not treason, base and accursed treason, given me up like a chained slave to your power, yonder walls must have first been beaten piecemeal down by your engines, and buried me beneath their ruins, and famine clutched all whom the sword had spared, ere we had owned you master. What is life, when liberty and independence are gone?'

'But why, let me ask,' said Aurelian, 'were you moved to assert an independency of Rome? How many peaceful and prosperous years have rolled on since Trajan and the Antonines, while you and Rome were at harmony—a part of us and yet independent—allies rather than a subject province—using our power for your defence, yet owning no allegiance! Why was this order disturbed? What madness ruled to turn you against the power of Rome?'

'The same madness,' replied Zenobia, 'that tells Aurelian he may yet possess the whole world, and sends him here into the far east to wage needless war with a woman—ambition! Yet had Aurelian always been upon the Roman throne, or one resembling him, it had perhaps been different. There then could have been nought but honour in any alliance that had bound together Rome and Palmyra. But was I, was the late renowned Odenatus, to confess allegiance to base souls such as Aureolus, Gallienus, Balista? While the thirty tyrants were fighting for the Roman crown, was I to sit still, waiting humbly to become the passive prey of whosoever might please to call me his? By the immortal gods, not so! I asserted my supremacy, and made it felt; and in times of tumult and confusion to Rome, while her eastern provinces were one scene of discord and civil broil, I came in, and reduced the jarring elements; and out of parts broken and sundered, and hostile, I constructed a fair and well proportioned whole. And when once created, and I had tasted the sweets of sovereign and despotic power—what they are, thou knowest—was I tamely to yield the whole at the word or threat even of Aurelian? It could not be. So many years as had passed and seen me queen, not of Palmyra only, but of the east—a sovereign honoured and courted at Rome, feared by Persia, my alliance sought by all the neighbouring dominions of Asia—had served but to foster in me that love of rule which descended to me from a long line of kings. Sprung from a royal line, and so long upon a throne, it was superior force alone, divine or human, that should drag me from my right. Thou hast been but four years king, Aurelian, monarch of the great Roman world, yet wouldst thou not, but with painful unwillingness, descend and mix with the common herd. For me, ceasing to reign, I would cease to live.'

'Thy speech,' said Aurelian, 'shows thee well worthy to reign. It is no treason to Rome, Carus, to lament that the fates have cast down from a throne, one who filled its seat so well. Hadst thou hearkened to the message of Petronius, thou mightest still, lady, have sat upon thy native seat. The crown of Palmyra might still have girt thy brow.'

'But not of the east,' rejoined the queen.

'Fight against ambition, Carus, thou seest how, by aiming at too much, it loses all. It is the bane of humanity. When I am dead, may ambition then die, nor rise again.'

'May it be so!' replied his general; 'it has greatly cursed the world. It were better perhaps that it died now.'

'It cannot,' replied Aurelian; 'its life is too strong. I lament too, great queen, for so I may well call thee, that upon an ancient defender of our Roman honour, upon her who revenged Rome upon the insolent Persian, this heavy fate should fall. I would willingly have met for the first time in a different way, the brave conqueror of Sapor, the avenger of the wrongs and insults of the virtuous Valerian. The debt of Rome to Zenobia is great, and shall yet, in some sort at least, be paid.

Curses upon those who moved thee to this war. They have brought this calamity upon thee, queen, not I, nor thou. What ill-designing aspirants have urged thee on? This is not a woman's war.'

'Was not that a woman's war,' replied the queen, 'that drove the Goths from upper Asia? Was not that a woman's war that hemmed Sapor in his capital, and seized his camp? and that which beat Heraclianus, and gained thereby Syria and Mesopotamia? and that which worsted Probus, and so won the crown of Egypt? Does it ask for more, to be beaten by Romans, than to conquer these? Rest assured, great prince, that the war was mine. My people were indeed with me, but it was I who roused, fired, and led them on. I had indeed great advisers. Their names are known throughout the world. Why should I name the renowned Longinus, the princely Gracchus, the invincible Zabdas, the honest Otho. Their names are honoured in Rome as well as here. They have been with me; but without lying or vanity, I may say I have been their head.'

'Be it so; nevertheless, thy services shall be remembered. But let us now to the affairs before us. The city has not surrendered—though thy captivity is known, the gates still are shut. A word from thee would open them.'

'It is a word I cannot speak,' replied the queen, her countenance expressing now, instead of sorrow, indignation; 'wouldst thou that I too should turn traitor?'

'It surely would not be that,' replied the emperor. 'It can avail naught to contend further—it can but end in a wider destruction, both of your people and my soldiers.'

'Longinus, I may suppose,' said Zenobia, 'is now supreme. Let the emperor address him, and what is right will be done.' Aurelian turned, and held a brief conversation with some of his officers.

'Within the walls,' said the emperor, again addressing the queen, 'thou hast sons. Is it not so?'

'It is not they,' said the queen quickly, her countenance growing pale, 'it is not they, or either of them, who have conspired against me?'

'No—not quite so. Yet he who betrayed thee calls himself of thy family. Thy sons surely were not in league with him. Soldiers,' cried the emperor, 'lead forth the great Antiochus, and his slave.'

At his name the queen started—the princess uttered a faint cry, and seemed as if she would have fallen.

A fold of the tent was drawn aside, and the huge form of Antiochus appeared, followed by the queen's slave, her head bent down and eyes cast upon the ground. If a look could have killed, the first glance of Zenobia, so full of a withering contempt, would have destroyed her base kinsman. He heeded it but so much as to blush, and turn away his face from her. Upon Sindarina the queen gazed with a look of deepest sorrow. The beautiful slave stood there where she entered, not lifting her head, but her bosom rising and falling with some great emotion—conscious, as it seemed, that the queen's look was fastened upon her, and fearing to meet it. But it was so only for a moment, when raising her head, and revealing a countenance swollen with grief, she rushed towards the queen, and threw herself at her feet, embracing them, and covering them with kisses. Her deep sobs took away all power of speech. The queen only said, 'My poor Sindarina.'

The stern voice of Aurelian was first heard, 'Bear her away—bear her from the tent.'

A guard seized her, and forcibly separating her from Zenobia, bore her weeping away.

'This,' said Aurelian, turning now to Zenobia, 'this is thy kinsman, as he tells me—the prince Antiochus.'

The queen replied not.

'He has done Rome a great service.' Antiochus raised his head, and strained his stooping shoulders. 'He has the merit of ending a weary and disastrous war. It is a rare fortune to fall to any one. 'Tis a work to grow great upon. Yet, prince,' turning to Antiochus, 'the work is not complete. The city yet holds out. If I am to reward thee with the sovereign power, as thou sayest, thou must open the gates. Canst thou do it?'

'Great prince,' replied the base spirit eagerly, 'it is provided for. Allow me but a few moments, and a place proper for it, and the gates, I warrant, shall quickly swing upon their hinges.'

'Ah! do you say so? That is well. What, I pray, is the process?'

'At a signal which I shall make, noble prince, and which has been agreed upon, every head of every one of the queen's party rolls in the dust—Longinus, Gracchus, and his daughter, Seleucus, Gabrayas, and a host more—their heads fall. The gates are then to be thrown open.'

'Noble Palmyrene, you have the thanks of all. Of the city, then, we are at length secure. For this, thou wouldst have the rule of it under Rome, wielding a sceptre in the name of the Roman senate, and paying tribute as a subject province. Is it not so?'

'It is. That is what I would have, and would do, most excellent Aurelian.'

'Who are thy associates in this? Are the queen's sons, Herennianus, Timolaus, Vabalathus, of thy side, and partners in this enterprise?'

'They are not knowing to the design to deliver up to thy great power, the queen, their mother; but they are my friends, and most surely do I count upon their support. As I shall return king of Palmyra, they will gladly share my power.'

'But if friends of thine, they are enemies of mine,' rejoined Aurelian, in terrific tones; 'they are seeds of future trouble; they may sprout up into kings also, to Rome's annoyance. They must be crushed. Dost thou understand me?'

'I do, great prince. Leave them to me. I will do for them. But, to say the truth, they are too weak to disturb any—friends or enemies.'

'Escape not so. They must die,' roared Aurelian.

'They shall—they shall,' ejaculated the alarmed Antiochus; 'soon as I am within the walls, their heads shall be sent to thee.'

'That now is as I would have it. One thing more thou hast asked—that the fair slave who accompanies thee, be spared to thee, to be thy queen.'

'It was her desire—hers—noble Aurelian, not mine.'

'But didst thou not engage to her as much?'

'Truly I did. But among princes such words are but politic ones. That is well understood. Kings marry for the state. I would be higher matched,' and the sensual demon cast his eyes significantly towards the princess Julia.

'Am I understood?' continued Antiochus, Aurelian making no response. 'The princess Julia I would raise to the throne.' The monster seemed to dilate to twice his common size, as his mind fed upon the opening glories.

Aurelian had turned from him, looking first at his Roman attendants, then at the queen and Julia—his countenance kindling with some swelling passion.

'Do I understand thee?' he then said. 'I understand thee to say that for the bestowment of the favours and honours thou hast named, thou wilt do the things thou hast now specifically promised. Is it not so?'

'It is, gracious king.'

'Dost thou swear it.'

'I swear it by the great god of light.'

The countenance of the emperor now grew black with, as it seemed, mingled fury and contempt. Antiochus started, and his cheek paled. A little light reached his thick brain.

'Romans,' cried Aurelian, 'pardon me for so abusing your ears. And you, our royal captives. I knew not that such baseness lived—still less that it was here. Thou foul stigma upon humanity! why opens not the earth under thee, but that it loathes and rejects thee? Is a Roman like thee, dost thou think, to reward thy unheard-of treacheries? Thou knowest no more what a Roman is, than what truth and honour are. Soldiers, seize yonder miscreant, write traitor on his back, and spurn him forth the camp. His form and his soul both offend alike. Hence, monster!'

Antiochus was like one thunderstruck. Trembling in every joint, he sought to appeal to the emperor's mercy, but the guard stopped his mouth, and dragged him from the tent. His shrieks pierced the air, as the soldiers scourged him beyond the encampment.

'It was not for me,' said Aurelian, as these ceased to be heard, 'to refuse what fate threw into my hands. Though I despised the traitorous informer, I could not shut my ear to the facts he revealed, without myself betraying the interests of Rome. But, believe me, it was information I would willingly have spared. My infamy were as his to have rewarded the traitor. Fear not, queen, I pledge the word of a Roman and an emperor for thy safety. Thou art safe both from Roman and Palmyrene.'

'What I have but now been witness of,' replied the queen, 'assures me that in the magnanimity of Aurelian I may securely rest.'

As the queen uttered these words, a sound as of a distant tumult, and the uproar of a multitude, caught the ears of all within the tent.

'What mean these tumultuous cries?' inquired Aurelian of his attending guard. 'They increase and approach.'

'It may be but the soldiers at their game with Antiochus,' replied Probus.

But it was not so. At the moment, a centurion, breathless, and with his head bare, rushed madly into the tent.

'Speak!' said the emperor; 'what is it?'

'The legions,' said the centurion, as soon as he could command his words, 'are advancing, crying out for the queen of Palmyra. They have broken from their camp and their leaders, and in one mixed body come to surround the emperor's tent.'

As he ended, the fierce cries of the enraged soldiery were distinctly heard, like the roaring of a forest torn by a tempest. Aurelian baring his sword, and calling upon his friends to do the same, sprang towards the entrance of the tent. They were met by the dense throng of the soldiers, who now pressed against the tent, and whose savage yells could now be heard.

'The head of Zenobia! Deliver the queen to our will! Throw out the head of Zenobia, and we will return to our quarters! She belongs to us!'

At the same moment the sides of the tent were thrown up, showing the whole plain filled with the heaving multitude, and being itself instantly crowded with the ringleaders and their more desperate associates. Zenobia, supporting the princess, who clung to her, and pale through a just apprehension of every horror, but otherwise firm and undaunted, cried out to Aurelian, 'Save us, oh emperor! from this foul butchery.'

'We will die else,' replied the emperor, who with the word sprang upon a soldier making towards the queen, and with a blow clove him to the earth. Then swinging around him that sword which had drunk the blood of thousands, and followed by the gigantic Sandaron, by Probus, and Carus, a space around the queen was soon cleared. 'Back, ruffians,' cried Aurelian, in a voice of thunder, 'for you are no longer Romans: back to the borders of the tent. There I will hear your complaints.' The soldiers fell back, and their ferocious cries ceased.

'Now,' cried the emperor, addressing them, 'what is your will, that thus in wild disorder you throng my tent?'

One from the crowd replied—'Our will is that the queen of Palmyra be delivered to us, as our right, instantly. Thousands and thousands of our bold companions lie buried upon these accursed plains, slain by her and her fiery engines. We demand her life. It is but justice, and faint justice too.'

'Her life! her life!' arose in one shout from the innumerable throng.

The emperor raised his hand, waving his sword dripping with the blood of the slain soldier; the noise subsided;—and his voice, clear and loud, like the tone of a trumpet, went to the farthest bounds of the multitude.

'Soldiers,' he cried, 'you ask for justice, and justice you shall have.' 'Aurelian is ever just,' cried many voices. 'But you shall not have the life of the queen of Palmyra'—he paused: a low murmur went through the crowd—' or you must first take the life of your emperor, and of those who stand with me.' The soldiers were silent. 'In asking the life of Zenobia,' he continued, 'you know not what you ask. Are any here who went with Valerian to the Persian war?' A few voices responded, 'I was there—and I—and I.' 'Are there any here whose parents, or brothers, or friends, fell into the tiger clutches of the barbarian Sapor, and died miserably in hopeless captivity?' Many voices every where throughout the crowd were heard in reply, 'Yes, yes, mine were there, and mine.' 'Did you ever hear it said,' continued Aurelian, 'that Rome lifted a finger for their rescue, or for that of the good Valerian?' They were silent, some crying, 'No, no.' 'Know, then, that when Rome forgot her brave soldiers and her emperor, Zenobia remembered and avenged them, and Rome, fallen into contempt with the Persian, was raised to her ancient renown by the arms of her ally, the brave Zenobia—and her dominions throughout the east saved from the grasp of Sapor only by her valour. While Gallienus wallowed in sensuality and forgot Rome, and even his own great father, the queen of Palmyra stood forth, and with her royal husband, the noble Odenatus, was in truth the saviour of the empire. And is it her life you would have? Were that a just return? Were that Roman magnanimity? And grant that thousands of your brave companions lie buried upon these plains: it is but the fortune of war. Were they not slain in honourable fight, in the siege of a city, for its defence unequalled in all the annals of war? Cannot Romans honour courage and military skill, though in an enemy? But you ask for justice. I have said you shall have justice. You shall. It is right that the heads and advisers of this revolt, for such the senate deems it, should be cut off. It is the ministers of princes who are the true devisers of a nation's acts. These, when in our power, shall be yours. And now, who, soldiers, stirred up this mutiny, bringing inexpiable shame upon our brave legions? Who are the leaders of the tumult?' Enough were found to name them—'Firmus, Carinus, the Centurions Plancus, Tatias, Burrhus, Valens, Crispinus.'

'Guards, seize them and hew them down. Soldiers! to your tents.' The legions fell back as tumultuously as they had come together—the faster, as the dying groans of the slaughtered ringleaders fell upon their ears.

The tent of the emperor was once more restored to order. After a brief conversation, in which Aurelian expressed his shame for the occurrence of such disorders in the presence of the queen, the guard were commanded to convey back to the palace of Seleucus, whence they had been taken, Zenobia and the princess."

Such are the principal matters contained in the communications of Nichomachus.

When the facts contained in them became known, the senate, the council, the army, and the people, agreed in the belief, that the queen's safety and their own would now be best secured by an immediate capitulation. Accordingly, heralds bearing letters from Longinus, in the name of the council, proceeded to the Roman camp. No other terms could be obtained than a verbal promise that the city, the walls, and the common people, should be spared—but the surrender, beyond that, must be unconditional.

Upon learning the terms prescribed by the conqueror, many were for further resistance. "The language of

Aurelian," they said, " is ambiguous. He will spare the city, walls, and common people. Are our senators and councillors to be sacrificed? Are they, who have borne the burden of the day, now to be selected as the only ones who are to suffer? It shall not be so."

Generous sentiments like these were heard on all sides, but they were answered and overcome, by Gracchus especially, and others. Said Gracchus to the people, " Doubtless, punishment will be inflicted by Rome upon some. Our resistance is termed by her rebellion, revolt, conspiracy; the leaders will be sought and punished. It is ever her course. But this is a light evil compared with a wide-spread massacre of this whole population, the destruction of these famous temples, the levelling of these proud walls. Aurelian has said that these shall be spared. His word, though an unwritten and informal one, may be trusted. My counsel is, that it be at once accepted. What if a few grey heads among us are taken off? That will not touch the existence or prosperity of Palmyra. You can spare them. Your children will soon grow up to take our places, and fill them, as I hope, with more wisdom."

But such words only served at first the more to strengthen the people in their resolution, that their rulers should not be the only sacrifice. None were loved throughout the city more than Gracchus and Otho—none revered like Longinus. It was a long and painful struggle between affection and the convictions of reason before it ended, and the consent of the people was obtained to deliver up the city to the mercy of Aurelian. But it was obtained.

I was sitting with Fausta and Calpurnius, speaking of the things that had happened, and of the conduct of the queen, when Gracchus entered and joined us, informing us that " ambassadors were now gone to the camp of Aurelian, clothed with authority to deliver up the city into his hands. So that now the end has drawn on, and Palmyra ceases to exist."

Fausta, although knowing that this must happen, and

might at any moment, could not hear the fatal words announcing the death of her country, as she deemed it, and quenching for ever in darkness the bright dreams upon which she had fed so long, without renewed grief. We were a long time silent.

"Something yet remains," at length Gracchus resumed, "for us to resolve upon and do. Before many hours have elapsed, a Roman army will fill the streets of the city, perhaps our houses also, and a general plunder may be commenced of all the valuables we possess. It will be useless to conceal what it will be well enough known, from the manner in which we live, must be beneath our roof. It will but expose our lives. Yet, Fausta, your jewels, valued by you as gifts, and other things precious for the same or a like reason, may easily be secreted, nor yet be missed by the licensed robbers. See to this, my child—but except this, there is now nought to do concerning such affairs, but to sit still and observe the general wreck. But there are other and weightier matters to be decided upon, and that at once."

"Concerning the care of yourselves, you mean," said Fausta.

"I do," replied Gracchus.

"I," said Fausta, "would remain here, where I am."

"It is that which I wish," replied her father; "I commit you to the care of Lucius. For Calpurnius, he must leave you, and as he would live, fly, if that yet be possible, beyond the walls, or conceal himself within them."

"Never!" said Calpurnius; "I can do neither. I have never shunned a danger, and I cannot."

"Let pride and passion now," said Gracchus, "go fast asleep. We have no occasion for them; they are out of place, dealing as we now do with stern necessities. Your life will be especially sought by Aurelian—it is a life that cannot be spared. Fausta needs you. In you she must find, or nowhere, father—husband—friend. Lucius, when these troubles are over, will return to

Rome, and I—shall be in the keeping of Aurelian. You must live—for her sake, if not for your own."

"For mine too, surely, if for hers," replied Calpurnius.

"Father," said Fausta, throwing her arms around him, "why, why must you fall into the hands of Aurelian! Why not, with Calpurnius, fly from these now hated walls?"

"My daughter!" replied Gracchus, "let not your love of me make you forgetful of what I owe my own name and our country's. Am I not bound by the words of Aurelian?—'He will spare the city and the common people,' reserving for himself their rulers and advisers. Were they all to fly or shrink into concealment, can we doubt that the fury of the fierce Roman would then discharge itself upon the helpless people, and men, women, and children, suffer in our stead? And shall I fly while the rest are true to their trust?"

"The gods forbid!" sobbed Fausta.

"Now you are yourself again. Life is of little account with me. For you I would willingly hold on upon it, though in any event my grasp would be rapidly growing weaker and weaker; age would come and weaken it. But for myself, I can truly say, I survey the prospect of death with indifference. Life is one step; death is another. I have taken the first, I am as ready to take the second. But to preserve life—agreeable as I have found it—by any sacrifice ——"

"Oh, that were dying twice!" said Fausta; "I know it!"

"Be thankful, then, that I shall die but once, and so dry your tears. Of nothing am I more clear, than that if the loss of my head will bring security to the city and the people, I can offer it to the executioner with scarce a single regret. But let us leave this. But few hours remain to do what is yet to be done."

It was so, indeed. Already the commotion in the streets indicated that the entrance of the Roman army was each moment expected.

It was determined that Calpurnius should avail himself of the old conduit, and fly beyond the walls. To this he consented, though with pain, and bidding us farewell, departed. Fausta retired to fulfil the injunctions of her father, while Gracchus employed himself in arranging a few papers, to be entrusted to my keeping.

In the course of a few hours, the gates of the city were thrown open, and the army of the conqueror made its unobstructed entrance. Soon as the walls were secured, the towers of the gates, and the arms of the queen's remaining forces, Aurelian himself approached, and by the Roman gate passed into a city that had cost him so dear to gain. He rode through its principal streets and squares, gazing with admiration at the magnificence which every where met his view. As he arrived at the far-famed Temple of the Sun, and was told to what deity it was dedicated, he bared his head, flung himself from his horse, and on foot, followed by an innumerable company of Romans, ascended its long flight of steps, and then within its walls returned solemn thanks to the great god of light, the protecting deity of his house, for the success that had crowned his arms.

When this act of worship had been performed, and votive offerings had been hung upon the columns of the temple, the emperor came forth, and after visiting and inspecting all that was beautiful and rare, made proclamation of his will concerning the city and its inhabitants. This was, that all gold and silver, precious stones, all pictures, statues, and other works of art, were to be placed in the hands of the Romans, and that all the members of the queen's senate and council, with the nobility, were to be delivered up as prisoners of war—together with certain specified portions of the army. Beyond these requisitions, the persons and property of the citizens were to be respected. No violence of any kind on the part of the soldiers would be allowed, or pardoned, if committed.

Immediately upon this, the Roman army was converted into a body of labourers and artisans, employed in the construction of wains of every form and size, for the transportation across the desert to the sea-coast, of whatever would adorn the triumph of Aurelian, or add to the riches of the great capital of the world. Vast numbers of elephants and camels were collected from the city, and from all the neighbouring territory, with which to drag the huge and heavy laden waggons through the deep sands and over the rough and rocky plains of Syria. The palaces of the nobles and the wealthy merchants have been stripped of every embellishment of art and taste. The private and public gardens, the fountains, the porticoes, have each and all been robbed of every work, in either marble or brass, which had the misfortune or the merit to have been wrought by artists of distinguished names. The palaces of the queen and of Longinus were objects of especial curiosity and desire, and, as it were, their entire contents, after being secured with utmost art from possibility of injury, have been piled upon carriages prepared for them, ready for their journey towards Rome. It was pitiful to look on and see this wide desolation of scenes, that so little while ago had offered to the eye all that the most cultivated taste could have required for its gratification. The citizens stood around in groups, silent witnesses of the departing glories of their city and nation.

But the sight saddest of all to behold, was that of the senators and councillors of Palmyra, led guarded from the city to the camp of Aurelian. All along the streets through which they passed, the people stood in dumb and motionless array, to testify, in that expressive manner, their affection and their grief. Voices were, indeed, occasionally heard invoking the blessings of the gods upon them, or imprecating curses upon the head of the scourge Aurelian. Whenever Longinus and Gracchus appeared, their names were uttered in the tones with which children would cry out to venerated parents, whom they beheld for the last time—beheld borne away from them, by a power they could not resist, to captivity or death. No fear of the legion that surrounded them, availed to repress or silence such testimonies of regard. And if confidence was reposed in the Roman soldiery, that they would not, because conquerors and the power was theirs, churlishly deny them the freedom to relieve in that manner their overburdened hearts, it was not—happy was I, as a Roman, to witness it—misplaced. They resented it not either by word, or look, or act, but moved on like so many statues in mail, turning neither to the one hand nor the other, nor apparently so much as hearing the reproaches which were by some lavished upon them and their emperor.

Livia, Faustula, and the other inmates of the palace, have joined Zenobia and Julia, by order of Aurelian, at the house of Seleucus. The Cæsars, Herrenianus and Timolaus, have fled or concealed themselves—Vabalathus has surrendered himself, and has accompanied the princesses to the Roman camp.

How desolate is the house of Gracchus, deprived of its princely head!—especially as the mind cannot help running forward and conjecturing the fate which awaits him. Fausta surrenders herself to her grief—loss of country and of parent, at one and the same moment, is loss too great for her to bear with fortitude. Her spirit, so alive to affection and every generous sentiment, is almost broken by these sorrows and disappointments. I did not witness the parting between her and Gracchus, and happy am I that I did not. Her agony was in proportion to her love and her sensibility. I have not met her since. She remains within her own apartments, seen only by her favourite slaves. A double darkness spreads around while Fausta too is withdrawn.

It appeared to me now, my Curtius, as if something might be done on my part in behalf of Gracchus. According to the usages of Rome, the chief persons among the prisoners, and who might be considered as the leaders of the rebellion, I knew would die either at once, or, at farthest, when Aurelian should re-enter Rome as the conqueror of the east. I considered that by reason of the growing severity of the emperor towards all, friends as well as foes—amounting, as many now deem, to cruelty—the danger to Gracchus was extreme, beyond any power perhaps to avert. Yet I remembered, at the same time, the generous traits in Aurelian's character—his attachment towards old friends, his gratitude for services rendered him in the early part of his life, while making his way up through the lower posts of the army. It seemed to me that he was open to solicitation; that he would not refuse to hear me—a friend, and son of Cneius Piso—with what object soever I might present myself before him; and that, consequently, there was from this quarter a ray of hope, however small, for the father of our beloved Fausta.

Accordingly, so soon as the affairs at first calling for the entire devotion of Aurelian were through, and I knew that his leisure would allow of an interruption, I sought the Roman camp, and asked an audience of the emperor. It was immediately granted.

As I entered his tent, Aurelian was seated at a table holding in his hand a parchment scroll, which he seemed intently considering. His stern countenance lowered over it like a thunder-cloud. I stood there where I had entered a few moments, before he seemed aware of the presence of any one. His eye then falling almost accidentally upon me, he suddenly rose, and with the manner of his ancient friendship, warmly greeted me.

"I am glad," said he, "to meet so true a Roman in these distant parts."

"I am still a true Roman," I replied, "notwithstanding I have been, during this siege, upon the side of the enemy."

"I doubt it not. I am not ignorant of the causes that led you to Palmyra, and have detained you there. Henceforward your Roman blood must be held of the purest, for as I learn, and since I have seen can believe, they are few who have come within the magic circle of the late queen, who have not lost their name and freedom, themselves fastening on the chains of her service."

"You have heard truly. Her court and camp are filled with those who at first perhaps sought her capital, as visitors of curiosity or traffic, but being once within the marvellous influence of her presence, have remained there her friends or servants. She is irresistible."

"And well nigh so in war too. In Rome they make themselves merry at my expense, inasmuch as I have been warring thus with a woman—not a poet in the garrets of the Via Cœli, but has entertained the city with his couplets upon the invincible Aurelian, beset here in the east by an army of women, who seem likely to subdue him by their needles or their charms. Nay, the senate looks on and laughs. By the immortal gods! they know not of what they speak. Julius Cæsar himself, Piso, never displayed a better genius than this woman. Twice have I saved my army but by stratagem. I give the honour of those days to Zenobia. It belongs to her rather than to me. Palmyra may well boast of Antioch and Emesa. Your brother did her good service there. I trust, for your sake and for mine, he will not fall into my hands."

That dark and cruel frown which marks Aurelian, grew above and around his eyes.

"I never," he continued, "forgive a traitor to his country."

"Yet," I ventured to say, ".surely the circumstances of his captivity, and long abandonment, may plead somewhat in extenuation of his fault."

"Never. His crime is beyond the reach of pardon."

Aurelian had evidently supposed that I came to seek favour for Calpurnius. But this I had not intended to do, as Calpurnius had long ago resolved never again to dwell within the walls of Rome. I then opened the subject of my visit.

"I have come," I said, "not to seek the pardon of Calpurnius Piso. Such, to my grief, is his hostility towards Rome, that he would neither seek nor accept mercy at her hands. He has forsworn his country, and never willingly will set foot within her borders. He dwells henceforward in Asia. But there is another —"

"You would speak of Gracchus. It cannot be. Longinus excepted, he is the first citizen of Palmyra. If the queen be spared, these must suffer. It is due to the army, and to justice, and to vengeance. The soldiers have clamoured for the blood of Zenobia, and it has been at no small cost that hers and her daughter's life have been redeemed. But, I have sworn it, they shall live; my blood shall flow before theirs. Zenobia has done more for Rome than many an emperor. Besides, I would that Rome should see with her own eyes who it is has held even battle with Roman legions so long, that they may judge me to have had a worthy antagonist. She must grace my triumph."

"I truly thank the gods," I said, "that it is so resolved. Fortune has placed me, while in her dominions, near the queen; and though a Roman, I have come to love and revere her, even like a Palmyrene. Would that the like clemency might be shown towards Gracchus. There is no greatness like mercy."

"I may not, noble Piso, win glory to myself at the cost of Rome. On the field of battle I and Rome win together. In pardoning her enemies fallen into my power, I may indeed crown myself with the praise of magnanimity in the eye of the world, while by the same act I wound my country. No rebellion is quelled, till the heads that moved and guided it are off—off. Who is ignorant that Longinus, that subtle Greek, has been the master-spring in this great revolt? and hand in hand with him, Gracchus? Well should I deserve the gibes and sneers of the Roman mob, if I turned my back upon the great work I have achieved, leaving behind me spirits like these to brew fresh trouble. Nor, holding to this as it may seem to you harsh decision, am I forgetful, Piso, of our former friendship—nor of the helping hand often stretched out to do me service, of Cneius Piso, your great parent. I must trust in this to your generosity or justice, to construe me aright. Fidelity to Rome must come before private friendship, or even gratitude. Am I understood?"

"I think so."

"Neither must you speak to me of Longinus, the learned Greek, the accomplished scholar, the great philosopher. He has thrown aside the scholar and the philosopher in putting on the minister. He is to me known only as the queen's chief adviser, Palmyra's strength, the enemy of Rome. As such he has been arrayed against me—as such he has fallen a prisoner into my hands—as such he must feel the sword of the Roman executioner. Gracchus, I would willingly for thy sake, Piso, spare him—the more, as I hear thou art betrothed to his far-famed daughter, she who, upon the fields of Antioch and Emesa, filled with amazement even Roman soldiers."

To say that instead of me it was Calpurnius to whom she was betrothed, would seem to have sealed the fate of Gracchus at the moment there was a gleam of hope. I only said,

"She was the life of the queen's army. She falls but little below her great mistress."

"I believe it. These women of Palmyra are the true wonder of the age. When for the first time I found myself before Zenobia and her daughter, it is no shame for me to confess that it was hard for the moment to believe myself Aurelian and conqueror. I was ready to play the subject—I scarce kept myself from an oriental prostration. Never, Piso, was such beauty seen in Rome. Rome now has an empress worthy of her, unless a Roman emperor may sue in vain. Think you not with me? You have seen the princess Julia?"

You can pity me, Curtius and Lucilia. I said only,

"I have. Her beauty is rare indeed, but by many, nay, by most, her sister, the princess Livia, is esteemed before her."

"Ha! Nay, but that cannot be. The world itself holds not another like the elder princess, much less the same household." He seemed as if he would have added more, but his eye fell upon the scroll before him, and it changed the current of his thoughts and the expression of his countenance, which again grew dark as when I first entered the tent. He muttered over, as to himself, the names of "Gracchus," "Fausta," "the very life of their cause," "the people's chief trust," and other broken sentences of the same kind. He then suddenly recommenced:

"Piso, I know not that even I have power to grant thy suit. I have saved, with some hazard, the life of the queen and her daughter; in doing it I promised to the soldiers, in their place, the best blood of Palmyra, and theirs it is by right. It will not be easy to wrest Gracchus from their hands. It will bring danger to myself, to the queen, and to the empire. It may breed a fatal revolt. But, Piso, for the noble Portia's sake, the living representative of Cneius Piso, my early friend, for thine, and chiefly for the reason that thou art affianced to the warlike daughter of the princely Palmyrene——"

"Great prince," said I, for it was now my turn to speak, "pardon me that I break in upon your speech, but I cannot by a deception, however slight and unintentional, purchase the life even of a friend."

"To what does this tend?"

"It is not I who am affianced to the daughter of Gracchus, but Calpurnius Piso, my brother, and the enemy of Rome. If my hope for Gracchus rests but where you have placed it, it must be renounced. Rumour has dealt falsely with you."

"I am sorry for it. You know me, Piso, well enough to believe me—I am sorry for it. That plea would have availed me more than any. Yet it is right that he should die. It is the custom of war. The legions clamour for his death—it has been promised—it is due to justice and revenge. Piso, he must die."

I, however, did not cease to importune. As Aurelian had spoken of Portia, I too spoke of her, and refrained not from bringing freshly before his memory the characters of both my parents, and especially the services of my father. The emperor was noways displeased, but, on the contrary, as I recurred to the early periods of his career, when he was a centurion in Germany, under tutelage to the experienced Cucius Piso, he himself took up the story, and detained me long with the history of his life and actions, while serving with and under my father, and then afterwards when in Gaul, in Africa, and in the east. Much curious narrative, the proper source of history, I heard from the great actor himself, during this long interview. It was terminated by the entrance of Sandaron, upon pressing business with the emperor, whereupon I withdrew, Gracchus not being again named, but leaving his fate in the hands of the master of the world, and yet—how often has it been so with our emperors!—the slave of his own soldiers. I returned to the city.

The following day I again saw Fausta—now pale, melancholy, and silent. I told her of my interview with Aurelian, and of its doubtful issue. She listened to me with a painful interest, as if wishing a favourable result, yet not daring to hope. When I had ended, she said, "You have done all, Lucius, that can be done, yet it avails little or nothing. Would that Aurelian had thought women worthy his regard so much as to have made me a prisoner too. I can now feel how little one may fear death, dying in a certain cause. Palmyra is now dead, and I care no more for life. And if Gracchus is to die too, how much rather would I die with him, than live without him! And this is not, as it may seem, infidelity to Calpurnius. I love him better than I ever thought to have loved any thing besides Palmyra and Gracchus. But my love for these is from my infancy, and is in reason stronger than the other. The gods make it so, not I. I love Calpurnius with all that is left. When does the army depart?"

"To-morrow, as I learn. I shall follow it to Emesa, for it is there, so it is reported, that the fate of the prisoners will be decided."

"Do so, Lucius; and by bribery, cunning, or force, find your way to the presence of Gracchus. Be not denied. Tell him—but no; you know what I would say, I cannot"—and a passionate flood of tears came to her relief.

The preparations of the army are now completed. The city has been drained of its wealth and its embellishments. Scarce any thing is left but the walls and buildings, which are uninjured, the lives and the industry of the inhabitants. Sandaron is made governor of the city and province, with, as it seems to me, a very incompetent force to support his authority. Yet the citizens are, as they have been since the day the contest was decided, perfectly peaceable—nay, I rather should say, stupid and lethargic. There appears to be, on the part of Aurelian, no apprehension of future disturbance.

I have stood upon the walls, and watched till the last of the Romans has disappeared beyond the horizon. Two days have been spent in getting into motion and beyond the precincts of the city and suburbs, the army with its innumerable waggons, its long trains of elephants, and camels, and horses. Not only Palmyra, but the whole east, seems to have taken its departure for the Mediterranean. For the carriages were hardly to be numbered which have borne away for the Roman amphitheatres wild animals of every kind, collected from every part of Asia, together with innumerable objects of curiosity and works of art.

LETTER XVI.

I WRITE to you, Curtius, as from my last you were doubtless led to expect, from Emesa, a Syrian town of some consequence, filled now to overflowing with the

Roman army. Here Aurelian reposes for a while, after the fatigues of the march across the desert, and here justice is to be inflicted upon the leaders of the late revolt, as by Rome it is termed.

The prisons are crowded with the great, and noble, and good, of Palmyra. All those with whom I have for the last few months mingled so much, whose hospitality I have shared, whose taste, accomplishments, and elegant displays of wealth, I have admired, are now here immured in dungeons, and awaiting that death which their virtues, not their vices or their crimes, have drawn upon them. For I suppose it will be agreed, that if ever mankind do that which claims the name and rank of virtue, it is when they freely offer up their lives for their country, and for a cause which, whatever may be their misjudgment in the case, they believe to be the cause of liberty. Man is then greater in his disinterestedness, in the spirit with which he renounces himself, and offers his neck to the axe of the executioner, than he can be clothed in any robe of honour, or sitting upon any throne of power. Which is greater in the present instance, Longinus, Gracchus, Otho, or Aurelian, I cannot doubt for a moment, although I fear that you, Curtius, were I to declare my opinion, would hardly agree with me. Strange that such a sacrifice as this which is about to be made, can be thought to be necessary. It is not necessary, nor can Aurelian himself in his heart deem it so. It is a peace-offering to the blood-thirsty legions, who, well do I know it, for I have been of them, love no sight so well as the dying throes of an enemy. It is, I am told, with an impatience hardly to be restrained within the bounds of discipline, that they wait for the moment when their eyes shall be feasted with the flowing blood and headless trunks of the brave defenders of Palmyra. I see that this is so, whenever I pass by a group of soldiers, or through the camp. Their conversation seems to turn upon nothing else than the vengeance due to them upon those who have thinned their ranks of one-half their numbers, and who, themselves shielded by their walls, looked on and beheld in security the slaughter which they made.

They cry out for the blood of every Palmyrene brought across the desert. My hope for Gracchus is small. Not more, however, because of this clamour of the legions, than on account of the stern and almost cruel nature of Aurelian himself. He is himself a soldier. He is one of the legions. His sympathies are with them, one of whom he so long has been, and from whom he sprang. The gratifications which he remembers himself so often to have sought, and so dearly to have prized, he is willing to bestow upon those who he knows feel as he once did. He may speak of his want of power to resist the will of the soldiers; but I almost doubt his sincerity, since nothing can equal the terror and reverence with which he is regarded throughout the army; reverence for his genius, terror for his passions, which, when excited, rage with the fury of a madman, and wreak themselves upon all upon whom the least suspicion falls, though among his most trusted friends. To this terror, as you well know, his bodily strength greatly adds.

It was my first office to seek the presence of Gracchus. I found, upon inquiry, that both he and Longinus were confined in the same prison, and in the charge of the same keeper. I did not believe that I should experience difficulty in gaining admission to them, and I found it so.

Applying to the jailor for admittance to Gracchus the Palmyrene, I was told that but few were allowed to see him, and such only whose names had been given him. Upon giving him my name, he said that it was one which was upon his list, and I might enter. "Make the most of your time," he added, "for to-morrow is the day set for the general execution."

"So soon?" I said.

"Ay," he replied, "and that is scarce soon enough to keep the soldiers quiet. Since they have lost the queen, they are suspicious lest the others, or some of them, may escape too, so that they are well guarded, I warrant you."

"Is the queen," I asked, "under your guard, and within the same prison?"

"The queen!" he rejoined, and lowering his tone, added, "she is far enough from here. If others know it not, I know that she is well on her way to Rome. She has let too much Roman blood for her safety within reach of Roman swords, I can tell you—Aurelian, notwithstanding. That butchery of the centurions did neither any good."

"You say to-morrow is the day appointed for the execution?"

"So I said. But you will scarce believe it when you see the prisoners. They seem rather as if they were for Rome upon a journey of pleasure, than so soon for the axe. But walk in. And when you would be let out, make a signal by drawing the cord which you will find within the inner ward."

I passed in, and meeting another officer of the prison, was by him shown the door that led to the cell of Gracchus, and the cord by which I was to make the necessary signal.

I unbarred the door, and entered. Gracchus, who was pacing to and fro in his apartment, upon seeing who his visitor was, greeted me in his cordial, cheerful way. His first inquiry was, "Is Fausta well?"

"I left her well—well as her grief would allow her to be."

"My room is narrow, Piso, but it offers two seats. Let us sit. This room is not our hall in Palmyra, nor the banqueting room; this window is too small, nay, it is in some sort but a crevice, and this ceiling is too low, and these webs of the spider, the prisoner's friend, are not our purple hangings; but it might all be worse. I am free of chains, and I can walk the length of my room and back again, and there is light enough from our chink to see a friend's face by. Yet far as these things are from worst, I trust not to be annoyed or comforted by them long. You have done kindly, Piso, to seek me out thus remote from Palmyra, and death will be lighter for your presence. I am glad to see you."

"I could not, as you may easily suppose, remain in Palmyra, and you here and thus. For Fausta's sake and my own, I must be here. Although I should not speak a word, nor you, there is a happiness in being near and in seeing."

"There is. Confinement for a long period of time were robbed of much of its horror, if there were near you but a single human countenance, and that a stranger's, upon which you might look—especially if you might read there pity and affection. Then, if this countenance should be that of one known and beloved, it would be almost like living in society, even though speech were prohibited. Tyrants know this—these walls are the proof of it. Aurelian is not a tyrant in this sense. He is not without magnanimity. Are you here with his knowledge?"

"By his express provision. The jailor had been furnished with my name. You are right surely, touching the character of Aurelian. Though rude and unlettered, and severe almost to cruelty, there are generous sentiments within which shed a softening light, if inconstant, upon the darker traits. I would conceal nothing from you, Gracchus, as I would do nothing without your approbation. I know your indifference to life. I know that you would not purchase a day by any unworthy concession, by any doubtful act or word. Relying with some confidence upon the generosity of Aurelian ——"

"Why, Lucius, so hesitating and indirect! You would say that you have appealed to Aurelian for my life, and that hope is not extinct in your mind of escape from this appointed death."

"That is what I would say. The emperor inclines to spare your life, but wavers. Shall I seek another interview with him? And is there any argument which you would that I should urge, or, would you rather that I should forbear? It is, Gracchus, because I feared lest I had been doing you a displeasing and undesired service, that I have now spoken."

"Piso, it is the simple truth, when I say, that I anticipate the hour and the moment of death with the same indifference and composure that I do any, the most common event. I have schooled myself to patience. Acquiescence in the will of the gods—if gods there are —or, which is the same thing, in the order of events, is the temper which, since I have reflected at all, I have cultivated, and to which I can say I have fully attained. I throw myself upon the current of life, unresisting, to be wafted whithersoever it will. I look with desire neither to this shore nor to the opposite, to one port nor another, but wherever I am borne and permitted to act, I straightway find there and in that my happiness. Not that one allotment is not in itself preferable to another, but that there being so much of life over which man has no control, and cannot, if he would, secure his felicity, I think it wiser to renounce all action and endeavour concerning it—receiving what is sent or happens with joy if it be good, without complaint if it be evil. In this manner have I secured an inward calm, which has been as a fountain of life. My days, whether they have been dark ones, or bright, as others term them, have flowed along a smooth and even current. Under misfortune, I believe I have enjoyed more from this my inward frame, than many a son of prosperity has in the very height of his glory. That which so disturbs the peace of multitudes, even of philosophers—the prospect of death—has occasioned me not one moment's disquiet. It is true, I know not what it is—do I know what life is?—but that is no reason why I should fear it. One thing I know, which is this, that it will come—as it comes to all—and that I cannot escape it. It may take me where it will, I shall be content. If it be but a change, and I live again elsewhere, I shall be glad, especially if I am then exempt from evils in my condition which assail me here; if it be extinction of being, it will but resemble those nights when I sleep without dreaming—it will not yield any delights, but it will not bring affright or torment. I desire not to entertain, and I do not entertain, either hope or fear. I am passive. My will is annihilated. The object of my life has been to secure the greatest amount of pleasure—that being the best thing of which we can conceive. This I have done by acting right. I have found happiness—or that which we agree to call so—in acting in accordance with that part of my nature which prescribes the lines of duty. Not in any set of philosophical opinions, not in expectations in futurity, not in any fancies or dreams, but in the substantial reality of virtuous action. I have sought to treat both myself and others in such a way, that afterwards I should not hear from either a single word of reproach. In this way of life I have for the most part succeeded, as any one can who will apply his powers, as he may, if he will. I have at this hour, which, it may be, is the last of my life, no complaints to make or hear against myself. So, too, in regard to others. At least, I know not that there is one living whom I have wronged, and to whom I owe the least reparation. Now, therefore, by living in the best manner for this life on earth, I have prepared myself in the best manner for death, and for another life, if there be one. If there be none, still what I have enjoyed I have enjoyed, and it has been more than any other manner of life could have afforded. So that, in any event, I am like a soldier armed at all points. To me, Piso, to die is no more than to go on to live. Both are events. To both I am alike indifferent. I know nothing about either. As for the pain of death, it is not worthy a moment's thought, even if it were considerable. But it appears to me that it is not. I have many times witnessed it, and it has ever seemed that death, so far from being represented by any word signifying pain, would be better expressed by one that should stand for insensibility. The nearer death the nearer apathy. There is pain which often precedes it, in various forms of sickness. But this is sickness, not death. Such pains we often endure and recover—worse often than apparently are endured by those who die."

"I perceive then, Gracchus, that I have given you neither pain nor pleasure by anything I have done."

"Not that exactly. It has given me pleasure that you have sought to do me a service. For myself, it will weigh but little whether you succeed or fail. Your intercession has not displeased me. It cannot affect my good name. For Fausta's sake—" at her name he paused as if for strength—"and because she wishes it, I would rather live than die. Otherwise my mind is even-poised, inclining neither way."

"But would it not afford you, Gracchus, a sensible pleasure, if, supposing you are now to die, you could anticipate with certainty a future existence? You are now, you say, in a state of indifference as to life or death. Above all, you are delivered from all apprehensions concerning death and futurity. This is, it cannot be denied, a great felicity. You are able to sit here calm and composed. But it seems to me, if you were possessed of a certain expectation of immortality, you would be very much animated and transported, as it were, with the prospect of the wonderful scenes so soon to be revealed. If, with such a belief, you could turn back your eye upon as faultless and virtuous a life as you have passed, you would cast it forward with feelings far from those of indifference."

"What you assert is very true. Doubtless it would be as you say. I can conceive that death can be approached not only with composure, but with a bursting impatience—just as the youthful traveller pants to leap from the vessel that bears him to a foreign land. This would be the case if we were as secure of another and happier life as we are certain that we live now. In future ages, perhaps through the discoveries of reason, perhaps by disclosures from superior beings, it may be so universally, and death come to be regarded even with affection, as the great deliverer and rewarder.

But at present it is very different. I have found no evidence to satisfy me in any of the systems of ancient or modern philosophers, from Pythagoras to Seneca, and our own Longinus, either of the existence of a God, or of the reality of a future life. It seems to me oftentimes, in certain frames of mind, but they are transient, as if both were true ; they feel true, but that is all. I find no evidence beyond this inward feeling at all complete and sufficient—and this feeling is nothing ; it is of the nature of a dream ; I cannot rely upon it. So that I have, as I still judge, wisely intrenched myself behind indifference. I have never indulged in idle lamentations over evils that could not be removed, nor do I now. Submission is the law of my life, the sum of my philosophy."

"The Christians," I here said, "seem to possess that which all so much desire, a hope, amounting to a certain expectation, of immortality. They all, so I am informed, the poor and the humble, as well as the rich and the learned, live while they live, as feeling themselves to be only passengers here ; and when they die, die as those who pass from one stage of a journey to another. To them death loses its character of death, and is associated rather in their minds with life. It is a beginning rather than an ending ; a commencement, not a consummation ; being born, not dying."

"So I have heard, but I have never considered their doctrine. The Christian philosophy or doctrine is almost the only one of all which lay claim to such distinction, that I have not studied. I have been repelled from that, I suppose, by seeing it in so great proportion the property of the vulgar. What they so rejoiced in, it has appeared to me, could not at the same time be what would yield me either pleasure or wisdom. At least in other things the vulgar and the refined seek their knowledge and their pleasures from very different sources. I cannot conceive of the same philosophy approving itself to both classes. Do you learn, Piso, when the time for the execution of the prisoners is appointed ?"

"To-morrow, as I heard from the jailor."

"To-morrow. It is well. Yet I marvel that the jailor told not me. I am somewhat more concerned to know the hour than you, yet to you he has imparted what he has withheld from me. He is a partial knave. Have you yet seen Longinus?"

"I have not, but shall visit him in the morning."

"Do so. He will receive you with pleasure. Tell me if he continues true in his affections for the queen. His is a great trial, labouring, as at first he did, to turn her from the measures that have come to this end—now dying, because at last, out of friendship for her, rather than any thing else, he espoused her cause. Yet it is almost the same with me. And for myself, the sweetest feeling of this hour is, that I die for Zenobia—and that, perhaps, my death is in part the sacrifice that spares her. Incomparable woman! how the hearts of those who have known thee are bound to thee, so that thy very errors and faults are esteemed to be virtues!"

Our conversation here ended, and I turned from the prison, resolved to seek the presence of Aurelian. I did so. He received me with urbanity, as before, but neither confirmed my hopes nor fears. I returned again to the cell of Gracchus, with whom, in various, and to me most instructive conversation, we passed the remainder of the day.

In the morning, with a spirit heavy and sad, burdened indeed with a grief such as I never before had experienced, I turned to seek the apartment of Longinus. It was not far from that of Gracchus. The keeper of the prison readily admitted me, saying, "that free intercourse was allowed the prisoners with all whom it was their desire to see, and that there were several friends of Longinus already with him." With these words he let fall a heavy bar, and the door of the cell creaked upon its hinges.

The room into which I passed seemed a dungeon, rather than any thing else or better, for the only light it had came from a small barred window, far above the reach. Longinus was seated near a massy central column, to which he was bound by a chain; his friends were around him, with whom he appeared to have been engaged in earnest conversation. He rose as I approached him, and saluted me with that grace that is natural to him, and which is expressive, not more of his high breeding, than of an inward benevolence that goes forth and embraces all who draw near him.

"Although," said he, "I am forsaken of that which men call fortune, yet I am not forgotten by my friends. So that the best things remain. Piso, I rejoice truly to see you. These whom you behold, are pupils and friends whom you have often met at my house—if this dim light will allow you to distinguish them."

"My eyes are not yet so used to darkness as to see with much distinctness, but I recognise well-known faces."

After mutual salutations, Longinus said, "Let me now first inquire concerning the daughter of Gracchus, that bright emanation from the Deity. I trust in the gods, she is well."

"I left her," I replied, "overwhelmed by sorrow. To lose at once country, parent, and friends, is loss too great, I fear, for her. Death to Gracchus, will be death also to her."

"The temper of Fausta is too sanguine, her heart too warm. She was designed for a perpetual prosperity. The misfortunes that overtake her friends she makes more than her own. Others' sufferings—her own she could bear—falling upon her so thickly, will, if they leave her life, impart a lasting bitterness to it. It were better, perhaps, that she died with us. Gracchus you have found altogether Gracchus!"

"I have. He is in the prison as he was in his own palace. His thoughts will sometimes wander to his daughter—oftener than he would—and then in the mirror of the face you behold the inward sorrow of the heart, but it is only a momentary ruffling of the surface, and straightway it is calm again. Except this only, and he sits upon his hard seat in the same composure as if at the head of the senate."

"Gracchus," said Longinus in reply, "is naturally great. He is a giant; the ills of life, the greater and the lesser, which assail and subdue so many, can make nothing of him. He is impenetrable, immoveable. Then he has aided nature by the precepts of philosophy. What he wanted of insensibility to evil, he has added from a doctrine, to which he himself clings tenaciously, to which he refers, and will refer, as the spring of his highest felicity, but from which I—so variously are we constituted—shrink with unfeigned horror. Doubtless, you all know what it is?"

"We do."

"I grant it thus much, that it steels the mind against pain; that it is unrivalled in its power to sear and harden the soul; and that if it were man's common lot to be exposed to evil, and evil chiefly, it were a philosophy to be greatly coveted. But it is deadening, benumbing, in its influences. It oppresses the soul, and overlays it. It delivers it by rendering it insensible, not by imparting a new principle of vitality beyond the reach of earthly ill. It does the same service that a stupifying draught does to him who is about to submit to the knife of the surgeon, or the axe of the executioner. But is it not nobler to meet such pains, fortified in no other way than by a resolute purpose to bear them as well as the nature the gods have given you will allow? And suppose you shrink or give signs of suffering, that does not impeach the soul. It is rather the gods themselves who cry out through you. You did not, it was your corporeal nature; something besides your proper self. It is to be no subject of humiliation to us, or of grief, that when the prospect of acute suffering is before us—or, still more, when called to endure it—we give many tokens of a keen sensibility, so it be that at the same time we remain unshaken in our principles, and ready to bear what we must."

"And what," asked the young Cleoras, a favourite

disciple of the philosopher, "is it in your case that enables you to meet misfortune and death without shrinking? If you take not shelter behind indifference, what other shield do you find to be sufficient?"

"I know," said Longinus, "that you ask this question not because you have never heard from me, virtually at least, its answer, but because you wish to hear from me at this hour whether I adhere with firmness to the principles I have ever inculcated respecting death, and whether I myself derive from them the satisfactions I have declared them capable to impart. It is right and well that you do so. And I, on my part, take pleasure in repeating and reaffirming what I have maintained and taught. But I must be brief in what I say, more so than I have been in replying to your other inquiries, Cleoras and Bassus, for I perceive, by the manner in which the rays of the sun shoot through the bars of the window, that it is not long before the executioner will make his appearance. It affords me, then, I say, a very especial satisfaction to declare, in the presence of so many worthy friends, my continued attachment and hearty devotion to the truths I have believed and taught concerning the existence of a God, and the reality of a future and immortal life. Upon these two great points I suffer from no serious doubts, and it is from this belief that I now derive the serenity and peace which you witness. All the arguments which you have often heard from me in support of them, now seem to me to be possessed of a greater strength than ever—I will not repeat them, for they are too familiar to you, but only reaffirm them, and pronounce them, as in my judgment affording a ground for our assurance, in the department of moral demonstration, as solid and sufficient as the reasonings of Euclid afford in the science of geometry. I believe in a supreme God and sovereign ruler of the world, by whose wisdom and power all things and beings have been created, and are sustained, and in whose presence I live and enjoy, as implicitly as I believe the fifth proposition of Euclid's first book. I believe in a future life with the like strength. It is behind these truths, Cleoras, that I intrench myself at this hour; these make the shield which defends me from the assaults of fear and despair, that would otherwise, I am sure, overwhelm me."

"But how do they defend you, Longinus?" asked Cleoras; "by simply rendering you inaccessible to the shafts which are directed against you, or by any other and higher operation upon the soul?"

"Were it only," replied the philosopher, "that truth made me insensible and indifferent, I should pray rather to be left to the tutelage of nature. I both despise and abhor doctrines that can do no more than this. I desire to bless the gods that the philosophy I have received and taught has performed for me a far more essential service. This elevates and expands. It renders nature, as it were, superior to itself and its condition. It causes the soul to assert its entire supremacy over its companion the body, and its dwelling place the earth, and, in the perfect possession of itself, to inhabit a better world of its own creation. It infinitely increases all its sensibilities, and adds, to the constitution received from nature, what may be termed new senses, so vividly does it come to apprehend things, which to those who are unenlightened by this excellent truth, are as if they had no existence, their minds being invested with no faculty or power whereby to discern and esteem them. So far from carrying those who embrace it farther towards insensibility and indifference, which may truly be called a kind of death, it renders them intensely alive, and it is through the transforming energies of this new life that the soul is made not insensible to pain, but superior to it, and to all the greater ills of existence. It soars above them. The knowledge and the belief that fill it furnish it with wings by which it is borne far aloft, even at the very time that the body is in the deepest affliction. Gracchus meets death with equanimity, and that is something. It is better than to be convulsed with vulgar and excessive fear. But it is a state of the soul very inferior to what exists in those who truly receive the doctrines which I have taught. I, Cleoras, look upon death as a release, not from a life which has been wholly evil, for I have, through the favour of the gods, enjoyed much, but from the dominion of the body, and the appetites which clog the soul, and greatly hinder it in its efforts after a perfect virtue and a true felicity. It will open a way for me into those elysian realms, in whose reality all men have believed, a very few excepted, though few or none could prove it. Even as the great Roman could call that 'oh glorious day!' that should admit him to the council of the gods, and the society of the great and good who had preceded him, so can I in like manner designate the day and hour which are now present. I shall leave you whom I have known so long; I shall be separated from scenes familiar and beloved through a series of years; the arts and the sciences, which have ministered so largely to my happiness, in these forms of them, I shall lose; the very earth itself, venerable to my mind for the events which have passed upon it, and the genius it has nurtured and matured, and beautiful, too, in its array of forms and colours, I shall be conversant with no more. Death will divide me from them all. But it will bear me to worlds and scenes of a far exceeding beauty. It will introduce me to mansions inconceivably more magnificent than any thing which the soul has experience of here. Above all, it will bring me into the company of the good of all ages, with whom I shall enjoy the pleasures of an uninterrupted intercourse. It will place me where I shall be furnished with ample means for the prosecution of all those inquiries which have engaged me on earth, exposed to none or fewer of the hindrances which have here thronged the way. All knowledge and all happiness will then be attainable. Is death to be called an evil, or is it to be feared or approached with tears and regrets, when such are to be its issues?"

"By no means," said Cleoras; "it is rather to be desired. If my philosophy were as deep and secure as yours, oh Longinus, I should beg to exchange places with you. I should willingly suffer a brief pain to be rewarded so largely. But I find within me no such strong assurance."

"That," replied Longinus, "is for want of reflection. It is only by conversing with itself that the soul rises to any height of faith. Argument from abroad is of but little service in the comparison. I have often discoursed with you concerning these things, and have laid open before you the grounds upon which my convictions rest. But I have ever taught that consciousness was the true source of belief, and that of this you could possess yourselves only through habits of profound attention. What I believe, I feel. I cannot communicate the strength of my belief to another, because it is mysteriously generated within, interweaving itself with all my faculties and affections, and abundantly imparting itself to them, but at the same time inseparable from them, in such a sense that I can offer it as I can a portion of my reason or my knowledge, to any whom I might desire to benefit. It is, in truth, in its origin, the gift of God, strengthened and exalted infinitely by reflection. It is an instinct. Were it otherwise, why could I not give to you all I possess myself, and possess because I had by labour acquired it? Whereas, though I believe so confidently myself, I find no way in which to bestow the same good upon you. But each one will possess it, I am persuaded, in the proportion in which he prepares himself by a pure life and habitual meditation. It will then reveal itself with new strength every day. So will it also be of service to contemplate the characters and lives of those who have lived illustriously, both for their virtue and their philosophy. To study the character of Plato, will be more beneficial in this regard than to ponder the arguments of the Phœdo. Those arguments are trivial, fanciful, and ingenious, rather than convincing. And the great advantage to be derived from the perusal of that treatise is, as it shall be regarded as a sublime expression of the confidence with which its author entertained the hope of immortality. It is as a part of Plato's biography, of the history of his mind, that it is valuable. Through meditation, through inward purity, through the contemplation of bright examples, will the soul be best prepared for the birth of that feeling or conviction that shall set before you, with the distinctness and certainty of actual vision, the prospect of immortality."

"But there are, Longinus, after all, no waverings of the mind, no impertinent doubts, no overcasting shadows, which at all disturb your peace, or impair the vividness of your faith? Are you wholly superior to fear—the fear of suffering and death?"

"That is not, Cleoras, so much to ask whether I still consider my philosophy as sufficient, and whether it be so, as whether or not I am still a man, and, therefore, a mixed and imperfect being. But if you desire the assurance, I can answer you, and say, that I am but a man, and, therefore, notwithstanding my philosophy, subject to infirmity and to assaults from the body, which undoubtedly occasion me some distress. But these seasons are momentary. I can truly affirm, that although there have been, and still are, conflicts, the soul is ever conqueror, and that, too, by very great odds. My doubts and fears are mere flitting shadows, my hope a strong and unchanging beam of light. The body sometimes slips from beyond my control, and trembles, but the soul is at the very same time secure in herself, and undaunted. I present the same apparent contradiction that the soldier often does upon the field of battle—he trembles and turns pale as he first springs forward to encounter the foe, but his arm is strong and his soul determined at the very same moment, and no death or suffering in prospect avails to alarm or turn him back. Do not, therefore, although I should exhibit signs of fear, imagine that my soul is terrified, or that I am forsaken of those steadfast principles to which I have given in my allegiance for so long a time."

"We will not, Longinus," said they all.

Longinus here paused, and seemed for a time buried in meditation. We were all silent—or the silence was broken only by the sobs of those who could not restrain their grief.

"I have spoken to you, my friends," he at length resumed, " of the hope of immortality, of the strength it yields, and of its descent from God. But think not that this hope can exist but in the strictest alliance with virtue. The hope of immortality without virtue, is a contradiction in terms. The perpetuation of vice, or of any vicious affections or desires, can be contemplated only with horror. If the soul be without virtue, it is better that it should perish. And if deep stained with vice, it is to be feared that the very principle of life may be annihilated. As, then, you would meet the final hour, not only with calmness but with pleasant expectations, cherish virtue in your souls; reverence the divinity; do justly by all; obey your instincts, which point out the right and the wrong; keep yourselves pure; subdue the body. As virtue becomes a habit and a choice, and the soul, throughout all its affections and powers, harmonises with nature and God, will the hope of immortality increase in strength till it shall grow to a confident expectation. Remember that virtue is the golden key, and the only one that unlocks the gates of the celestial mansions."

I here asked Longinus if he was conscious of having been influenced in any of his opinions by Christianity. "I know," I said, " that in former conversations you have ever objected to that doctrine. Does your judgment remain the same?"

"I have not read the writings of the Christians, yet am I not wholly ignorant of them, since it were impossible to know with such familiarity the princess Julia, and not arrive at some just conceptions of what that religion is. But I have not received it. Yet, even as a piece of polished metal takes a thousand hues from surrounding objects, so does the mind; and mine may have been unconsciously coloured and swayed by the truths of Christianity, which I have heard so often stated and defended. Light may have fallen upon it from that quarter as well as from others. I doubt not that it has. For although I cannot myself admit that doctrine, yet am I now, and have ever been, persuaded of its excellence; and that upon such as can admit it, it must exert a power altogether beneficial. But let us now, for the little time that remains, turn to other things. Piso, know you aught concerning the queen? I have not seen her since the day of her flight, nor have I heard concerning her that which I could trust."

I then related at length all that I knew.

"Happy would it have been for her and for all, had my first counsels prevailed! Yet am I glad that fortune spares her. May she live to hear of Palmyra once more restored to opulence and glory. I was happy in her service. I am now happy, if by my death, as by my life, I can avert from her evil that otherwise might have overtaken her. For her or for the princess, there is no extremity I would not endure, as there have been no services I have not rejoiced to perform. The only favour I have asked of Aurelian was, to be permitted a last interview with my great pupils; it did not agree with my opinions of him, that I was denied so reasonable a request."

"Perhaps," said I, "it is in my power to furnish the reason, having been informed, since reaching Emesa, that the queen, with her attendants and the princesses, had been sent on secretly towards Rome, that they might be placed beyond the risk of violence on the part of the legions. He himself was doubtful of his power to protect them." "For the sake of both am I glad to hear the explanation," replied Longinus.

As he uttered these words, the sound of steps was heard, as of several approaching the door of the room.

Then the heavy bar of the door was let fall, and the key turned in the wards of the lock. We knew that the last moments of Longinus had arrived. Although knowing this so well, yet we still were not ready for it, and a horror as of some unlooked-for calamity came over us. Cleoras wept without restraint; and threw himself down before Longinus, embraced his knees, and, as the officers entered and drew near, warned them away with threatening language. It was with difficulty that Longinus calmed him. He seemed to have lost the possession of his reason.

The jailor, followed by a guard, now came up to Longinus, and informed him that the hour appointed for his execution had arrived.

Longinus replied, "that he was ready to go with him, but must first, when his chains were taken off, be permitted to address himself to the gods. For we ought to undertake no enterprise of moment, especially ought we not to venture into any unknown and untried scenes, without first asking their guidance, who alone have power to carry us safely through."

"This we readily grant," replied the jailor, who then taking his hammer, struck off the chain that was bound around the middle of his body.

Longinus, then, without moving from where he sat, bent his head, and covering his face with his hands, remained a few moments in that posture. The apartment was silent as if no one had been in it. Even Cleoras was by that sight taught to put a restraint upon the expression of his feelings.

When these few moments were ended, Longinus raised his head, and with a bright and smiling countenance, said to the jailor that he was now ready.

He then went out, in company with the guard and soldiers, we following in sad procession. The place of execution was in front of the camp, all the legions being drawn around to witness it, Aurelian himself being present among them.

Soon as we came in sight of that fatal place, and of

the executioner standing with his axe lifted upon his shoulder, Longinus suddenly stopped, his face became pale, and his frame trembled. He turned and looked upon us, who were immediately behind him, and held up his hand, but without speaking, which was as much as to say, "You perceive that what I said was very likely to happen has come to pass, and the body has obtained a momentary triumph." He paused, however, not long, making then a sign to the soldiers that he was ready to proceed. After a short walk from that spot, we reached the block and the executioner.

"Friend," said he now to the executioner, "I hope your axe is sharp, and that you are skilful in your art; and yet it is a pity if you have had so much practice as to have become very dexterous in it."

"Ten years' service in Rome," he replied, "may well make one so, or he must be born with little wit. Distrust not my arm, for it has never failed yet. One blow, and that a light one, is all I want, if it be, as it ought, a little slanting. As for this edge—feel it if thou wilt—it would do for thy beard."

Longinus had now divested himself of whatever parts of his garments would obstruct the executioner in his duty, and was about to place his head in the prescribed place, when he first turned to us and again held out his hands, which now trembled no longer.

"You see," said he, in a cheerful voice, "that the soul is again supreme. Love and cultivate the soul, my good friends, and you will then be universal conquerors, and throughout all ages. It will never betray you. Now, my new friend, open for me the gates of immortality, for you are in truth a celestial porter." So saying, he placed himself as he was directed to do, and at a single blow, as he had been promised, the head of Longinus was severed from the body.

Neither the head nor the body was delivered to the soldiers, or allowed to be treated with disrespect. This favour we had obtained of Aurelian. So, after the executioner had held up the head of the philosopher, and shown it to the soldiers, it was, together with the body, given to our care, and by us sent to Palmyra.

On this same day perished Otho, Seleucus, Gabrayas, Nicanor—all, in a word, of the queen's council, and almost all of the senate. Some were reserved for execution at another time, and among these I found, as I went sadly towards the cell of Gracchus, was the father of Fausta. The keeper of the prison admitted me with a more cheerful air than before, and with a significant shake of the head. I heeded him but little, pressing on to meet Gracchus.

"So," I exclaimed, "it is not to-day ——"

"No," rejoined Gracchus, visibly moved, "nor to-morrow, Piso. Read here." And placing a parchment in my hand, he turned away.

It contained a full and free remission of punishment, and permission to return immediately to Palmyra.

"The gods be praised—the gods be praised!" I cried as I embraced him. "Is not this better, Gracchus?"

"It is," said he, with emphasis, "a great boon—I do not deny it. For Fausta's sake I rejoice; as for myself, all is strictly true which I have said to you. But I forget all now, save Fausta and her joy, and renewed life. Would, oh would that Longinus could have returned to Palmyra with me!" and then, for the first time, Gracchus gave way to grief, and wept aloud.

In the morning we set off for Palmyra. Farewell.

LETTER XVII.

I write again from Palmyra.

We arrived here after a day's hard travel. The sensation occasioned by the unexpected return of Gracchus, seemed to cause a temporary forgetfulness of their calamities on the part of the citizens. As we entered the city at the close of the day, and they recognised their venerated friend, there were no bounds to the tumultuous expressions of their joy. The whole city was abroad. It were hard to say whether Fausta herself was more pained by excess of pleasure, than was each citizen who thronged the streets as we made our triumphal entry.

A general amnesty of the past having been proclaimed by Sandaron immediately after the departure of Aurelian with the prisoners whom he chose to select, we found Calpurnius already returned. At Fausta's side he received us as we dismounted in the palace-yard. I need not tell you how we passed our first evening. Yet it was one of very mixed enjoyment. Fausta's eye, as it dwelt upon the beloved form of her father, seemed to express unalloyed happiness. But then, again, as it was withdrawn at those moments when his voice kept not her attention fixed upon himself, she fell back upon the past and the lost, and the shadows of a deep sadness would gather over her. So, in truth, was it with us all, especially when at the urgency of the rest I related to them the interviews I had had with Longinus, and described to them his behaviour in the prison and at the execution.

"I think," said Fausta, " that Aurelian, in the death of Longinus, has injured his fame far more than by the capture of Zenobia and the reduction of Palmyra he has added to it. Posterity will not readily forgive him for putting out, in its meridian blaze, the very brightest light of the age. It surely was an unnecessary act."

"The destruction of prisoners, especially those of rank and influence, is," said I, " according to the savage usages of war; and Aurelian defends the death of Longinus by saying, that in becoming the first adviser of Zenobia, he was no longer Longinus the philosopher, but Longinus the minister and rebel."

"That will be held," she replied, " as a poor piece of sophistry. He was still Longinus. And in killing Longinus the minister, he basely slew Longinus the renowned philosopher, the accomplished scholar, the man of letters and of taste, the great man of the age— for you will not say that either in Rome or Greece there now lives his equal."

"Fausta," said Gracchus, "you are right. And had Aurelian been any more or higher than a soldier, he would not have dared to encounter the odium of the act, but in simple truth he was, I suppose, and is utterly insensible to the crime he has committed, not against an individual or Palmyra, but against the civilised world and posterity—a crime that will grow in its magnitude as time rolls on, and will for ever, and to the remotest times, blast the fame and the name of him who did it. Longinus belonged to all times and people, and by them will be avenged. Aurelian could not understand the greatness of his victim, and was ignorant that he was drawing upon himself a reproach greater than if he had sacrificed in his fury the queen herself, and half the inhabitants of Palmyra. He will find it out when he reaches Rome. He will find himself as notorious there as the murderer of Longinus, as he will be as conqueror of the east."

"There was one sentiment of Aurelian," I said, "which he expressed to me when I urged upon him the sparing of Longinus, to which you must allow some greatness to attach. I had said to him that it was greater to pardon than to punish, and that for that reason. 'Ah,' he replied, interrupting me, 'I may not gain to myself the fame of magnanimity at the expense of Rome. As the chief enemy of Rome in this rebellion, Rome requires his punishment, and Rome is the party to be satisfied, not I.'"

"I grant that there is greatness in the sentiment. If he was sincere, all we can say is, that he misjudged in supposing that Rome needed the sacrifice. She needed it not. There were enough heads like mine, of less worth, that would do for the soldiers—for they are Rome in Aurelian's vocabulary."

"Men of humanity and of letters," I replied, "will, I suppose, decide upon this question one way, politicians and soldiers another."

"That, I believe," rejoined Gracchus, "is nearly the truth."

When wearied by a prolonged conversation, we sought the repose of our pillows, each one of us happier by a large and overflowing measure, than but two days before we had ever thought to be again.

The city is to all appearance tranquil and acquiescent under its bitter chastisement. The outward aspect is calm and peaceful. The gates are thrown open, and the merchants and traders are returning to the pursuits of traffic; the gentry and nobles are engaged in refitting and re-embellishing their rifled palaces. And the common people have returned in quiet to the several channels of their industry.

I have made, however, some observations which lead me to believe that all is not so settled and secure as it seems to be, and that, however the greater proportion of the citizens are content to sit down patiently under the rule of their new masters, others are not of their mind. I can perceive that Antiochus, who, under the general pardon proclaimed by Sandaron, has returned to the city, is the central point of a good deal of interest among a certain class of citizens. He is again at the head of the same licentious and desperate crew as before; a set of men, like himself, large in their resources, lawless in their lives, and daring in the pursuit of whatever object they set before them. To one who knows the men, their habits and manners, it is not difficult to see that they are engaged in other plans than appear upon the surface. Yet are their movements so quietly ordered as to occasion no general observation or remark. Sandaron, ignorant whence danger might be expected to arise, appears not to indulge suspicions of one or another. Indeed, from the smallness of the garrison, from the whole manner both of the governor and those who are under him, soldiers and others, it is evident that no thought of a rising on the part of the populace has entered their minds.

A few days have passed, and Gracchus and Fausta, who inclined not to give much heed to my observations, both think with me; indeed, to Gracchus communication has been made of the existence of a plot to rescue the city from the hands of the Romans, in which he had been solicited to join.

Antiochus himself has sought and obtained an interview with Gracchus.

Gracchus has not hesitated to reject all overtures from that quarter. We thus learn that the most desperate measures are in agitation; weak and preposterous, too, as they are desperate, and must in the end prove ruinous. Antiochus, we doubt not, is a tool in the hands of others, but he stands out as the head and centre of the conspiracy. There is a violent and strong party, consisting chiefly of the disbanded soldiers, but of some drawn from every class of the inhabitants, whose object is, by a sudden attack, to snatch the city from the Roman garrison, and, placing Antiochus on the throne, proclaim their independence again, and prepare themselves to maintain and defend it. They make use of Antiochus because of his connection with Zenobia, and the influence he would exert through that prejudice, and because of his sway over other families among the richest and most powerful, especially the two princes, Herennianus and Timolaus, and because of his fool-hardiness. If they should fail, he, they imagine, will be the only or the chief sacrifice—and he can well be spared. If they succeed, it will be an easy matter afterwards to dispose of him, if his character or measures as their king should displease them, and exalt some other and worthier in his room.

"And what, father," said Fausta, "said you to Antiochus?"

"I told him," replied Gracchus, "what I thought, that the plan struck me not only as frantic and wild, but foolish; that I myself should engage in no plot of any kind, having in view any similar object, much less in such a one as he proposed. I told him, that if Palmyra was destined ever to assert its supremacy and independence of Rome, it could not be for many years to come, and then by watching for some favourable juncture in the affairs of Rome in other parts of the world. It might very well happen, I thought, that in the process of years, and when Palmyra had wholly recruited her strength, after her late and extreme sufferings, that there might occur some period of revolution or inward commotion in the Roman empire, such as would leave her remote provinces in a comparatively unprotected state. Then would be the time for reasserting our independence; then we might spring upon our keepers with some good prospect of overpowering them, and taking again to ourselves our own government. But now, I tried to convince him, it was utter madness—or worse, stupidity—to dream of success in such an enterprise. The Romans were already inflamed and angry, not half appeased by the bloody offering that had just been made; their strength was undiminished—for what could diminish the strength of Rome?—and a rising could no sooner take place than her legions would again be upon us, and our sufferings might be greater than ever. I entreated him to pause, and to dissuade those from action who were connected with him. I did not hesitate to set before him a lively picture of his own hazard in the affair; that he, if failure ensued, would be the first victim. I urged, moreover, that a few, as I held his number to be, had no right to endanger, by any selfish and besotted conduct, the general welfare, the lives and property of the citizens; that not till he felt he had the voice of the people with him, ought he to dare to act; and that although I should not betray his counsels to Sandaron, I should to the people, unless I received from him ample assurance that no movement should be made without a full disclosure of the project to all the principal citizens, as representatives of the whole city."

"And how took he all that?" we asked.

"He was evidently troubled at the vision I raised of his own head borne aloft upon a Roman pike, and not a little disconcerted at what I laboured to convince him were the rights of us all in the case. I obtained from him, in the end, a solemn promise that he would communicate what I had said to his companions, and that they would forbear all action till they had first obtained the concurrence of the greater part of the city. I assured him, however, that in no case, and under no conceivable circumstances, could he or any calculate upon any co-operation of mine. Upon any knowledge which I might obtain of intended action, I should withdraw from the city."

"It is a sad fate," said Fausta, "that having just escaped with our lives and the bare walls of our city and dwellings from the Romans, we are now to become the prey of a wicked faction among ourselves. But can you trust the word of Antiochus, that he will give you timely notice if they go on to prosecute the affair? Will they not now work in secret all the more, and veil themselves even from the scrutiny of citizens?"

"I hardly think they can escape the watchful eyes that will be fixed upon them," replied Gracchus, " nor do I believe that, however inclined Antiochus might be to deceive me, those who are of his party would agree to such baseness. There are honourable men, however deluded, in his company."

Several days have passed, and our fears are almost laid. Antiochus and the princes have been seen as usual frequenting the more public streets, lounging in the Portico, or at the places of amusement. And the evenings have been devoted to gaiety and pleasure; Sandaron himself, and the officers of his legion, being frequent visitors at the palace of Antiochus, and at that of the Cæsars, lately the palace of Zenobia.

During this interval we have celebrated, with all becoming rites, the marriage of Fausta and Calpurnius, hastened at the urgency of Gracchus, who feeling still very insecure of life, and doubtful of the continued tranquillity of the city, wished to bestow upon Calpurnius the rights of a husband, and to secure to Fausta the protection of one. Gracchus seems happier and lighter of heart since this has been done—so do we all.

It was an occasion of joy, but as much of tears also. An event which we had hoped to have been graced by the presence of Zenobia, Julia, and Longinus, took place almost in solitude and silence. But of this I have written fully to Portia.

That which we have apprehended has happened. The blow has been struck, and Palmyra is again, in name at least, free and independent.

Early on the morning after the marriage of Fausta, we were alarmed by the sounds of strife and commotion in the streets, by the cries of those who pursued, and of those who fled and fought. It was as yet hardly light. But it was not difficult to know the cause of the uproar, or the parties engaged. We seized our arms, and prepared ourselves for defence, against whatever party, Roman or Palmyrene, should make an assault. The preparation was, however, needless, for the contest was already decided. The whole garrison, with the brave Sandaron at their head, has been massacred, and the power of Palmyra is in the hands of Antiochus and his adherents. There has been, in truth, no fighting; it has been the murder rather of unprepared and defenceless men. The garrison was cut off in detail while upon their watch, by overwhelming numbers. Sandaron was dispatched in his quarters, and in his bed, by the very inhuman wretches at whose tables he had just been feasted, from whom he had but a few hours before parted, giving and receiving the signs of friendship. The cowardly Antiochus it was who stabbed him as he sprang from his sleep, encumbered and disabled by his night clothes. Not a Roman has escaped with his life.

Antiochus is proclaimed king, and the streets of the city have resounded with the shouts of this deluded people, crying, "Long live Antiochus!" He has been borne in tumult to the great portico of the Temple of the Sun, where, with the ceremonies prescribed for the occasion, he has been crowned king of Palmyra and of the east.

While these things were in progress—the new king

entering upon his authority, and the government forming itself—Gracchus chose and acted his part.

"There is little safety," he said, "for me now, I fear, any where, but least of all here. But were I secure of life, Palmyra is now to be a desecrated and polluted place, and I would fain depart from it. I could not remain in it, though covered with honour, to see Antiochus in the seat of Zenobia, and Critias in the chair of Longinus. I must go, as I respect myself, and as I desire life. Antiochus will bear me no good will, and no sooner will he have become easy in his seat and secure of his power, than he will begin the work for which his nature alone fits him, of cold-blooded revenge, cruelty, and lust. I trust, indeed, that his reign will end before that day shall arrive—but it may not—and it will be best for me and for you, my children, to remove from his sight. If he sees us not, he may forget us."

We all gladly assented to the plan which he then proposed. It was to withdraw, privately as possible, to one of his estates in the neighbourhood of the city, and there await the unfolding of the scenes that remained yet to be enacted. The plan was at once carried into effect. The estate to which we retreated was about four Roman miles from the walls, situated upon an eminence, and overlooking the city and the surrounding plains. Soon as the shadows of the evening of the first day of the reign of Antiochus had fallen, we departed from Palmyra, and within an hour found ourselves upon a spot as wild and secluded as if it had been within the bosom of a wilderness. The building consists of a square tower of stone, large and lofty, built originally for purposes of war and defence, but now long occupied by those who have pursued the peaceful labours of husbandry. The wildness of the region, the solitariness of the place, the dark and frowning aspect of the impregnable tower, had pleased the fancy of both Gracchus and Fausta, and it has been used by them as an occasional retreat, at those times when, wearied of the sound and sight of life, they have needed perfect repose. A few slaves are all that are required to constitute a sufficient household.

Here, Curtius, notwithstanding the troubled aspect of the times, have we passed a few days of no moderate enjoyment. Had there been no other, it would have been enough to sit and witness the happiness of Calpurnius and Fausta. But there have been and are other sources of satisfaction, as you will not doubt. We have now leisure to converse, at such length as we please, upon a thousand subjects which interest us. Seated upon the rocks at nightfall, or upon the lofty battlements of the tower, or at hot noon reclining beneath the shade of the terebinth or palm, we have tasted once again the calm delights we experienced at the queen's mountain palace. In this manner have we heard from Calpurnius accounts every way instructive and entertaining, of his life while in Persia—of the character and acts of Sapor—of the condition of that empire, and its wide-spread population. Nothing seems to have escaped his notice and investigation. At these times and places too, do I amuse and enlighten the circle around me by reading such portions of your letters and of Portia's as relate to matters generally interesting—and thus, too, do we discuss the times, and speculate upon the events with which the future labours in relation to Palmyra.

In the meantime, we learn that the city is given up to festivity and excess. Antiochus himself possessing immense riches, is devoting these, and whatever the treasury of the kingdom places within his reach, to the entertainment of the people with shows and games after the Roman fashion; and seems really to have deluded the mass of the people so far as to have convinced them that their ancient prosperity has returned, and that he is the father of their country, a second Odenatus. He has succeeded in giving to his betrayal of the queen the character and merit of a patriotic act, at least with the creatures who uphold him—and there are no praises so false and gross that they are not heaped upon him, and imposed upon the people in proclamations and edicts. The ignorant—and where is it that they are not the greater part?—stand by, wonder, and believe. They cannot penetrate the wickedness of the game that has been played before them, and by the arts of the king and his minions, have already been converted into friends and supporters.

The defence of the city is not, we understand, wholly neglected. But having before their eyes some fear of retribution, troops are again levied and organised, and the walls beginning to be put into a state of preparation. But this is all of secondary interest, and is postponed to any object of more immediate and sensual gratification.

But there are large numbers of the late queen's truest friends, who with Gracchus look on in grief, and terror even, at the order of things that has arisen, and prophesying with him a speedy end to it, either from interior and domestic revolution, or a return of the Roman armies, accompanied in either case, of course, by a wide-spread destruction—have with him also secretly withdrawn from the city, and fled either to some neighbouring territory, or retreated to the fastnesses of the rural districts. Gracchus has not ceased to warn all whom he knows and chiefly esteems, of the dangers to be apprehended, and urge upon them the duty of a timely escape.

Messengers have arrived from Antiochus to Gracchus, with whom they have held long and earnest conference, the object of which has been to induce him to return to the city, and resume his place at the head of the senate, the king well knowing that no act of his would so much strengthen his power as to be able to number Gracchus among his friends. But Gracchus has not so much as wavered in his purpose to keep aloof from Antiochus and all concern with his affairs. His contempt and abhorrence of the king would not, however, he says, prevent his serving his country, were he not persuaded that in so short a time violence of some sort from without or within would prostrate king and government in the dust.

It was only a few days after the messengers from Antiochus had paid their visit to Gracchus, that as we were seated upon a shaded rock, not far from the tower, listening to Fausta as she read to us, we were alarmed by the sudden irruption of Milo upon our seclusion, breathless, except that he could just exclaim, "The Romans! the Romans!" As soon as he could command his speech, he said that the Roman army could plainly be discerned from the higher points of the land, rapidly approaching the city, of which we might satisfy ourselves by ascending the tower.

"Gods! can it be possible," exclaimed Gracchus, "that Aurelian can himself have returned? He must have been well on his way to the Hellespont ere the conspiracy broke out."

"I can easily believe it," I replied, as we hastened towards the old tower, "from what I have known and witnessed of the promptness and miraculous celerity of his movements."

As we came forth upon the battlements of the tower, not a doubt remained that it was indeed the Romans pouring in again like a flood upon the plains of the now devoted city. Far as the eye could reach to the west, clouds of dust indicated the line of the Roman march, while the van was already within a mile of the very gates. The roads leading to the capital in every direction, seemed covered with those, who, at the last moment, ere the gates were shut, had fled, and were flying, to escape the impending desolation. All bore the appearance of a city taken by surprise and utterly unprepared—as we doubted not was the case, from what we had observed of its actual state, and from the suddenness of Aurelian's return and approach.

"Now," said Fausta, "I can believe that the last days of Palmyra have arrived. It is impossible that Antiochus can sustain the siege against what will now be the tenfold fury of Aurelian and his enraged soldiers."

A very few days will suffice for its reduction, if long before it be not again betrayed into the power of the assailants.

We have watched with intense curiosity and anxiety the scene that has been performing before our eyes. We are not so remote but what we can see with considerable distinctness whatever takes place, sometimes advancing and choosing our point of observation upon some nearer eminence.

After one day of preparation and one of assault, the city has fallen, and Aurelian again entered in triumph —this time in the spirit of revenge and retaliation. It is evident, as we look on horror-struck, that no quarter is given, but that a general massacre has been ordered, both of soldier and citizen. We can behold whole herds of the defenceless populace escaping from the gates or over the walls, only to be pursued, hunted, and slaughtered by the remorseless soldiers. And thousands upon thousands have we seen driven over the walls, or hurled from the battlements of the lofty towers, to perish, dashed upon the rocks below. Fausta cannot endure these sights of horror, but retires and hides herself in her apartments.

No sooner had the evening of this fatal day set in, than a new scene of terrific sublimity opened before us, as we beheld flames beginning to ascend from every part of the city. They grew and spread, till they presently appeared to wrap all objects alike in one vast sheet of fire. Towers, pinnacles, and domes, after glittering awhile in the fierce blaze, one after another fell and disappeared in the general ruin. The Temple of the Sun stood long untouched, shining almost with the brightness of the sun itself, its polished shafts and sides reflecting the surrounding fire with an intense brilliancy. We hoped that it might escape, and were certain that it would, unless fired from within—as from its insulated position the flames from the neighbouring buildings could not reach it. But we watched not long ere from its western extremity the fire broke forth, and warned us that that peerless monument of human genius, like all else, would soon crumble to the ground. To our amazement, however, and joy, the flames, after having made great progress, were suddenly arrested, and by some cause extinguished—and the vast pile stood towering in the centre of the desolation, of double size, as it seemed, from the fall and disappearance of so many of the surrounding structures.

"This," said Fausta, "is the act of a rash and passionate man. Aurelian, before to-morrow's sun has set, will himself repent it. What a single night has destroyed, a century could not restore. This blighted and ruined capital, as long as its crumbling remains shall attract the gaze of the traveller, will utter a blasting malediction upon the name and memory of Aurelian. Hereafter he will be known, not as conqueror of the east, and the restorer of the Roman empire, but as the executioner of Longinus and the ruthless destroyer of Palmyra."

"I fear that you prophesy with too much truth," I replied. "Rage and revenge have ruled the hour, and have committed horrors which no reason and no policy, either of the present or of any age, will justify."

"It is a result ever to be expected," said Gracchus, "so long as mankind will prefer an ignorant, unlettered soldier as their ruler. They can look for nothing different from one whose ideas have been formed by the camp alone, whose vulgar mind has never been illuminated by study and the knowledge of antiquity. Such a one feels no reverence for the arts, for learning, for philosophy, or for man as man—he knows not what these mean—power is all he can comprehend, and all he worships. As long as the army furnishes Rome with her emperors, so long may she know that her name will, by acts like these, be handed down to posterity covered with the infamy that belongs to the polished savage, the civilised barbarian. Come, Fausta, let us now in and hide ourselves from this sight—too sad and sorrowful to gaze upon."

"I can look now, father, without emotion," she replied; "a little sorrow opens all the fountains of grief —too much seals them. I have wept till I can weep no more. My sensibility is, I believe, by this succession of calamities, dulled till it is dead."

Aurelian, we learn, long before the fire had completed its work of destruction, recalled the orders he had given, and laboured to arrest the progress of the flames. In this he to a considerable extent succeeded, and it was owing to this that the great temple was saved, and others among the most costly and beautiful structures.

On the third day after the capture of the city and the massacre of the inhabitants, the army of the "conqueror and destroyer" withdrew from the scene of its glory, and again disappeared beyond the desert. I sought not the presence of Aurelian while before the city, for I cared not to meet him drenched in the blood of women and children. But as soon as he and his legions were departed, we turned towards the city, as children to visit the dead body of a parent.

No language which I can use, my Curtius, can give you any just conception of the horrors which met our view on the way to the walls and in the city itself. For more than a mile before we reached the gates, the roads, and the fields on either hand, were strewed with the bodies of those who, in their attempts to escape, had been overtaken by the enemy and slain. Many a group of bodies did we notice, evidently those of a family, the parents and the children, who, hoping to reach in company some place of security, had all, and without resistance apparently, fallen a sacrifice to the relentless fury of their pursuers. Immediately in the vicinity of the walls, and under them, the earth was concealed from the eye by the multitudes of the slain, and all objects were stained with the one hue of blood. Upon passing the gates, and entering within those walls which I had been accustomed to regard as embracing, in their wide and graceful sweep, the most beautiful city of the world, my eye met naught but black and smoking ruins, fallen houses and temples, the streets choked with piles of still blazing timbers and the half-burned bodies of the dead. As I penetrated farther into the heart of the city, and to its better built and more spacious quarters, I found the destruction to be less—that the principal streets were standing, and many of the more distinguished structures. But every where—in the streets—upon the porticoes of private and public dwellings—upon the steps and within the very walls of the temples of every faith—in all places, the most sacred as well as the most common, lay the mangled carcases of the wretched inhabitants. None, apparently, had been spared. The aged were there, with their bald or silvered heads—little children and infants—women, the young, the beautiful, the good—all were there, slaughtered in every imaginable way, and presenting to the eye spectacles of horror and of grief enough to break the heart and craze the brain. For one could not but go back to the day and the hour when they died, and suffer with these innocent thousands a part of what they suffered, when the gates of the city giving way, the infuriated soldiery poured in, and with death written in their faces and clamouring on their tongues, their quiet houses were invaded, and, resisting or unresisting, they all fell together beneath the murderous knives of the savage foe. What shrieks then rent and filled the air!—what prayers of agony went up to the gods for life to those whose ears on mercy's side were adders'!—what piercing supplications that life might be taken and honour spared! The apartments of the rich and the noble presented the most harrowing spectacles, where the inmates, delicately nurtured, and knowing of danger, evil, and wrong only by name and report, had first endured all that nature most abhors, and then there, where their souls had died, were slain by their brutal violators with every circumstance of most demoniac cruelty. Happy for those who, like Gracchus, foresaw the tempest and fled! These calamities have fallen chiefly upon the adherents of Antiochus; but among them, alas! were some of the noblest and most honoured families of the capital. Their bodies now lie blackened and bloated upon their door-stones—their own halls have become their tombs.

We sought together the house of Gracchus. We found it partly consumed, partly standing and uninjured. The offices and one of the rear wings were burned and level with the ground, but there the flames had been arrested, and the remainder, comprising all the principal apartments, stands as it stood before. The palace of Zenobia has escaped without harm; its lofty walls and insulated position were its protection. The Long Portico, with its columns, monuments, and inscriptions, remains also untouched by the flames, and unprofaned by any violence from the wanton soldiery. The fire has fed upon the poorer quarters of the city, where the buildings were composed in greater proportion of wood, and spared most of the great thoroughfares, principal avenues, and squares of the capital, which, being constructed in the most solid manner of stone, resisted effectually all progress of the flames, and though frequently set on fire for the purpose of their destruction, the fire perished from a want of material, or it consumed but the single edifice where it was kindled.

The silence of death and of ruin rests over this once and but so lately populous city. As I stood upon a high point which overlooked a large extent of it, I could discern no signs of life, except here and there a detachment of the Roman guard dragging forth the bodies of the slaughtered citizens, and bearing them to be burned or buried. This whole people is extinct. In a single day these hundred thousands have found a common grave. Not one remains to bewail or bury the dead. Where are the anxious crowds, who, when their dwellings have been burned, eagerly rush in as the flames have spent themselves, to sorrow over their smoking altars, and pry with busy search among the hot ashes, if perchance they may yet rescue some lamented treasure, or bear away, at least, the bones of a parent or a child, buried beneath the ruins? They are not here.

It is broad day, and the sun shines bright, but not a living form is seen lingering about these desolated streets and squares. Birds of prey are already hovering round, and alighting without apprehension of disturbance wherever the banquet invites them; and soon as the shadows of evening shall fall, the hyena of the desert will be here to gorge himself upon what they have left, having scented afar off upon the tainted breeze the fumes of the rich feast here spread for him. These Roman grave-diggers from the legion of Bassus are alone upon the ground to contend with them for their prize. Oh, miserable condition of humanity! Why is it that to man have been given passions which he cannot tame, and which sink him below the brute? Why is it that a few ambitious are permitted by the great ruler, in the selfish pursuit of their own aggrandisement, to scatter in ruin, desolation, and death, whole kingdoms, making misery and destruction the steps by which they mount up to their seats of pride? Oh, gentle doctrine of Christ!—doctrine of love and of peace—when shall it be that I and all mankind shall know thy truth, and the world smile with a new happiness under thy life-giving reign?

Fausta, as she has wandered with us through this wilderness of woe, has uttered scarce a word. This appalling and afflicting sight of her beloved Palmyra, her pride and hope, in whose glory her very life was wrapt up, so soon become a blackened heap of ruins—its power departed, its busy multitudes dead, and their dwellings empty or consumed—has deprived her of all but tears. She has only wept. The sensibility which she feared was dead she finds endued with life enough—with too much for either her peace or safety.

As soon as it became known in the neighbouring districts that the army of Aurelian was withdrawn, and that the troops left in the camp and upon the walls were no longer commissioned to destroy, they who had succeeded in effecting their escape, or who had early retreated from the scene of danger, began to venture back. These were accompanied by great numbers of the country people, who now poured in either to witness with their own eyes the great horror of the times, or to seek for the bodies of children or friends, who, dwelling in the city for purposes of trade or labour, or as soldiers, had fallen in the common ruin. For many days might the streets, and walls, and ruins, be seen covered with crowds of men and women, who, weeping, sought among the piles of the yet unburied and decaying dead, dear relatives, or friends, or lovers, for whom they hoped to perform the last offices of unfailing affection; a hope that was, perhaps, in scarce a single instance fulfilled. And how could any but those in whom love had swallowed up reason, once imagine that where the dead were heaped fathoms deep, mangled by every shocking mode of death, and now defaced yet more by the processes of corruption, they could identify the forms which they last saw beautiful in all the bloom of health? But love is love—it feels and cannot reason!

Cerronius Bassus, the lieutenant of Aurelian, has with a humane violence laid hold upon this curious and gazing multitude, and changed them all into buriers of the dead they came to seek and bewail. To save the country from pestilence, himself, and his soldiers, he hastens the necessary work of interment. The plains are trenched, and into them the bodies of the citizens are indiscriminately thrown. There now lie in narrow space the multitudes of Palmyra.

The mangled bodies of Antiochus, Herennianus, and Timolaus, have been found among the slain.

We go no longer to the city, but remain at our solitary tower—now, however, populous as the city itself. We converse of the past and the future, but most of my speedy departure for Rome.

It is the purpose of Gracchus to continue for a season yet in the quiet retreat where he now is. He then will return to the capital, and become one of those to lay again the foundations of another prosperity.

"Nature," he says, "has given to our city a position and resources, which, it seems to me, no power of man can deprive her of, nor prevent their always creating and sustaining upon this same spot a large population. Circumstances like the present may oppress and overwhelm for a time, but time will again revive, and rebuild, and embellish. I will not for one sit down in inactivity or useless grief, but, if Aurelian does not hinder, shall apply the remainder of my days to the restoration of Palmyra. In Calpurnius and Fausta I shall look to find my lieutenants, prompt to execute the commissions entrusted to them by their commander."

"We shall fall behind," said Calpurnius, "I warrant you, in no quality of affection or zeal in the great task."

"Fausta," continued Gracchus, "has as yet no heart but for the dead and the lost. But, Lucius, when you shall have been not long in Rome, you will hear that she lives then but among the living, and runs before me and Calpurnius in every labour that promises advantage to Palmyra."

"It may be so," replied Fausta, "but I have no faith that it will. We have witnessed the death of our country; we have attended the funeral obsequies. I have no belief in any rising again from the dead."

"Give not way, my child," said Gracchus, "to grief and despair. These are among the worst enemies of man. They are the true doubters and deniers of the gods and their providence, who want a spirit of trust and hope. Hope and confidence are the best religion, and the truest worship. I who do not believe in the existence of the gods, am therefore to be commended for my religion more than many of the staunchest defenders of pagan, Christian, or Jewish superstitions, who too often, it seems to me, feel and act as if the world were abandoned of all divine care, and its affairs and events the sport of a blind chance. What is best for man and the condition of the world, must be most agreeable to the gods—to the creator and possessor of the world—be they one or many. Can we doubt which

2 B

is best for the remaining inhabitants of Palmyra, and the provinces around which are dependent upon her trade—to leave her in her ruin, finally and utterly to perish, or apply every energy to her restoration? Is it better that the sands of the desert should within a few years heap themselves over these remaining walls and dwellings, or that we who survive should cleanse, and repair, and rebuild, in the confident hope, before we in our turn are called to disappear, to behold our beloved city again thronged with its thousands of busy and laborious inhabitants? Carthage is again populous as in the days of Hamilcar. You, Fausta, may live to see Palmyra what she was in the days of Zenobia."

"The gods grant it may be so!" exclaimed Fausta; and a bright smile at the vision her father had raised up before her, illuminated her features. She looked for a moment as if the reality had been suddenly revealed to her, and had stood forth in all its glory.

"I do not despair," continued Gracchus, "of the Romans themselves doing something towards the restoration of that which they have wantonly and foolishly destroyed."

"But they cannot give life to the dead, and therefore it is but little that they can do at best," said Fausta. "They may, indeed, rebuild the Temple of the Sun, but they cannot give us back the godlike form of Longinus, and kindle within it that intellect that shed light over the world; they may raise again the walls of the citizen's humble dwelling, but they cannot reanimate the bodies of the slaughtered multitudes, and call them out from their trenches to people again the silent streets."

"They cannot indeed," rejoined Gracchus; "they cannot do every thing—they may not do any thing. But I think they will, and that the emperor himself, when reason returns, will himself set the example. And from you, Lucius, when once more in Rome, shall I look for substantial aid in disposing favourably the mind both of Aurelian and the senate."

"I can never be more happily employed," I replied,

"than in serving either you or Palmyra. You will have a powerful advocate also in Zenobia."

"Yes," said Gracchus, "if her life be spared, which must for some time be still quite uncertain. After gracing the triumph of Aurelian, she, like Longinus, may be offered as a new largess to the still hungering legions."

"Nay, there, I think, Gracchus, you do Aurelian hardly justice. Although he has bound himself by no oath, yet virtually is he sworn to spare Zenobia—and his least word is true as his sword."

Thus have we passed the last days and hours of my residence here. I should in vain attempt, my Curtius, to tell you how strongly I am bound to this place, to this kingdom and city, and, above all, to those who survive this destruction. No Palmyrene can lament with more sincerity than I, the whirlwind of desolation that has passed over them, obliterating almost their place and name; nor from any one do there ascend more fervent prayers that prosperity may yet return, and these wide-spread ruins again rise and glow in their ancient beauty. Rome has by former acts of unparalleled barbarism covered her name with reproach; but by none has she so drenched it in guilt as by this wanton annihilation—for so do I regard it—of one of the fairest cities and kingdoms of the earth. The day of Aurelian's triumph may be a day of triumph to him, but to Rome it will be a day of never-forgotten infamy.

LETTER XVIII.

FROM PISO TO FAUSTA.

I TRUST that you have safely received the letter which, as we entered the Tiber, I was fortunate enough to place on board a vessel bound directly to Berytus. In that I have told you of my journey and voyage, and have said many other things of more consequence still, both to you, Gracchus, and myself.

I now write to you from my own dwelling upon the Cœlian, where I have been these many days that have intervened since the date of my former letter. If you have waited impatiently to hear from me again, I hope now I shall atone for what may seem a too long delay, by telling you of those concerning whom you wish chiefly to hear and know—Zenobia and Julia.

But first let me say that I have found Portia in health, and as happy as she could be after her bitter disappointment in Calpurnius. This has proved a misfortune, less only than the loss of our father himself. That a Piso should live, and be other than a Roman; that he should live and bear arms against his country—this has been to her one of those inexplicable mysteries in the providence of the gods that has tasked her piety to the utmost. In vain has she scrutinised her life to discover what fault has drawn down upon her and her house this heavy retribution. Yet her grief is lightened by what I have told her of the conduct of Calpurnius at Antioch and Emesa. At such times, when I have related the events of those great days, and the part which my brother took, the pride of the Roman has yielded to that of the mother, and she has not been able to conceal her satisfaction. "Ah," she would say, "my brave boy!" "That was like him!" "I warrant Zabdas himself was not greater!" "What might he not be, were he but in Rome!"

Portia is never weary with inquiring into every thing relating to yourself and Gracchus. My letters, many and minute as they have been, so far from satisfying her, serve only as themes for new and endless conversations, in which, as well as I am able, I set before her my whole life while in Palmyra, and every event, from the conversation at the tables, or in the porticoes, to the fall of the city and the death of Longinus. So great is her desire to know all concerning the "hero Fausta," and so unsatisfying is the all that I can say, that I shall not wonder if, after the ceremony of the triumph, she should herself propose a journey to Palmyra, to see you once more with her own eyes, and once more fold you in her arms. You will rejoice to be told that she bewails, even with tears, the ruin of the city, and the cruel massacre of its inhabitants. She condemns the emperor, in language as strong as you or I should use. The slaughter of Sandaron and his troops she will by no means allow to be a sufficient justification of the act. And of her opinion are all the chief citizens of Rome.

I have found Curtius and Lucilia also in health. They are at their villa upon the Tiber. The first to greet me there were Laco and Cælia. Their gratitude was affecting and oppressive. Indeed, there is no duty so hard as to receive with grace the thanks of those whom you have obliged. Curtius is for once satisfied that I have performed with fidelity the part of a correspondent. He even wonders at my diligence. The advantage is, I believe for the first time, fairly on my side—though you can yourself bear testimony, having heard all his epistles, how many he wrote, and with what vividness and exactness he made Rome to pass before us. I think he will not be prevented from writing to you by any thing I can say. He drops in every day, Lucilia sometimes with him, and never leaves us till he has exhausted his prepared questions concerning you, and the great events which have taken place—there remaining innumerable points, to a man of his exact turn of mind, about which he must insist upon fuller and more careful information. I think he will draw up a history of the war. I hope he will—no one could do it better.

Aurelian, you will have heard, upon leaving Palmyra, instead of continuing on the route upon which he set out towards Emesa and Antioch, turned aside to Egypt, in order to put down, by one of his sudden movements, the Egyptian merchant Firmus, who with a genius for war greater than for traffic, had placed himself at the head of the people, and proclaimed their independence of Rome. As the friend and ally of Zenobia—although he could render her during the siege no assistance—I must pity his misfortunes and his end. News has just reached us that his armies have been defeated, he himself taken and put to death, and his new-made kingdom reduced again to the condition of a Roman province. We now every hour look to hear of the arrival of the emperor and his armies.

Although there has been observed some secrecy concerning the progress and places of residence of Zenobia, yet we learn, with a good degree of certainty, that she is now at Brundusium, awaiting the further orders of Aurelian, having gone over-land from Byzantium to Apollonia, and there crossing the Adriatic. I have not been much disturbed by the reports which have prevailed, because I thought I knew too much of the queen to think them well grounded. Yet I confess I have suffered somewhat, when, upon resorting to the capitol or the baths, I have found the principal topic to be the death of Zenobia—according to some, of grief, on her way from Antioch to Byzantium—or, as others had it, of hunger, she having resolutely refused all nourishment. I have given no credit to the rumour, yet as all stories of this kind are a mixture of truth and error, so in this case I can conceive easily that it has some foundation in reality, and I am led to believe from it that the sufferings of the queen have been great. How indeed could they be otherwise? A feebler spirit than Zenobia's, and a feebler frame, would necessarily have been destroyed. With what impatience do I wait the hour that shall see her in Rome! I am happily already relieved of all anxiety as to her treatment by Aurelian —no fear need be entertained for her safety. Desirous, as far as may be, to atone for the rash severity of his orders in Syria, he will distinguish, with every possible mark of honour, the queen, her family, and such other of the inhabitants of Palmyra as have been reserved to grace his triumph.

For this august ceremony the preparations are already making. It is the sole topic of conversation, and the single object towards which seem to be bent the whole genius and industry of the capital. It is intended to surpass in magnificence all that has been done by former emperors or generals. The materials for it are collecting from every part of the empire, and the remotest regions of Asia and Africa. Every day there arrive cargoes either of wild beasts or of prisoners, destined to the amphitheatre. Illustrious captives also from Asia, Germany, and Gaul, among whom are Tetricus and his son. The Tiber is crowded with vessels bringing in the treasures drawn from Palmyra—her silver and gold—her statuary and works of art—and every object of curiosity and taste that was susceptible of transportation across the desert and the ocean.

It is now certain that the queen has advanced as far as Tusculum, where with Julia, Livia, Faustula, and Vabalathus, they will remain—at a villa of Aurelian's, it is said—till the day of the triumph. Separation seems the more painful as they approach nearer. Although knowing that they would be scrupulously prohibited from all intercourse with any beyond the precincts of the villa itself, I have not been restrained from going again and again to Tusculum, and passing through it and around it, in the hope to obtain, were it but a distant glimpse, of persons to whom I am bound more closely than to any others on earth. But it has been all in vain. I shall not see them, till I behold them a part of the triumphal procession of their conqueror.

Aurelian has arrived, the long expected day has come, and is gone. His triumph has been celebrated, and with a magnificence and a pomp greater than the traditionary glories of those of Pompey, Trajan, Titus, or even the secular games of Philip.

I have seen Zenobia!

The sun of Italy never poured a flood of more golden light upon the great capital and its surrounding plains than on the day of Aurelian's triumph. The airs of Palmyra were never more soft. The whole city was early abroad; and added to our own overgrown population, there were the inhabitants of all the neighbouring towns and cities, and strangers from all parts of the empire, so that it was with difficulty and labour only, and no little danger too, that the spectacle could be seen. I obtained a position opposite the capitol, from which I could observe the whole of this proud display of the power and greatness of Rome.

A long train of elephants opened the show, their huge sides and limbs hung with cloth of gold and scarlet, some having upon their backs military towers or other fanciful structures, which were filled with the natives of Asia or Africa, all arrayed in the richest costumes of their countries. These were followed by wild animals, and those remarkable for their beauty, from every part of the world, either led—as in the case of lions, tigers, leopards—by those who, from long management of them, possessed the same power over them as the groom over his horse; or else drawn along upon low platforms, upon which they are made to perform a thousand antic tricks, for the amusement of the gaping and wondering crowds. Then came not many fewer than two thousand gladiators, in pairs, all arranged in such a manner as to display to the greatest advantage their well-knit joints, and projecting and swollen muscles. Of these a great number have already perished on the arena of the Flavian, and in the sea fights in Domitian's theatre. Next, upon gilded waggons, and arrayed so as to produce the most dazzling effect, came the spoils of the wars of Aurelian—treasures of art, rich cloths and embroideries, utensils of gold and silver, pictures, statues, and works in brass, from the cities of Gaul, from Asia, and from Egypt. Conspicuous here, over all, were the rich and gorgeous contents of the palace of Zenobia. The huge wains groaned under the weight of vessels of gold and silver, of ivory, and the most precious woods of India. The jewelled wine-cups, vases, and golden statuary of Demetrius, attracted the gaze and excited the admiration of every beholder. Immediately after these came a crowd of youths richly habited in the costumes of a thousand different tribes, bearing in their hands, upon cushions of silk, crowns of gold and precious stones, the offerings of the cities and kingdoms of all the world, as it were, to the power and fame of Aurelian. Following these, came the ambassadors of all nations, sumptuously arrayed in the habits of their respective countries. Then an innumerable train of captives, showing plainly, in their downcast eyes, in their fixed and melancholy gaze, that hope had taken its departure from their breasts. Among these were many women from the shores of the Danube, taken in arms fighting for their country, of enormous stature, and clothed in the warlike costume of their tribes.

But why do I detain you with these things, when it is of one only that you wish to hear? I cannot tell you with what impatience I waited for that part of the procession to approach where were Zenobia and Julia. I thought its line would stretch on for ever. And it was the ninth hour before the alternate shouts and deep silence of the multitudes announced that the conqueror was drawing near the capitol. As the first shout arose, I turned towards the quarter whence it came, and beheld, not Aurelian, as I expected, but the Gallic Emperor Tetricus—yet slave of his army and of Victoria—accompanied by the prince his son, and followed by other illustrious captives from Gaul. All eyes were turned with pity upon him, and with indignation, too, that Aurelian should thus treat a Roman, and once a senator. But sympathy for him was instantly lost in a stronger feeling of the same kind for Zenobia; who came immediately after. You can imagine, Fausta, better than I can describe them, my sensations, when I saw our beloved friend—her whom I had seen treated never otherwise than as a sovereign queen, and with all the imposing pomp of the Persian ceremonial—now on foot, and exposed to the rude gaze of the Roman populace, toiling beneath the rays of a hot sun, and the weight of jewels, such as, both for richness and beauty, were never before seen in Rome; and of chains of gold, which first passing around her neck and arms, were then borne up by attendant slaves. I could have wept to see her so ; yes, and did. My impulse was to break through the crowd and support her almost fainting form, but I well knew that my life would answer for the rashness on the spot. I could only, therefore, like the rest, wonder and gaze. And never did she seem to me, not even in the midst of her own court, to blaze forth with such transcendant beauty, yet touched with grief. Her look was not that of dejection, of one who was broken and crushed by misfortune ; there was no blush of shame. It was rather one of profound heartbreaking melancholy. Her full eyes looked as if privacy only was wanted for them to overflow with floods of tears. But they fell not. Her gaze was fixed on vacancy, or else cast towards the ground. She seemed like one unobservant of all around her, and buried in thoughts to which all else were strangers, and had nothing in common with. They were in Palmyra, and with her slaughtered multitudes. Yet though she wept not, others did ; and one could see all along, wherever she moved, the Roman hardness yielding to pity, and melting down before the all-subduing presence of this wonderful woman. The most touching phrases of compassion fell constantly upon my ear. And ever and anon, as in the road there would happen some rough or damp place, the kind souls would throw down upon it whatever of their garments they could quickest divest themselves of, that those feet, little used to such encounters, might receive no harm. And, as when other parts of the procession were passing by, shouts of triumph and vulgar joy frequently arose from the motley crowds, yet when Zenobia appeared, a death-like silence prevailed, or it was interrupted only by exclamations of admiration or pity, or of indignation at Aurelian for so using her. But this happened not long. For when the emperor's pride had been sufficiently gratified, and just there where he came over against the steps of the capitol, he himself, crowned as he was with the diadem of universal empire, descended from his chariot, and unlocking the chains of gold that bound the limbs of the queen, led and placed her in her own chariot—that chariot in which she had hoped herself to enter Rome in triumph—between Julia and Livia. Upon this, the air was rent with the grateful acclamations of the countless multitudes. The queen's countenance brightened for a moment as if with the expressive sentiment, "The gods bless you!" and was then buried in the folds of her robe. And when, after the lapse of many minutes, it was again raised and turned towards the people, every one might see that tears burning hot had coursed her cheeks, and relieved a heart which else might well have burst with its restrained emotion. Soon as the chariot which held her had disappeared upon the other side of the capitol, I extricated myself from the crowd, and returned home. It was not till the shades of evening had fallen that the last of the procession had passed the front of the capitol, and the emperor reposed within the walls of his palace. The evening was devoted to the shows of the theatres.

Seven days succeeding this first day of the triumph have been devoted to games and shows. I attended them not, but, escaping from the tumult and confusion of the city, passed them in a very different manner—you will at once conjecture where and with whom. It was, indeed, as you suppose, in the society of Zenobia, Julia, and Livia.

What the immediate destination of the queen was to be, I knew not, nor did any seem to know even so late as the day of the triumph. It was only known that her treatment was to be lenient. But on the day after, it became public in the city, that the emperor had bestowed upon her his magnificent villa, not far from Hadrian's, at Tibur, and at the close of the first day of the triumph, a chariot of Aurelian's in waiting had conveyed her there. This was to me transporting news, as it will be to you.

On the evening of that day I was at Tibur. Had I been a son or a brother, the queen could not have received me with more emotion. But I leave it to you, to imagine the first moments of our interview. When our greetings were over, the first thought, at least the first question of Zenobia, was concerning you and Gracchus. All her inquiries, as well as those of Julia, I was happily able to answer in the most exact manner, out of the fulness of your letter. When I had finished this agreeable duty, the queen said,

"Our happiness were complete as now it can be, could Fausta and Gracchus be but added to our numbers. I shall hope, in the lapse of days or months, to entice them away for a season from their melancholy home. And yet what better can I offer them here? There they behold their city in ruins; here their queen. There they already detect some tokens of reviving life; here they would have before them but the picture of decay and approaching death. But these things I ought not to say—Piso, you will be glad to learn the purposes of Aurelian concerning Palmyra. He has already set apart large sums for the restoration of its walls and temples—and, what is more and better, he has made Gracchus governor of the city and province, with liberal promises of treasure to carry into effect whatever designs he may conceive as most likely to people again the silent streets, and fill them again with the merchants of the east and west."

"Aurelian, I am persuaded," I replied, "will feel upon him the weight of the strongest motives to do all that he can to repair the injuries he has inflicted. Then, too, in addition to this, his nature is generous."

"It is so," said Julia. "How happy if he had been less subject to his passions! The proofs of a generous nature you see here, Piso, every where around us. This vast and magnificent palace, with its extensive grounds, has he freely bestowed upon us; and here, as your eye has already informed you, has he caused to be brought and arranged every article of use or luxury found in the palace at Palmyra, and capable of transportation."

"I could hardly believe," I said, "as I approached the great entrance, and beheld objects so familiar—still more, when I came within the walls, and saw around me all that I had seen in Palmyra, that I was indeed in the vicinity of Rome, and had not been by some strange power transported suddenly to Asia. In the rash violence of Aurelian in Syria, and in this reparation, both here and there, of the evil he has committed to the farthest extent possible, you witness a genuine revelation of his character. Would that principle rather than passion were the governing power of his life."

Although I have passed many days at Tibur, yet have I seen but little of Zenobia. She is silent and solitary. Her thoughts are evidently never with the present, but far back among the scenes of her former life. To converse is an effort. The lines of grief have fixed themselves upon her countenance; her very form and manner are expressive of a soul bowed and subdued by misfortune. Her pride seems no longer, as on the day of the triumph, to bear her up. It is Zenobia before me, but—like her own beautiful capital—it is Zenobia in ruins. That she suffers, too, from the reproaches of a mind now conscious of its errors, I cannot doubt. She blames Aurelian, but, I am persuaded, she blames with no less severity herself. It is, I doubt not, the image of her desolated country rising before her, that causes her so often, in the midst of discourse with us, or when she has been sitting long silent, suddenly to start and clasp her hands, and withdraw weeping to her apartments, or the seclusion of the garden.

"It will be long, very long," Julia has said to me, "before Zenobia will recover from this grief—if indeed she ever do. Would that the principles of that faith which we have learned to believe and prize, were also hers. Life would then still place before her a great object, which now she wants. The past absorbs her wholly—the future is nothing. She dwells upon glories that are departed for ever, and is able to anticipate no other, or greater, in this world—nor with certainty in any beyond it."

I said, "But doubtless she throws herself at this season upon her Jewish faith and philosophy. She has ever spoken of it with respect at least, if not with affection."

"I do not," Julia replied, "think that her faith in Judaism is of much avail to her. She has found pleasure in reading the sacred books of the Jews, and has often expressed warmly her admiration of the great principles of moral living and of religious belief found in them, but I do not think that she has derived from them that which she conceives to be the sum of all religion and philosophy, a firm belief and hope of immortality. I am sure she has not. She has sometimes spoken as if such a belief possessed likelihood, but never as if she entertained it in the way the Christian does."

* * * *

You will rejoice, dear Fausta, to learn that Zenobia no longer opposes me, but waits with impatience for the day when I shall be an inmate of her palace.

What think you is the news to-day in Rome? No other and no less than this—which you may well suppose has for some time been no news to me—that Livia is to be empress! It has just been made public with authority, and I dispatch my letter that you may be immediately informed of it. It has brought another expression upon the countenance of Zenobia.

Curtius and Lucilia have this moment come in full of these tidings, and interrupt me—they with Portia wish to be remembered to you with affection. I shall soon write again—telling you then especially of my interviews with Aurelian. Farewell.

THE END.

www.ingramcontent.com/pod-product-compliance
Lightning Source LLC
Chambersburg PA
CBHW022144300426
44115CB00006B/334